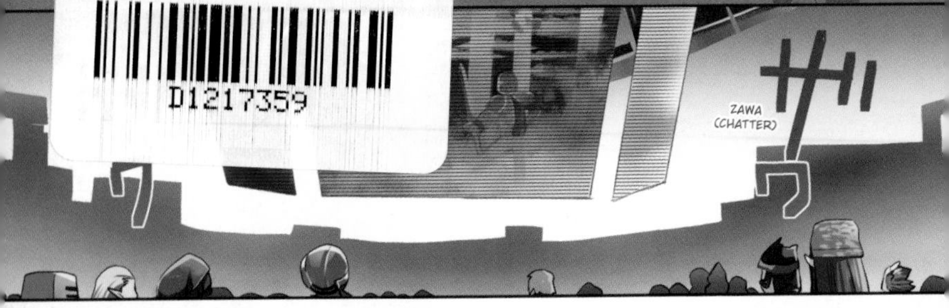
ZAWA
(CHATTER)

presented by: JIROU OIMOTO & YUUMIKAN

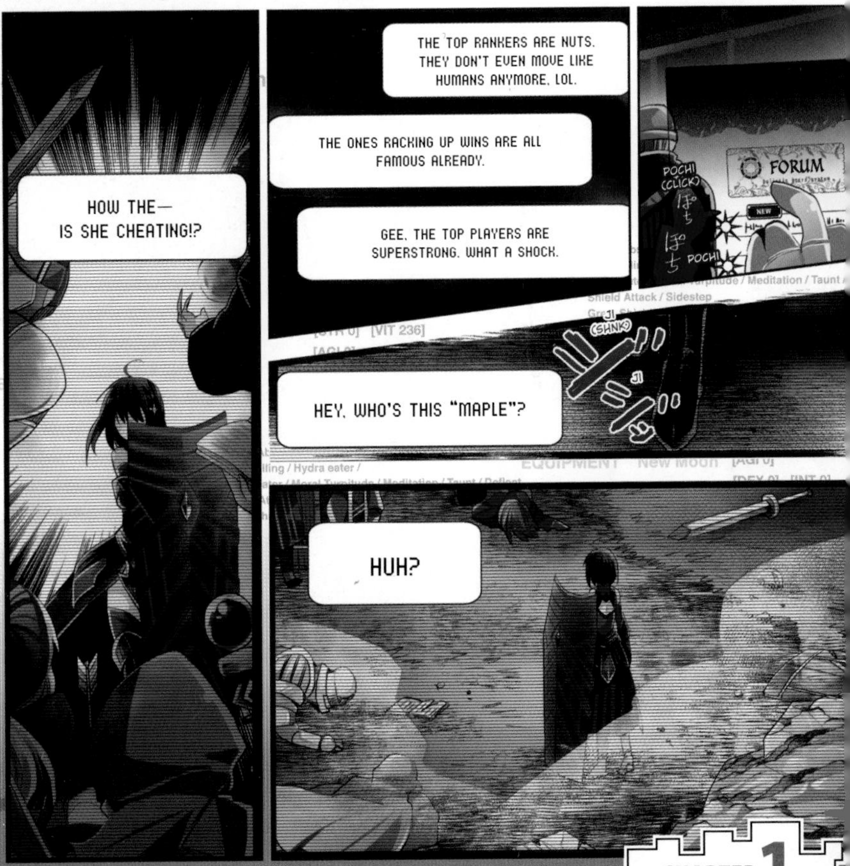
POCHI
(CLICK)
POCHI
FORUM
NEW
THE TOP RANKERS ARE NUTS. THEY DON'T EVEN MOVE LIKE HUMANS ANYMORE, LOL.
THE ONES RACKING UP WINS ARE ALL FAMOUS ALREADY.
GEE, THE TOP PLAYERS ARE SUPERSTRONG. WHAT A SHOCK.
JI
(SHNK)
JI
HEY, WHO'S THIS "MAPLE"?
HUH?
HOW THE—
IS SHE CHEATING!?

CHAPTER 1

Welcome to NewWorld Online.

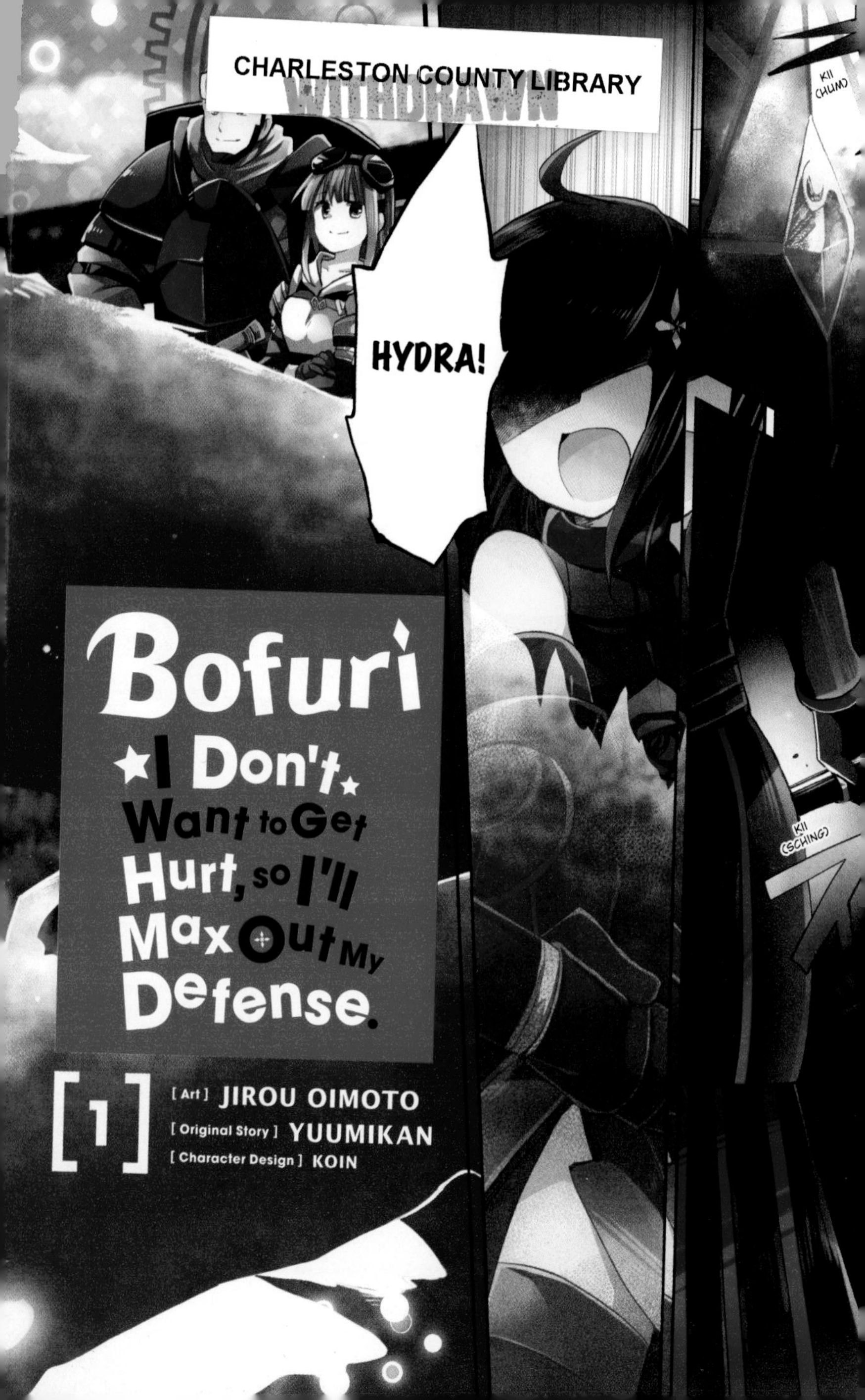
KII (CHUM)
HYDRA!
KII (SCHING)
Bofuri
★I Don't★ Want to Get Hurt, so I'll Max Out My Defense.
[1]
[Art] JIROU OIMOTO
[Original Story] YUUMIKAN
[Character Design] KOIN

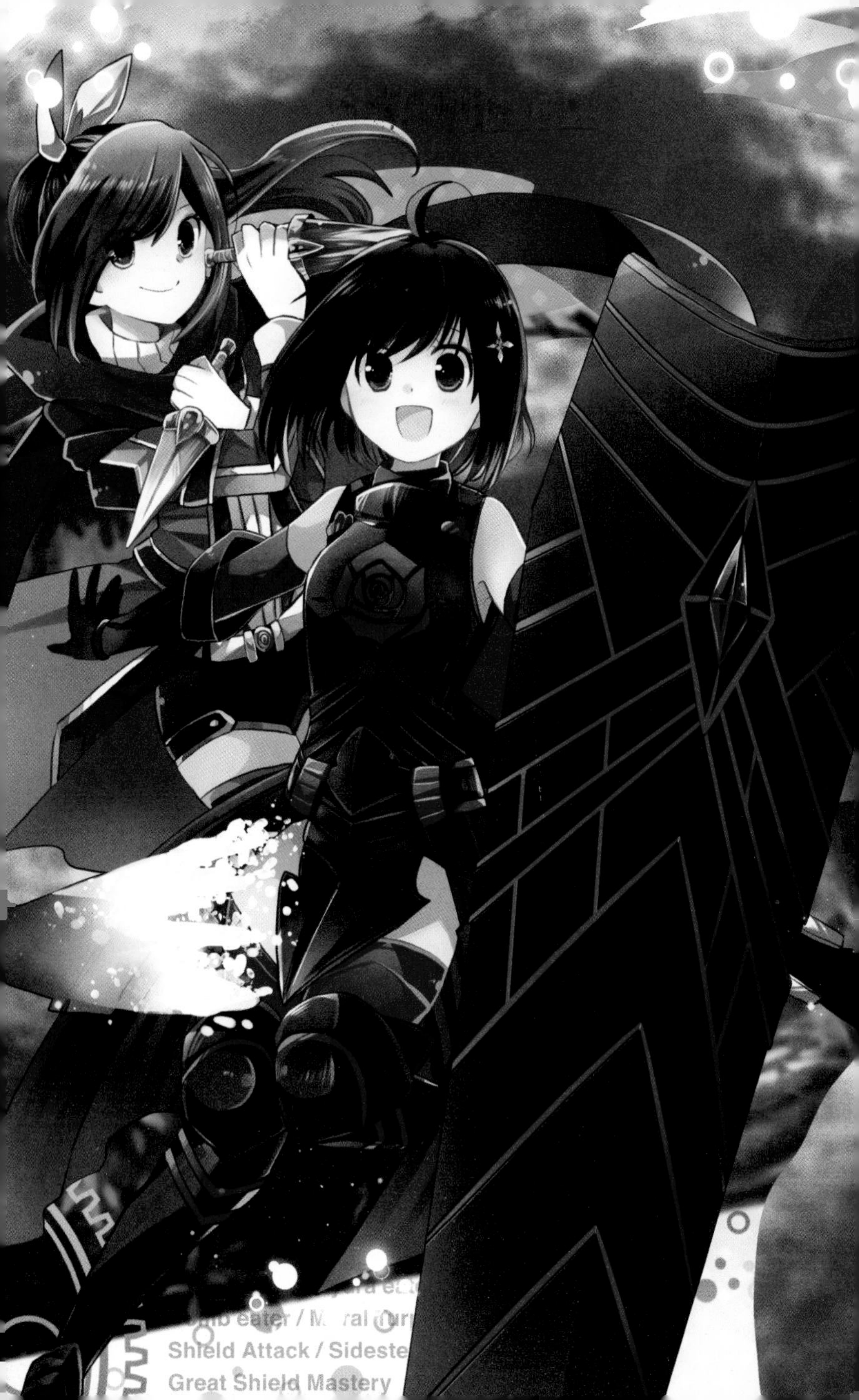

Shield Attack / Sideste
Great Shield Mastery

Welcome to NewWorld Online

Maple

LV 20 HP 40/40
MP 12/12 [STR 0]
[VIT 160(+66)]
[AGI 0] [DEX 0]
[INT 0]

CONTENTS

[1]

I Don't Want to Get Hurt,
so I'll Max Out My Defense.

Chapter 1 001
Chapter 2 035
Chapter 3 065
Chapter 4 091
Chapter 5 113
Chapter 6 137
Special 161

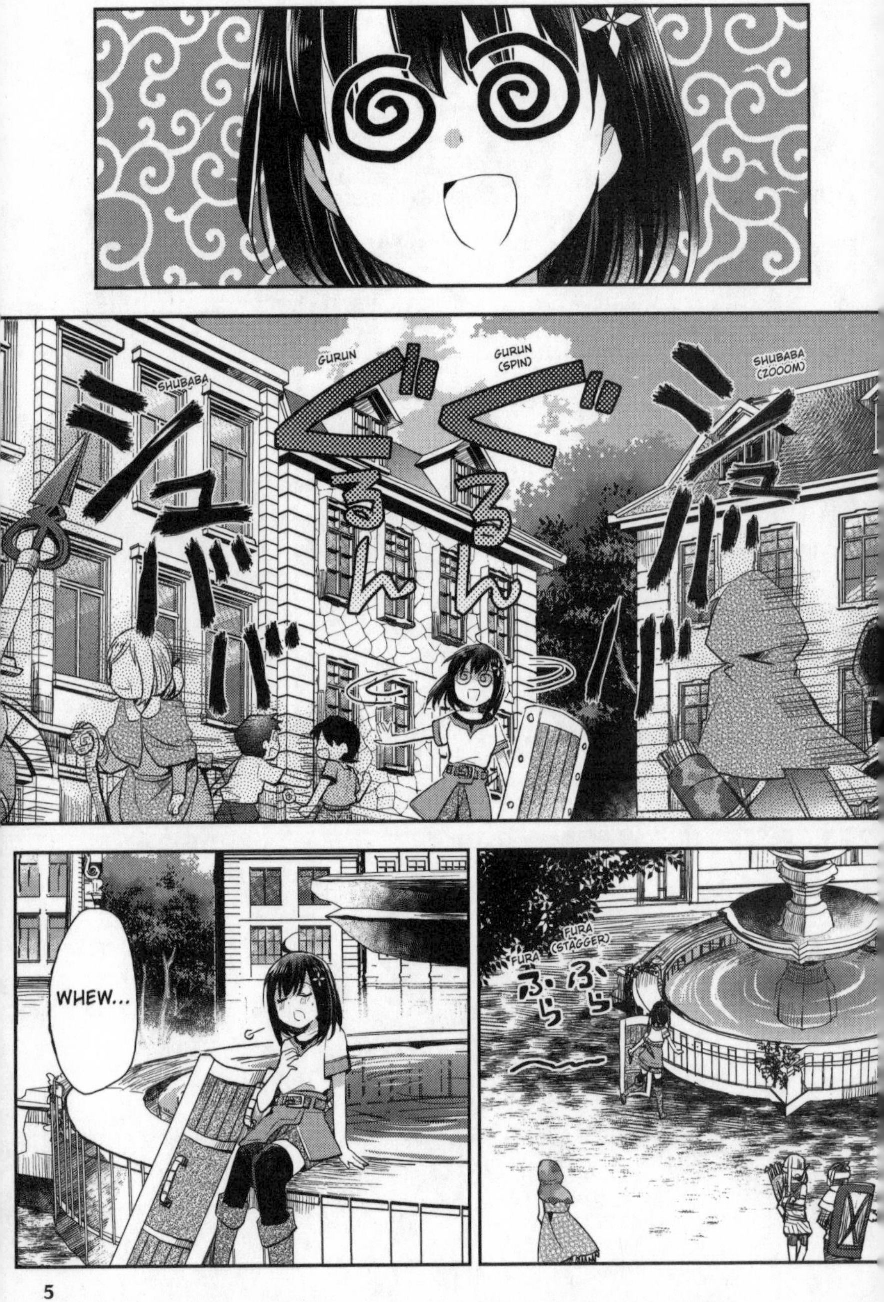
SHUBABA (ZOOOM)
GURUN (SPIN)
ぐるん
GURUN
ぐるん
SHUBABA
FURA (STAGGER)
ふら
FURA
ふら
WHEW...

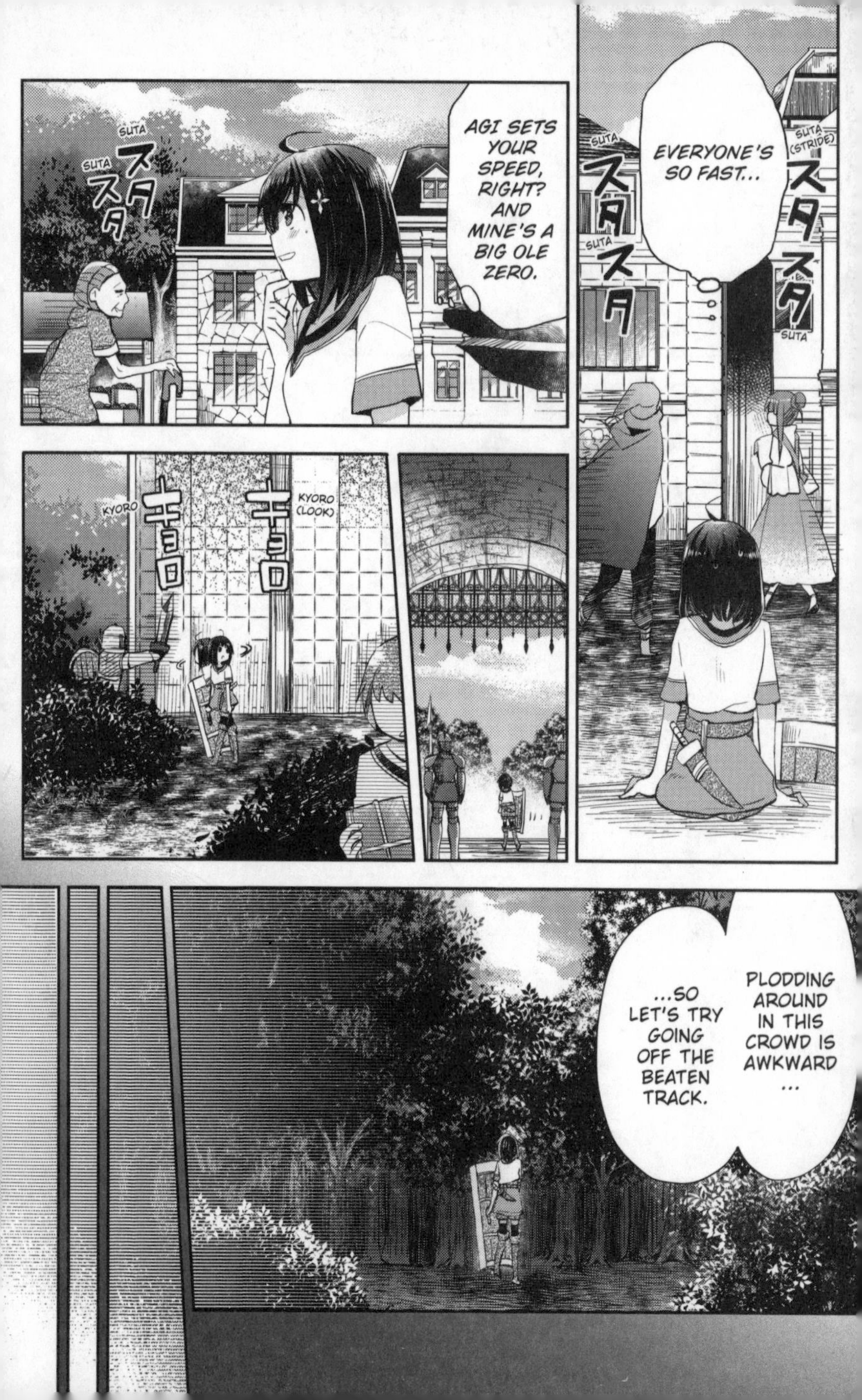
SUTA (STRIDE)
スタスタ
SUTA
SUTA
スタスタ
SUTA
EVERYONE'S SO FAST...
AGI SETS YOUR SPEED, RIGHT? AND MINE'S A BIG OLE ZERO.
SUTA
スタスタ
SUTA
KYORO (LOOK)
キョロ
KYORO
キョロ
PLODDING AROUND IN THIS CROWD IS AWKWARD...
...SO LET'S TRY GOING OFF THE BEATEN TRACK.

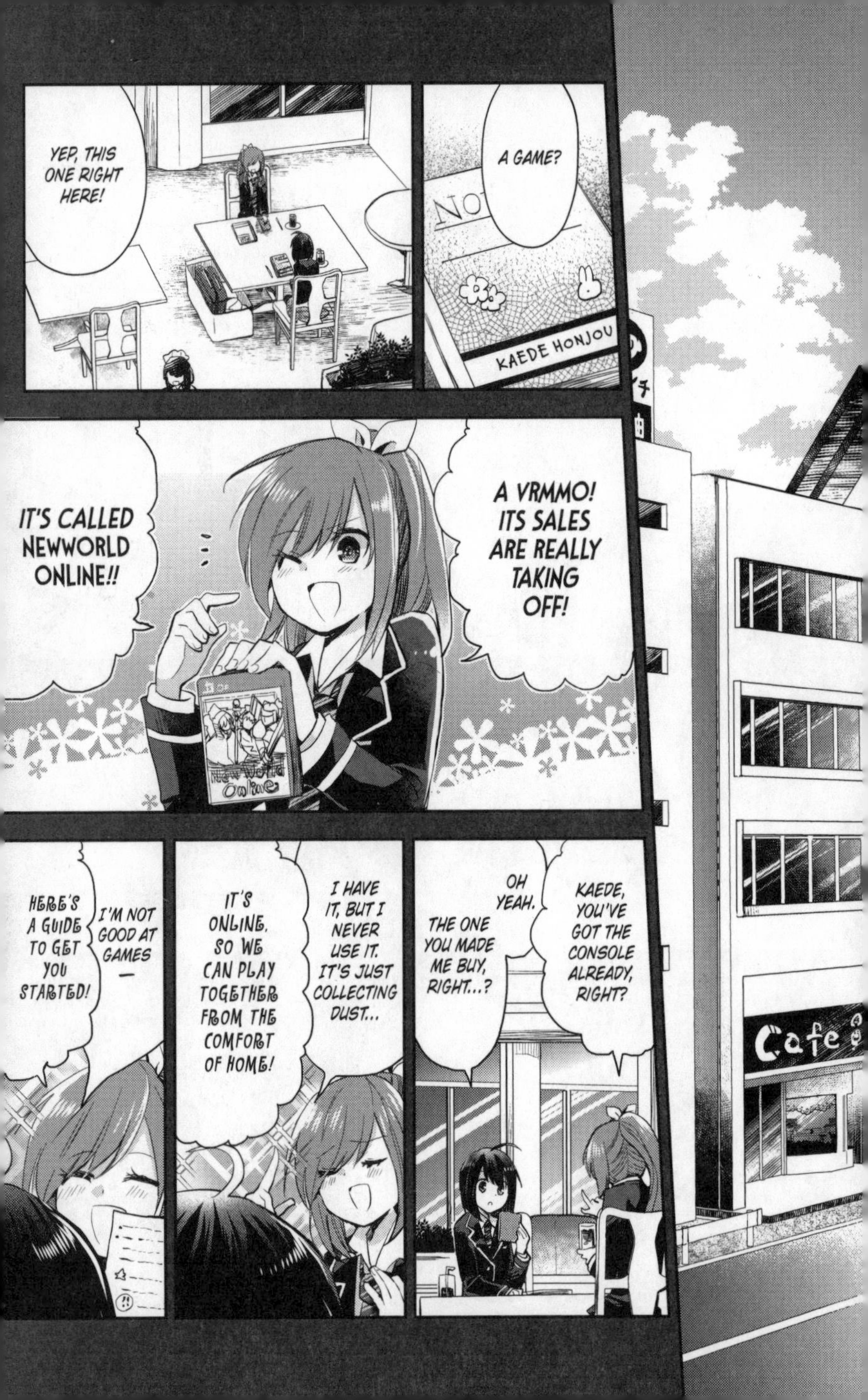
A GAME?
KAEDE HONJOU
YEP, THIS ONE RIGHT HERE!
A VRMMO! ITS SALES ARE REALLY TAKING OFF!
IT'S CALLED NEWWORLD ONLINE!!
New World Online
KAEDE, YOU'VE GOT THE CONSOLE ALREADY, RIGHT?
OH YEAH.
THE ONE YOU MADE ME BUY, RIGHT...?
I HAVE IT, BUT I NEVER USE IT. IT'S JUST COLLECTING DUST...
IT'S ONLINE, SO WE CAN PLAY TOGETHER FROM THE COMFORT OF HOME!
I'M NOT GOOD AT GAMES —
HERE'S A GUIDE TO GET YOU STARTED!
Cafe

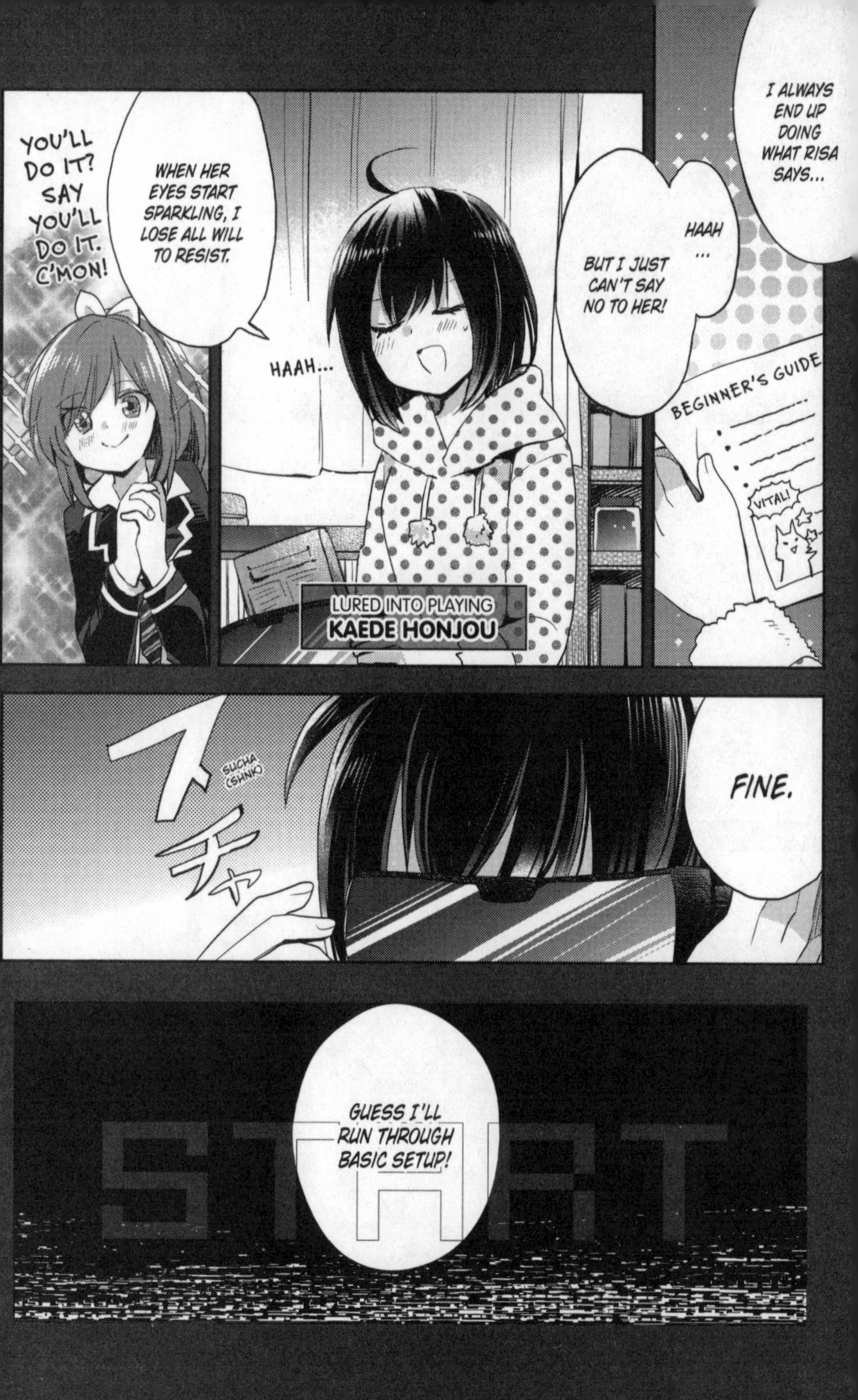
I ALWAYS END UP DOING WHAT RISA SAYS...
HAAH ...
BUT I JUST CAN'T SAY NO TO HER!
BEGINNER'S GUIDE
VITAL!
HAAH...
LURED INTO PLAYING
KAEDE HONJOU
WHEN HER EYES START SPARKLING, I LOSE ALL WILL TO RESIST.
YOU'LL DO IT? SAY YOU'LL DO IT. C'MON!
FINE.
SUCHA (SHNK)
GUESS I'LL RUN THROUGH BASIC SETUP!
START

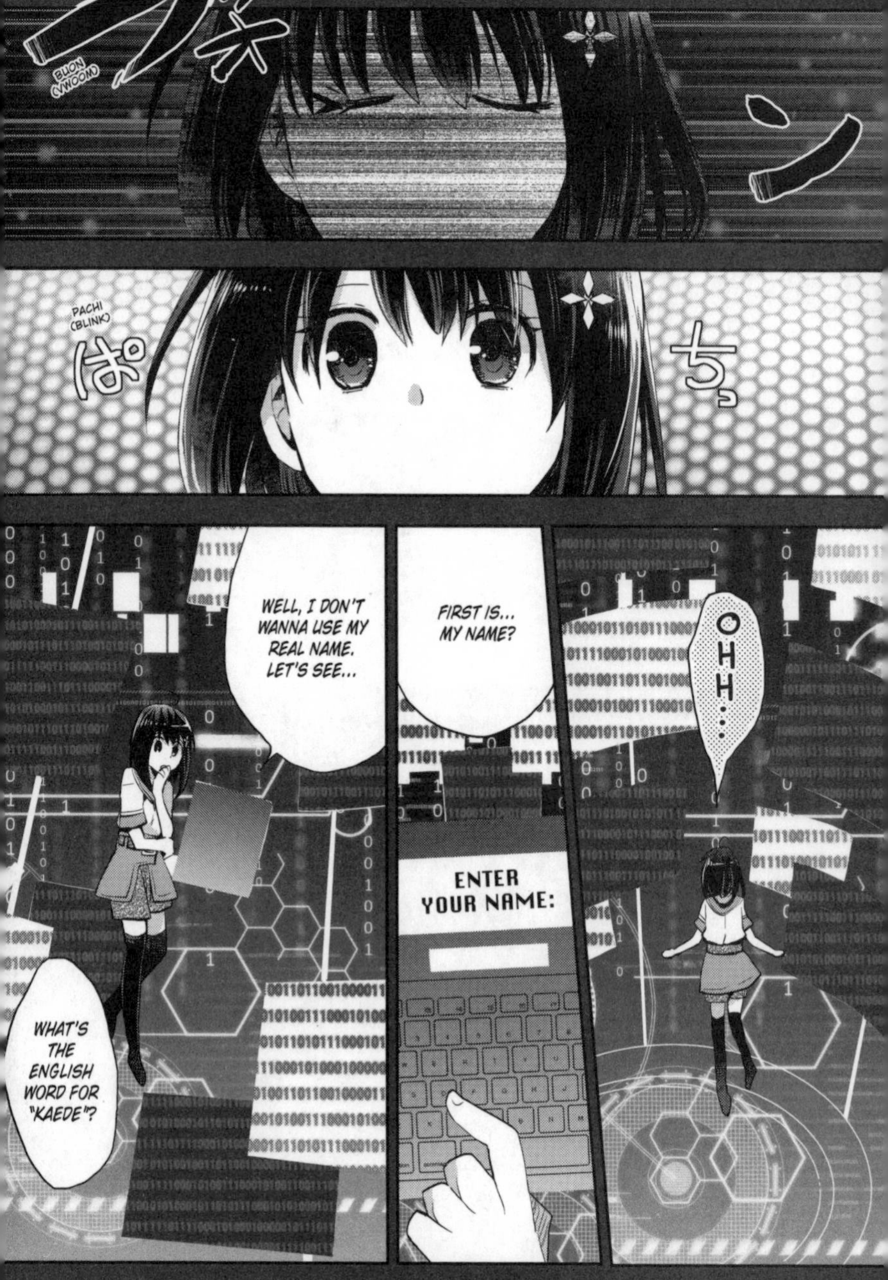
ブォン
BUON (VWOOM)
ぱちっ
PACHI (BLINK)
OHH...
FIRST IS... MY NAME?
ENTER YOUR NAME:
WELL, I DON'T WANNA USE MY REAL NAME. LET'S SEE...
WHAT'S THE ENGLISH WORD FOR "KAEDE"?

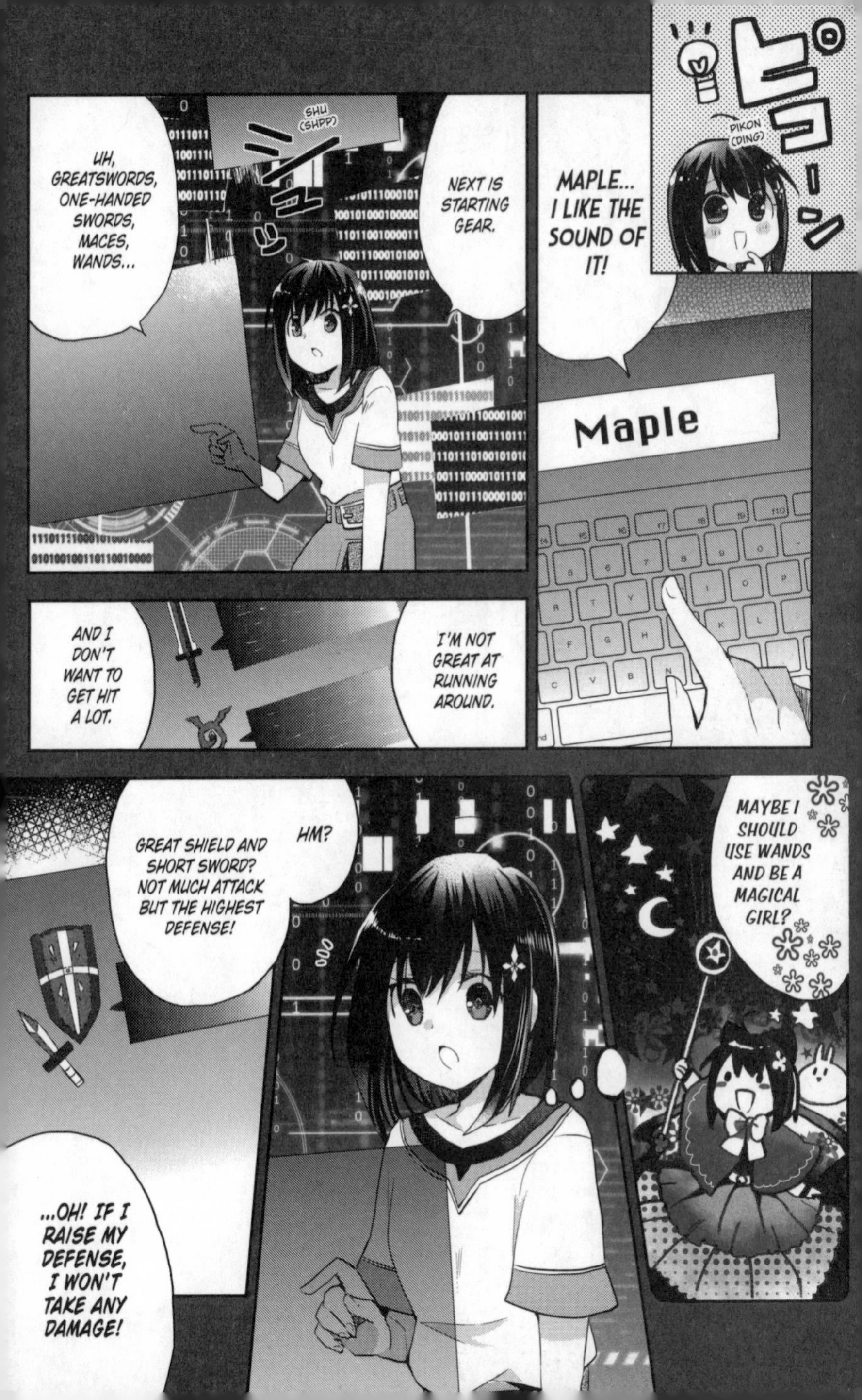
PIKON (DING)
MAPLE... I LIKE THE SOUND OF IT!
Maple
NEXT IS STARTING GEAR.
SHU (SHPP)
UH, GREATSWORDS, ONE-HANDED SWORDS, MACES, WANDS...
I'M NOT GREAT AT RUNNING AROUND.
AND I DON'T WANT TO GET HIT A LOT.
MAYBE I SHOULD USE WANDS AND BE A MAGICAL GIRL?
HM?
GREAT SHIELD AND SHORT SWORD? NOT MUCH ATTACK BUT THE HIGHEST DEFENSE!
...OH! IF I RAISE MY DEFENSE, I WON'T TAKE ANY DAMAGE!

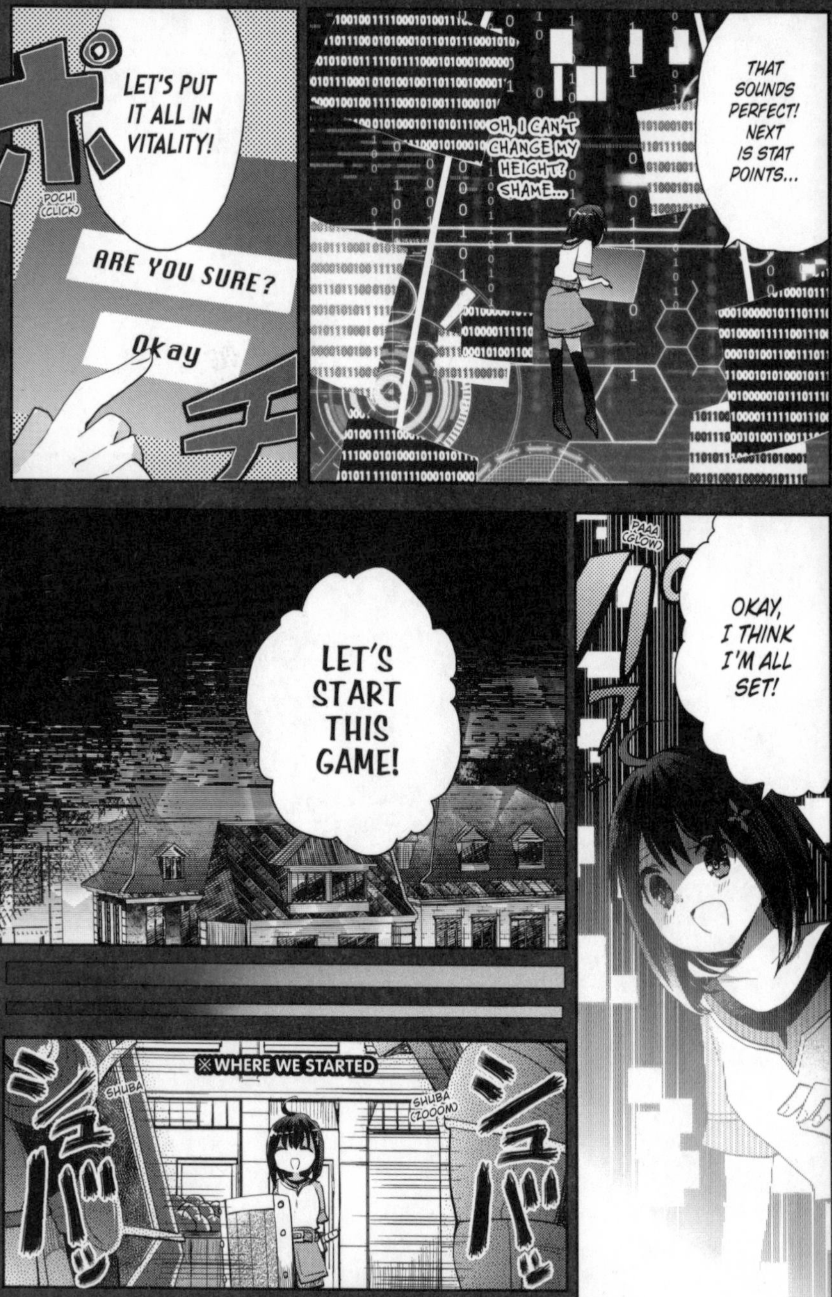
THAT SOUNDS PERFECT! NEXT IS STAT POINTS...
OH, I CAN'T CHANGE MY HEIGHT? SHAME...
LET'S PUT IT ALL IN VITALITY!
POCHI (CLICK)
ARE YOU SURE?
Okay
PAAA (GLOW)
OKAY, I THINK I'M ALL SET!
LET'S START THIS GAME!
※WHERE WE STARTED
SHUBA
SHUBA (ZOOOM)

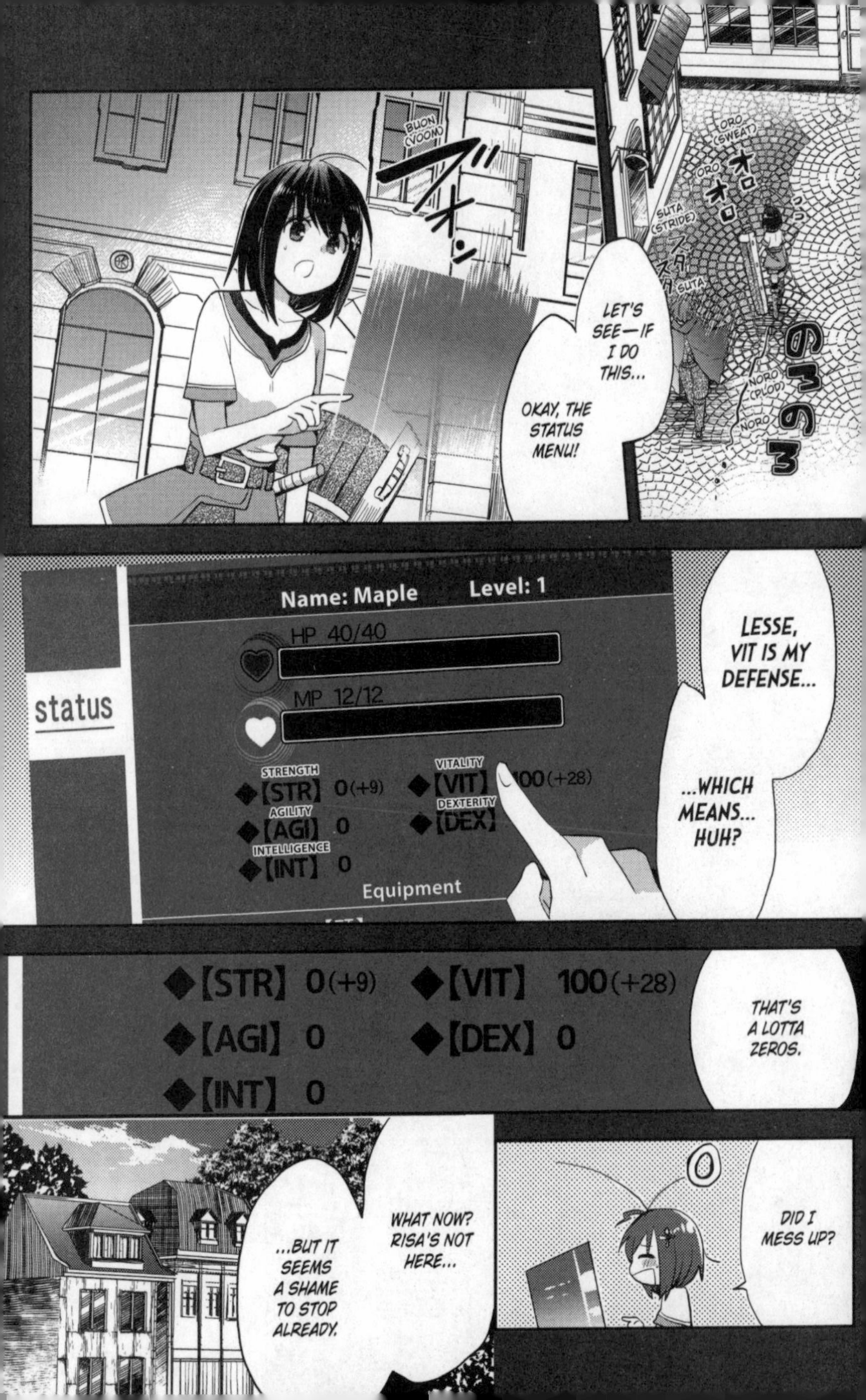
ORO (SWEAT)
ORO
オロオロ
SUTA (STRIDE)
SUTA
スタスタ
NORO (PLOD)
NORO
LET'S SEE—IF I DO THIS...
OKAY, THE STATUS MENU!
BUON (VOOM)
ブオン
Name: Maple
Level: 1
status
HP 40/40
MP 12/12
STRENGTH
◆【STR】 0(+9)
AGILITY
◆【AGI】 0
INTELLIGENCE
◆【INT】 0
VITALITY
◆【VIT】 100(+28)
DEXTERITY
◆【DEX】
Equipment
LESSE, VIT IS MY DEFENSE...
...WHICH MEANS... HUH?
◆【STR】 0(+9)
◆【VIT】 100(+28)
◆【AGI】 0
◆【DEX】 0
◆【INT】 0
THAT'S A LOTTA ZEROS.
DID I MESS UP?
WHAT NOW? RISA'S NOT HERE...
...BUT IT SEEMS A SHAME TO STOP ALREADY.

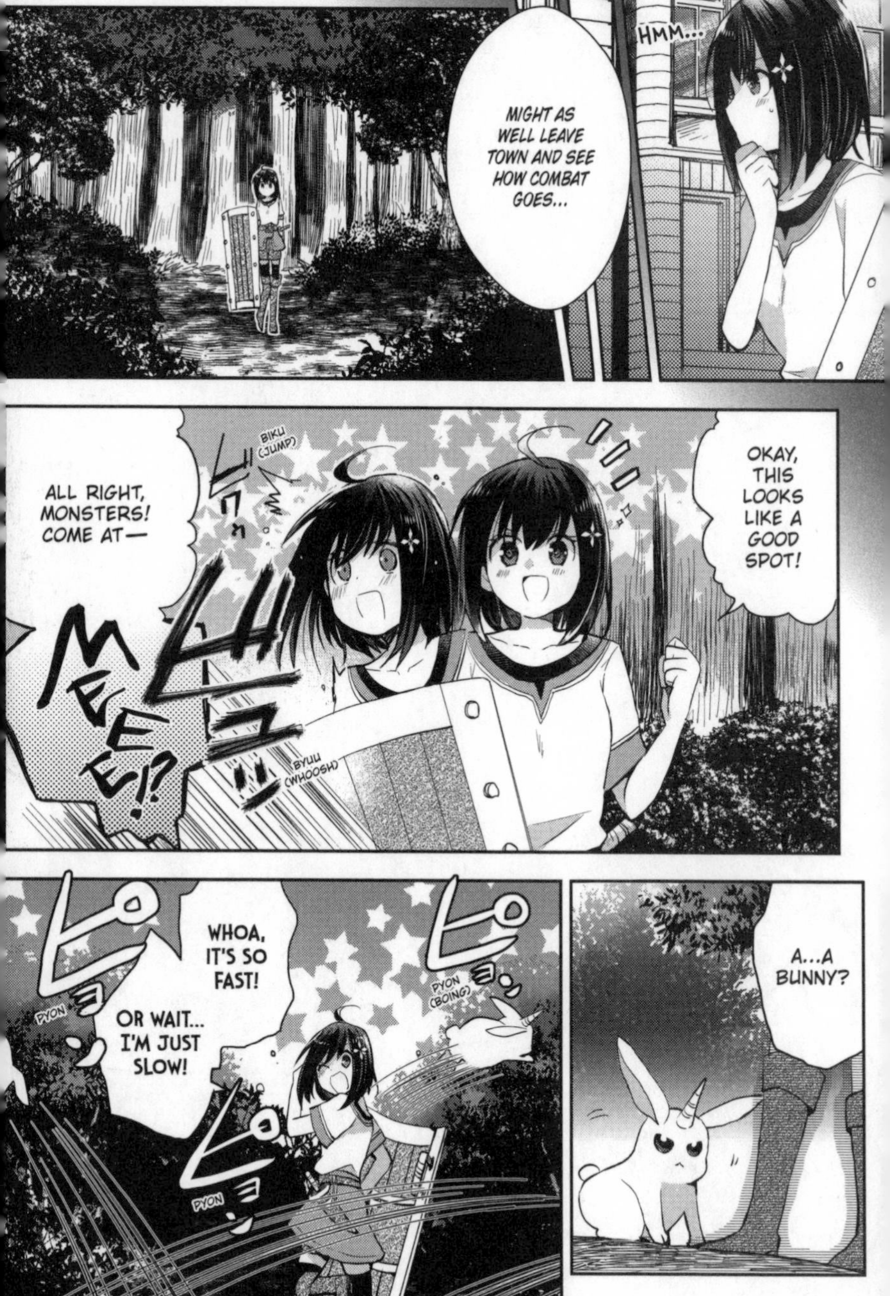
HMM...
MIGHT AS WELL LEAVE TOWN AND SEE HOW COMBAT GOES...
OKAY, THIS LOOKS LIKE A GOOD SPOT!
BIKU (JUMP)
ALL RIGHT, MONSTERS! COME AT—
MEEE!?
BYUU (WHOOSH)
A...A BUNNY?
PYON (BOING)
WHOA, IT'S SO FAST!
PYON
OR WAIT... I'M JUST SLOW!
PYON

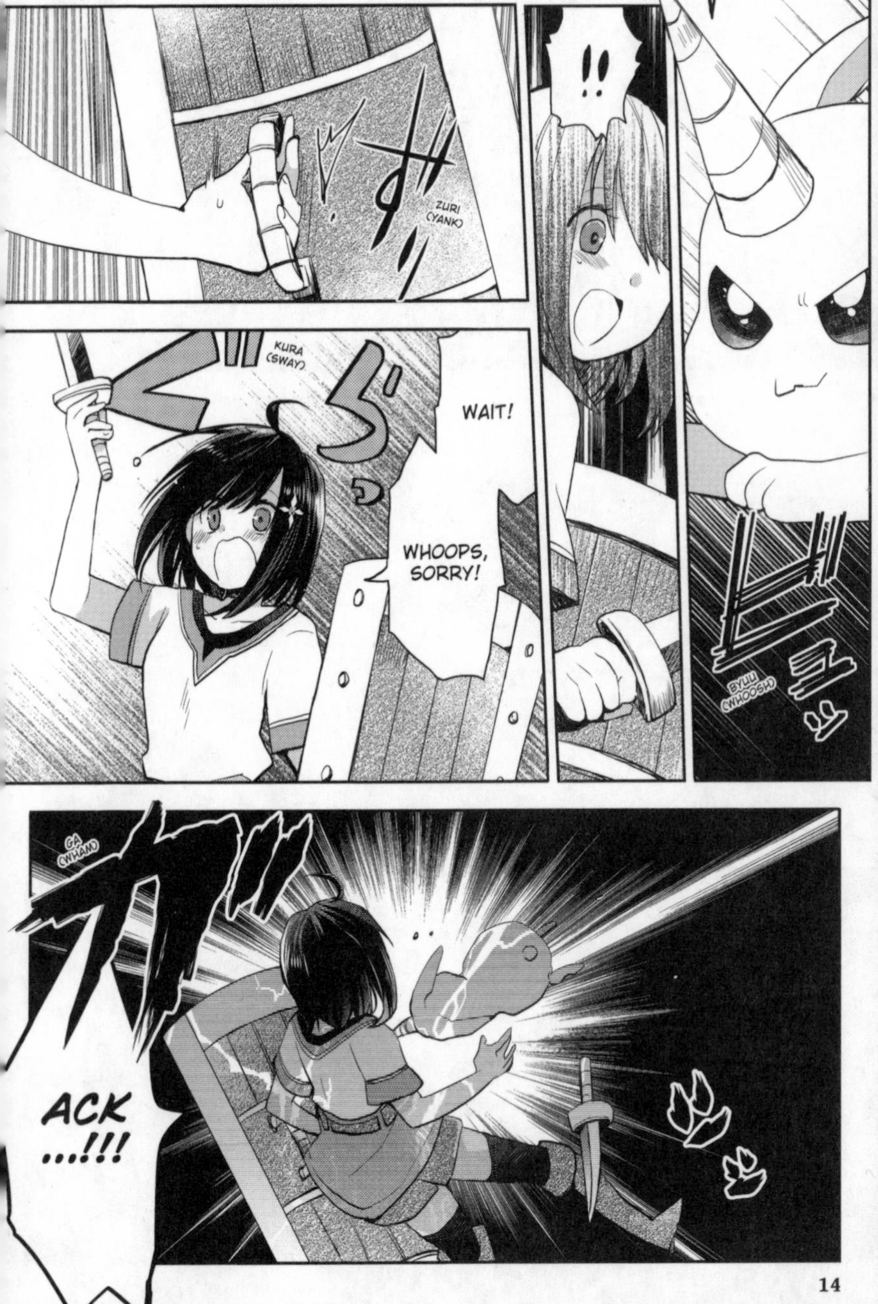
BYUU (WHOOSH)
ZURI (YANK)
KURA (SWAY)
WAIT!
WHOOPS, SORRY!
GA (WHAM)
ACK ...!!!

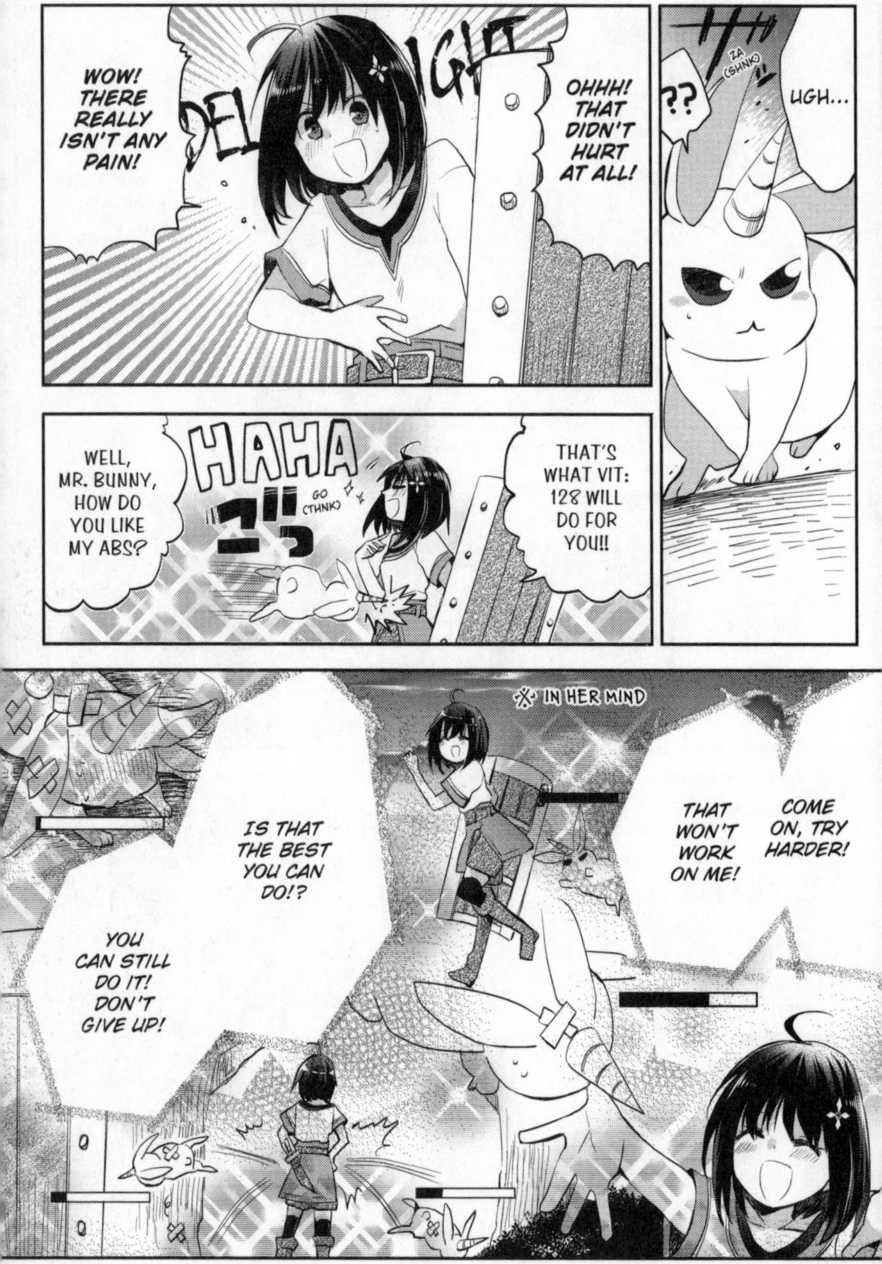
ZA (SHNK)
??
UGH...
OHHH! THAT DIDN'T HURT AT ALL!
DELIGHT
WOW! THERE REALLY ISN'T ANY PAIN!
THAT'S WHAT VIT: 128 WILL DO FOR YOU!!
HAHA
GO (THNK)
WELL, MR. BUNNY, HOW DO YOU LIKE MY ABS?
※ IN HER MIND
COME ON, TRY HARDER!
THAT WON'T WORK ON ME!
IS THAT THE BEST YOU CAN DO!?
YOU CAN STILL DO IT! DON'T GIVE UP!

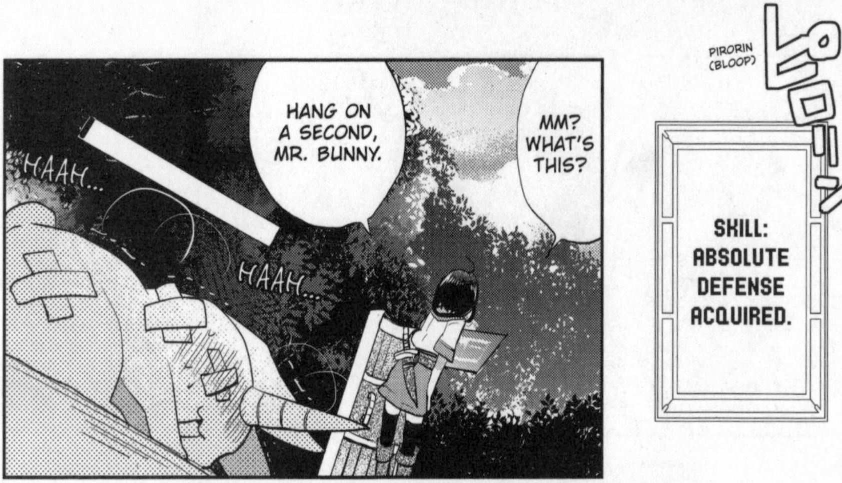
PIRORIN (BLOOP)
SKILL: ABSOLUTE DEFENSE ACQUIRED.
MM? WHAT'S THIS?
HANG ON A SECOND, MR. BUNNY.
HAAH...
HAAH...

★ **ABSOLUTE DEFENSE:** Doubles the user's Vitality. Costs 3x the points to raise STR, AGI, or INT.

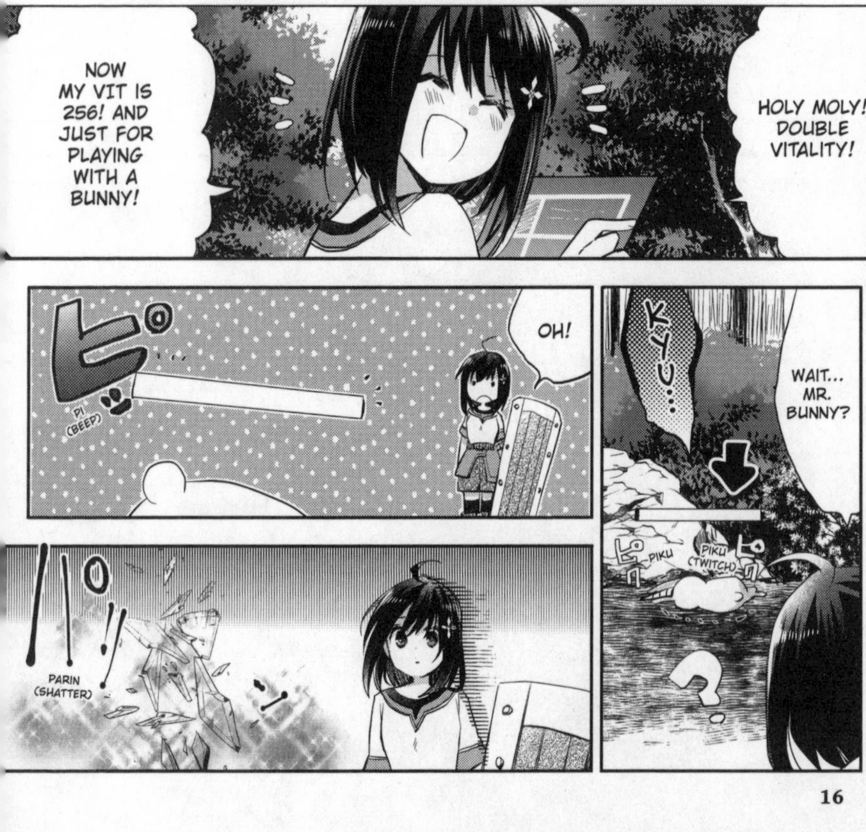
HOLY MOLY! DOUBLE VITALITY!
NOW MY VIT IS 256! AND JUST FOR PLAYING WITH A BUNNY!
KYUU...
WAIT... MR. BUNNY?
PIKU (TWITCH)
PIKU
OH!
PI (BEEP)
PARIN (SHATTER)

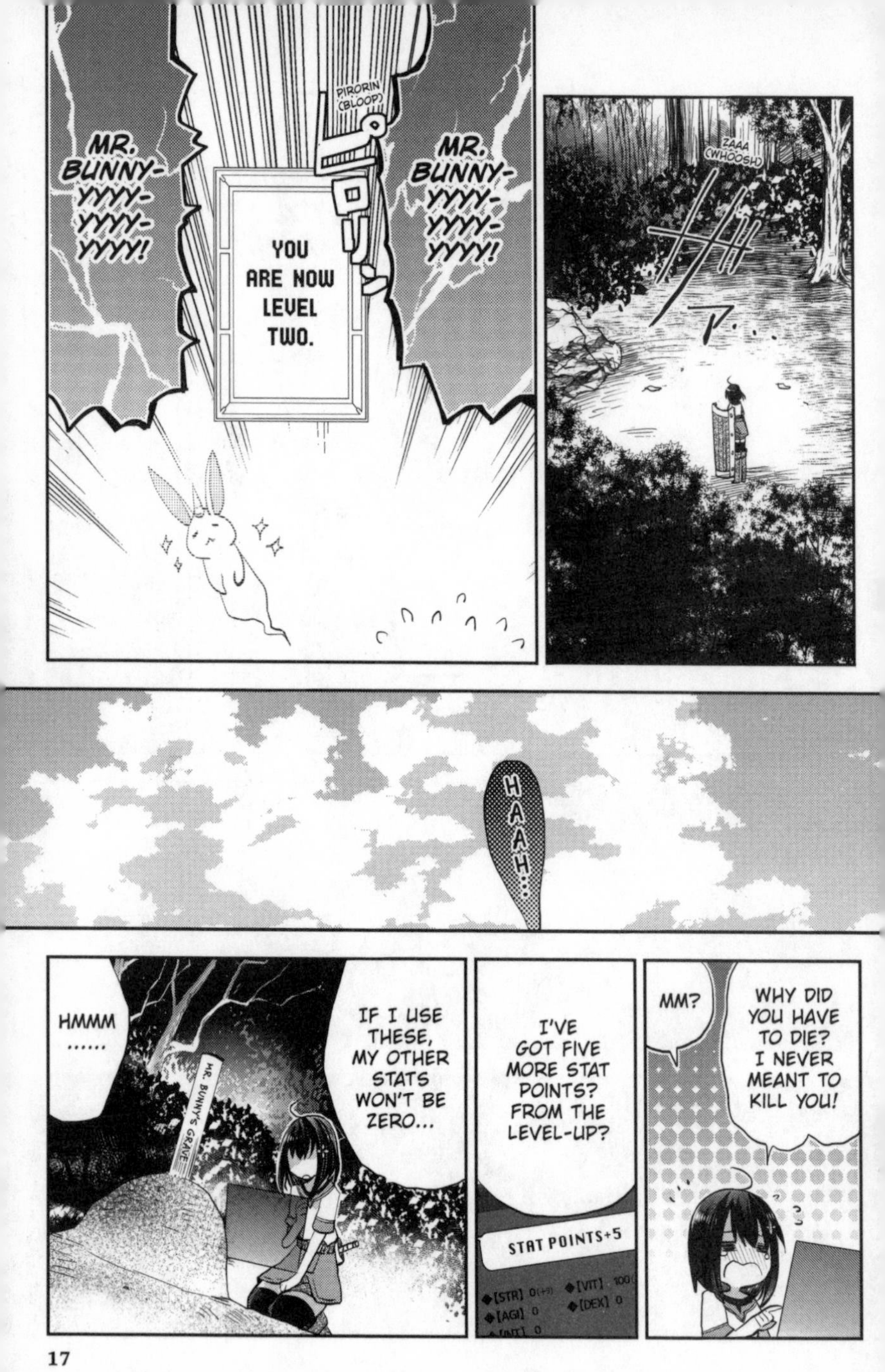
ZAAA (WHOOSH)
PIRORIN (BLOOP)
MR. BUNNY-YYYY-YYYY-YYYY!
YOU ARE NOW LEVEL TWO.
MR. BUNNY-YYYY-YYYY-YYYY!
HAAAH...
WHY DID YOU HAVE TO DIE? I NEVER MEANT TO KILL YOU!
MM?
I'VE GOT FIVE MORE STAT POINTS? FROM THE LEVEL-UP?
STAT POINTS+5
[STR] 0
[VIT] 100
[AGI] 0
[DEX] 0
[INT] 0
IF I USE THESE, MY OTHER STATS WON'T BE ZERO...
HMMM......
MR. BUNNY'S GRAVE

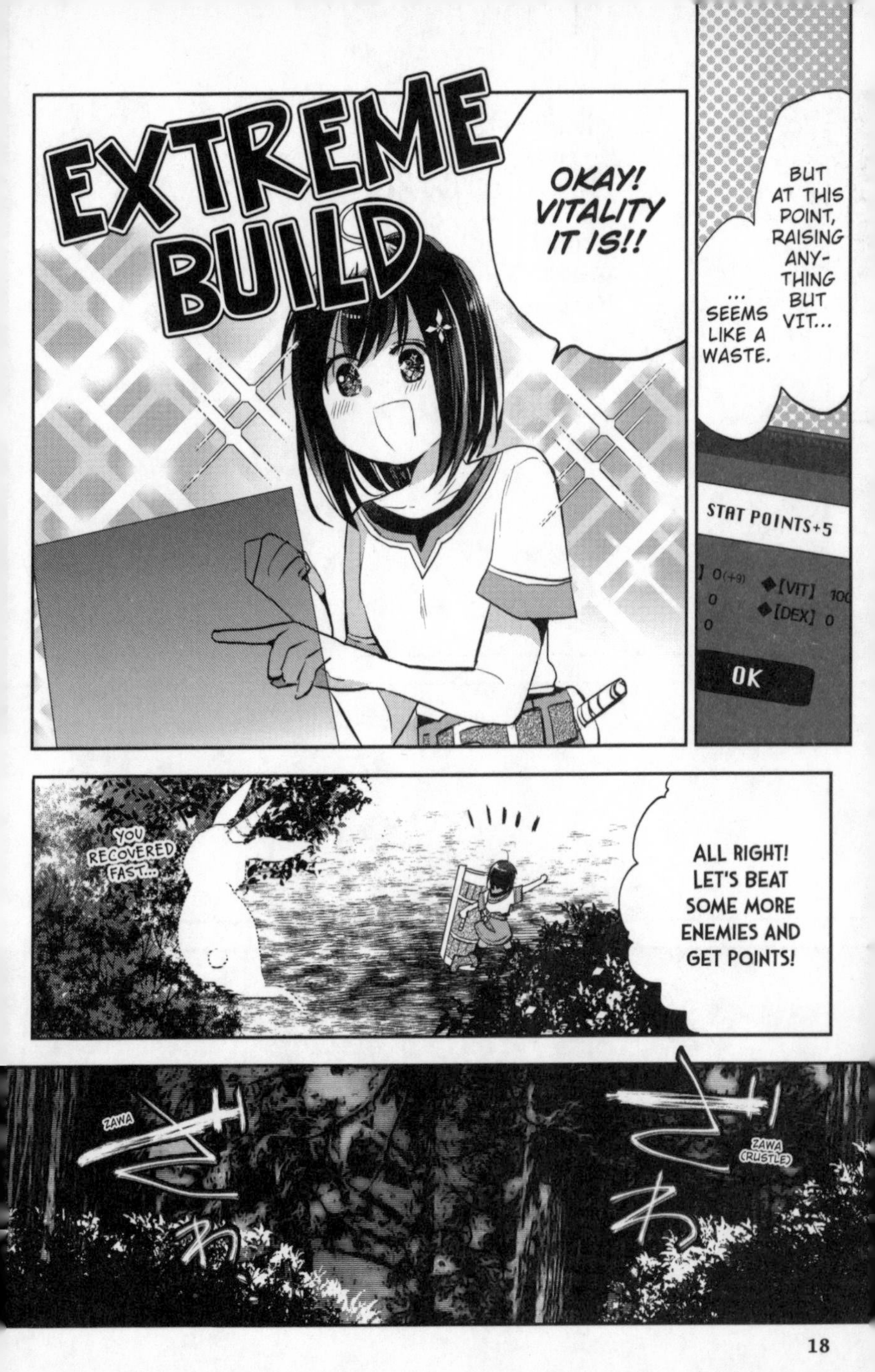
BUT AT THIS POINT, RAISING ANYTHING BUT VIT...
...SEEMS LIKE A WASTE.
STAT POINTS+5
[VIT]
[DEX] 0
OK
OKAY! VITALITY IT IS!!
EXTREME BUILD
ALL RIGHT! LET'S BEAT SOME MORE ENEMIES AND GET POINTS!
YOU RECOVERED FAST...
ZAWA (RUSTLE)
ZAWA

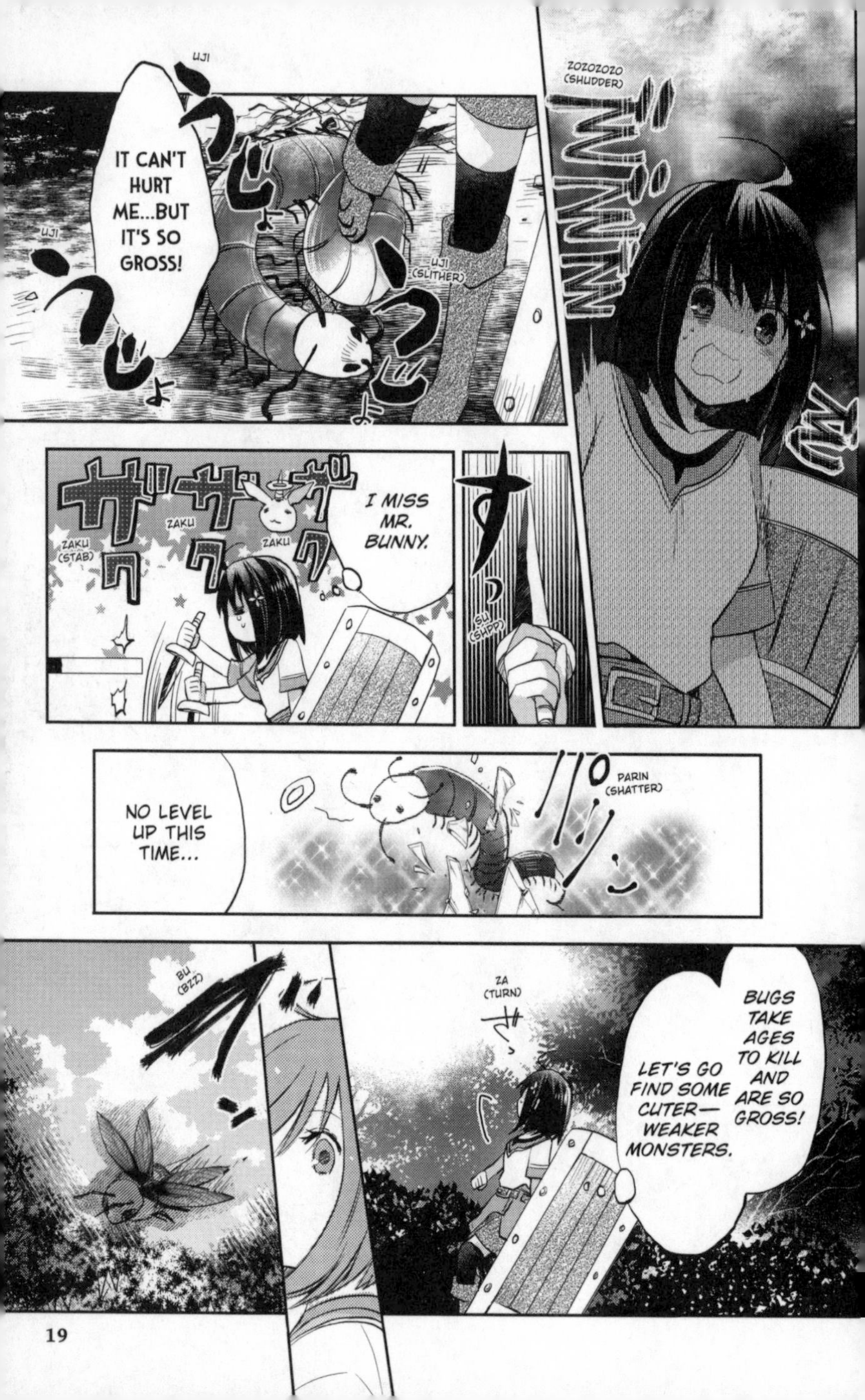
ZOZOZOZO
(SHUDDER)
UJI
IT CAN'T HURT ME...BUT IT'S SO GROSS!
UJI
UJI
(SLITHER)
SU
(SHPP)
I MISS MR. BUNNY.
ZAKU
ZAKU
ZAKU
(STAB)
PARIN
(SHATTER)
NO LEVEL UP THIS TIME...
BUGS TAKE AGES TO KILL AND ARE SO GROSS!
LET'S GO FIND SOME CUTER—WEAKER MONSTERS.
ZA
(TURN)
BU
(BZZ)

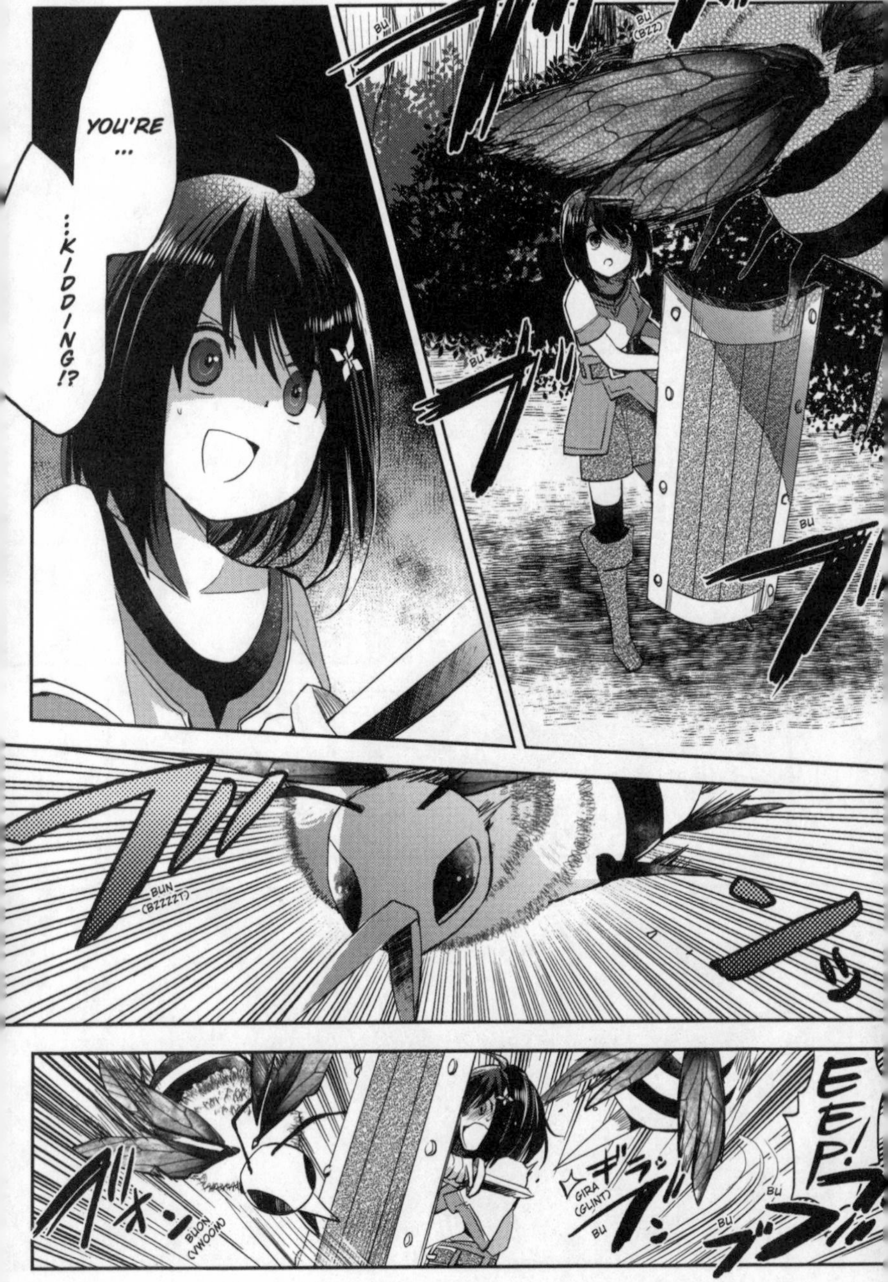
BU
(BZZ)
BU
BU
BU
YOU'RE
...
...KIDDING!?
BUN
(BZZZZT)
EEP!
BU
BU
BU
GIRA
(GLINT)
BUON
(VWOOM)

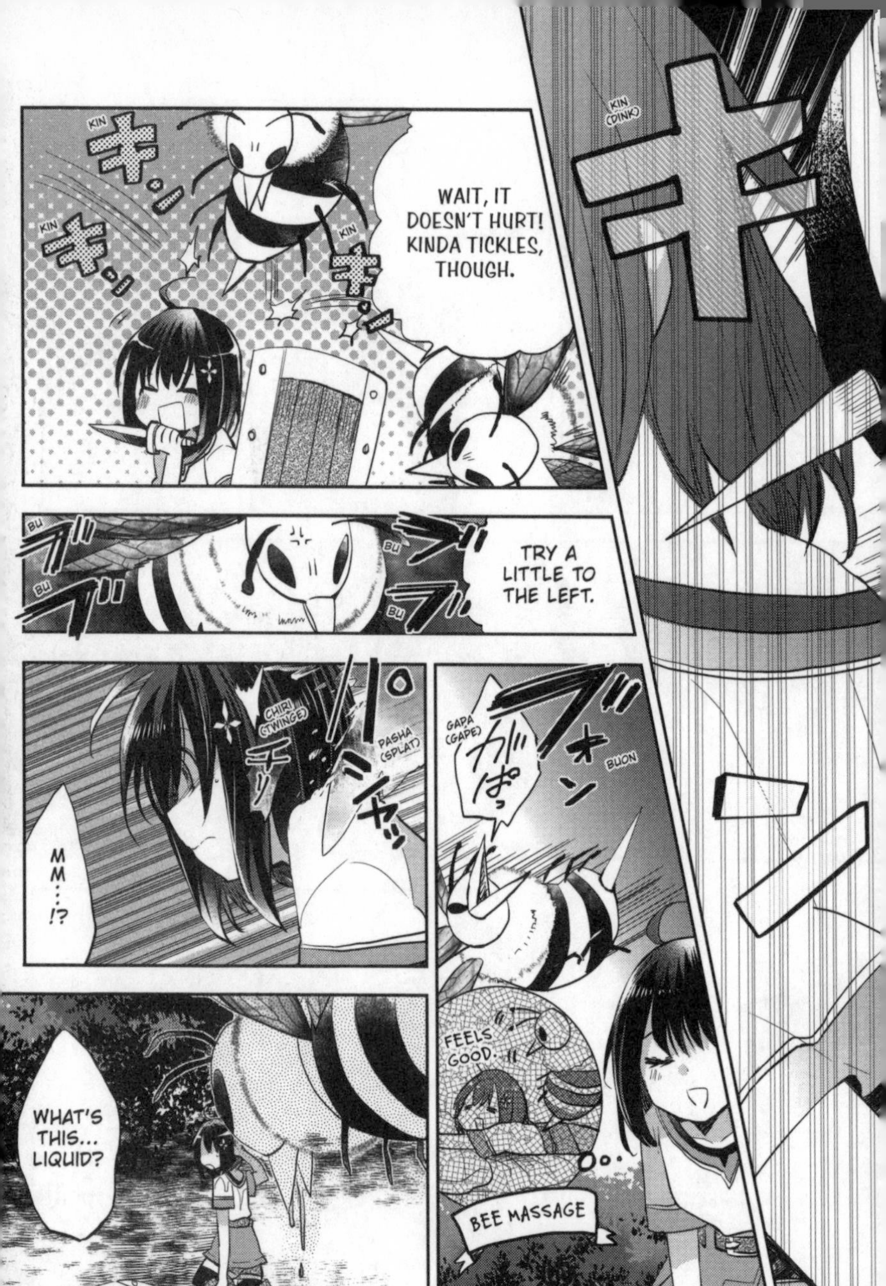
KIN (DINK)
KIN
KIN
KIN
WAIT, IT DOESN'T HURT! KINDA TICKLES, THOUGH.
BU
BU
BU
BU
TRY A LITTLE TO THE LEFT.
BUON
GAPA (GAPE)
PASHA (SPLAT)
CHIRI (TWINGE)
MM…!?
FEELS GOOD.
BEE MASSAGE
WHAT'S THIS… LIQUID?

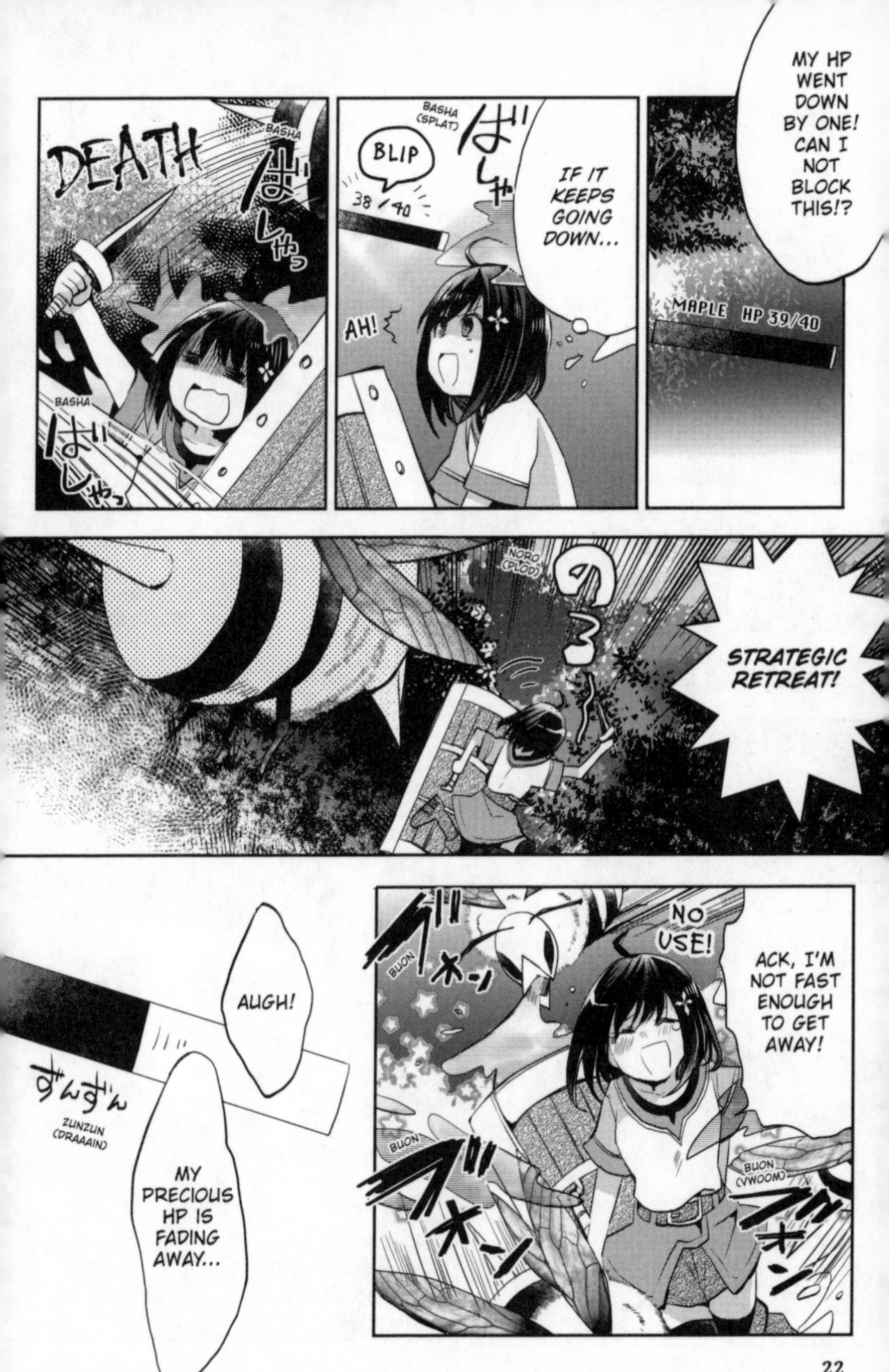
MY HP WENT DOWN BY ONE! CAN I NOT BLOCK THIS!?
MAPLE HP 39/40
BASHA (SPLAT)
ばしゃ
BLIP
38/40
IF IT KEEPS GOING DOWN...
AH!
DEATH
BASHA
BASHA
STRATEGIC RETREAT!
NORO (PLOD)
NO USE!
ACK, I'M NOT FAST ENOUGH TO GET AWAY!
BUON
BUON
BUON (VWOOM)
AUGH!
MY PRECIOUS HP IS FADING AWAY...
ずんずん
ZUNZUN (DRAAAIN)

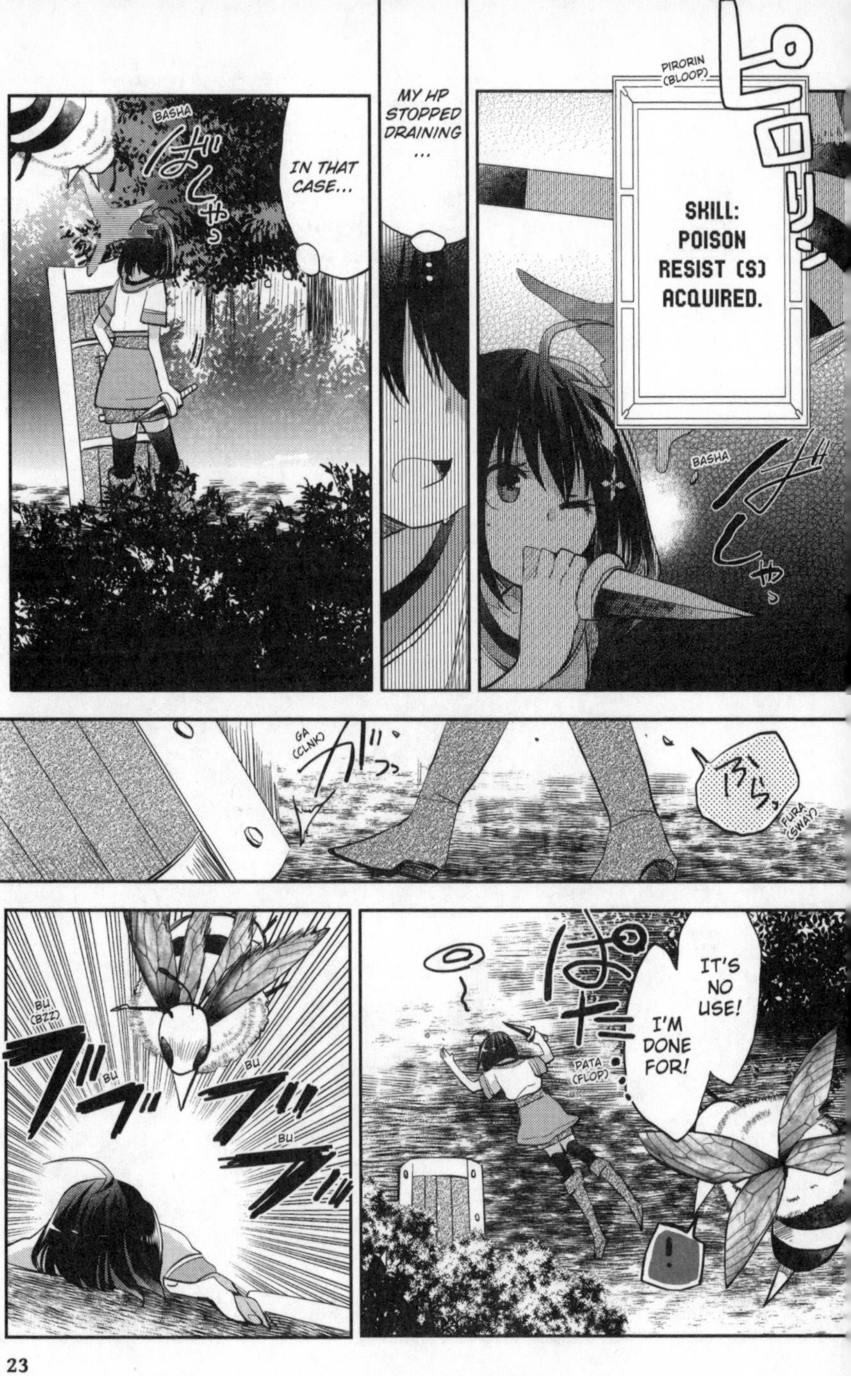
PIRORIN (BLOOP)
SKILL: POISON RESIST (S) ACQUIRED.
BASHA
MY HP STOPPED DRAINING...
IN THAT CASE...
BASHA
FURA (SWAY)
GA (CLNK)
IT'S NO USE!
I'M DONE FOR!
PATA (FLOP)
BU (BZZ)
BU
BU
BU

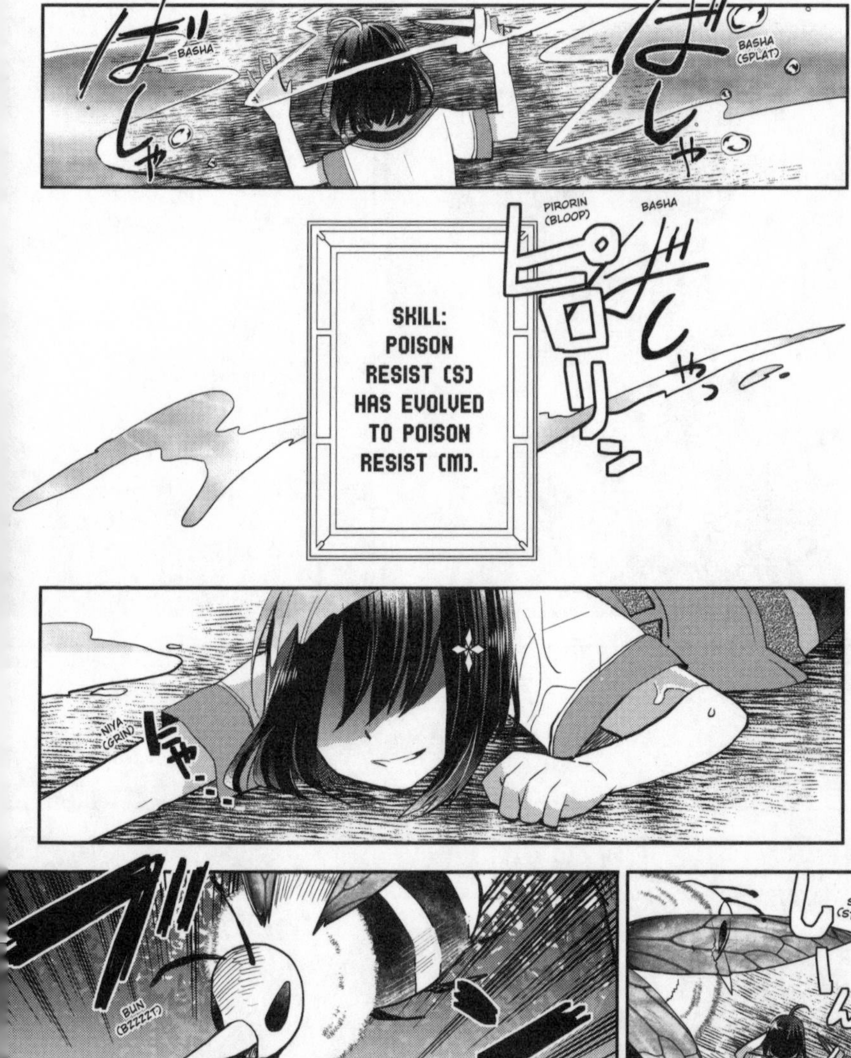
BASHA (SPLAT)
BASHA
BASHA
PIRORIN (BLOOP)
SKILL: POISON RESIST (S) HAS EVOLVED TO POISON RESIST (M).
NIYA (GRIN)
SHIN (STILL)
BUN (BZZZZT)

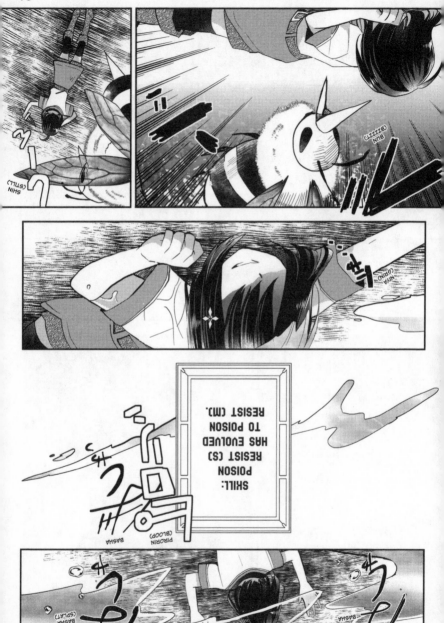

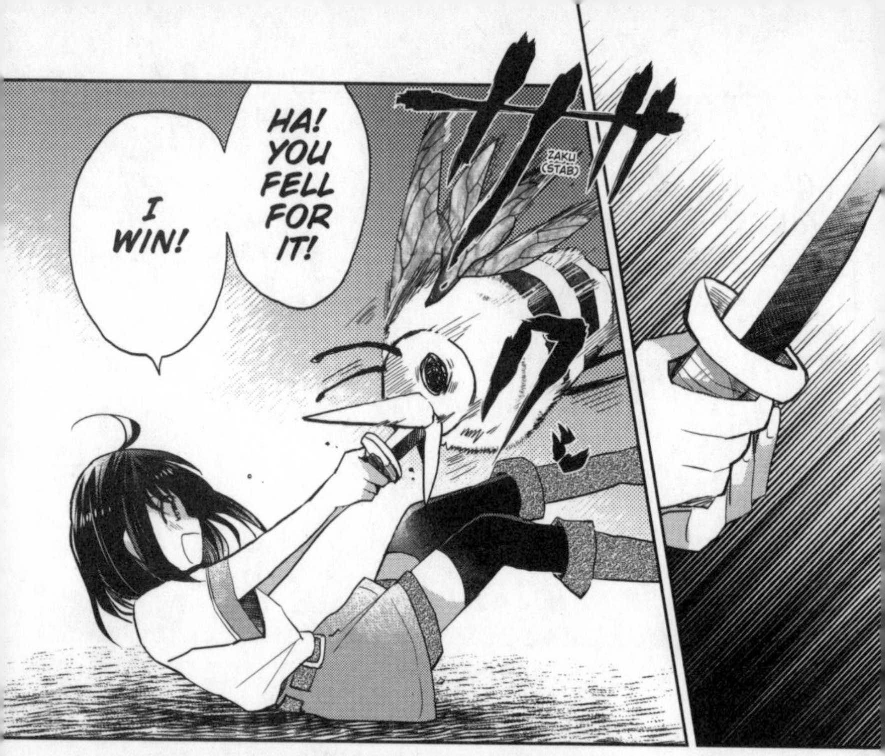
ZAKU (STAB)
HA! YOU FELL FOR IT!
I WIN!

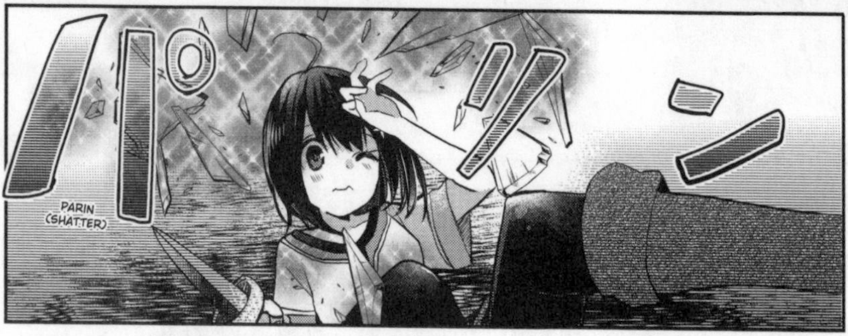
PARIN (SHATTER)

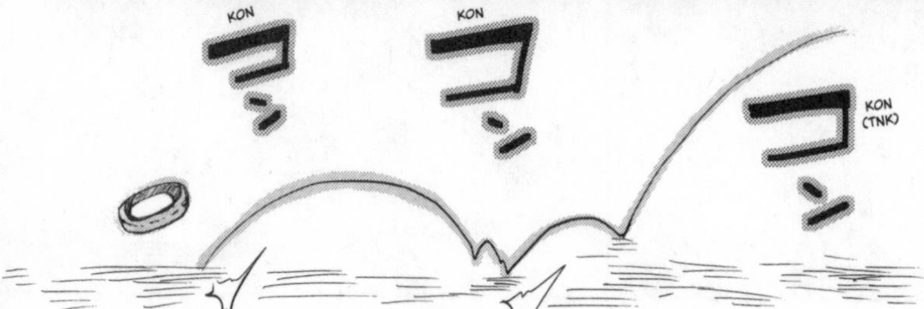
KON (TNK)
KON
KON

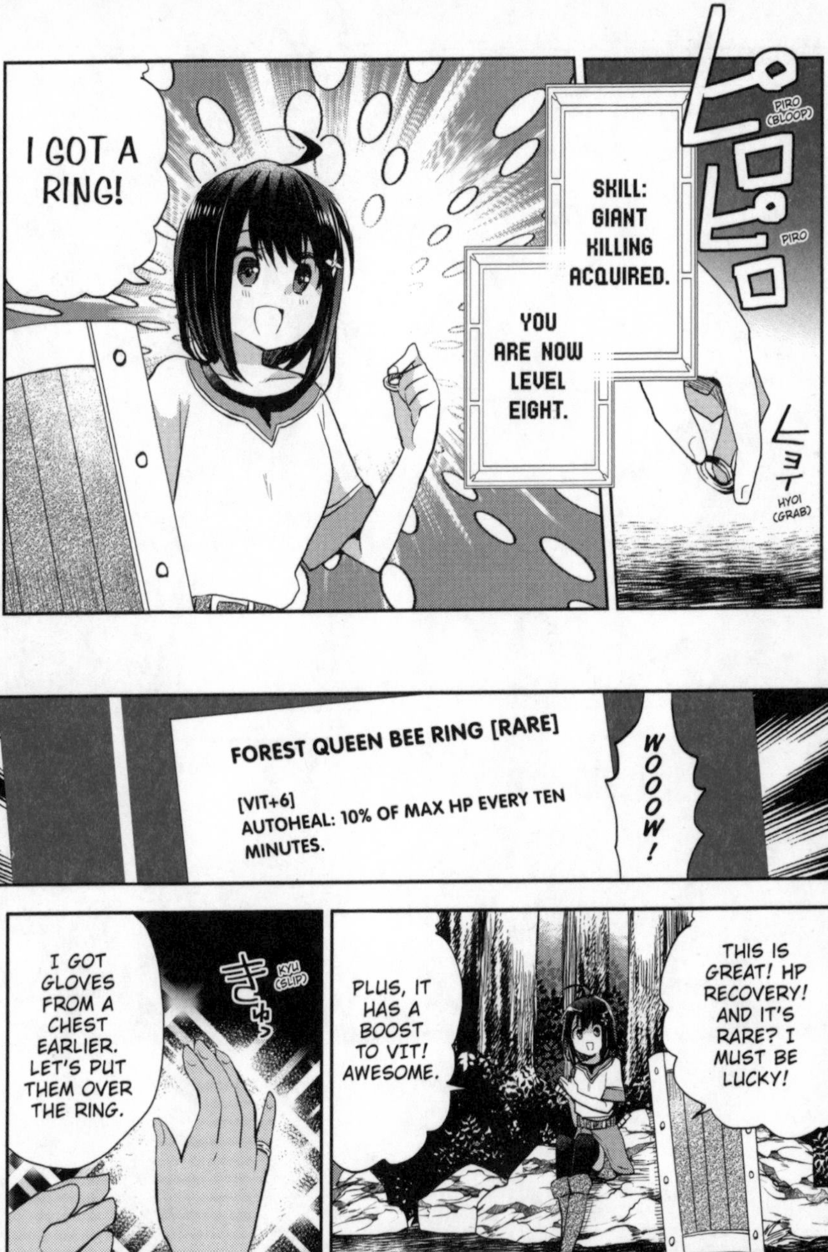
PIRO (BLOOP)
PIRO
SKILL: GIANT KILLING ACQUIRED.
YOU ARE NOW LEVEL EIGHT.
HYOI (GRAB)
I GOT A RING!
FOREST QUEEN BEE RING [RARE]
[VIT+6]
AUTOHEAL: 10% OF MAX HP EVERY TEN MINUTES.
WOOOOW!
THIS IS GREAT! HP RECOVERY! AND IT'S RARE? I MUST BE LUCKY!
PLUS, IT HAS A BOOST TO VIT! AWESOME.
KYU (SLIP)
I GOT GLOVES FROM A CHEST EARLIER. LET'S PUT THEM OVER THE RING.

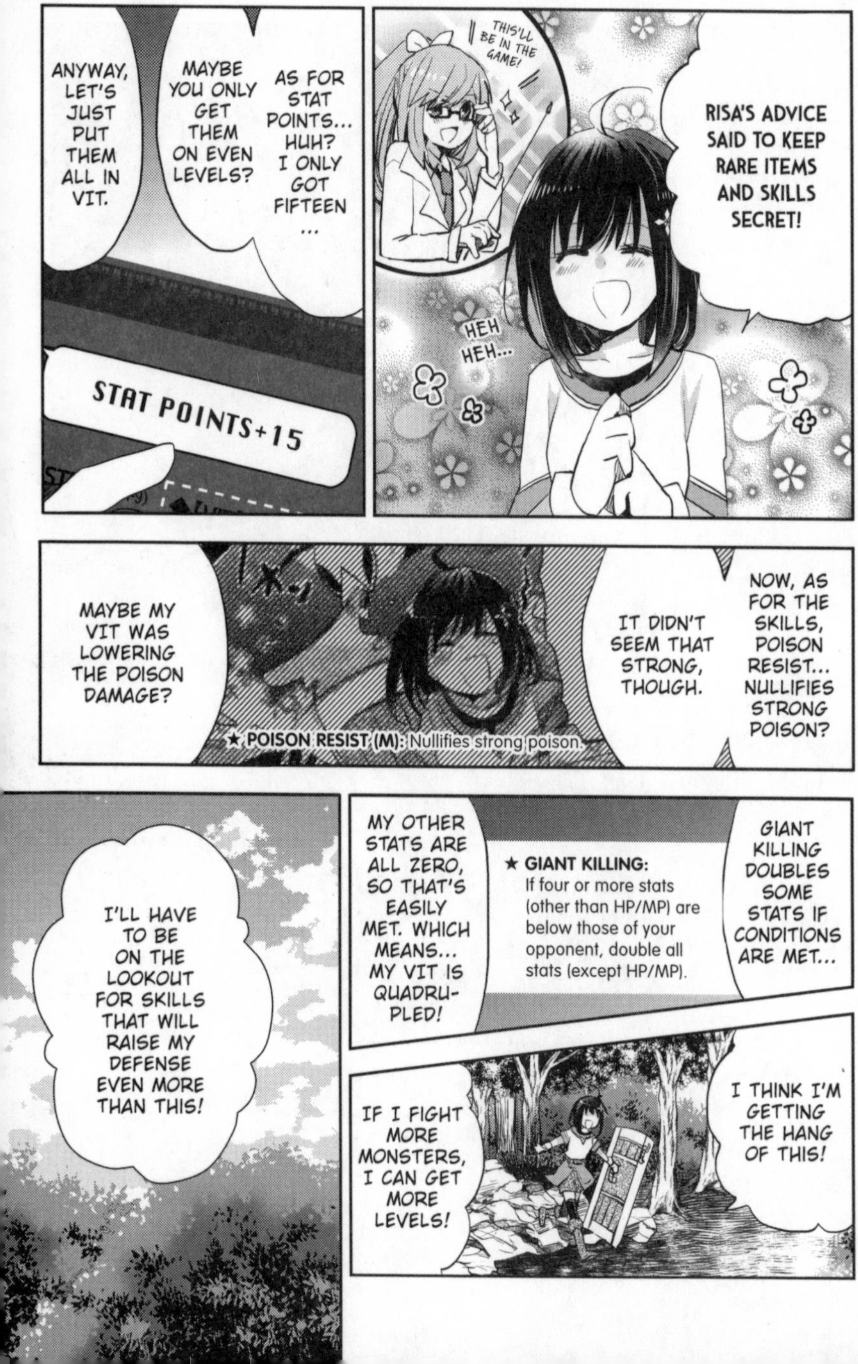
RISA'S ADVICE SAID TO KEEP RARE ITEMS AND SKILLS SECRET!
THIS'LL BE IN THE GAME!
HEH HEH...
AS FOR STAT POINTS... HUH? I ONLY GOT FIFTEEN ...
MAYBE YOU ONLY GET THEM ON EVEN LEVELS?
ANYWAY, LET'S JUST PUT THEM ALL IN VIT.
STAT POINTS+15
NOW, AS FOR THE SKILLS, POISON RESIST... NULLIFIES STRONG POISON?
IT DIDN'T SEEM THAT STRONG, THOUGH.
MAYBE MY VIT WAS LOWERING THE POISON DAMAGE?
★ POISON RESIST (M): Nullifies strong poison.
GIANT KILLING DOUBLES SOME STATS IF CONDITIONS ARE MET...
★ GIANT KILLING: If four or more stats (other than HP/MP) are below those of your opponent, double all stats (except HP/MP).
MY OTHER STATS ARE ALL ZERO, SO THAT'S EASILY MET. WHICH MEANS... MY VIT IS QUADRU-PLED!
I THINK I'M GETTING THE HANG OF THIS!
IF I FIGHT MORE MONSTERS, I CAN GET MORE LEVELS!
I'LL HAVE TO BE ON THE LOOKOUT FOR SKILLS THAT WILL RAISE MY DEFENSE EVEN MORE THAN THIS!

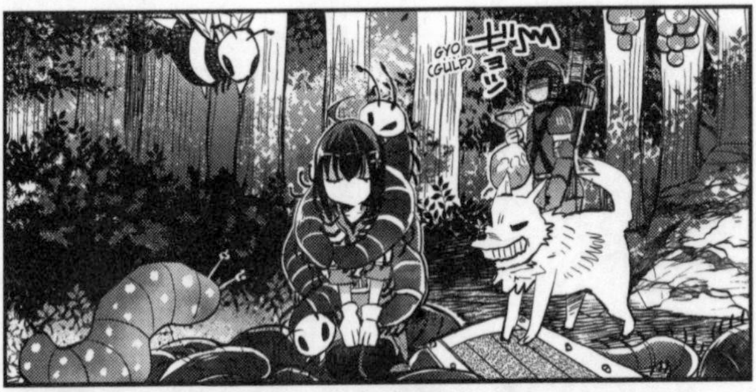
GYO (GULP)

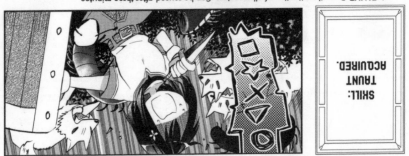

SKILL:
MEDITATION
ACQUIRED.

★ **MEDITATION:** Use to recover 1% of Max HP every ten seconds. Effect lasts ten minutes. Consumes no MP. Unable to attack while Meditating.

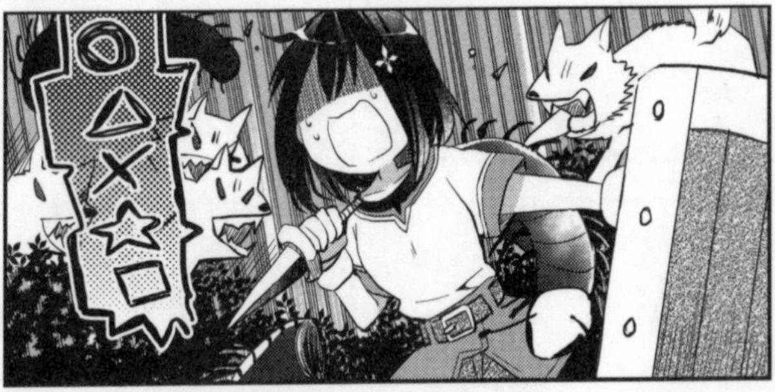

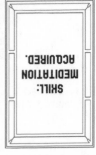

SKILL:
TAUNT
ACQUIRED.

★ **TAUNT:** Draw the attention of all monsters. Can be reused after three minutes.

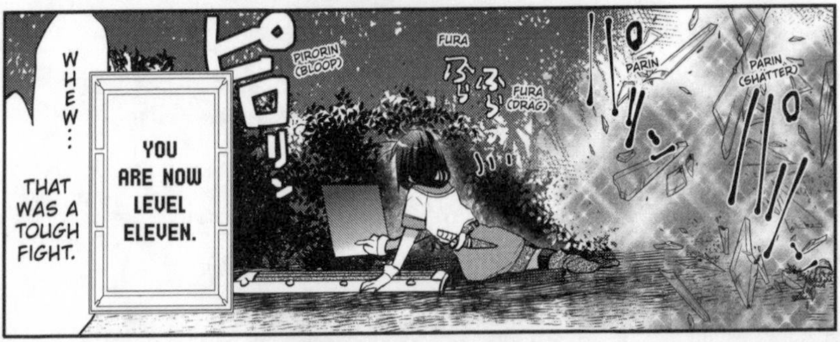
PARIN (SHATTER)
PARIN
FURA
FURA (DRAG)
PIRORIN (BLOOP)
YOU ARE NOW LEVEL ELEVEN.
WHEW... THAT WAS A TOUGH FIGHT.

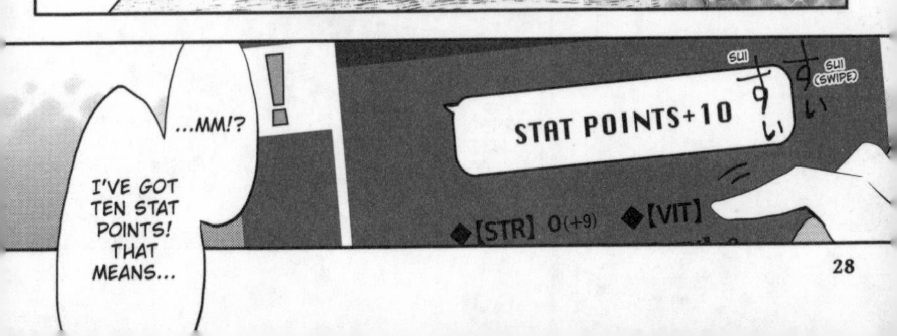
SUI (SWIPE)
SUI
STAT POINTS+10
[STR] 0(+9)
[VIT]
!
...MM!?
I'VE GOT TEN STAT POINTS! THAT MEANS...

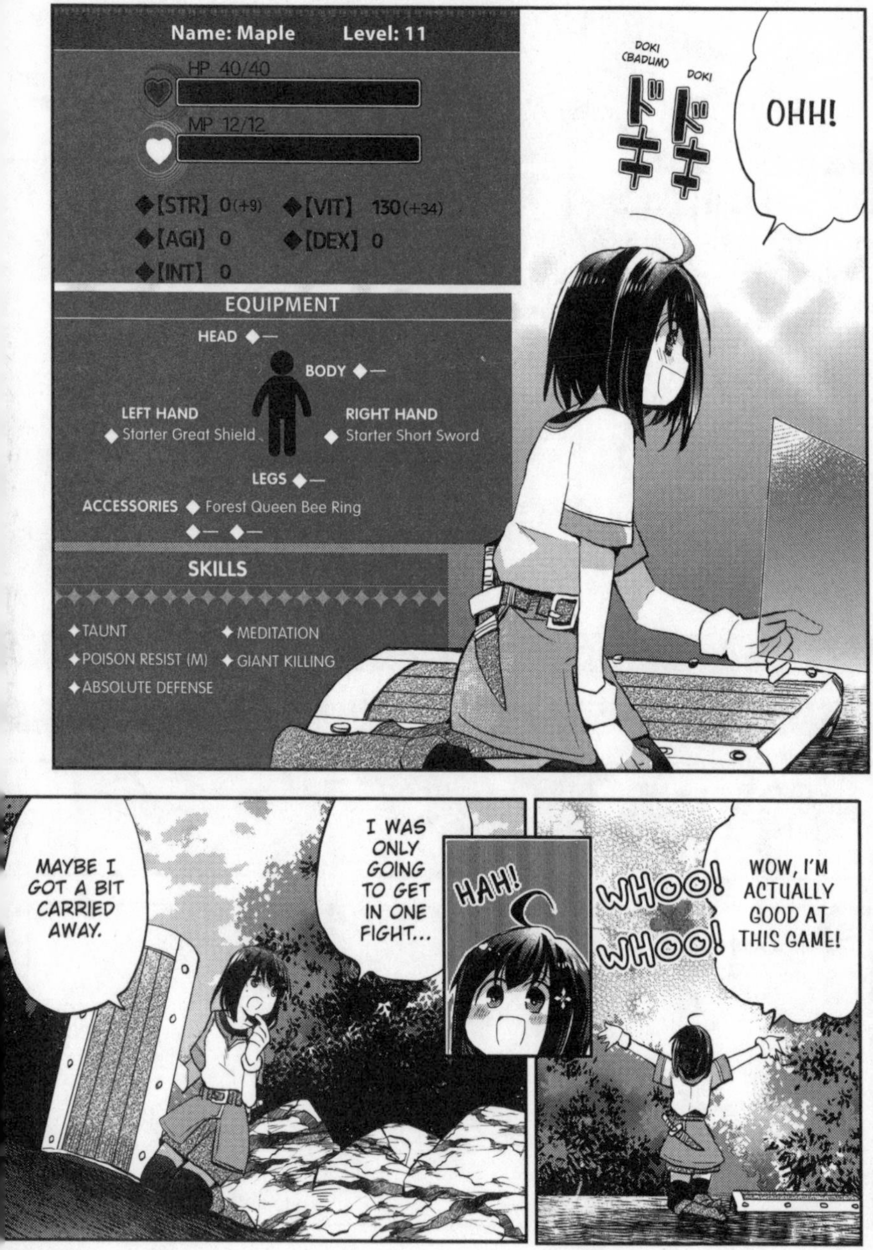
OHH!
DOKI (BADUM) DOKI
Name: Maple Level: 11
HP 40/40
MP 12/12
◆【STR】 0(+9) ◆【VIT】 130(+34)
◆【AGI】 0 ◆【DEX】 0
◆【INT】 0
EQUIPMENT
HEAD ◆—
BODY ◆—
LEFT HAND ◆ Starter Great Shield
RIGHT HAND ◆ Starter Short Sword
LEGS ◆—
ACCESSORIES ◆ Forest Queen Bee Ring
◆— ◆—
SKILLS
✦TAUNT ✦MEDITATION
✦POISON RESIST (M) ✦GIANT KILLING
✦ABSOLUTE DEFENSE
WOW, I'M ACTUALLY GOOD AT THIS GAME!
WHOO! WHOO!
HAH!
I WAS ONLY GOING TO GET IN ONE FIGHT...
MAYBE I GOT A BIT CARRIED AWAY.

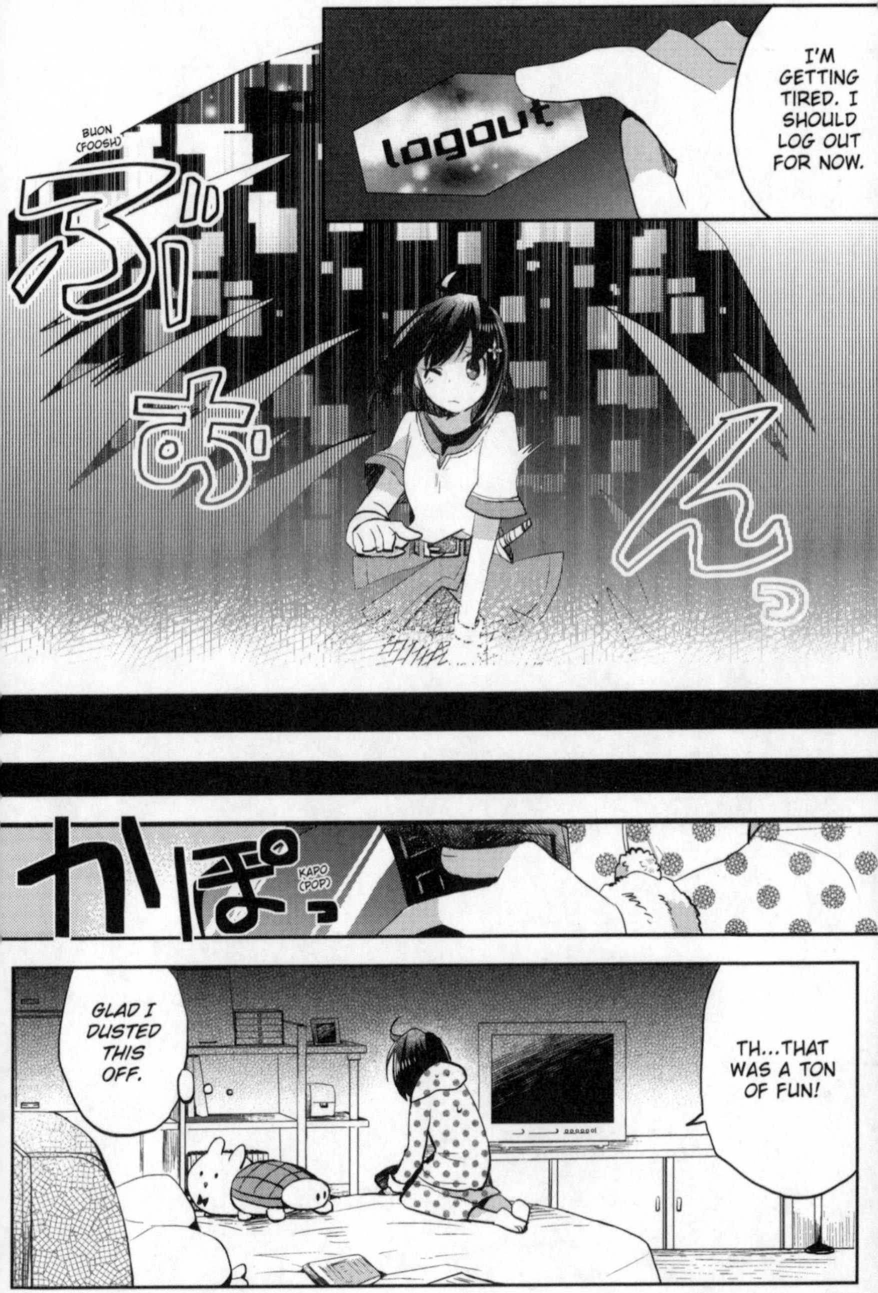
I'M GETTING TIRED. I SHOULD LOG OUT FOR NOW.
logout
BUON (FOOSH)
KAPO (POP)
TH...THAT WAS A TON OF FUN!
GLAD I DUSTED THIS OFF.

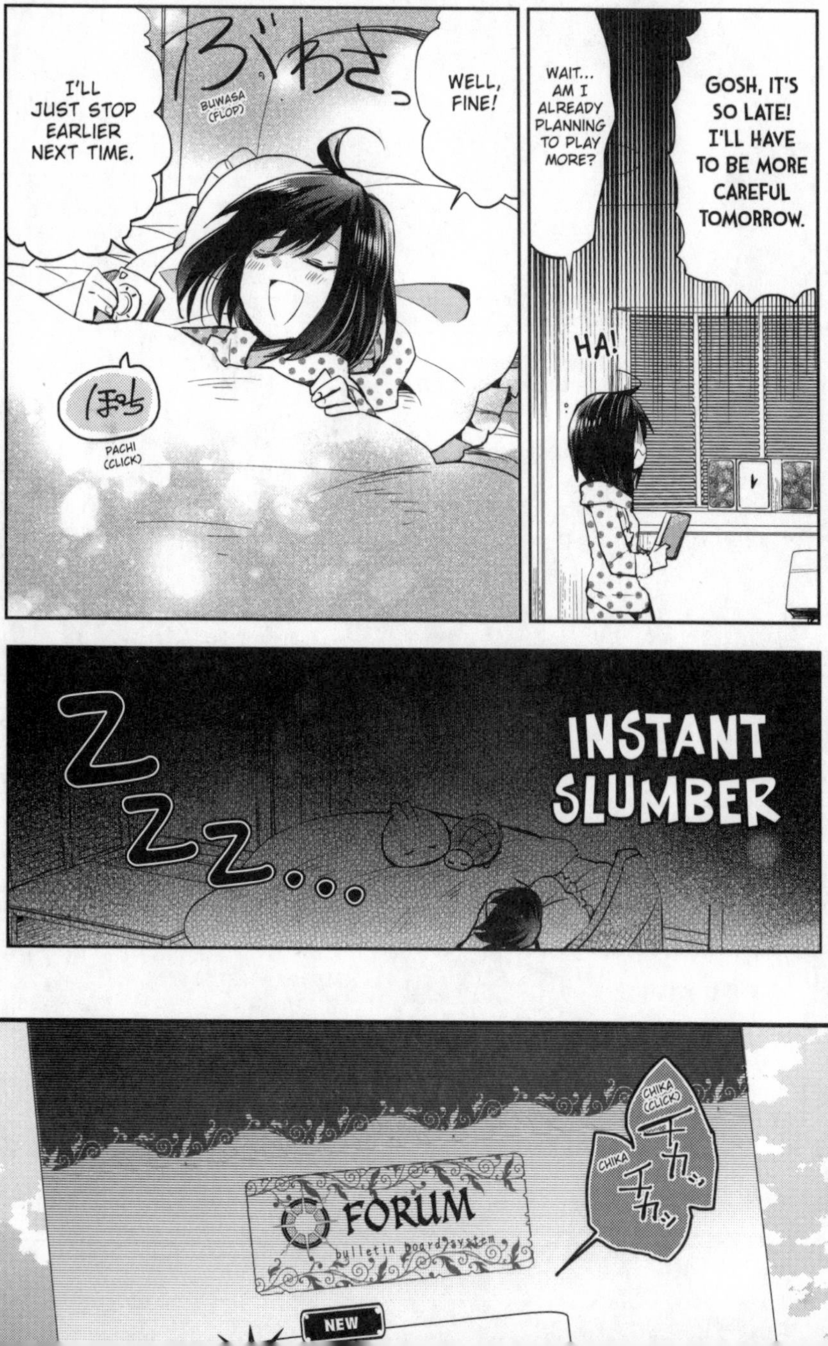
GOSH, IT'S SO LATE! I'LL HAVE TO BE MORE CAREFUL TOMORROW.
WAIT... AM I ALREADY PLANNING TO PLAY MORE?
HA!
WELL, FINE!
ぶわさっ
BUWASA (FLOP)
I'LL JUST STOP EARLIER NEXT TIME.
ぽちっ
PACHI (CLICK)
INSTANT SLUMBER
ZZZ...
チカッ チカッ
CHIKA CHIKA (CLICK)
FORUM
bulletin board system
NEW

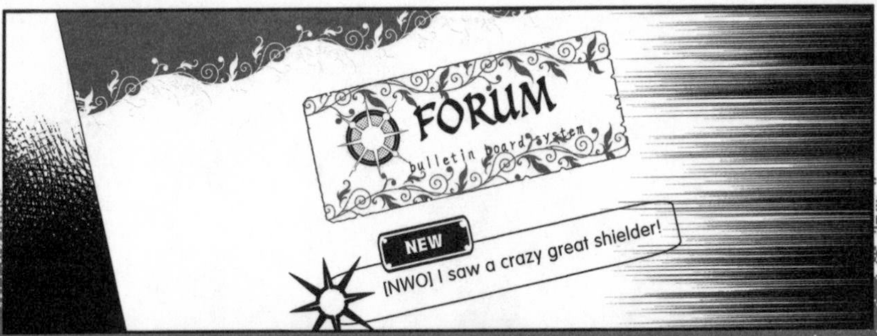
FORUM
bulletin board system
NEW
[NWO] I saw a crazy great shielder!

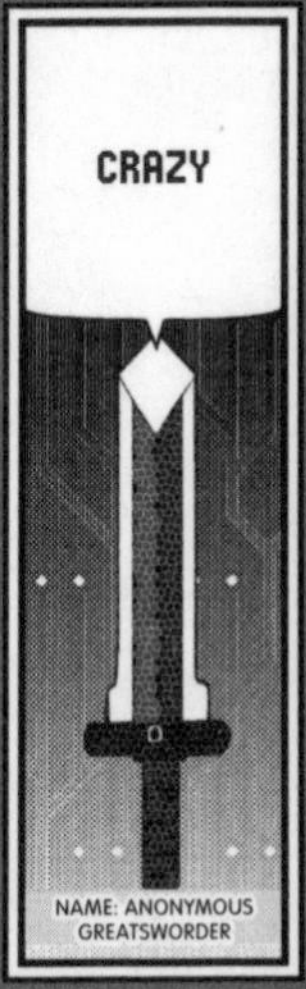
CRAZY
NAME: ANONYMOUS GREATSWORDER

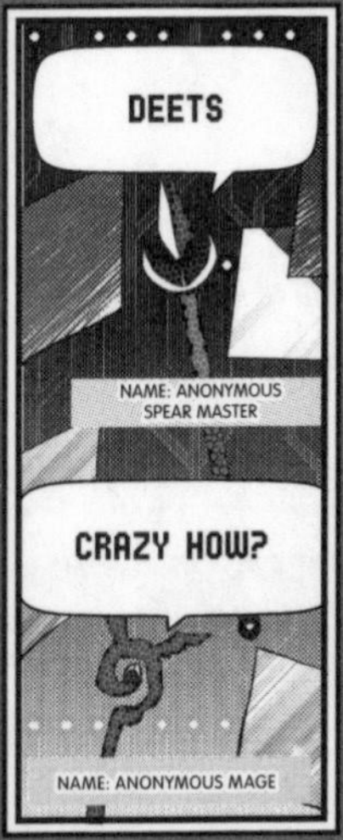
DEETS
NAME: ANONYMOUS SPEAR MASTER
CRAZY HOW?
NAME: ANONYMOUS MAGE

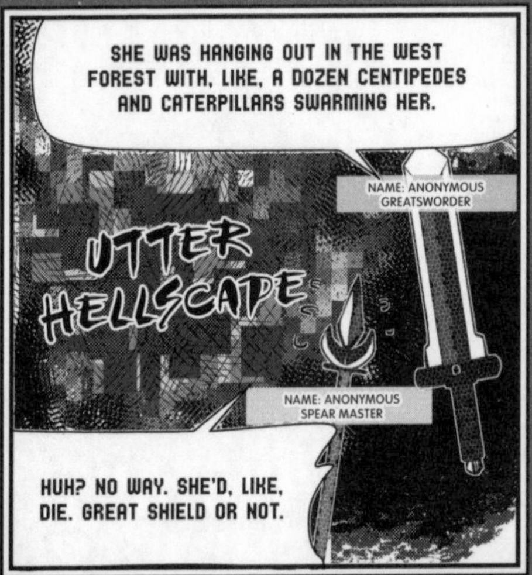
SHE WAS HANGING OUT IN THE WEST FOREST WITH, LIKE, A DOZEN CENTIPEDES AND CATERPILLARS SWARMING HER.
NAME: ANONYMOUS GREATSWORDER
UTTER HELLSCAPE
NAME: ANONYMOUS SPEAR MASTER
HUH? NO WAY. SHE'D, LIKE, DIE. GREAT SHIELD OR NOT.

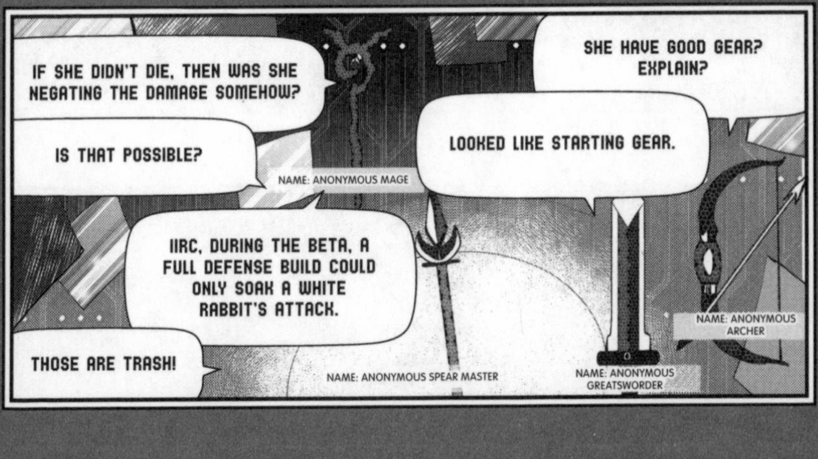
SHE HAVE GOOD GEAR? EXPLAIN?
LOOKED LIKE STARTING GEAR.
NAME: ANONYMOUS ARCHER
NAME: ANONYMOUS GREATSWORDER
IF SHE DIDN'T DIE, THEN WAS SHE NEGATING THE DAMAGE SOMEHOW?
IS THAT POSSIBLE?
NAME: ANONYMOUS MAGE
IIRC, DURING THE BETA, A FULL DEFENSE BUILD COULD ONLY SOAK A WHITE RABBIT'S ATTACK.
THOSE ARE TRASH!
NAME: ANONYMOUS SPEAR MASTER

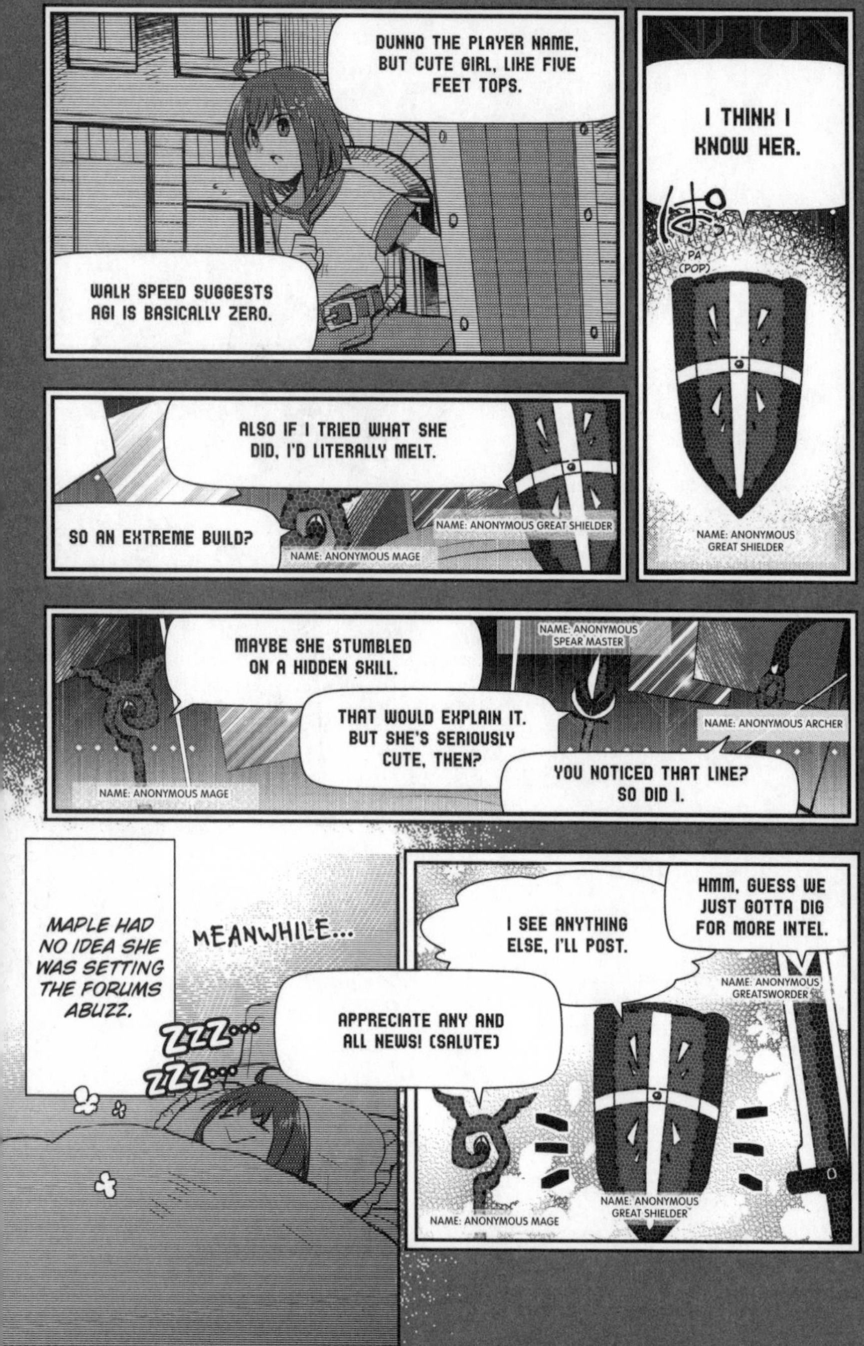
I THINK I KNOW HER.
PA (POP)
NAME: ANONYMOUS GREAT SHIELDER
DUNNO THE PLAYER NAME, BUT CUTE GIRL, LIKE FIVE FEET TOPS.
WALK SPEED SUGGESTS AGI IS BASICALLY ZERO.
ALSO IF I TRIED WHAT SHE DID, I'D LITERALLY MELT.
NAME: ANONYMOUS GREAT SHIELDER
SO AN EXTREME BUILD?
NAME: ANONYMOUS MAGE
NAME: ANONYMOUS SPEAR MASTER
NAME: ANONYMOUS ARCHER
MAYBE SHE STUMBLED ON A HIDDEN SKILL.
THAT WOULD EXPLAIN IT. BUT SHE'S SERIOUSLY CUTE, THEN?
YOU NOTICED THAT LINE? SO DID I.
NAME: ANONYMOUS MAGE
HMM, GUESS WE JUST GOTTA DIG FOR MORE INTEL.
NAME: ANONYMOUS GREATSWORDER
I SEE ANYTHING ELSE, I'LL POST.
APPRECIATE ANY AND ALL NEWS! (SALUTE)
NAME: ANONYMOUS GREAT SHIELDER
NAME: ANONYMOUS MAGE
MEANWHILE...
MAPLE HAD NO IDEA SHE WAS SETTING THE FORUMS ABUZZ.
ZZZ...
ZZZ...

Welcome to NewWorld Online.

I Don't Want to Get Hurt,

so I'll Max Out My Defense.

presented by: JIROU OIMOTO & YUUMIKAN

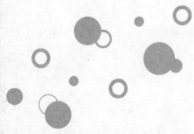

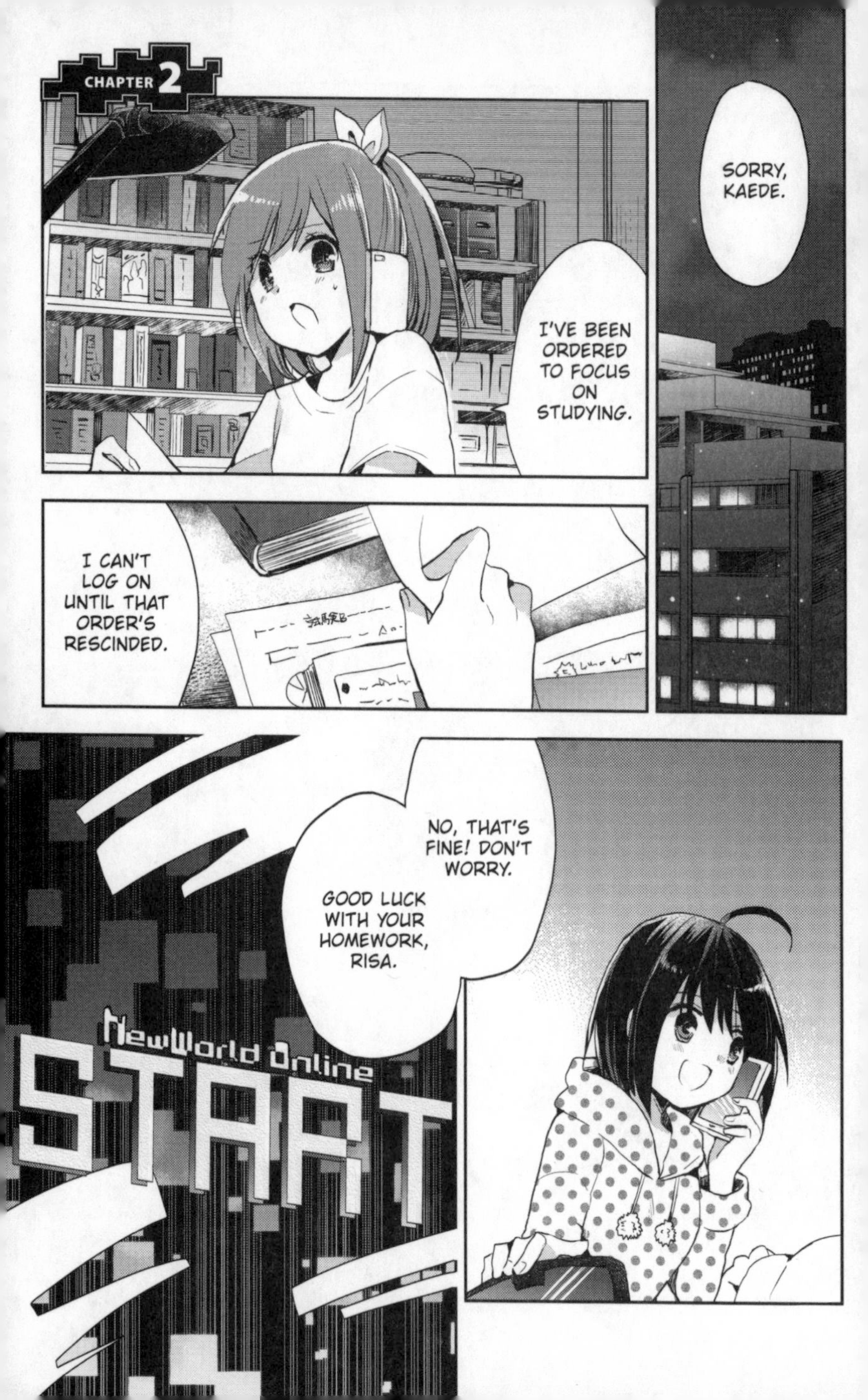
CHAPTER 2
SORRY, KAEDE.
I'VE BEEN ORDERED TO FOCUS ON STUDYING.
I CAN'T LOG ON UNTIL THAT ORDER'S RESCINDED.
NO, THAT'S FINE! DON'T WORRY.
GOOD LUCK WITH YOUR HOMEWORK, RISA.
NewWorld Online
START

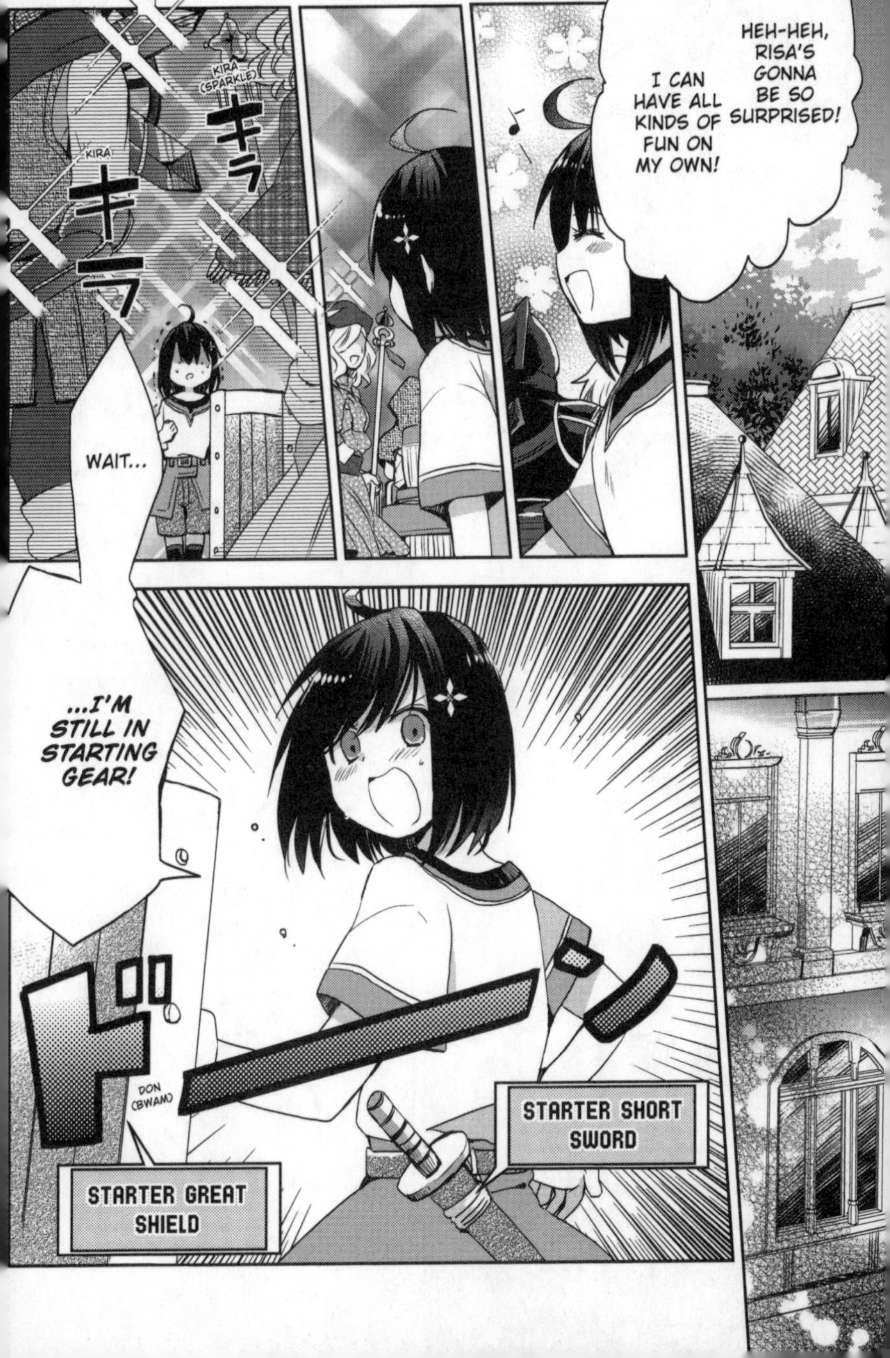
HEH-HEH, RISA'S GONNA BE SO SURPRISED!
I CAN HAVE ALL KINDS OF FUN ON MY OWN!
キラ KIRA (SPARKLE)
キラ KIRA
WAIT...
...I'M STILL IN STARTING GEAR!
STARTER SHORT SWORD
ド DON (BWAM)
STARTER GREAT SHIELD

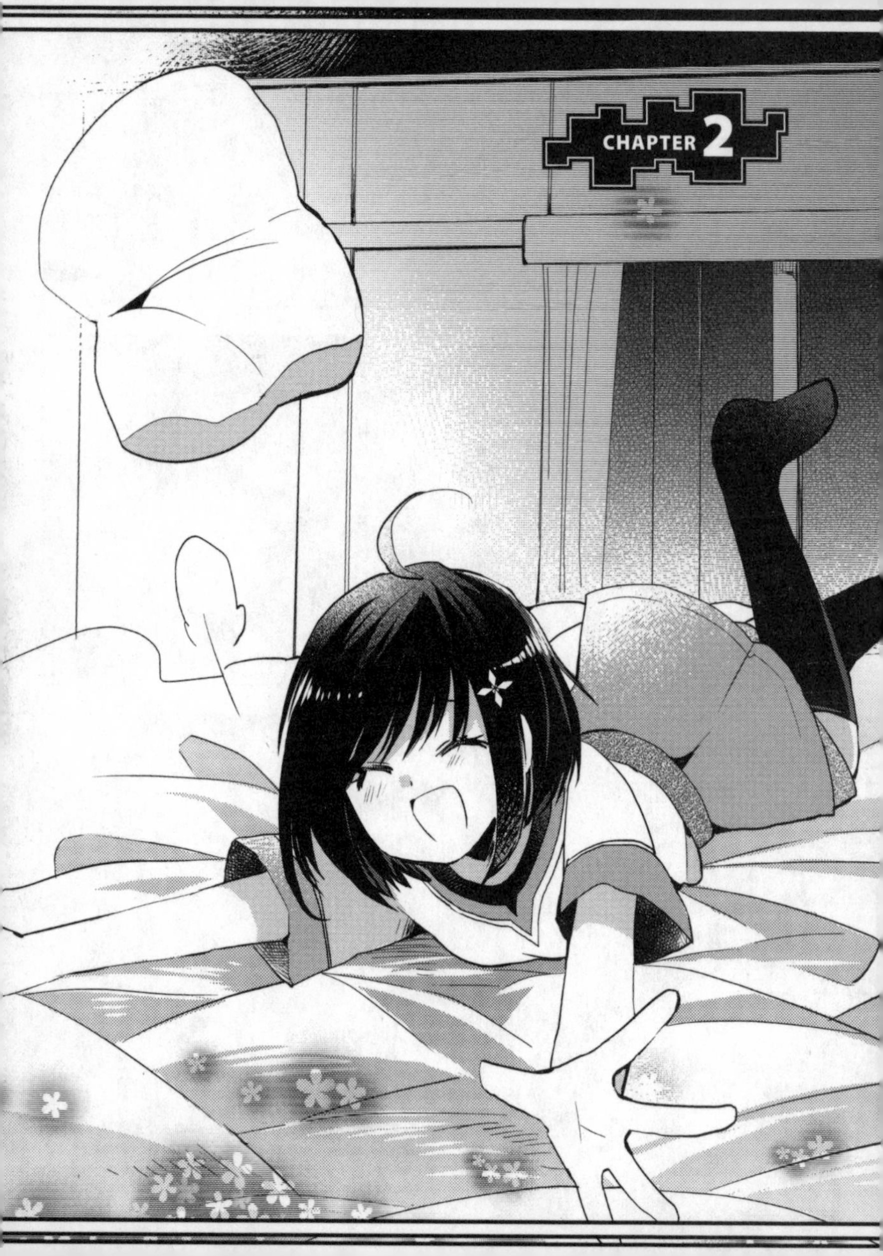
CHAPTER 2

SHUBABA

NORO
(PLOD)
NORO

SHUBABA
(ZOOM)

!

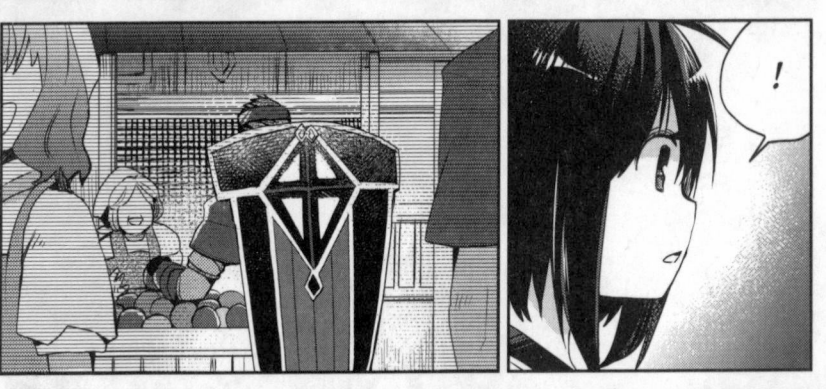

EXCUSE
ME!

WHERE DID
YOU GET
THAT COOL
SHIELD?

PIKU
(TWITCH)

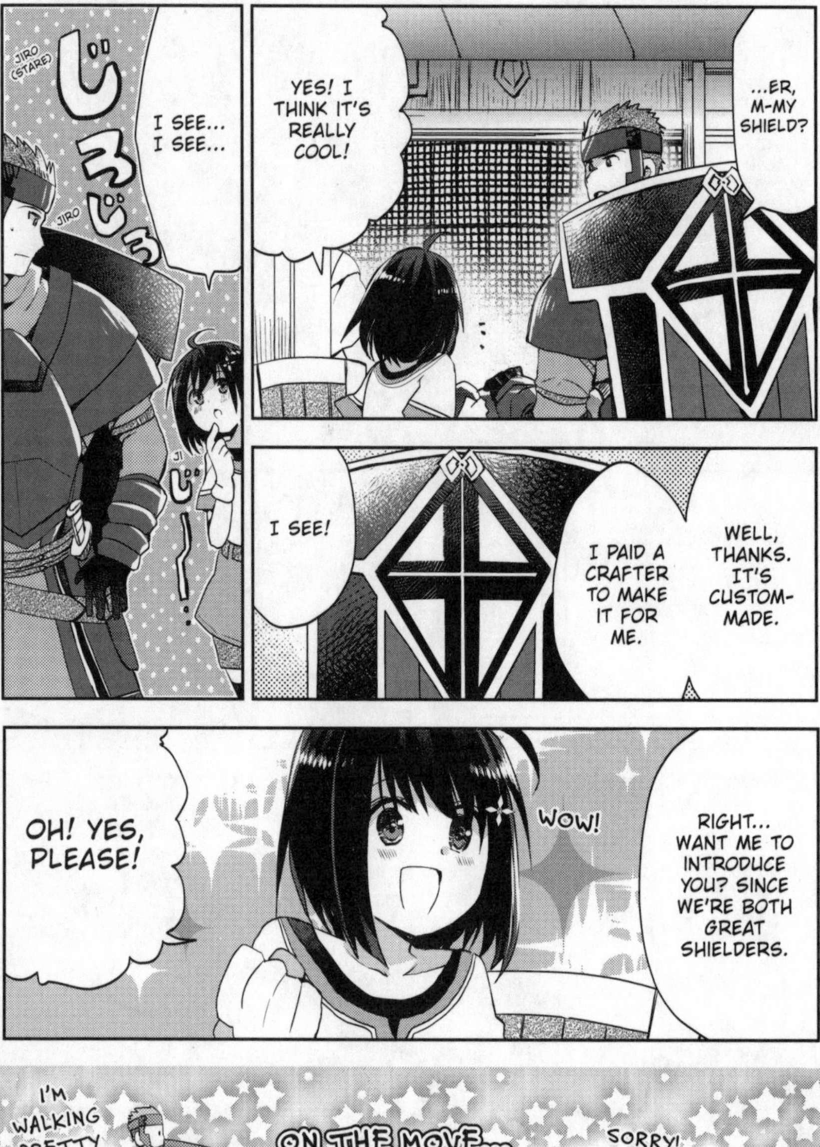
...ER, M-MY SHIELD?
YES! I THINK IT'S REALLY COOL!
WELL, THANKS. IT'S CUSTOM-MADE.
I PAID A CRAFTER TO MAKE IT FOR ME.
I SEE!
JIRO (STARE)
JIRO
I SEE... I SEE...
JI
RIGHT... WANT ME TO INTRODUCE YOU? SINCE WE'RE BOTH GREAT SHIELDERS.
WOW!
OH! YES, PLEASE!
ON THE MOVE...
SORRY!
NORO
NORO (PLOD)
I'M WALKING PRETTY SLOWLY...

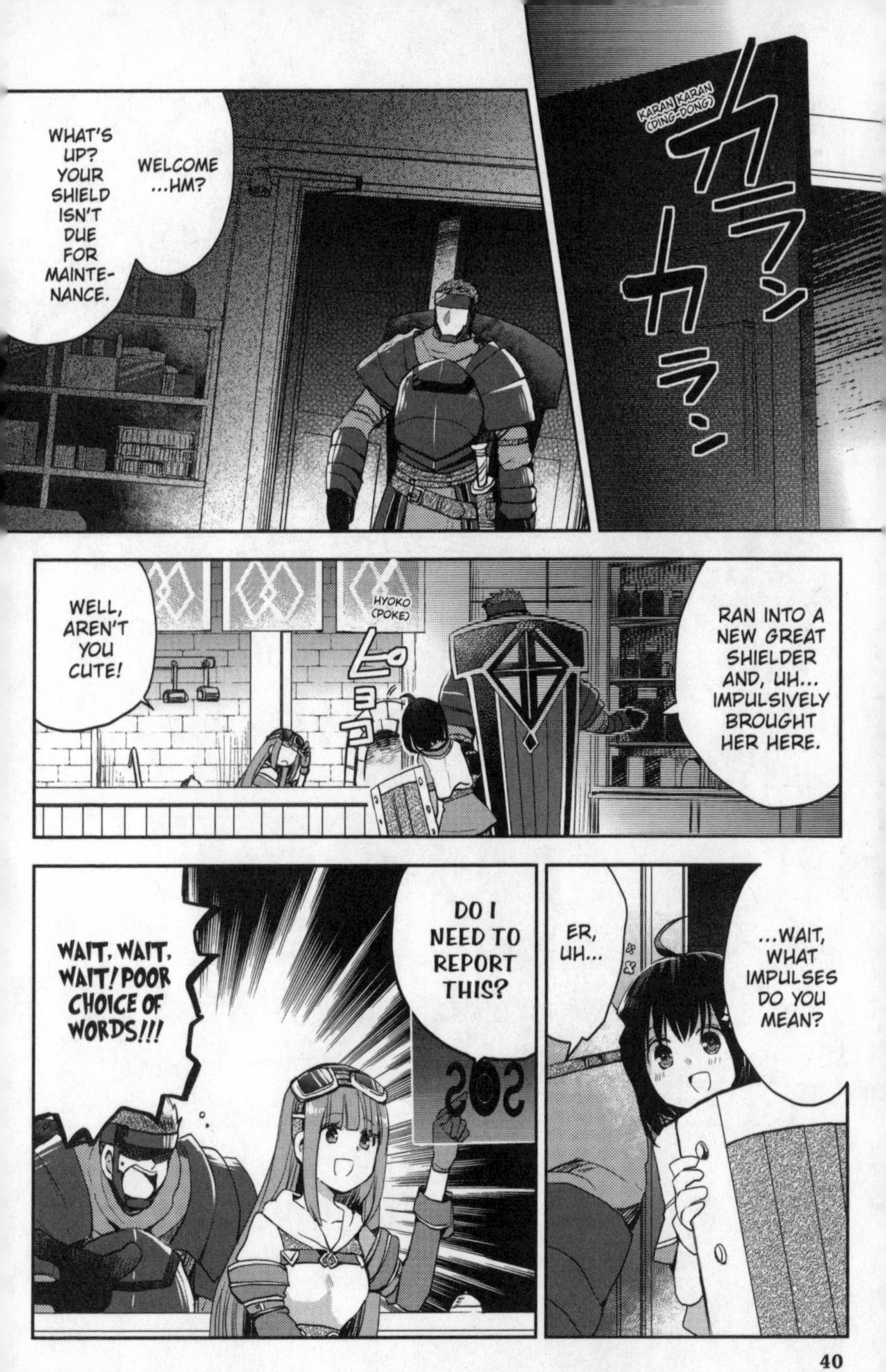
KARAN KARAN (DING-DONG)
WELCOME ...HM?
WHAT'S UP? YOUR SHIELD ISN'T DUE FOR MAINTE-NANCE.
RAN INTO A NEW GREAT SHIELDER AND, UH... IMPULSIVELY BROUGHT HER HERE.
HYOKO (POKE)
WELL, AREN'T YOU CUTE!
...WAIT, WHAT IMPULSES DO YOU MEAN?
ER, UH...
DO I NEED TO REPORT THIS?
SOS
WAIT, WAIT, WAIT! POOR CHOICE OF WORDS!!!

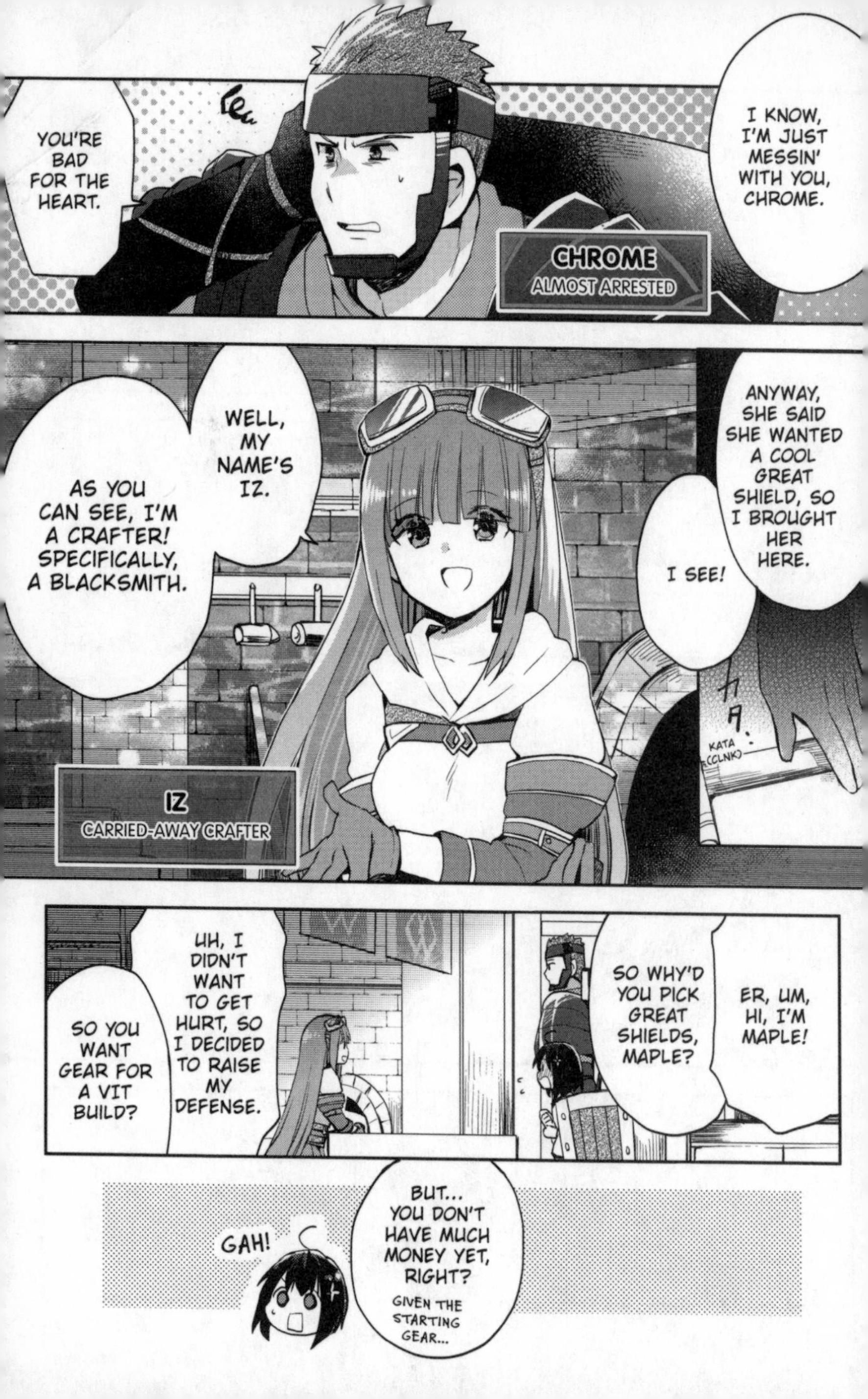
I KNOW, I'M JUST MESSIN' WITH YOU, CHROME.
YOU'RE BAD FOR THE HEART.
CHROME
ALMOST ARRESTED
ANYWAY, SHE SAID SHE WANTED A COOL GREAT SHIELD, SO I BROUGHT HER HERE.
I SEE!
KATA (CLNK)
WELL, MY NAME'S IZ.
AS YOU CAN SEE, I'M A CRAFTER! SPECIFICALLY, A BLACKSMITH.
IZ
CARRIED-AWAY CRAFTER
ER, UM, HI, I'M MAPLE!
SO WHY'D YOU PICK GREAT SHIELDS, MAPLE?
UH, I DIDN'T WANT TO GET HURT, SO I DECIDED TO RAISE MY DEFENSE.
SO YOU WANT GEAR FOR A VIT BUILD?
BUT... YOU DON'T HAVE MUCH MONEY YET, RIGHT?
GIVEN THE STARTING GEAR...
GAH!

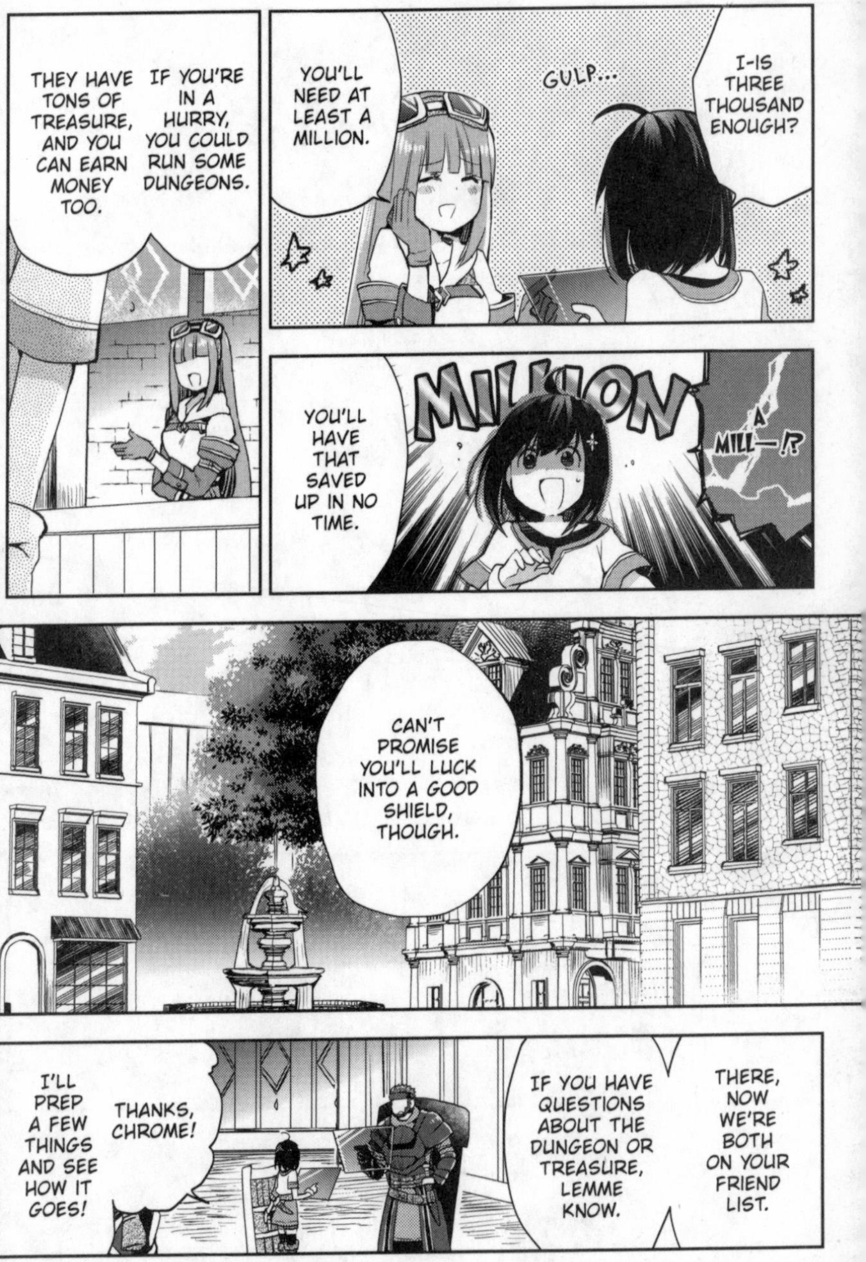
I-IS THREE THOUSAND ENOUGH?
GULP...
YOU'LL NEED AT LEAST A MILLION.
A MILL—!?
MILLION
YOU'LL HAVE THAT SAVED UP IN NO TIME.
IF YOU'RE IN A HURRY, YOU COULD RUN SOME DUNGEONS.
THEY HAVE TONS OF TREASURE, AND YOU CAN EARN MONEY TOO.
CAN'T PROMISE YOU'LL LUCK INTO A GOOD SHIELD, THOUGH.
THERE, NOW WE'RE BOTH ON YOUR FRIEND LIST.
IF YOU HAVE QUESTIONS ABOUT THE DUNGEON OR TREASURE, LEMME KNOW.
THANKS, CHROME!
I'LL PREP A FEW THINGS AND SEE HOW IT GOES!

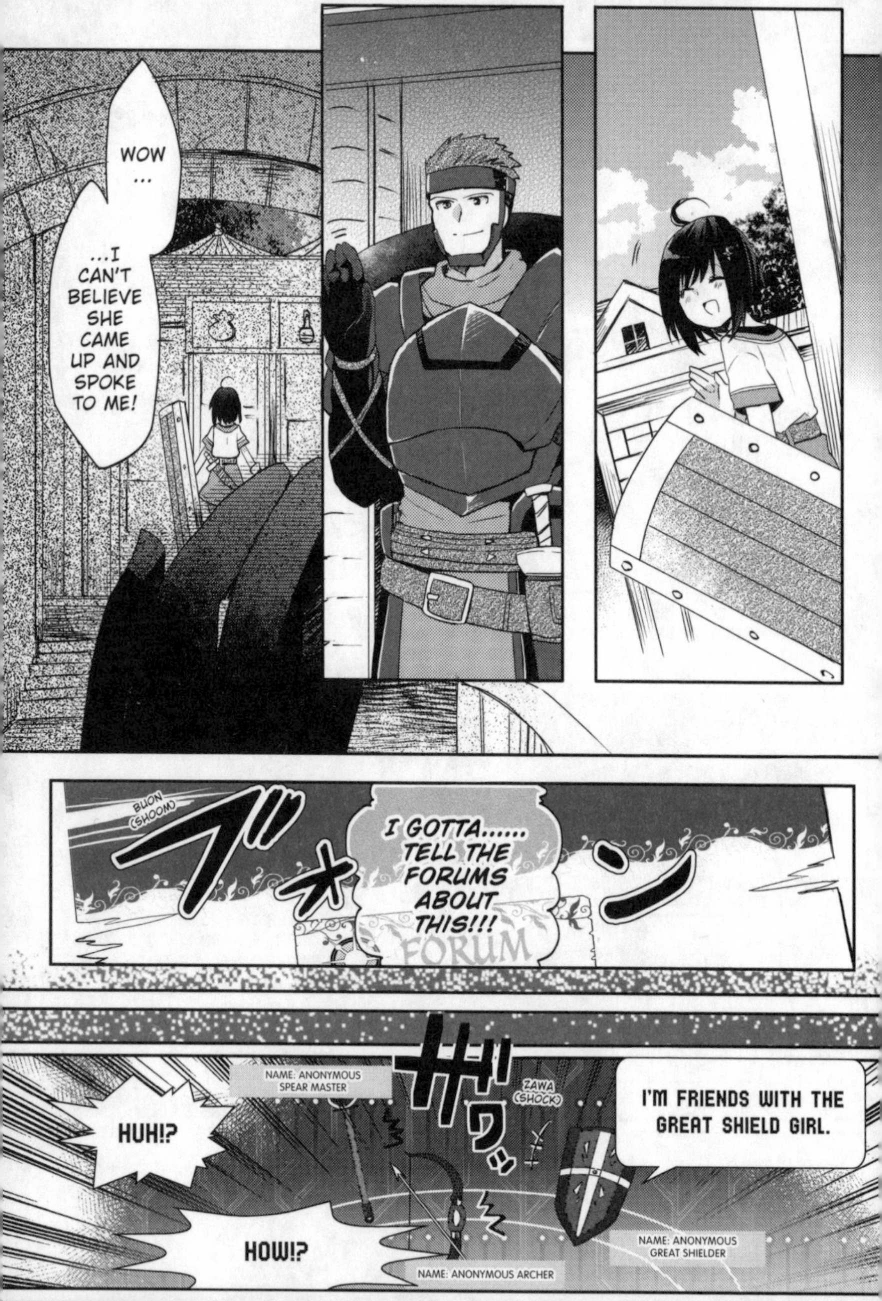
WOW ...
...I CAN'T BELIEVE SHE CAME UP AND SPOKE TO ME!
BUON (SHOOM)
I GOTTA...... TELL THE FORUMS ABOUT THIS!!!
FORUM
I'M FRIENDS WITH THE GREAT SHIELD GIRL.
ZAWA (SHOCK)
NAME: ANONYMOUS GREAT SHIELDER
NAME: ANONYMOUS SPEAR MASTER
HUH!?
NAME: ANONYMOUS ARCHER
HOW!?

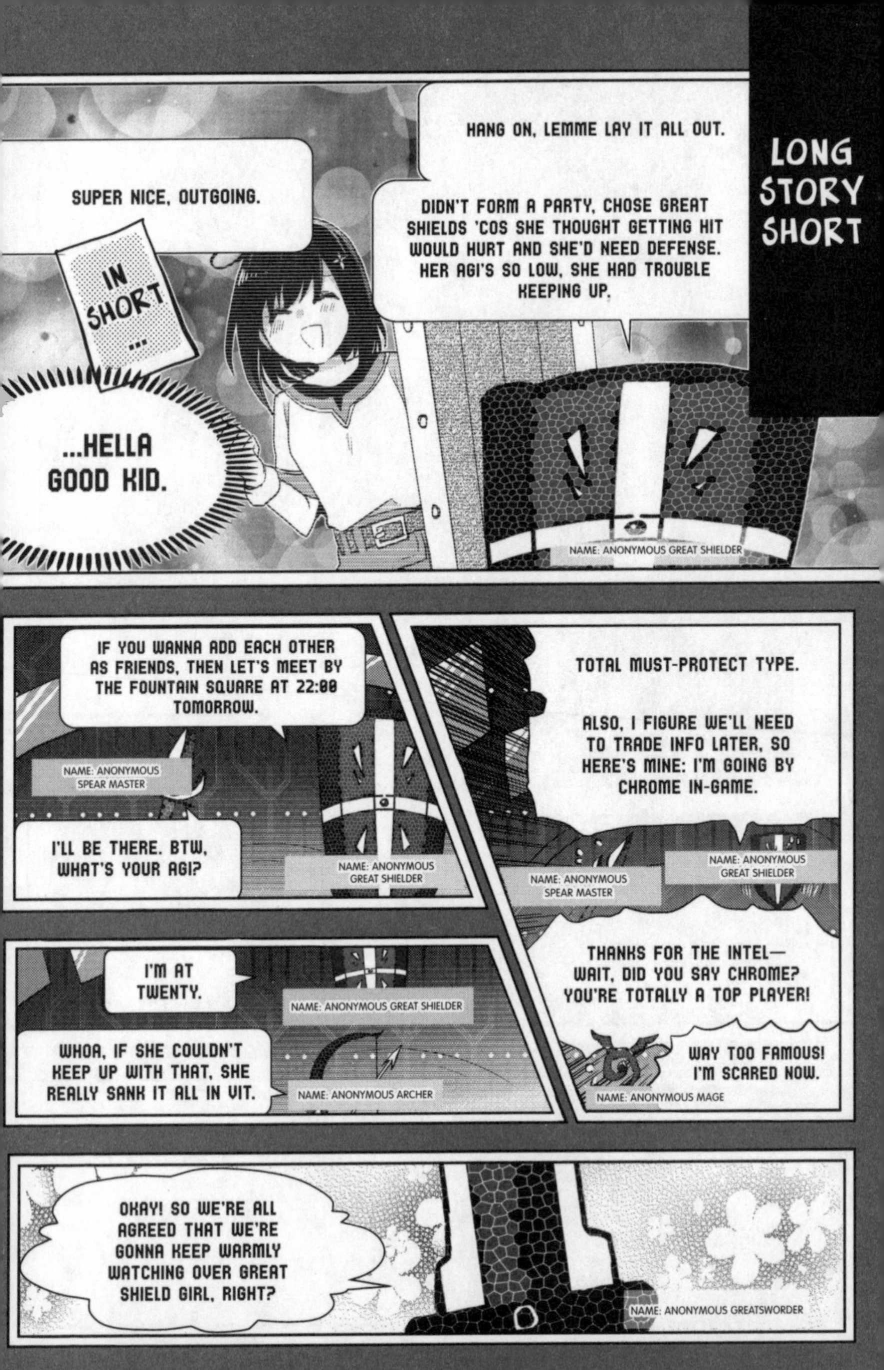
LONG STORY SHORT
HANG ON, LEMME LAY IT ALL OUT.
DIDN'T FORM A PARTY, CHOSE GREAT SHIELDS 'COS SHE THOUGHT GETTING HIT WOULD HURT AND SHE'D NEED DEFENSE. HER AGI'S SO LOW, SHE HAD TROUBLE KEEPING UP.
NAME: ANONYMOUS GREAT SHIELDER
SUPER NICE, OUTGOING.
IN SHORT ...
...HELLA GOOD KID.
TOTAL MUST-PROTECT TYPE.
ALSO, I FIGURE WE'LL NEED TO TRADE INFO LATER, SO HERE'S MINE: I'M GOING BY CHROME IN-GAME.
NAME: ANONYMOUS GREAT SHIELDER
NAME: ANONYMOUS SPEAR MASTER
THANKS FOR THE INTEL—WAIT, DID YOU SAY CHROME? YOU'RE TOTALLY A TOP PLAYER!
WAY TOO FAMOUS! I'M SCARED NOW.
NAME: ANONYMOUS MAGE
IF YOU WANNA ADD EACH OTHER AS FRIENDS, THEN LET'S MEET BY THE FOUNTAIN SQUARE AT 22:00 TOMORROW.
NAME: ANONYMOUS SPEAR MASTER
I'LL BE THERE. BTW, WHAT'S YOUR AGI?
NAME: ANONYMOUS GREAT SHIELDER
I'M AT TWENTY.
NAME: ANONYMOUS GREAT SHIELDER
WHOA, IF SHE COULDN'T KEEP UP WITH THAT, SHE REALLY SANK IT ALL IN VIT.
NAME: ANONYMOUS ARCHER
OKAY! SO WE'RE ALL AGREED THAT WE'RE GONNA KEEP WARMLY WATCHING OVER GREAT SHIELD GIRL, RIGHT?
NAME: ANONYMOUS GREATSWORDER

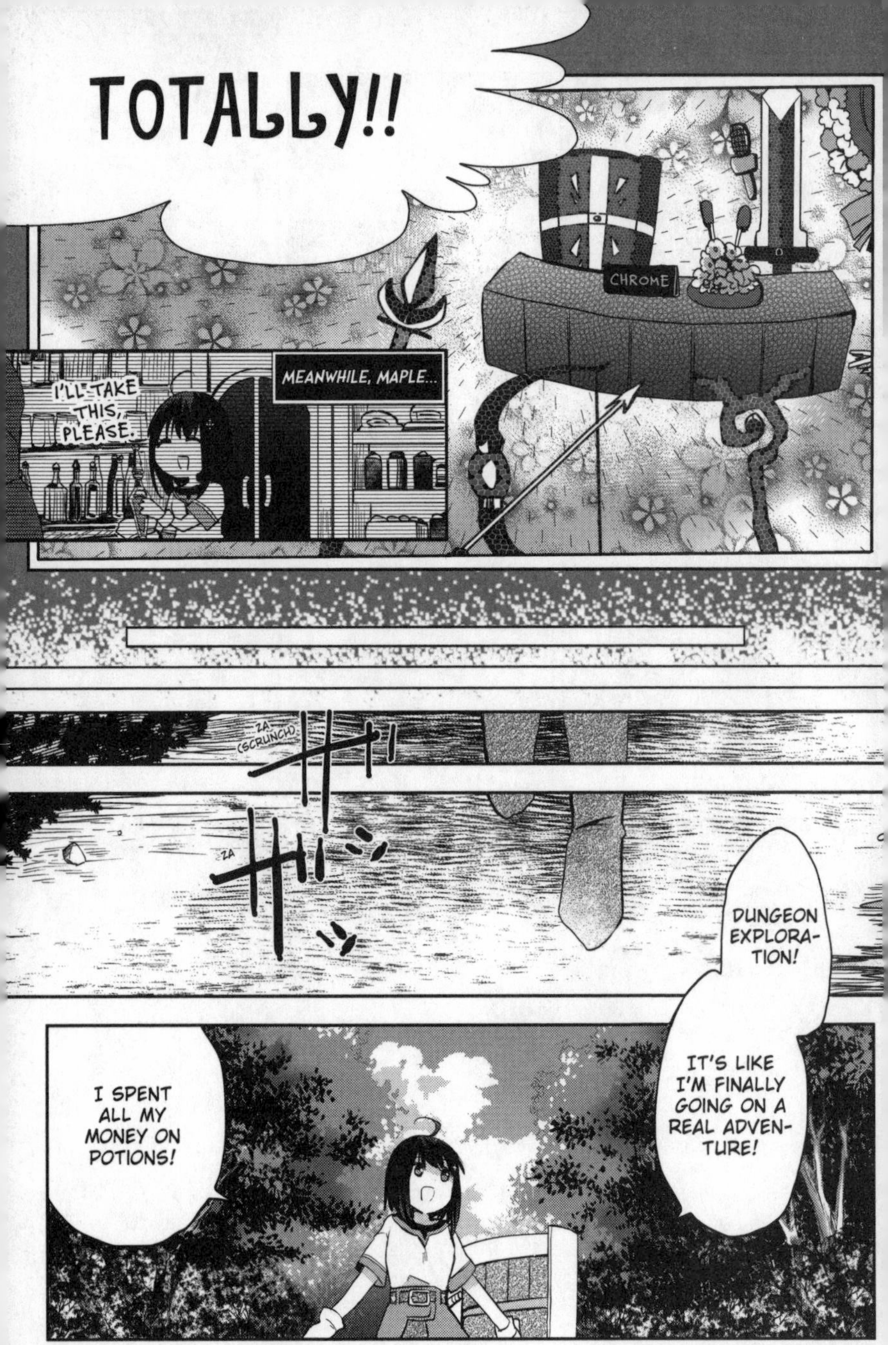
TOTALLY!!
CHROME
MEANWHILE, MAPLE...
I'LL TAKE THIS, PLEASE.
ZA (SCRUNCH)
ZA
DUNGEON EXPLORATION!
IT'S LIKE I'M FINALLY GOING ON A REAL ADVENTURE!
I SPENT ALL MY MONEY ON POTIONS!

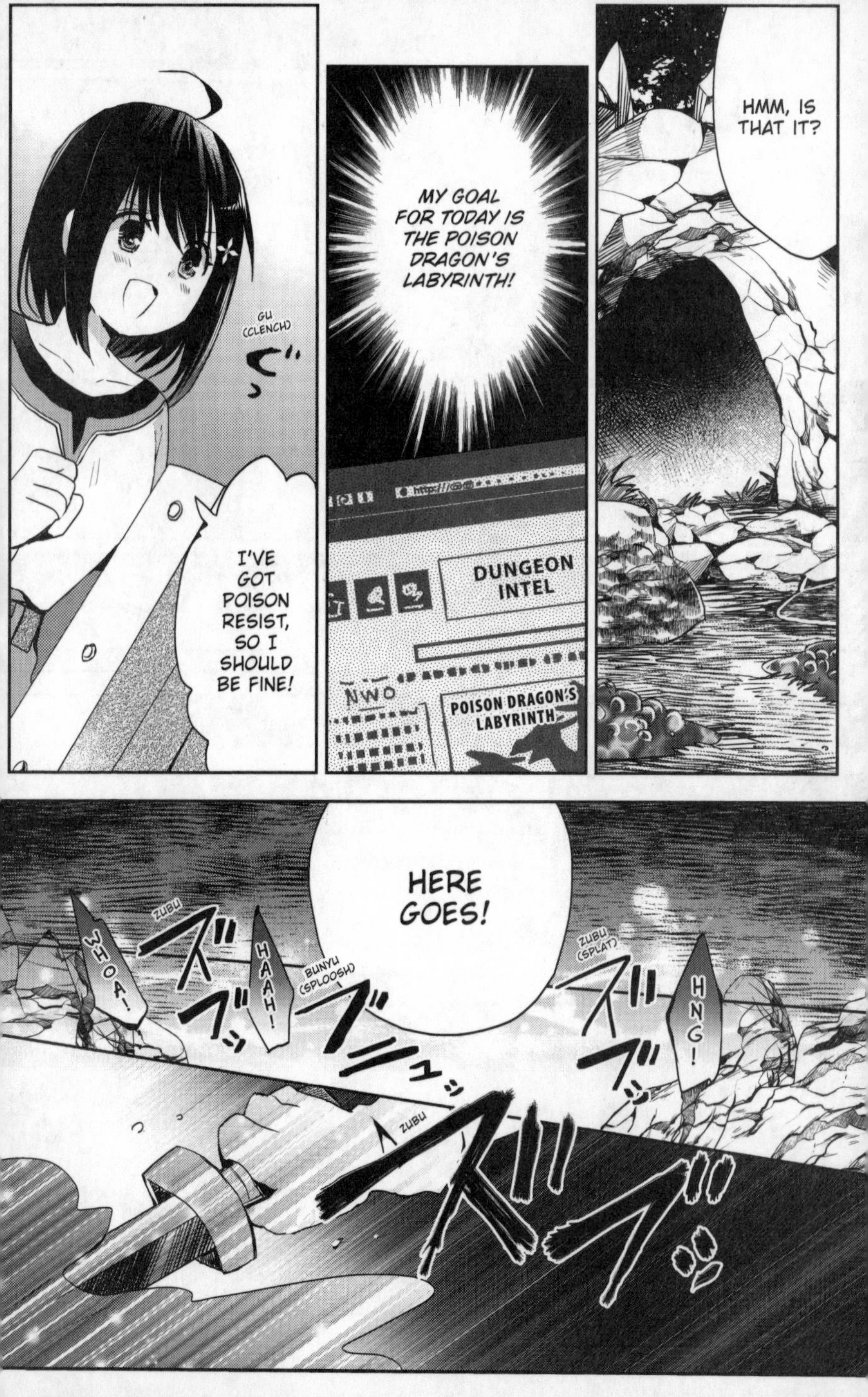
HMM, IS THAT IT?
MY GOAL FOR TODAY IS THE POISON DRAGON'S LABYRINTH!
DUNGEON INTEL
POISON DRAGON'S LABYRINTH
GU (CLENCH)
I'VE GOT POISON RESIST, SO I SHOULD BE FINE!
HERE GOES!
ZUBU (SPLAT)
HNG!
BUNYU (SPLOOSH)
HAAH!
ZUBU
WHOA!
ZUBU

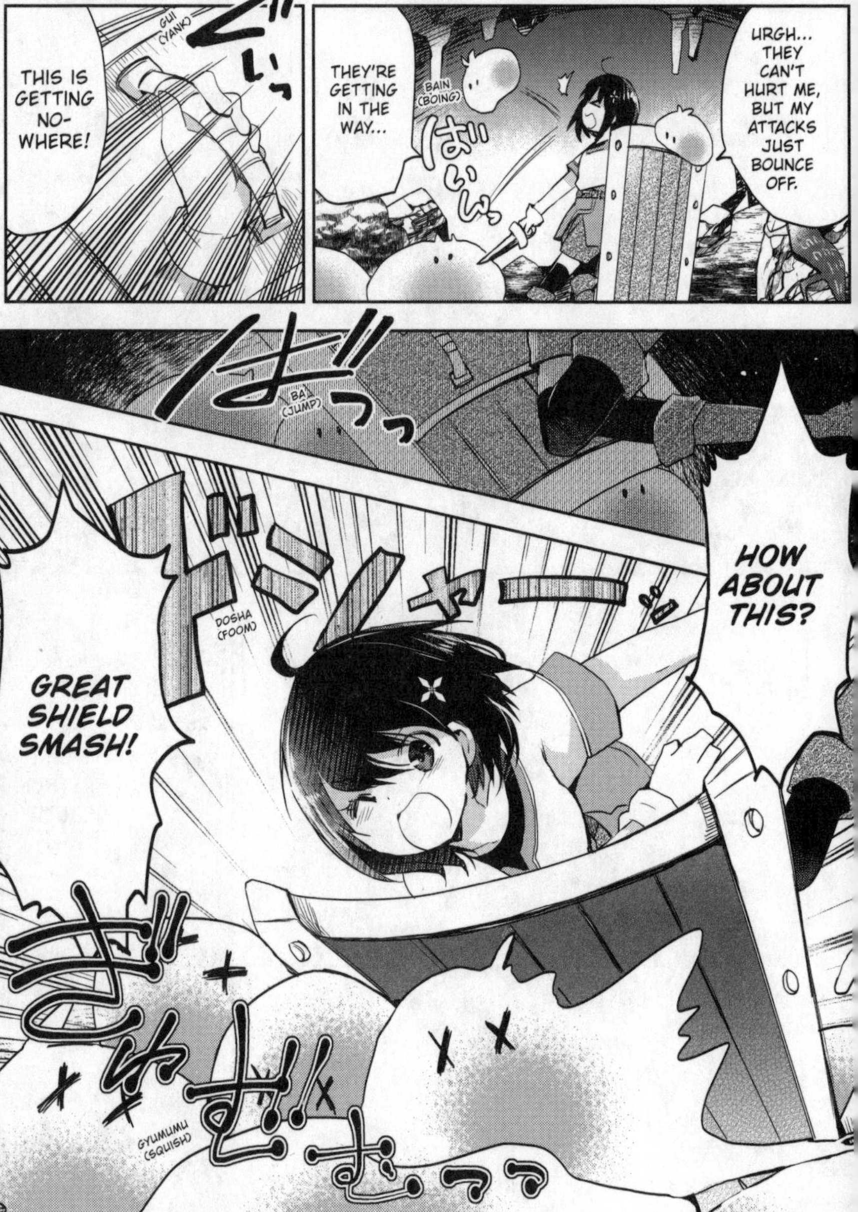
URGH... THEY CAN'T HURT ME, BUT MY ATTACKS JUST BOUNCE OFF.
THEY'RE GETTING IN THE WAY...
BAIN (BOING)
GUI (YANK)
THIS IS GETTING NO-WHERE!
BA (JUMP)
HOW ABOUT THIS?
DOSHA (FOOM)
GREAT SHIELD SMASH!
GYUMUMU (SQUISH)

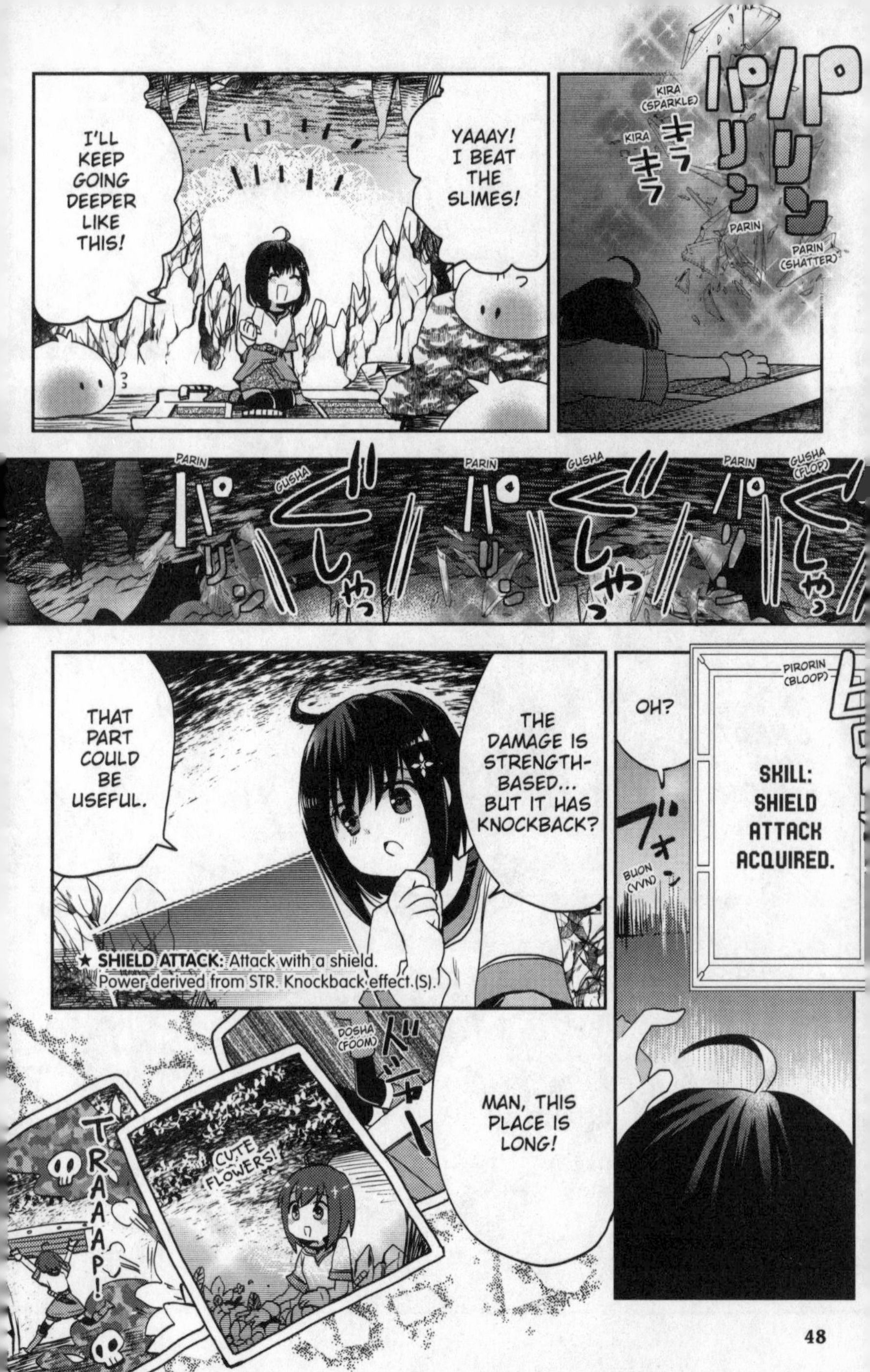
PARIN (SHATTER)
PARIN
KIRA (SPARKLE)
KIRA
YAAAY! I BEAT THE SLIMES!
I'LL KEEP GOING DEEPER LIKE THIS!
GUSHA (FLOP)
PARIN
GUSHA
PARIN
GUSHA
PARIN
PIRORIN (BLOOP)
SKILL: SHIELD ATTACK ACQUIRED.
OH?
BUON (VVN)
THE DAMAGE IS STRENGTH-BASED... BUT IT HAS KNOCKBACK?
THAT PART COULD BE USEFUL.
★ SHIELD ATTACK: Attack with a shield. Power derived from STR. Knockback effect.(S).
MAN, THIS PLACE IS LONG!
DOSHA (FOOM)
CUTE FLOWERS!
TRAAAP!

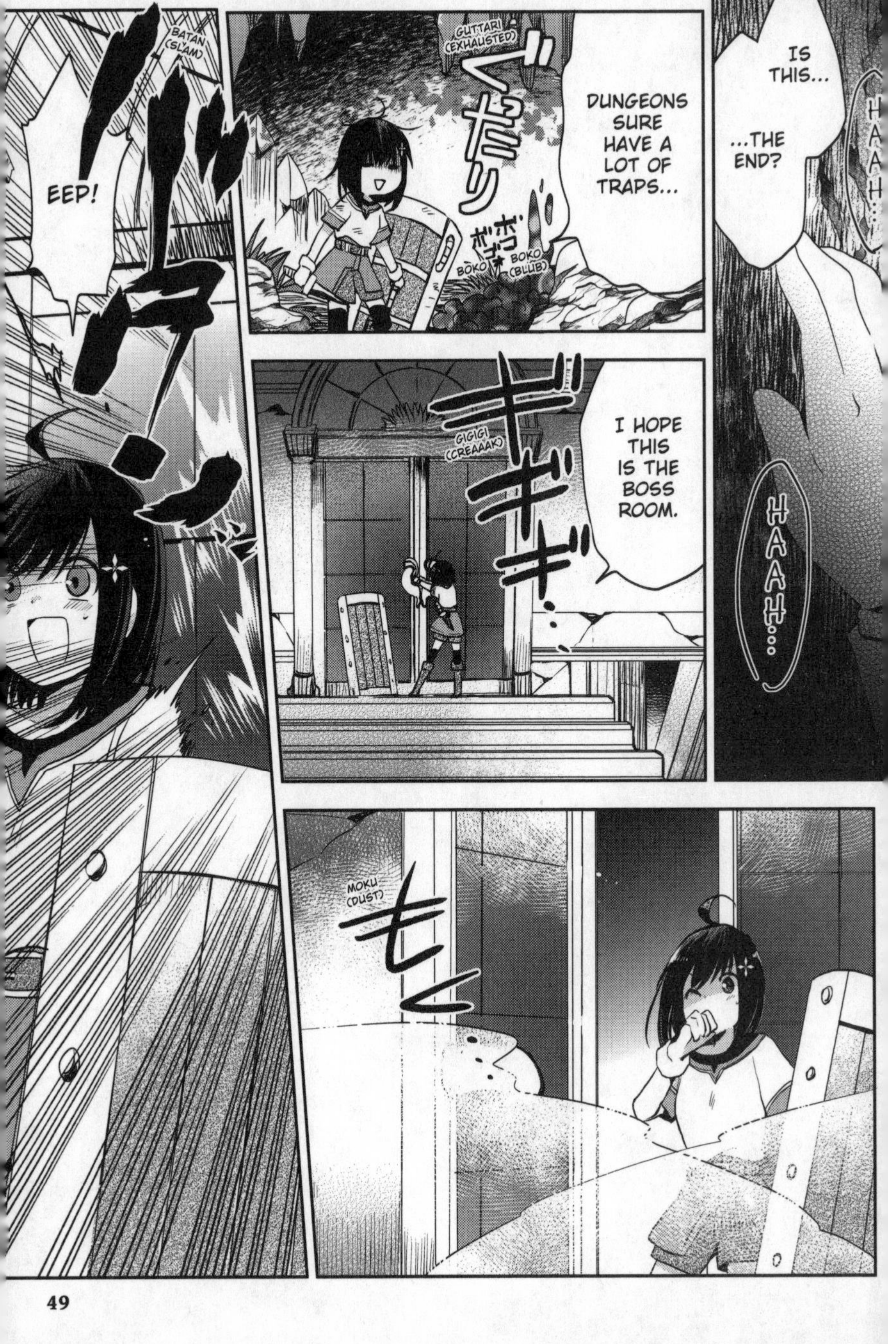
IS THIS...
...THE END?
HAAAH...
HAAAH...
GUTTARI (EXHAUSTED)
DUNGEONS SURE HAVE A LOT OF TRAPS...
BOKO ★ BOKO (BLUB)
GIGIGI (CREAAAK)
I HOPE THIS IS THE BOSS ROOM.
MOKU (DUST)
BATAN (SLAM)
EEP!

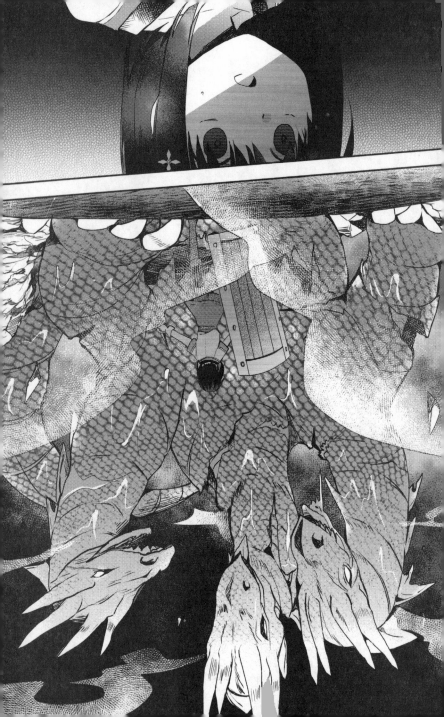

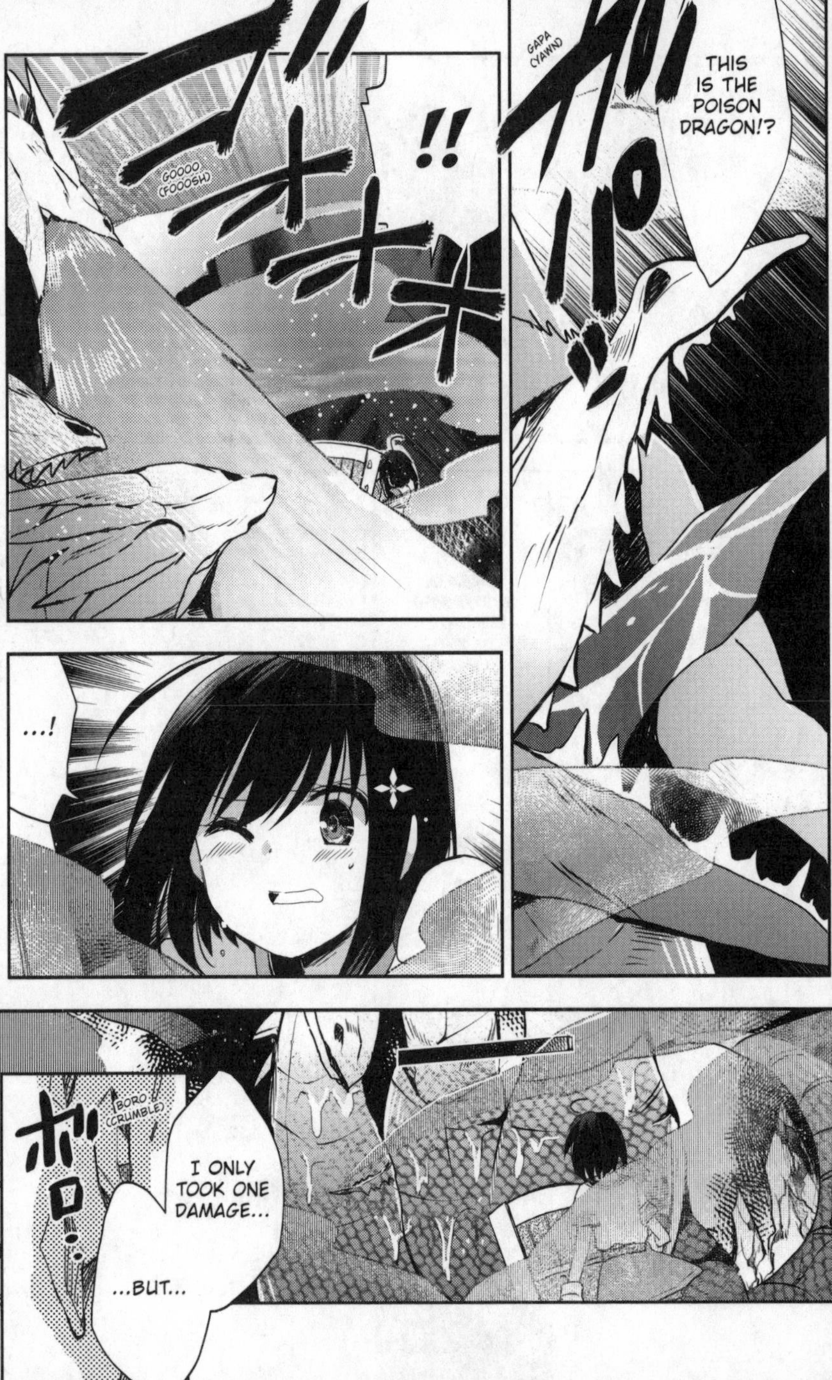
GAPA (YAWN)
THIS IS THE POISON DRAGON!?
GOOOO (FOOOSH)
...!
BORO (CRUMBLE)
I ONLY TOOK ONE DAMAGE...
...BUT...

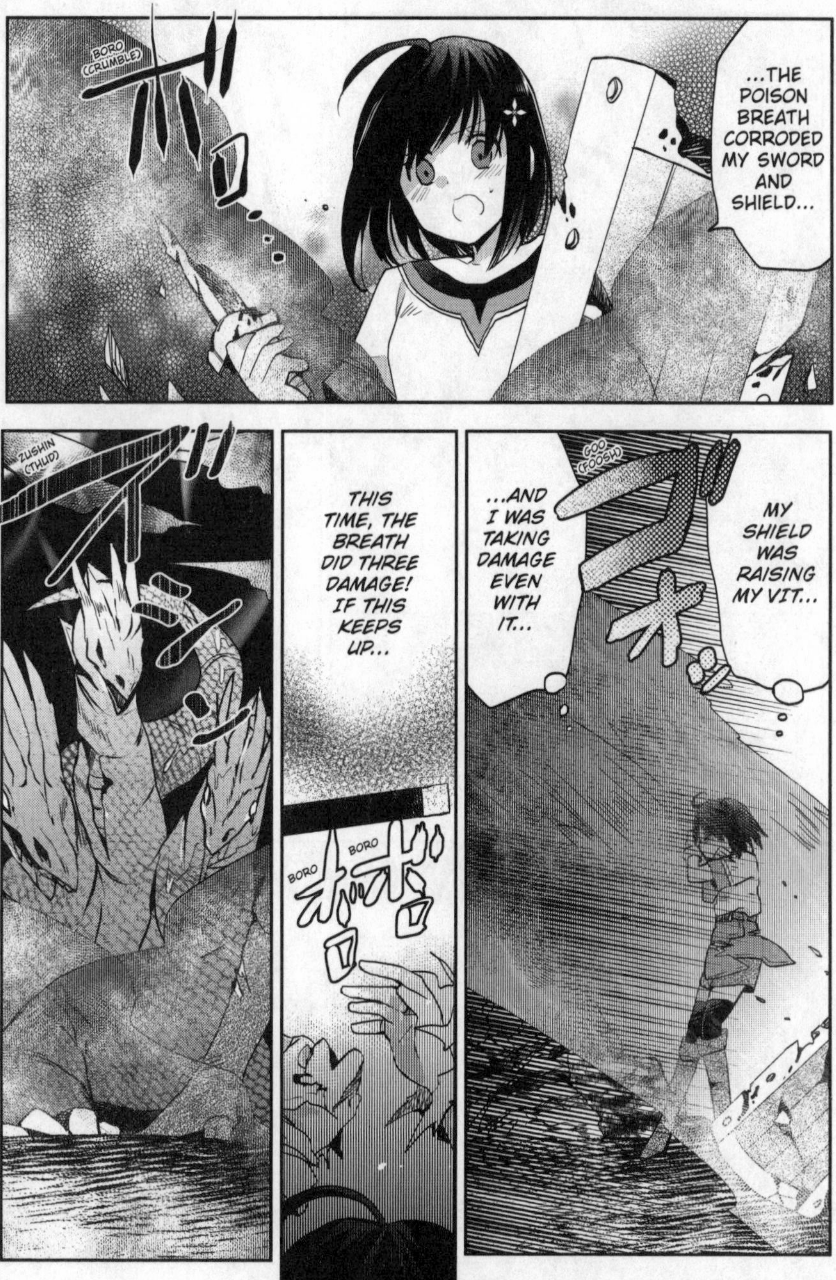
...THE POISON BREATH CORRODED MY SWORD AND SHIELD...
BORO (CRUMBLE)
MY SHIELD WAS RAISING MY VIT...
...AND I WAS TAKING DAMAGE EVEN WITH IT...
GOO (FOOSH)
THIS TIME, THE BREATH DID THREE DAMAGE! IF THIS KEEPS UP...
BORO BORO
ZUSHIN (THUD)

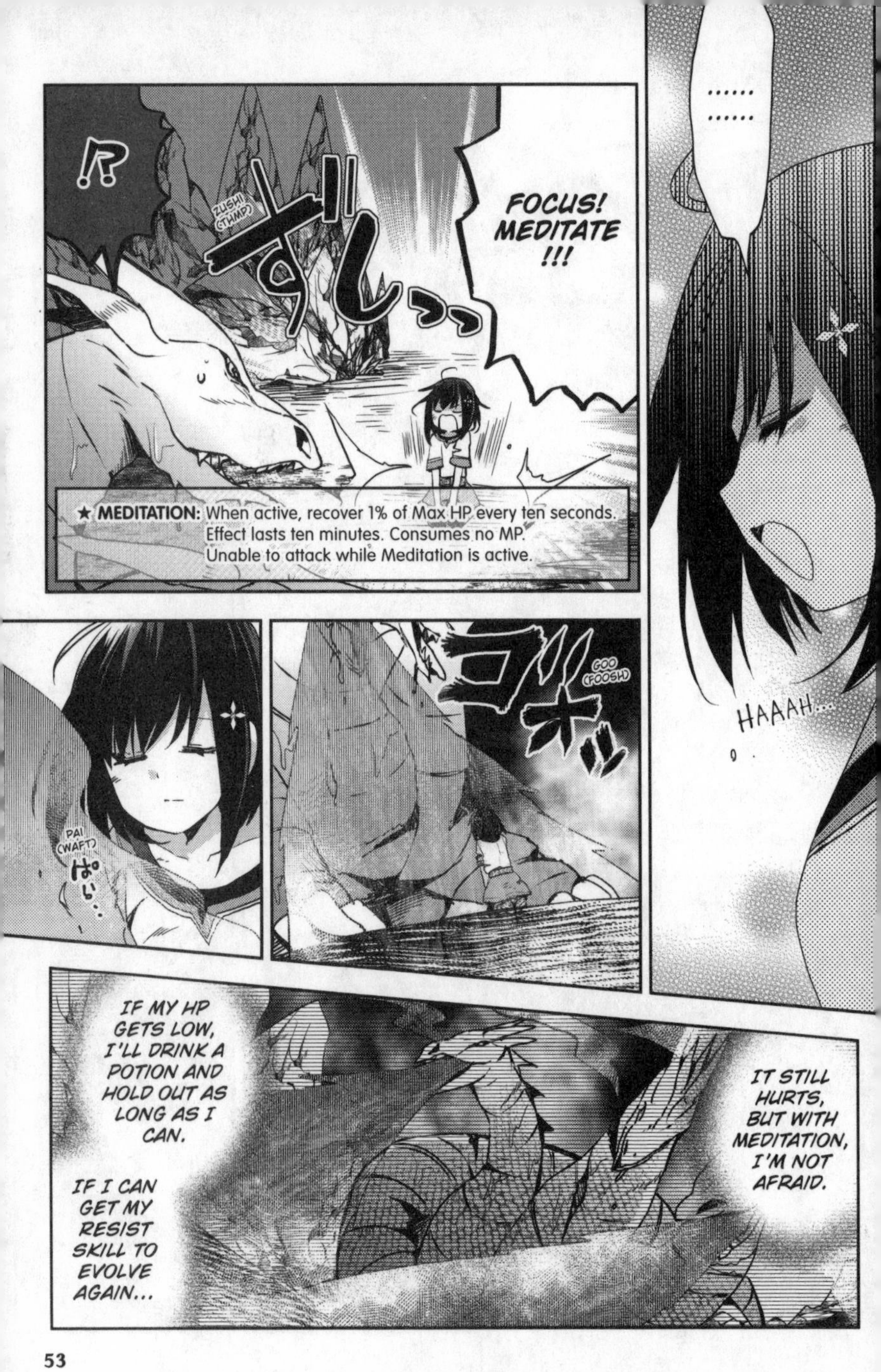
......
......
HAAAH...
FOCUS! MEDITATE !!!
ZUSHI (THMP)
!?
★ MEDITATION: When active, recover 1% of Max HP every ten seconds. Effect lasts ten minutes. Consumes no MP. Unable to attack while Meditation is active.
GOO (FOOSH)
PAI (WAFT)
IT STILL HURTS, BUT WITH MEDITATION, I'M NOT AFRAID.
IF MY HP GETS LOW, I'LL DRINK A POTION AND HOLD OUT AS LONG AS I CAN.
IF I CAN GET MY RESIST SKILL TO EVOLVE AGAIN...

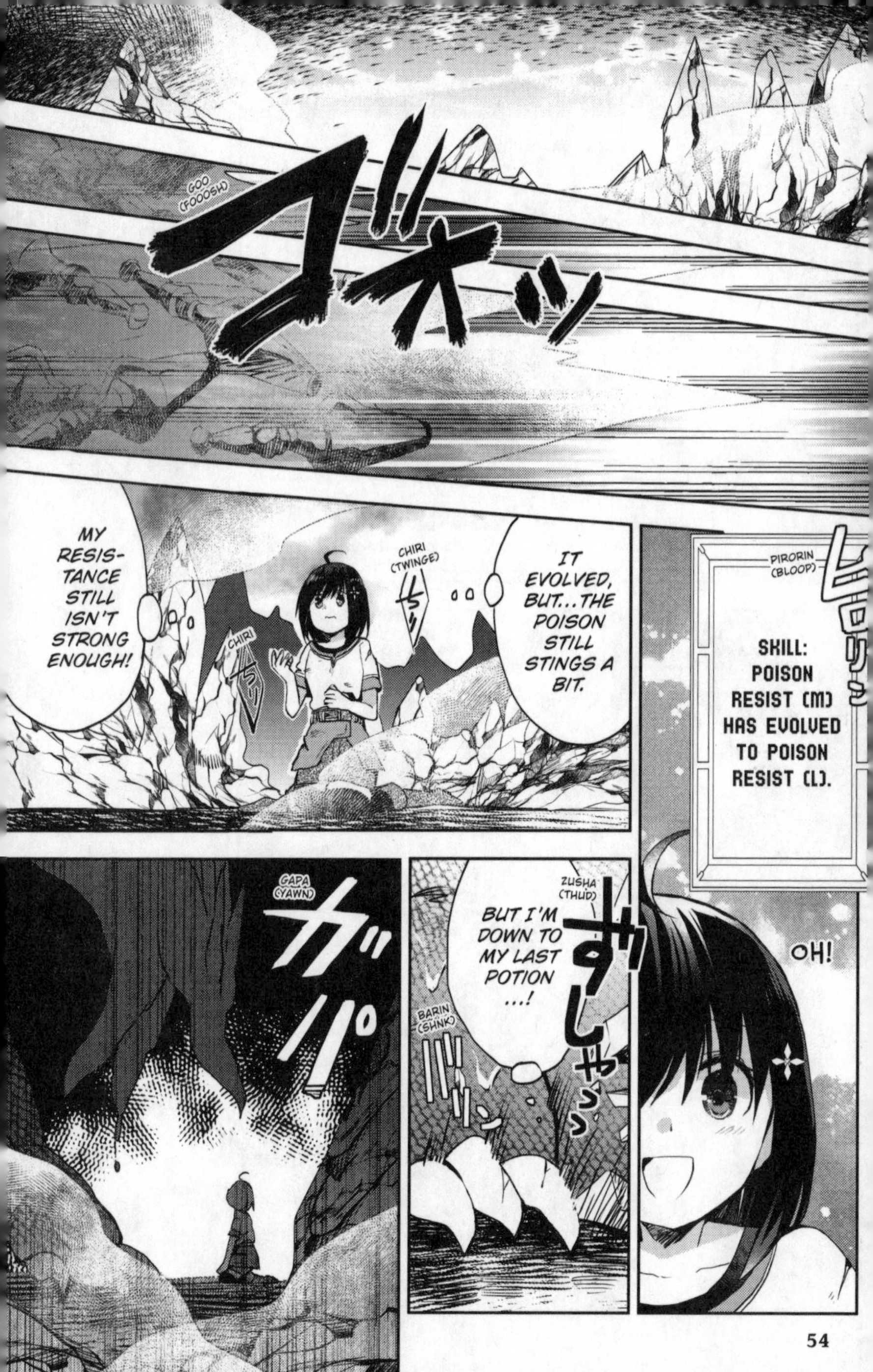
GOO (FOOOSH)
PIRORIN (BLOOP)
SKILL: POISON RESIST (M) HAS EVOLVED TO POISON RESIST (L).
IT EVOLVED, BUT...THE POISON STILL STINGS A BIT.
CHIRI (TWINGE)
CHIRI
MY RESISTANCE STILL ISN'T STRONG ENOUGH!
OH!
ZUSHA (THUD)
BUT I'M DOWN TO MY LAST POTION ...!
BARIN (SHNK)
GAPA (YAWN)

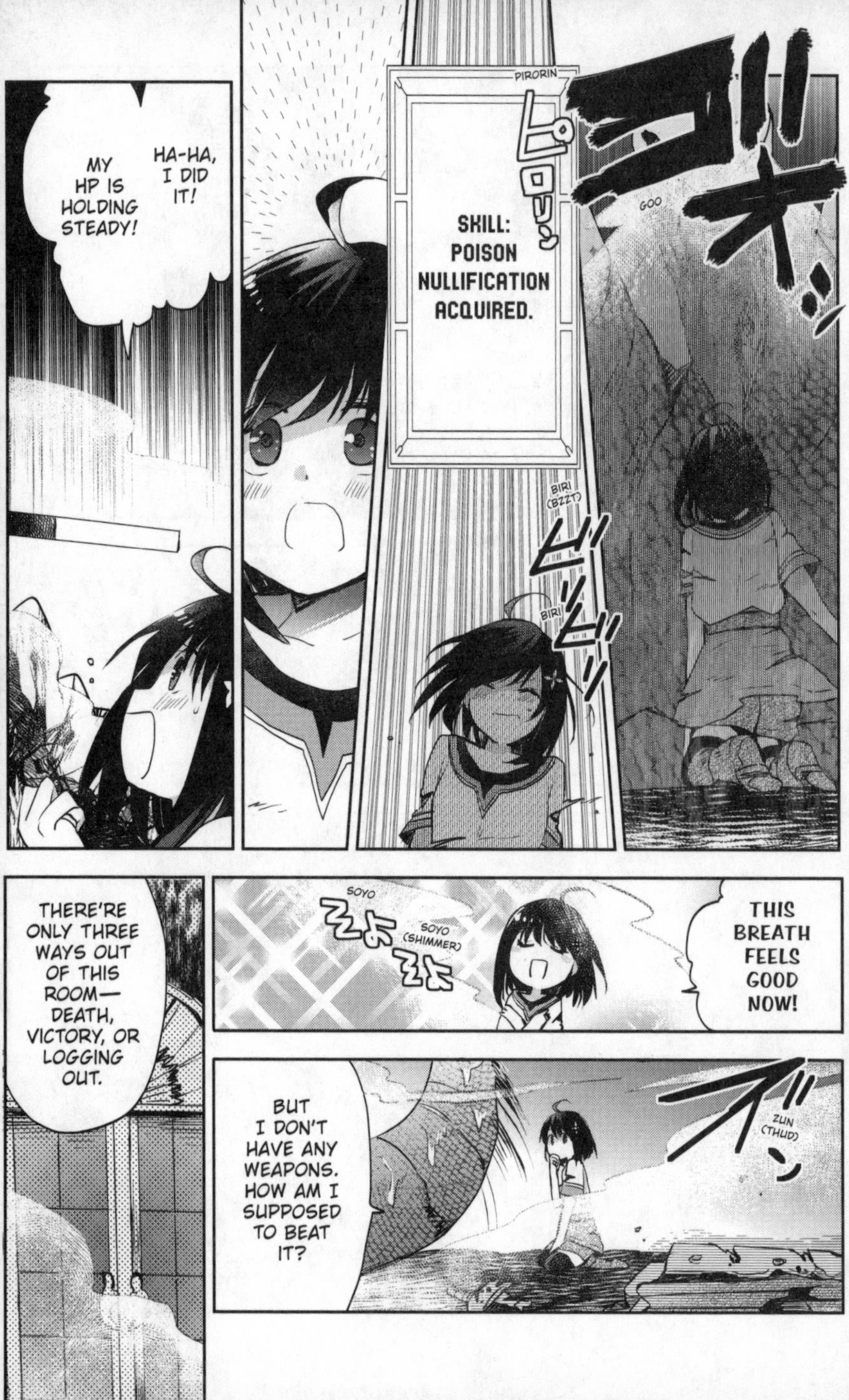
GOO
PIRORIN
SKILL: POISON NULLIFICATION ACQUIRED.
BIRI (BZZT)
BIRI
HA-HA, I DID IT!
MY HP IS HOLDING STEADY!
THIS BREATH FEELS GOOD NOW!
SOYO
SOYO (SHIMMER)
THERE'RE ONLY THREE WAYS OUT OF THIS ROOM—DEATH, VICTORY, OR LOGGING OUT.
ZUN (THUD)
BUT I DON'T HAVE ANY WEAPONS. HOW AM I SUPPOSED TO BEAT IT?

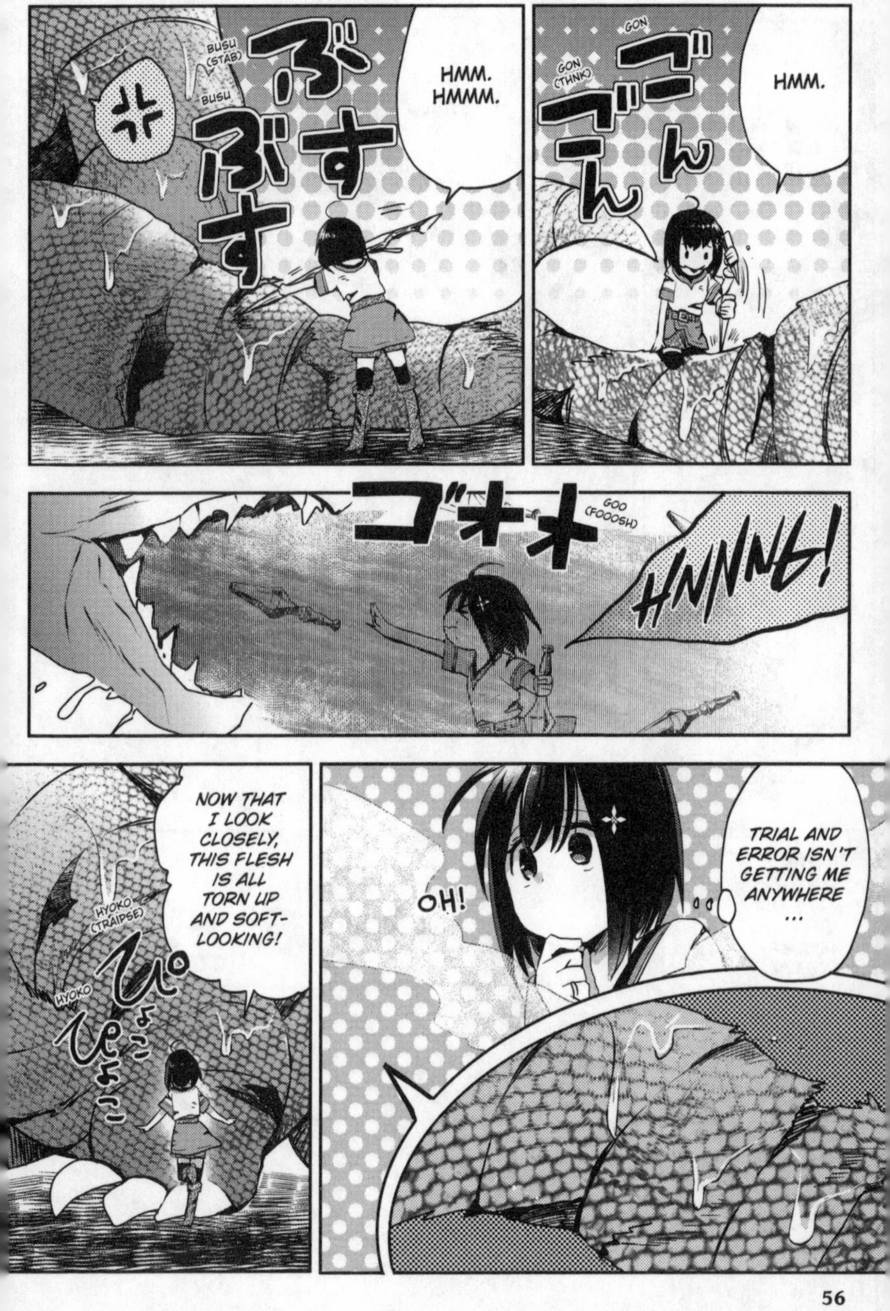
HMM.
ごんごん
GON (THNK)
GON
HMM. HMMM.
ぶすぶす
BUSU (STAB)
BUSU
ゴオォ
GOO (FOOOSH)
HNNNG!
TRIAL AND ERROR ISN'T GETTING ME ANYWHERE ...
OH!
NOW THAT I LOOK CLOSELY, THIS FLESH IS ALL TORN UP AND SOFT-LOOKING!
ぴょこぴょこ
HYOKO (TRAIPSE)
HYOKO

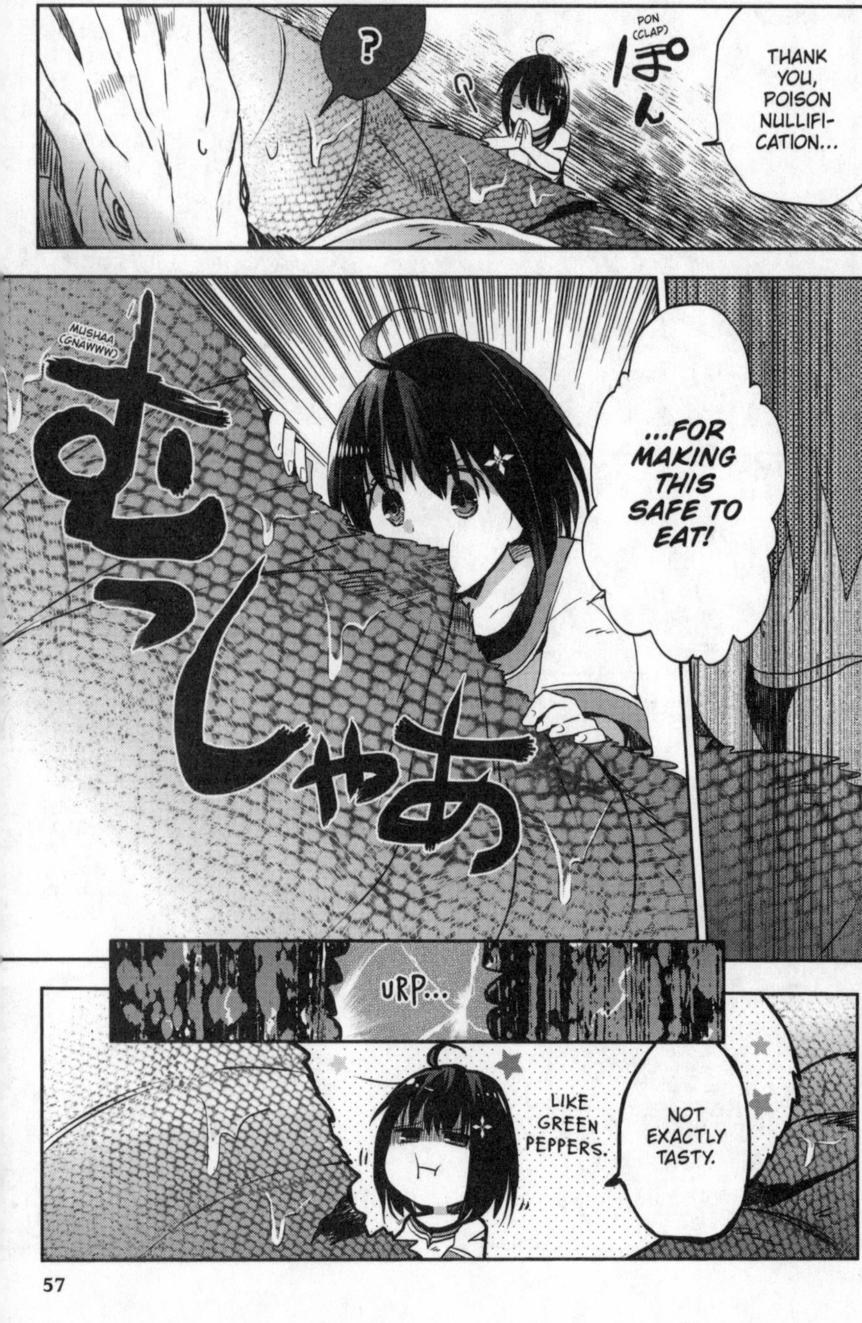
THANK YOU, POISON NULLIFICATION...
PON (CLAP)
ぽん
?
...FOR MAKING THIS SAFE TO EAT!
MUSHAA (GNAWWW)
むしゃあ
URP...
NOT EXACTLY TASTY.
LIKE GREEN PEPPERS.

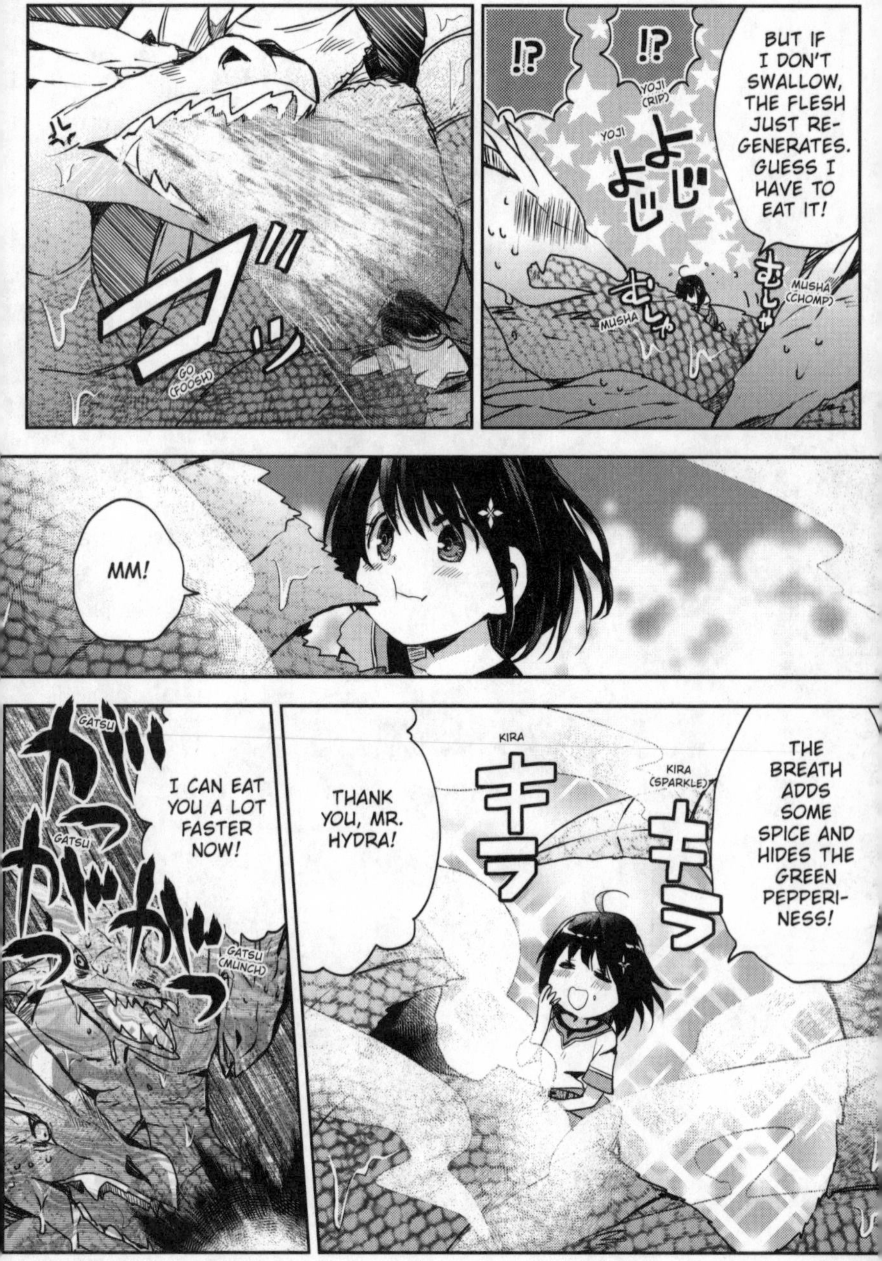
BUT IF I DON'T SWALLOW, THE FLESH JUST RE-GENERATES. GUESS I HAVE TO EAT IT!
!?
!?
YOJI (RIP)
YOJI
MUSHA (CHOMP)
MUSHA
GO (FOOSH)
MM!
THE BREATH ADDS SOME SPICE AND HIDES THE GREEN PEPPERI-NESS!
KIRA (SPARKLE)
KIRA
THANK YOU, MR. HYDRA!
I CAN EAT YOU A LOT FASTER NOW!
GATSU
GATSU
GATSU (MUNCH)

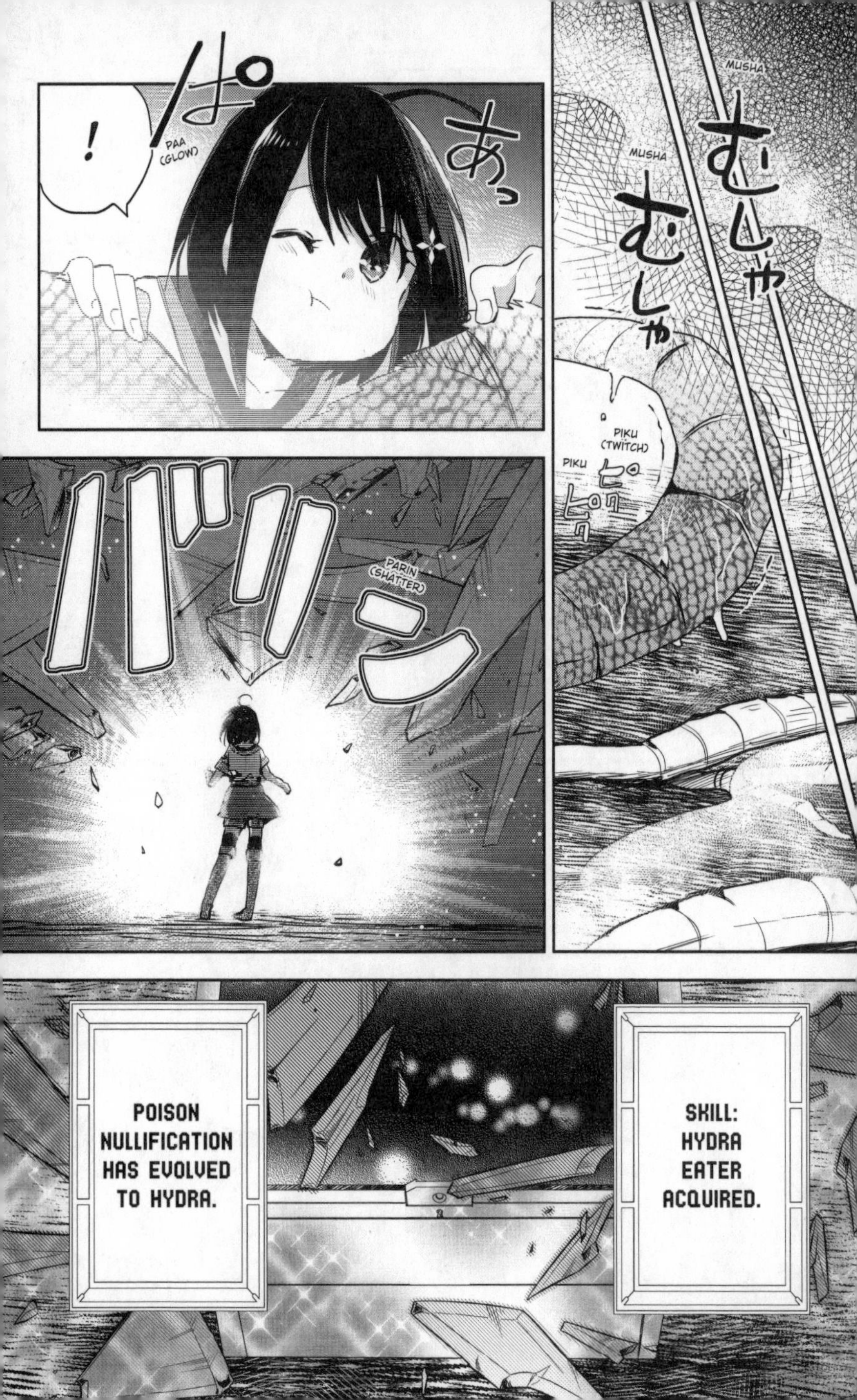
むしゃ
MUSHA
むしゃ
MUSHA
ピクピク
PIKU
PIKU (TWITCH)
あっ
!
ぱ
PAA (GLOW)
パリン
PARIN (SHATTER)
SKILL: HYDRA EATER ACQUIRED.
POISON NULLIFICATION HAS EVOLVED TO HYDRA.

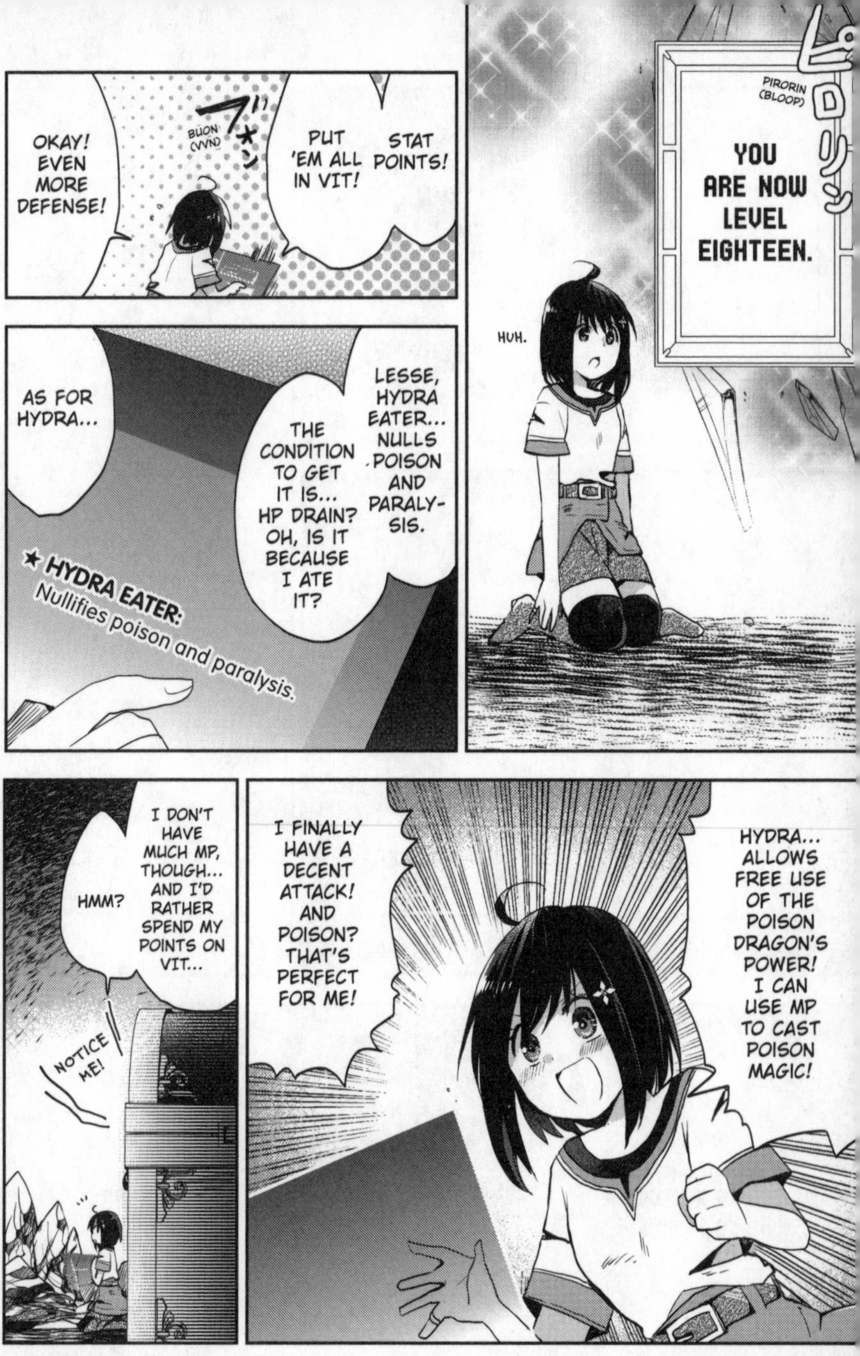
PIRORIN (BLOOP)
YOU ARE NOW LEVEL EIGHTEEN.
HUH.
STAT POINTS!
PUT 'EM ALL IN VIT!
BUON (VVN)
OKAY! EVEN MORE DEFENSE!
LESSE, HYDRA EATER... NULLS POISON AND PARALYSIS.
THE CONDITION TO GET IT IS... HP DRAIN? OH, IS IT BECAUSE I ATE IT?
AS FOR HYDRA...
★ HYDRA EATER: Nullifies poison and paralysis.
HYDRA... ALLOWS FREE USE OF THE POISON DRAGON'S POWER! I CAN USE MP TO CAST POISON MAGIC!
I FINALLY HAVE A DECENT ATTACK! AND POISON? THAT'S PERFECT FOR ME!
I DON'T HAVE MUCH MP, THOUGH... AND I'D RATHER SPEND MY POINTS ON VIT...
HMM?
NOTICE ME!
...

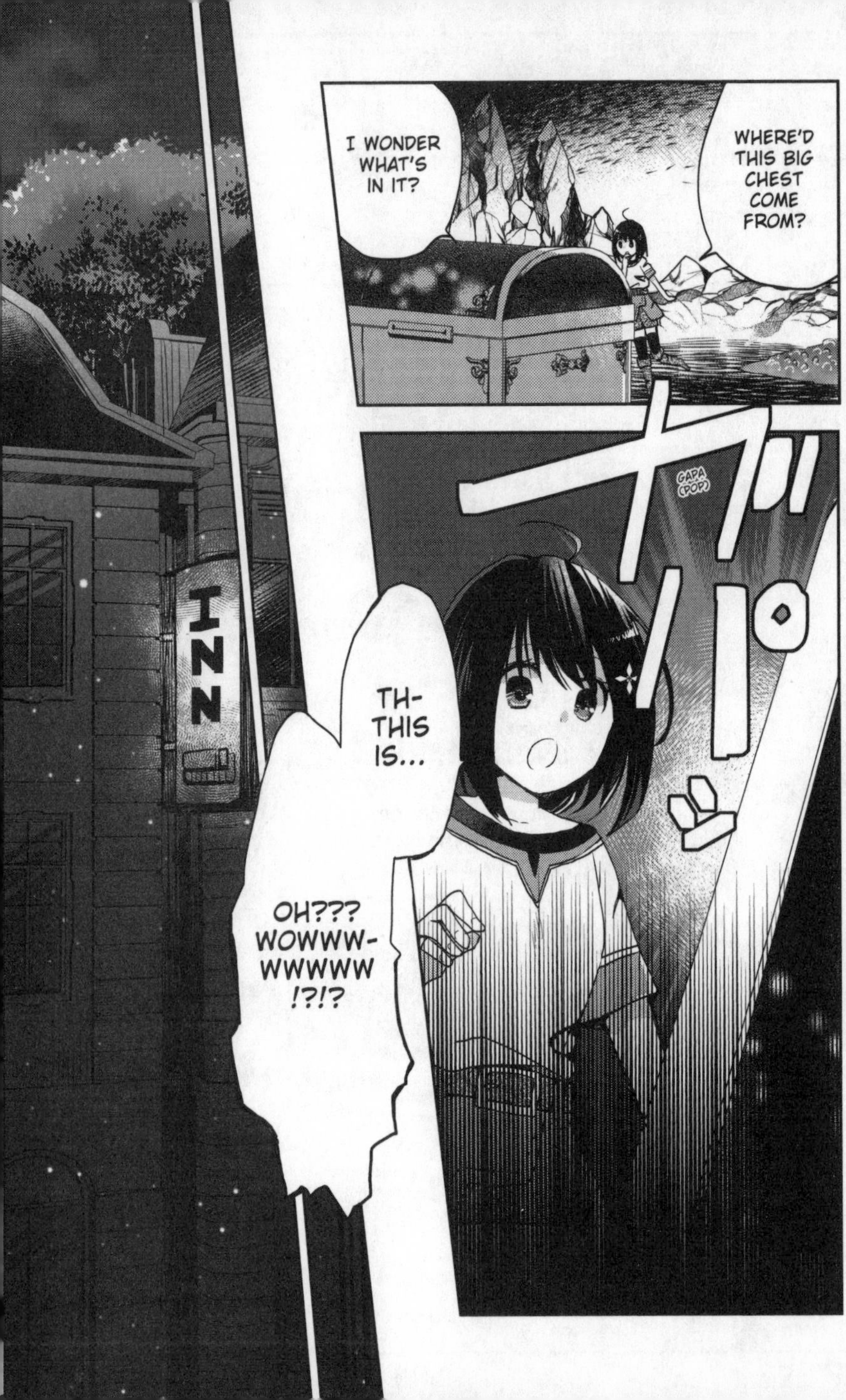
WHERE'D THIS BIG CHEST COME FROM?
I WONDER WHAT'S IN IT?
GAPA (POP)
TH- THIS IS...
OH??? WOWWW-WWWWW !?!?
INN

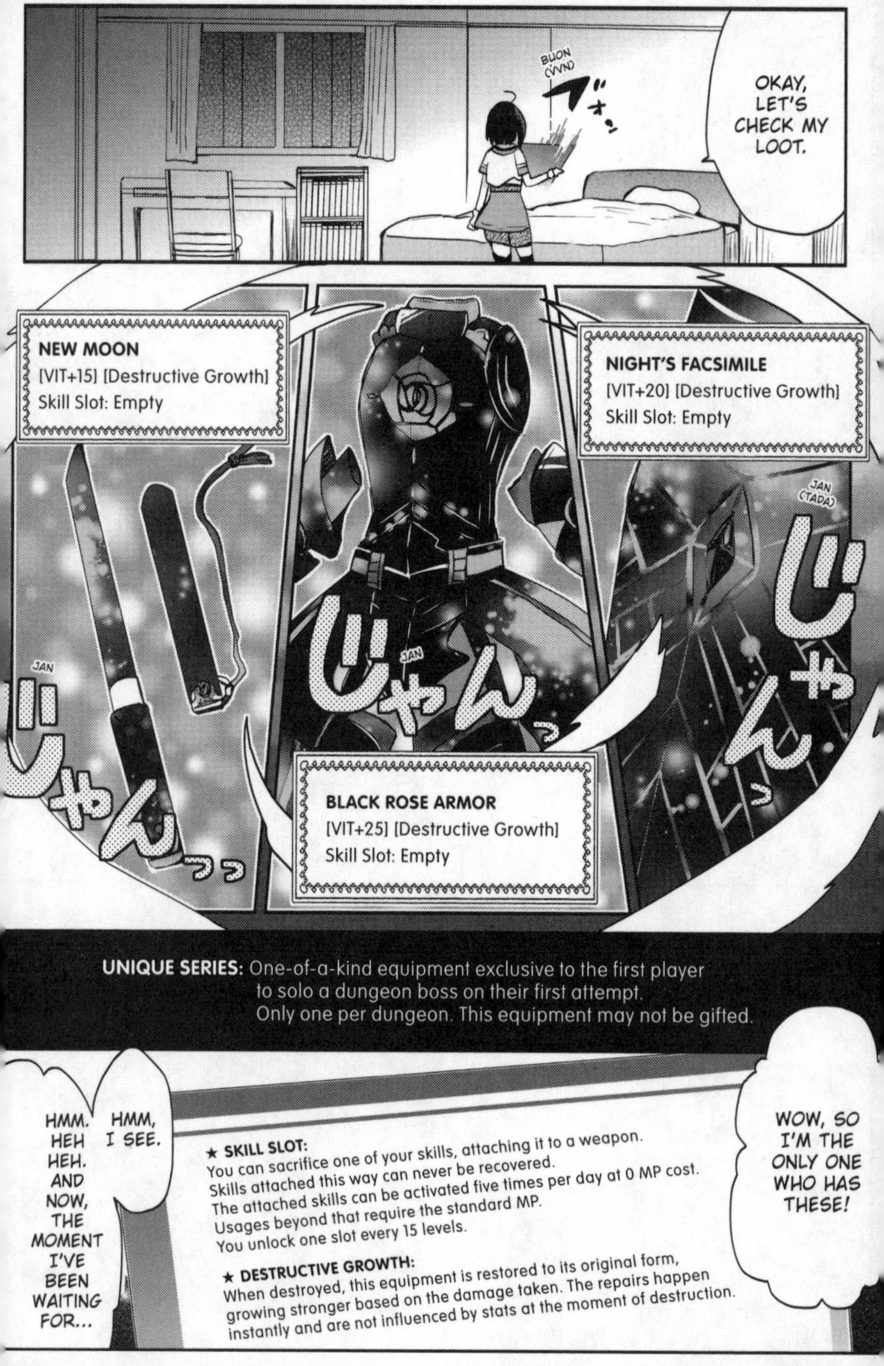
OKAY, LET'S CHECK MY LOOT.
BUON (VVN)
ブォンッ
NIGHT'S FACSIMILE
[VIT+20] [Destructive Growth]
Skill Slot: Empty
JAN (TADA)
じゃんっ
JAN
じゃんっ
BLACK ROSE ARMOR
[VIT+25] [Destructive Growth]
Skill Slot: Empty
NEW MOON
[VIT+15] [Destructive Growth]
Skill Slot: Empty
JAN
じゃんっっ
UNIQUE SERIES: One-of-a-kind equipment exclusive to the first player to solo a dungeon boss on their first attempt. Only one per dungeon. This equipment may not be gifted.
WOW, SO I'M THE ONLY ONE WHO HAS THESE!
★ SKILL SLOT:
You can sacrifice one of your skills, attaching it to a weapon.
Skills attached this way can never be recovered.
The attached skills can be activated five times per day at 0 MP cost.
Usages beyond that require the standard MP.
You unlock one slot every 15 levels.
★ DESTRUCTIVE GROWTH:
When destroyed, this equipment is restored to its original form, growing stronger based on the damage taken. The repairs happen instantly and are not influenced by stats at the moment of destruction.
HMM, I SEE.
HMM. HEH HEH. AND NOW, THE MOMENT I'VE BEEN WAITING FOR...

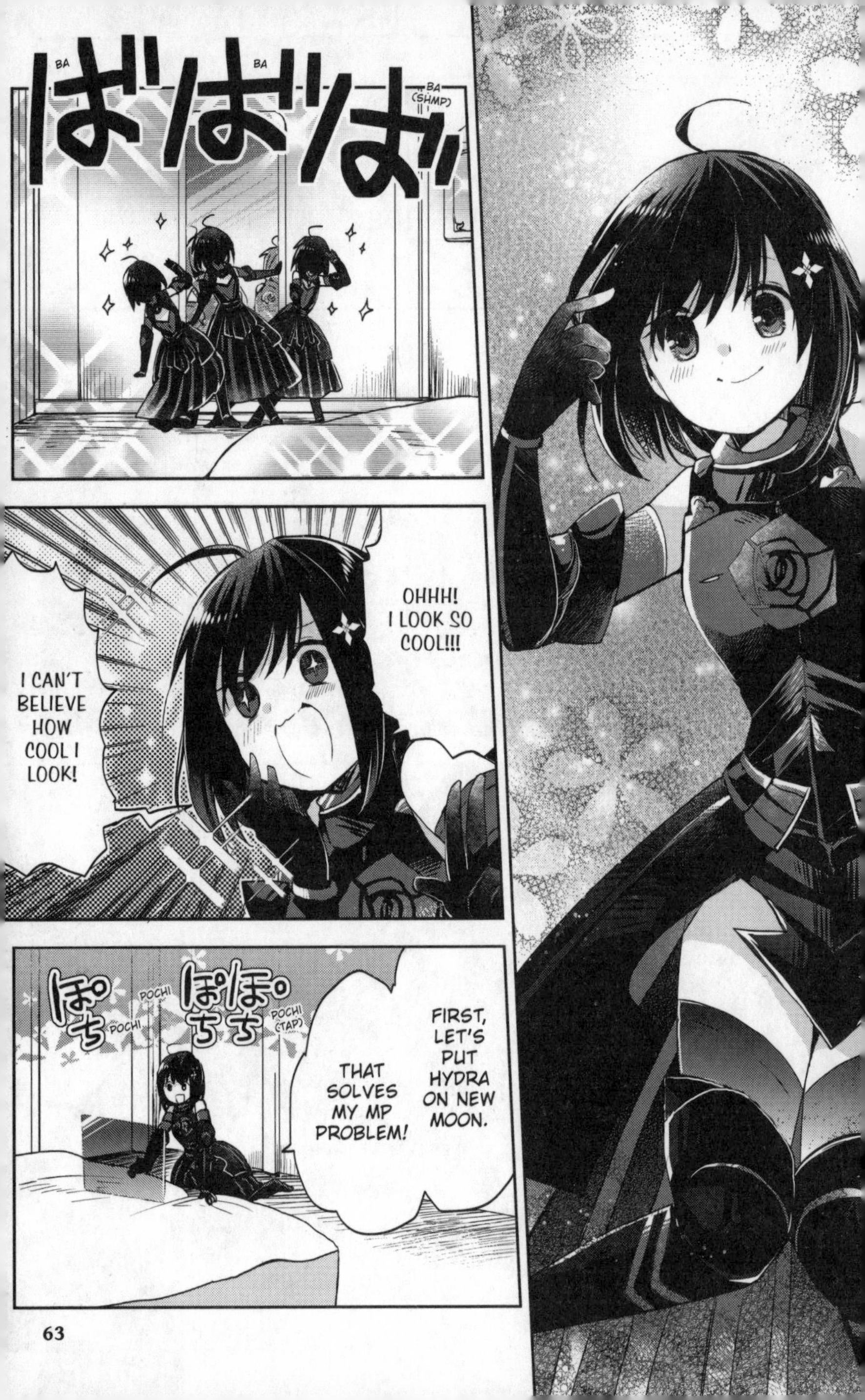
ばばばっ
BA BA BA (SHMP)
OHHH! I LOOK SO COOL!!!
I CAN'T BELIEVE HOW COOL I LOOK!
ぽち POCHI
ぽち POCHI
ぽちぽち POCHI (TAP)
FIRST, LET'S PUT HYDRA ON NEW MOON.
THAT SOLVES MY MP PROBLEM!

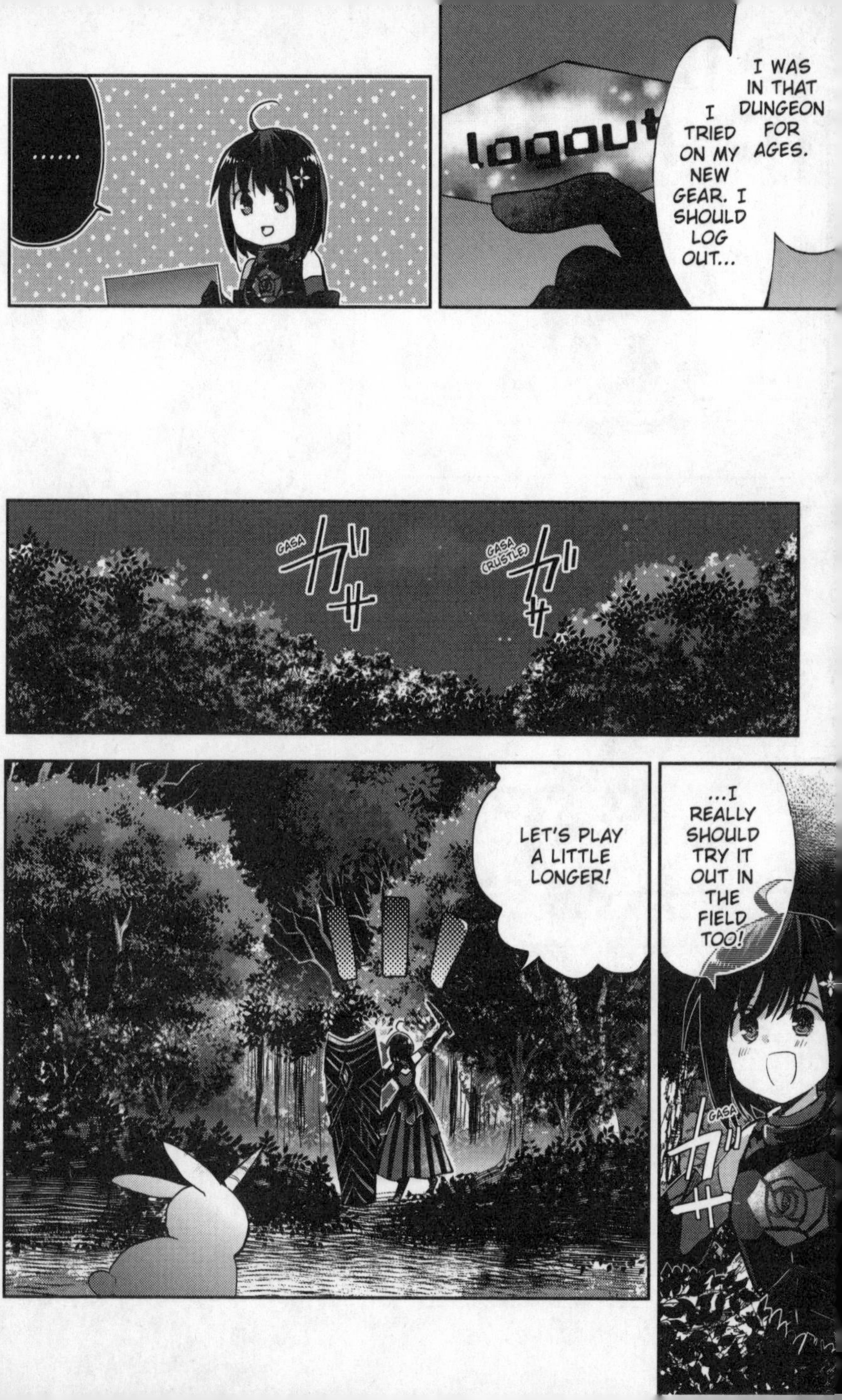
I WAS IN THAT DUNGEON FOR AGES.
I TRIED ON MY NEW GEAR. I SHOULD LOG OUT...
logout
......
GASA (RUSTLE)
GASA
...I REALLY SHOULD TRY IT OUT IN THE FIELD TOO!
GASA
LET'S PLAY A LITTLE LONGER!

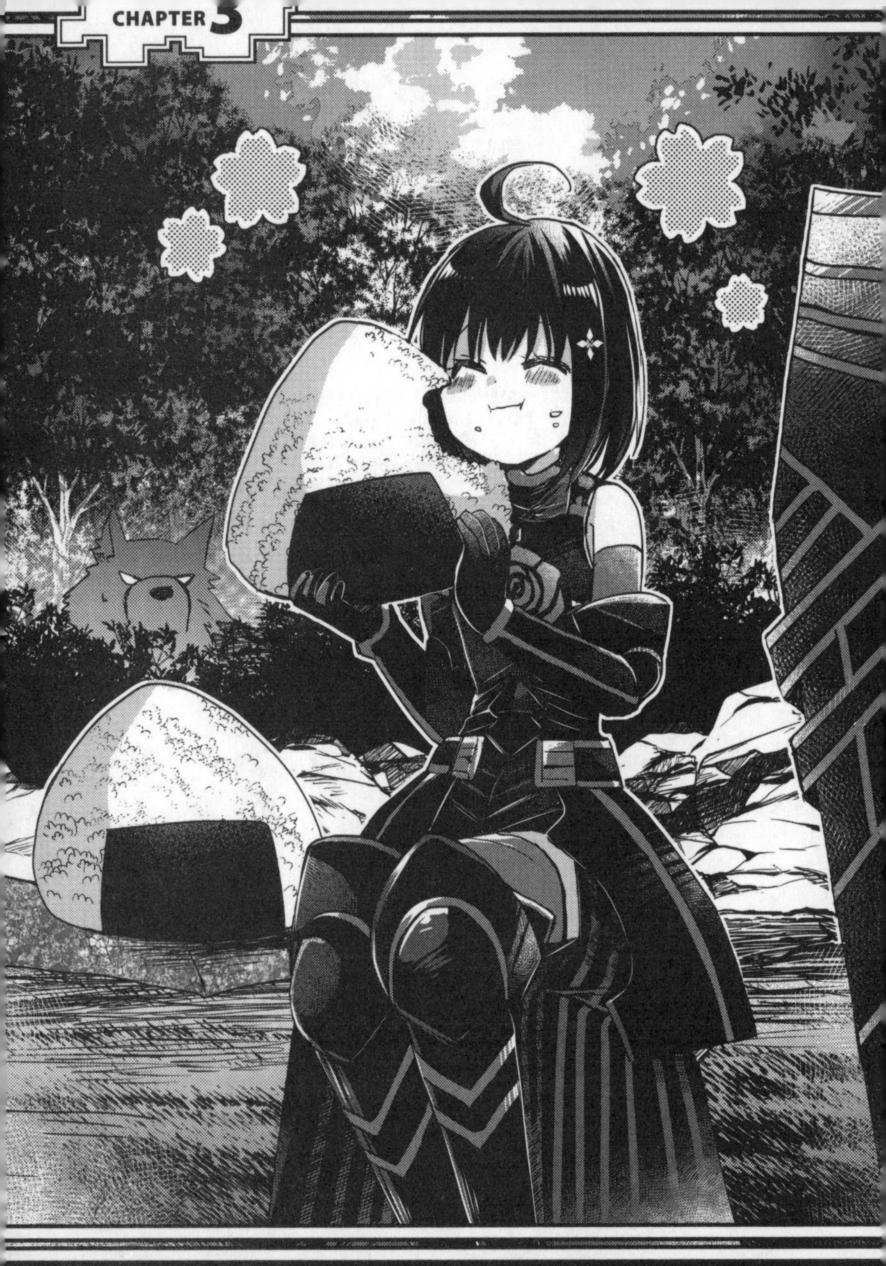
CHAPTER 3

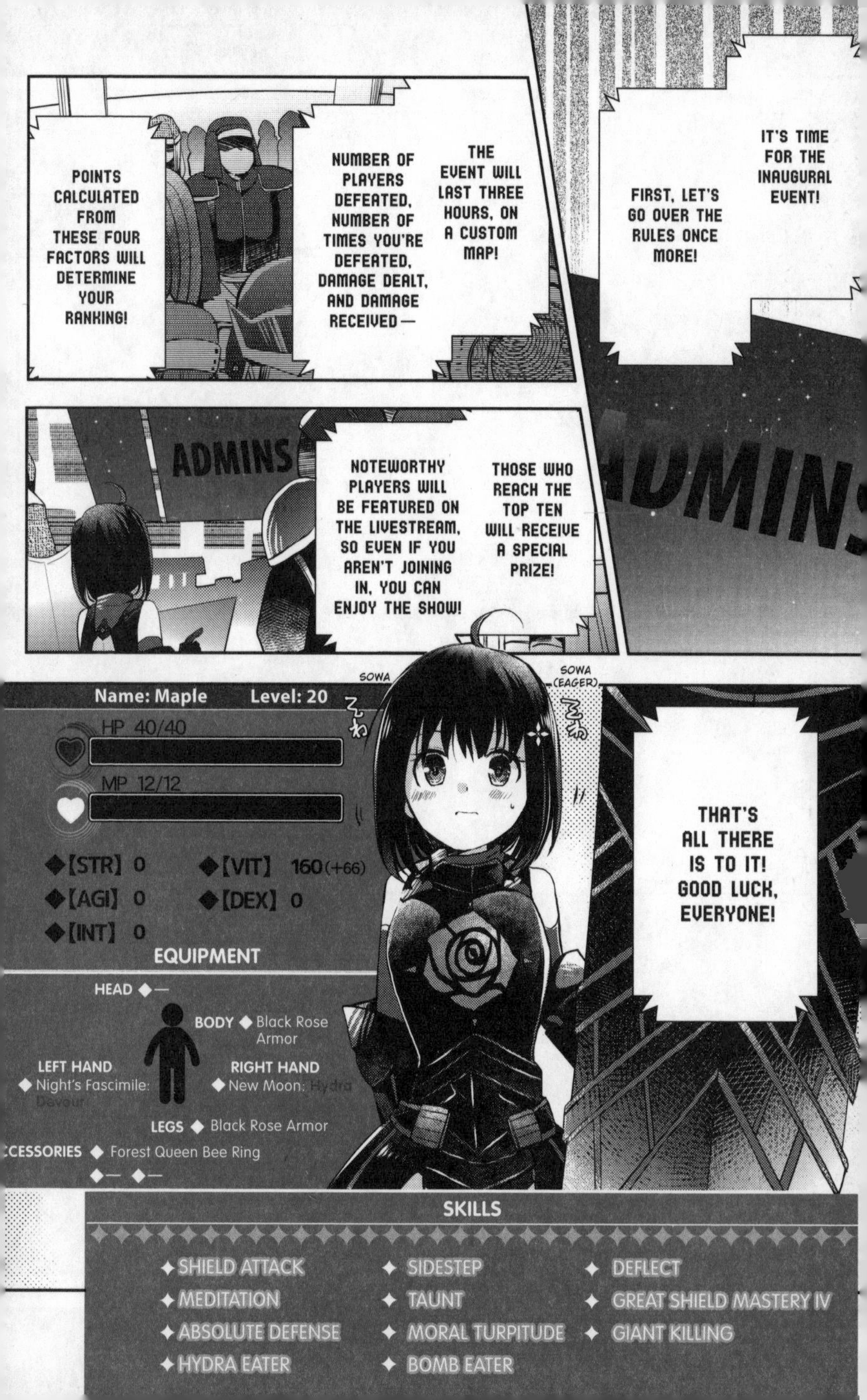
IT'S TIME FOR THE INAUGURAL EVENT!
FIRST, LET'S GO OVER THE RULES ONCE MORE!
THE EVENT WILL LAST THREE HOURS, ON A CUSTOM MAP!
NUMBER OF PLAYERS DEFEATED, NUMBER OF TIMES YOU'RE DEFEATED, DAMAGE DEALT, AND DAMAGE RECEIVED—
POINTS CALCULATED FROM THESE FOUR FACTORS WILL DETERMINE YOUR RANKING!
ADMINS
THOSE WHO REACH THE TOP TEN WILL RECEIVE A SPECIAL PRIZE!
NOTEWORTHY PLAYERS WILL BE FEATURED ON THE LIVESTREAM, SO EVEN IF YOU AREN'T JOINING IN, YOU CAN ENJOY THE SHOW!
ADMINS
SOWA (EAGER)
SOWA
THAT'S ALL THERE IS TO IT! GOOD LUCK, EVERYONE!
Name: Maple Level: 20
HP 40/40
MP 12/12
◆【STR】 0 ◆【VIT】 160(+66)
◆【AGI】 0 ◆【DEX】 0
◆【INT】 0
EQUIPMENT
HEAD ◆—
BODY ◆ Black Rose Armor
LEFT HAND ◆ Night's Fascimile: Devour
RIGHT HAND ◆ New Moon: Hydra
LEGS ◆ Black Rose Armor
CCESSORIES ◆ Forest Queen Bee Ring
◆— ◆—
SKILLS
✦ SHIELD ATTACK ✦ SIDESTEP ✦ DEFLECT
✦ MEDITATION ✦ TAUNT ✦ GREAT SHIELD MASTERY IV
✦ ABSOLUTE DEFENSE ✦ MORAL TURPITUDE ✦ GIANT KILLING
✦ HYDRA EATER ✦ BOMB EATER

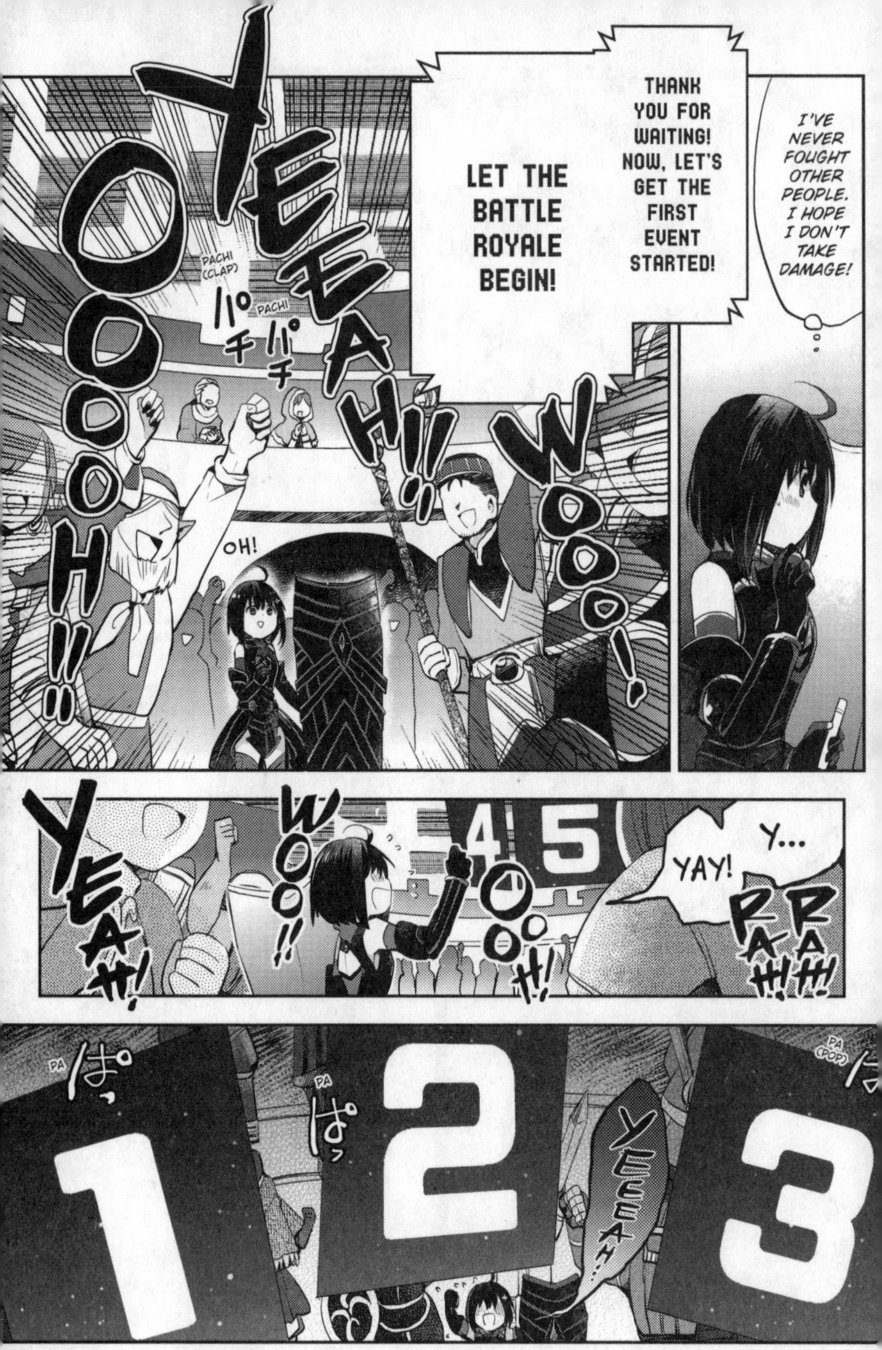
I'VE NEVER FOUGHT OTHER PEOPLE. I HOPE I DON'T TAKE DAMAGE!
THANK YOU FOR WAITING! NOW, LET'S GET THE FIRST EVENT STARTED!
LET THE BATTLE ROYALE BEGIN!
WOOO!
YEEAH!!
PACHI PACHI (CLAP)
OH!
OOOOOH!!
Y... YAY!
RAH! RAH!
WOOOOH!!
YEAH!
PA (POP)
YEEEAH...
PA
PA

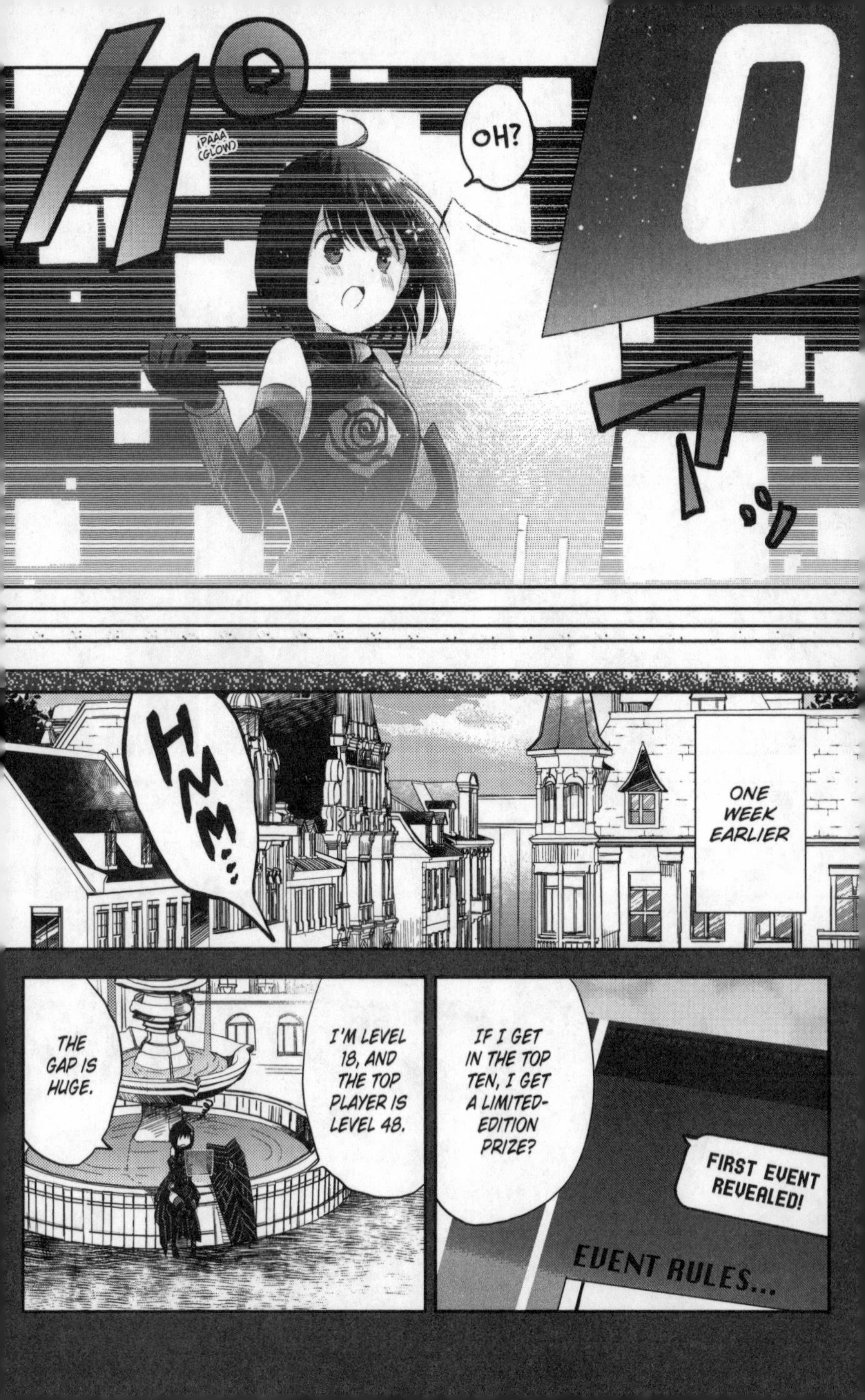
OH?
PAAA (GLOW)
ONE WEEK EARLIER
HMM...
FIRST EVENT REVEALED!
EVENT RULES...
IF I GET IN THE TOP TEN, I GET A LIMITED-EDITION PRIZE?
I'M LEVEL 18, AND THE TOP PLAYER IS LEVEL 48.
THE GAP IS HUGE.

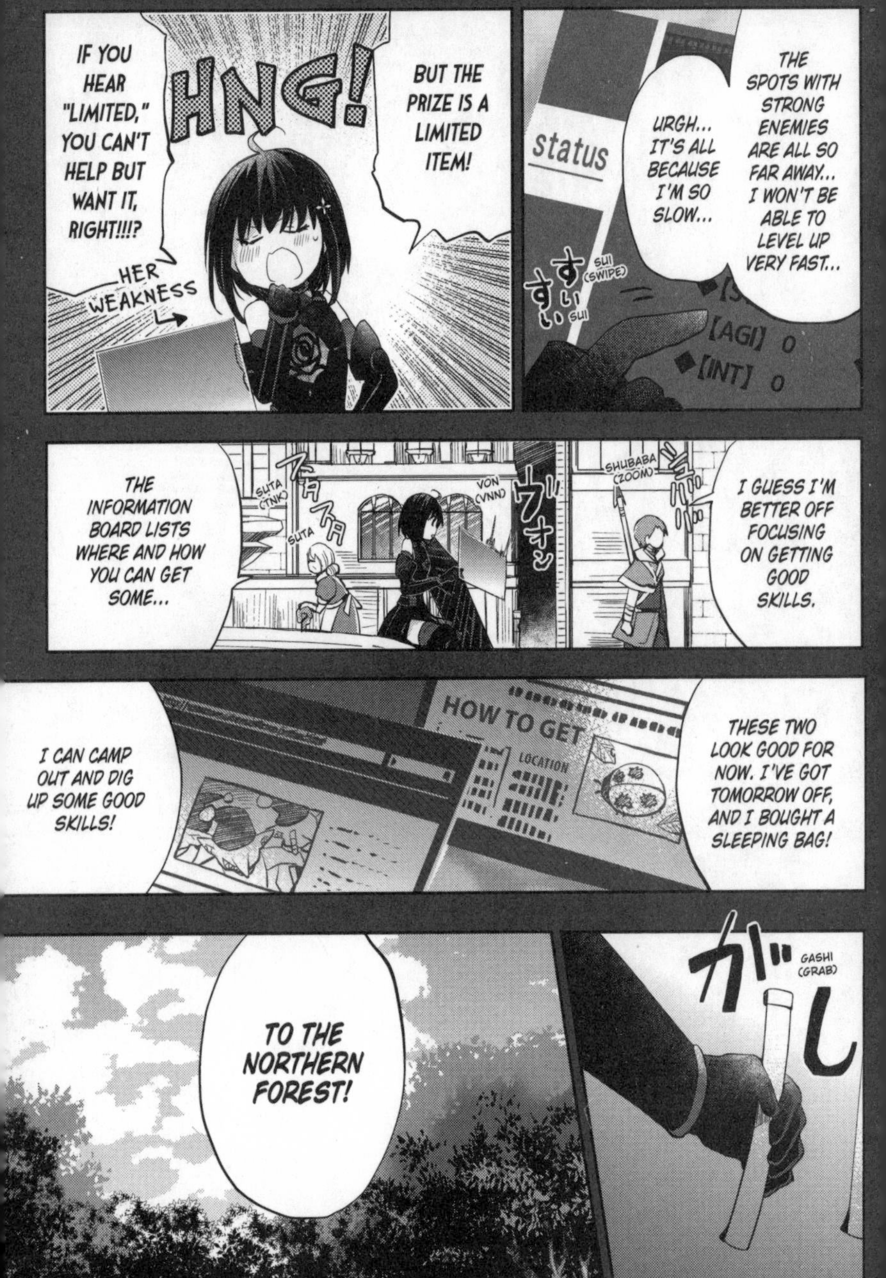

THE SPOTS WITH STRONG ENEMIES ARE ALL SO FAR AWAY... I WON'T BE ABLE TO LEVEL UP VERY FAST...
URGH... IT'S ALL BECAUSE I'M SO SLOW...
status
[AGI] 0
[INT] 0
すいすい SUI (SWIPE) SUI
BUT THE PRIZE IS A LIMITED ITEM!
HNG!
IF YOU HEAR "LIMITED," YOU CAN'T HELP BUT WANT IT, RIGHT!!!?
HER WEAKNESS
I GUESS I'M BETTER OFF FOCUSING ON GETTING GOOD SKILLS.
SHUBABA (ZOOM)
VON (VNN)
SUTA (TNK) SUTA
THE INFORMATION BOARD LISTS WHERE AND HOW YOU CAN GET SOME...
THESE TWO LOOK GOOD FOR NOW. I'VE GOT TOMORROW OFF, AND I BOUGHT A SLEEPING BAG!
HOW TO GET
LOCATION
I CAN CAMP OUT AND DIG UP SOME GOOD SKILLS!
GASHI (GRAB)
TO THE NORTHERN FOREST!

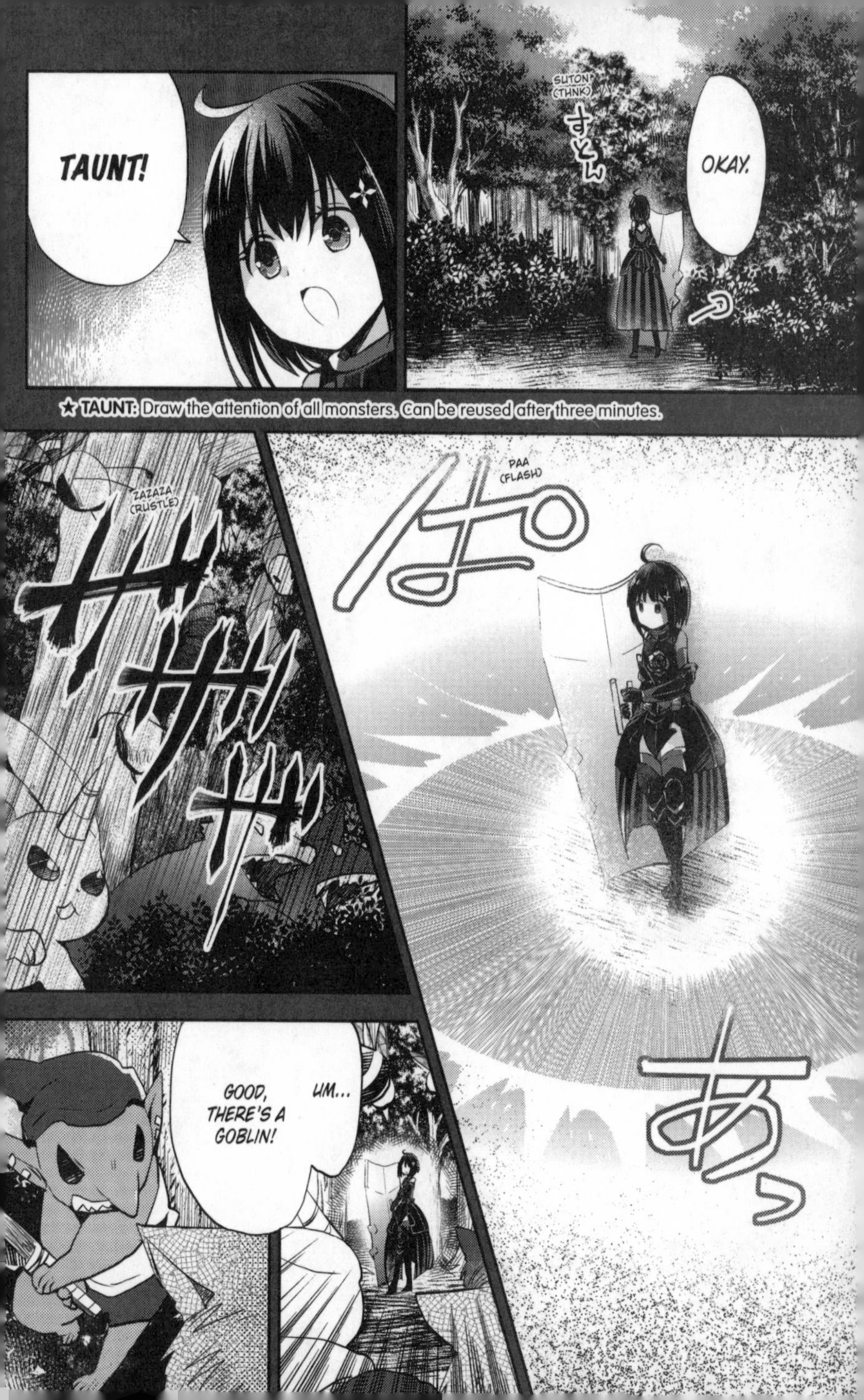
OKAY.
SUTON (THNK)
すとん
TAUNT!
★ TAUNT: Draw the attention of all monsters. Can be reused after three minutes.
PAA (FLASH)
ぱ
あっ
ZAZAZA (RUSTLE)
ザザザッ
UM...
GOOD, THERE'S A GOBLIN!

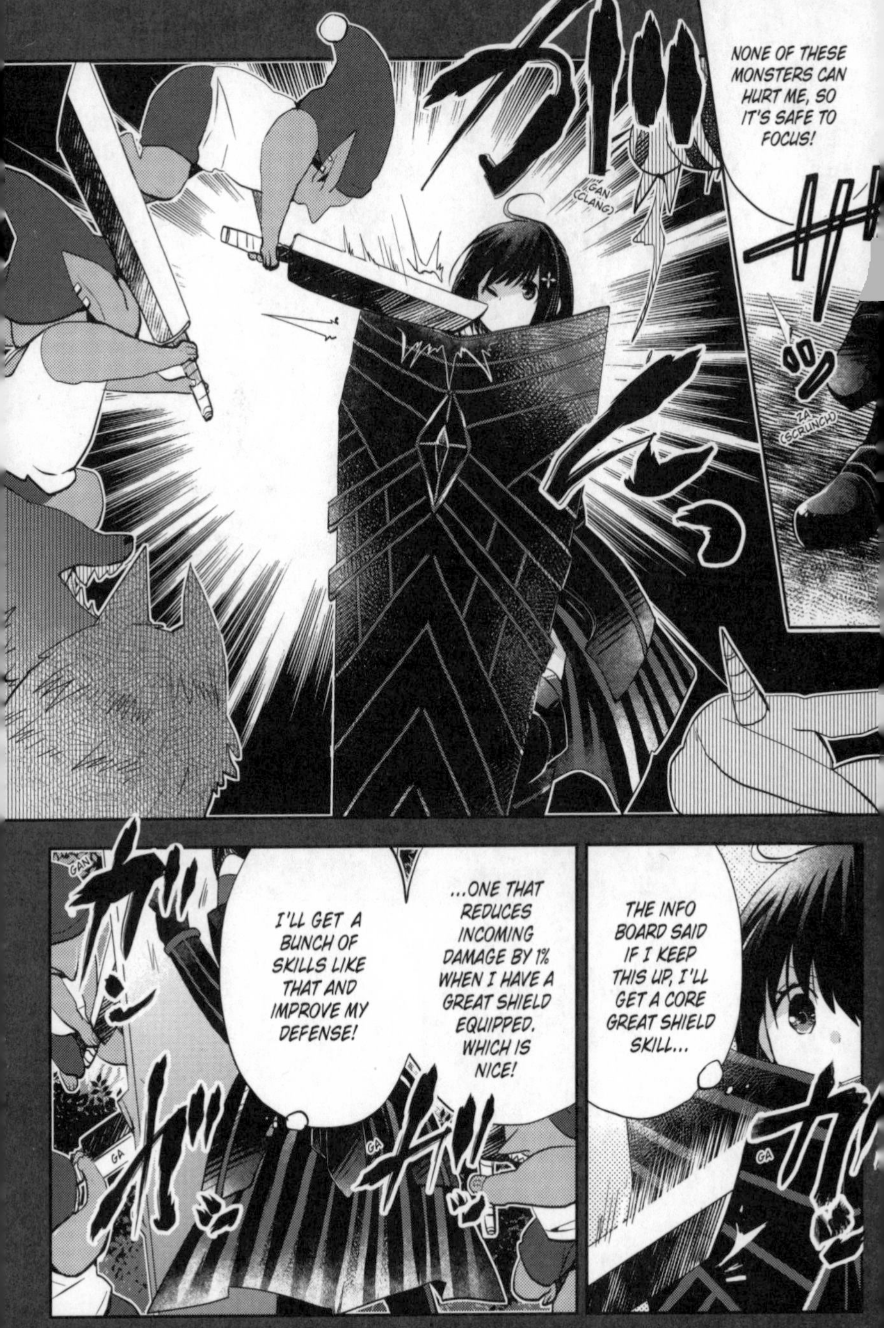
NONE OF THESE MONSTERS CAN HURT ME, SO IT'S SAFE TO FOCUS!
ZA (SCRUNCH)
GAN (CLANG)
THE INFO BOARD SAID IF I KEEP THIS UP, I'LL GET A CORE GREAT SHIELD SKILL...
GA
...ONE THAT REDUCES INCOMING DAMAGE BY 1% WHEN I HAVE A GREAT SHIELD EQUIPPED. WHICH IS NICE!
GA
I'LL GET A BUNCH OF SKILLS LIKE THAT AND IMPROVE MY DEFENSE!
GA
GAN

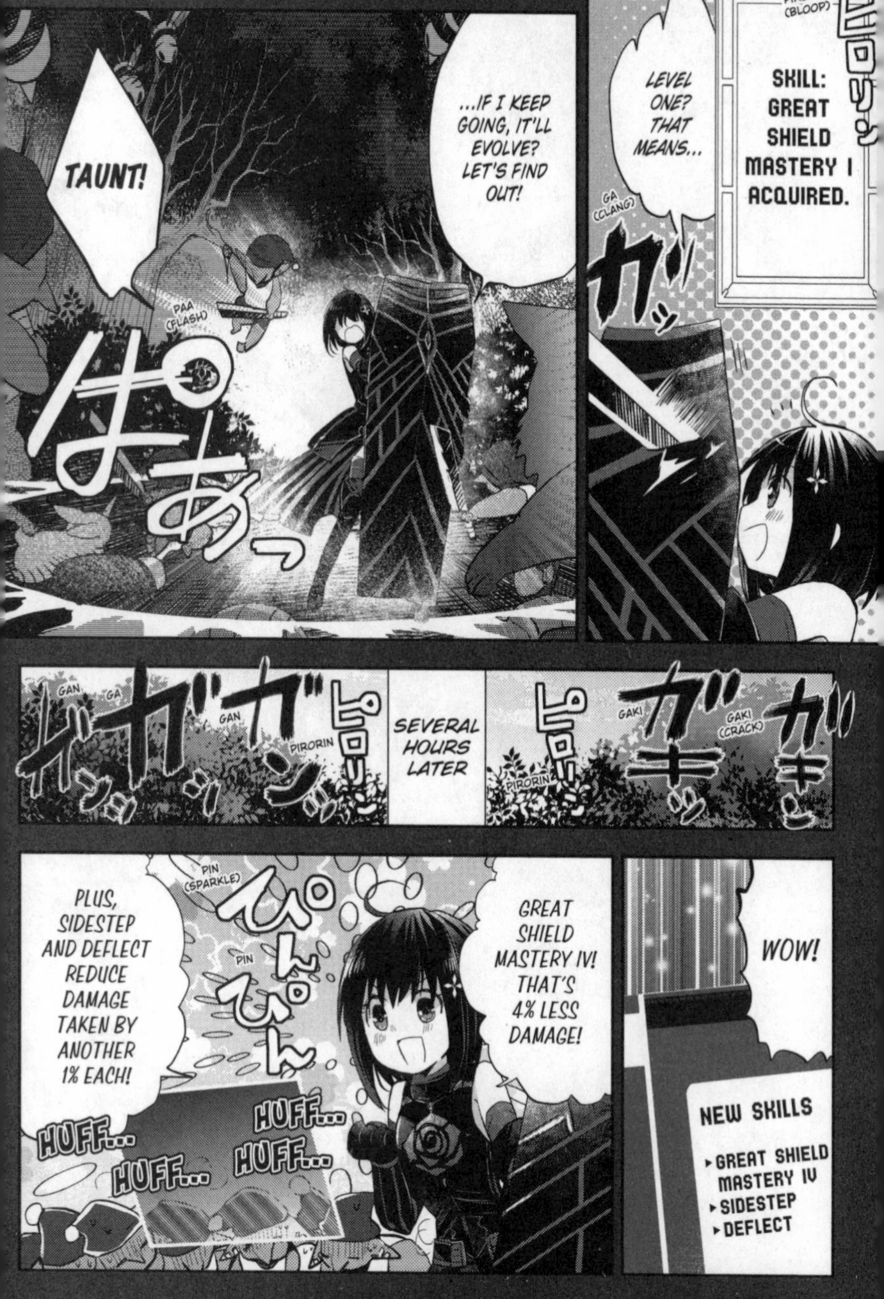

PIRORIN (BLOOP)
ピロリン
SKILL: GREAT SHIELD MASTERY I ACQUIRED.
LEVEL ONE? THAT MEANS...
GA (CLANG)
ガッ
...IF I KEEP GOING, IT'LL EVOLVE? LET'S FIND OUT!
TAUNT!
PAA (FLASH)
ぱあっ
GAKI GAKI (CRACK)
ガキッ ガキッ
PIRORIN
ピロリン
SEVERAL HOURS LATER
PIRORIN
ピロリン
GAN GAN GA
ガンガンガン
WOW!
NEW SKILLS
▸ GREAT SHIELD MASTERY IV
▸ SIDESTEP
▸ DEFLECT
GREAT SHIELD MASTERY IV! THAT'S 4% LESS DAMAGE!
PIN (SPARKLE) PIN
ぴんぴん
PLUS, SIDESTEP AND DEFLECT REDUCE DAMAGE TAKEN BY ANOTHER 1% EACH!
HUFF... HUFF... HUFF... HUFF...

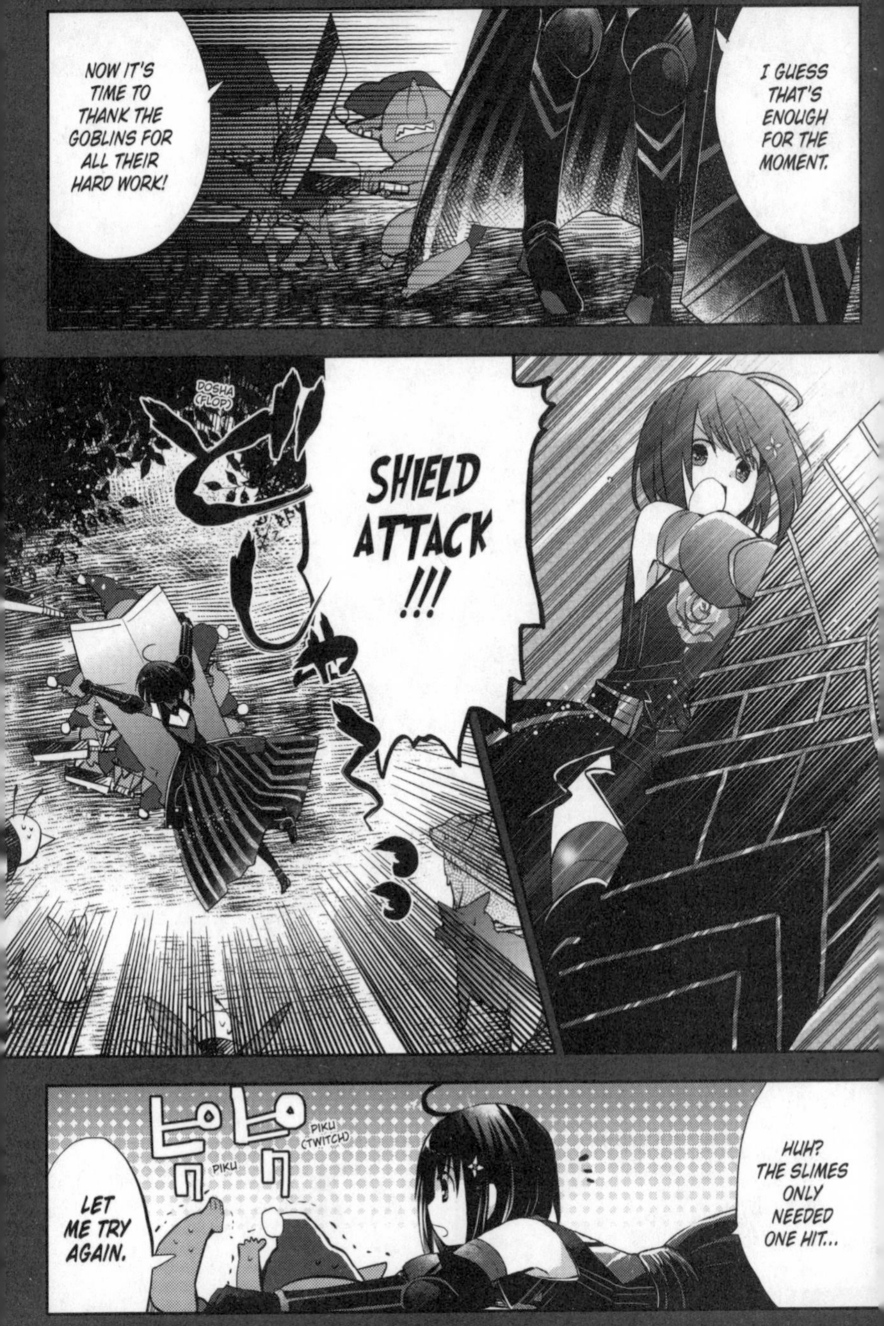
I GUESS THAT'S ENOUGH FOR THE MOMENT.
NOW IT'S TIME TO THANK THE GOBLINS FOR ALL THEIR HARD WORK!
SHIELD ATTACK !!!
DOSHA (FLOP)
HUH? THE SLIMES ONLY NEEDED ONE HIT...
PIKU (TWITCH)
PIKU
LET ME TRY AGAIN.

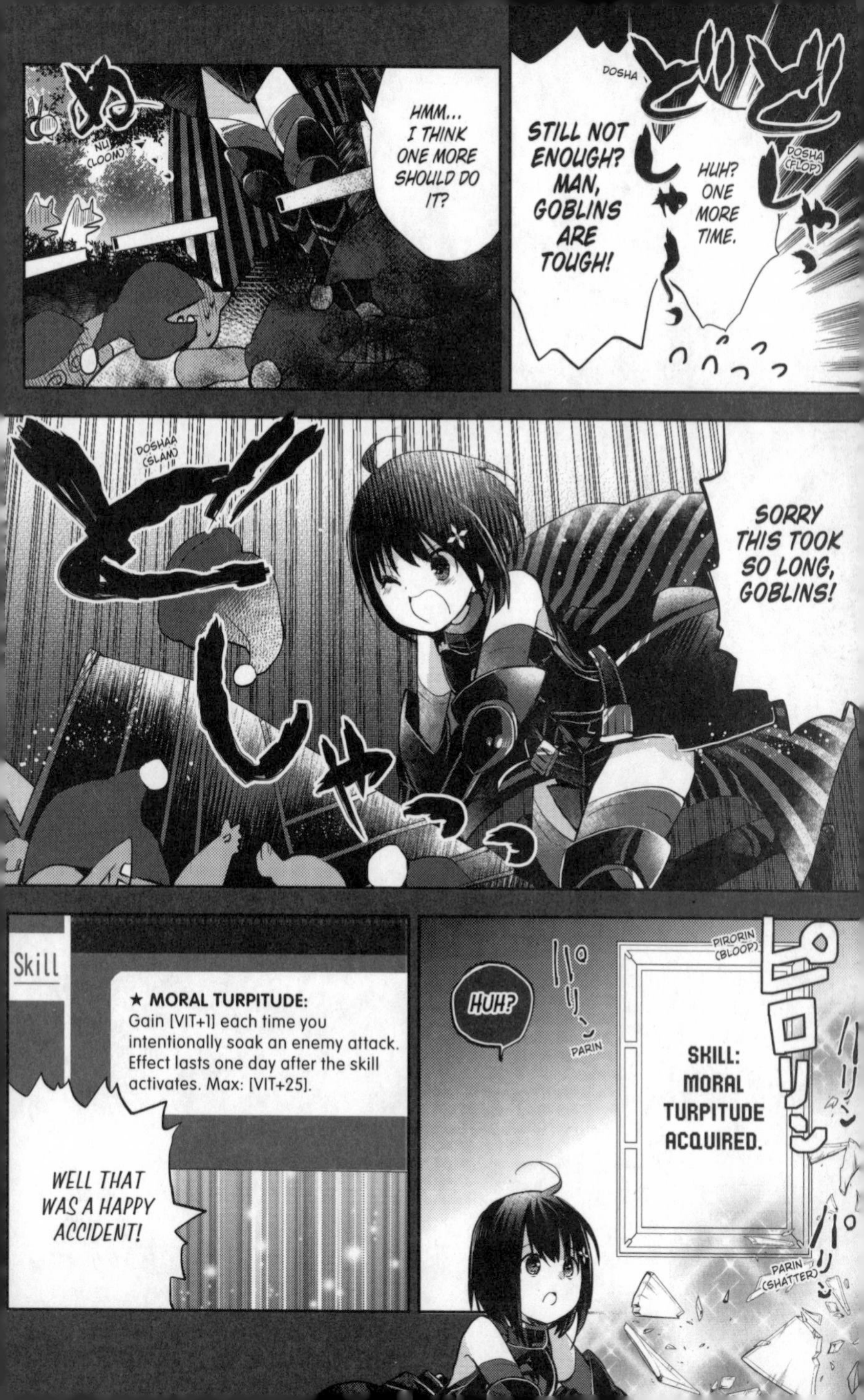
DOSHA
STILL NOT ENOUGH? MAN, GOBLINS ARE TOUGH!
HUH? ONE MORE TIME.
DOSHA (FLOP)
HMM... I THINK ONE MORE SHOULD DO IT?
NU (LOOM)
DOSHAA (SLAM)
SORRY THIS TOOK SO LONG, GOBLINS!
PIRORIN (BLOOP)
SKILL: MORAL TURPITUDE ACQUIRED.
PARIN
HUH?
PARIN (SHATTER)
Skill
★ MORAL TURPITUDE:
Gain [VIT+1] each time you intentionally soak an enemy attack. Effect lasts one day after the skill activates. Max: [VIT+25].
WELL THAT WAS A HAPPY ACCIDENT!

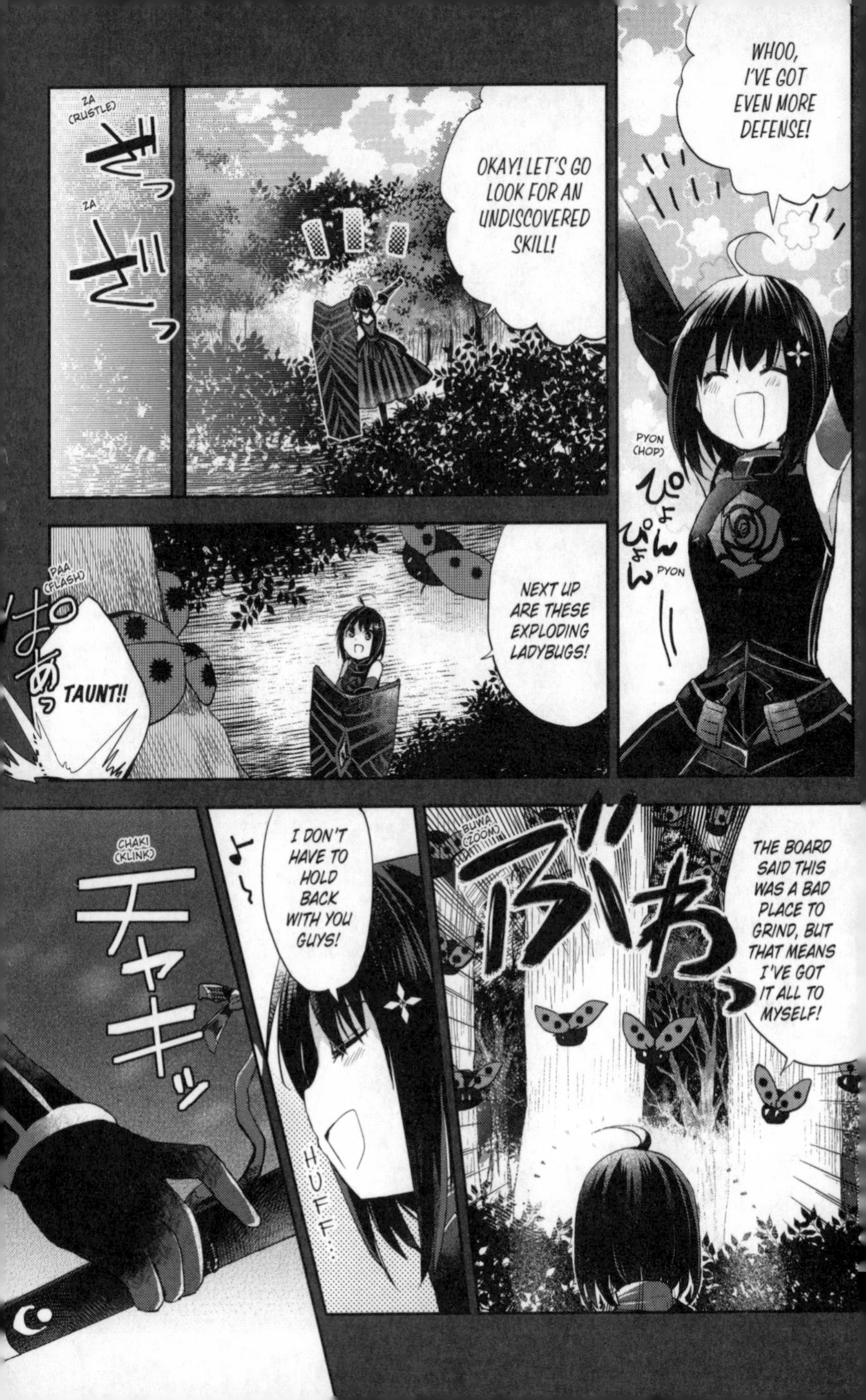
WHOO, I'VE GOT EVEN MORE DEFENSE!
PYON (HOP)
ぴょんぴょん
PYON
OKAY! LET'S GO LOOK FOR AN UNDISCOVERED SKILL!
ZA (RUSTLE)
ざっ
ZA
ざっ
NEXT UP ARE THESE EXPLODING LADYBUGS!
PAA (FLASH)
ぱあっ
TAUNT!!
BUWA (ZOOM)
ぶわっ
THE BOARD SAID THIS WAS A BAD PLACE TO GRIND, BUT THAT MEANS I'VE GOT IT ALL TO MYSELF!
I DON'T HAVE TO HOLD BACK WITH YOU GUYS!
♪~
HUFF...
CHAKI (KLINK)
チャキッ

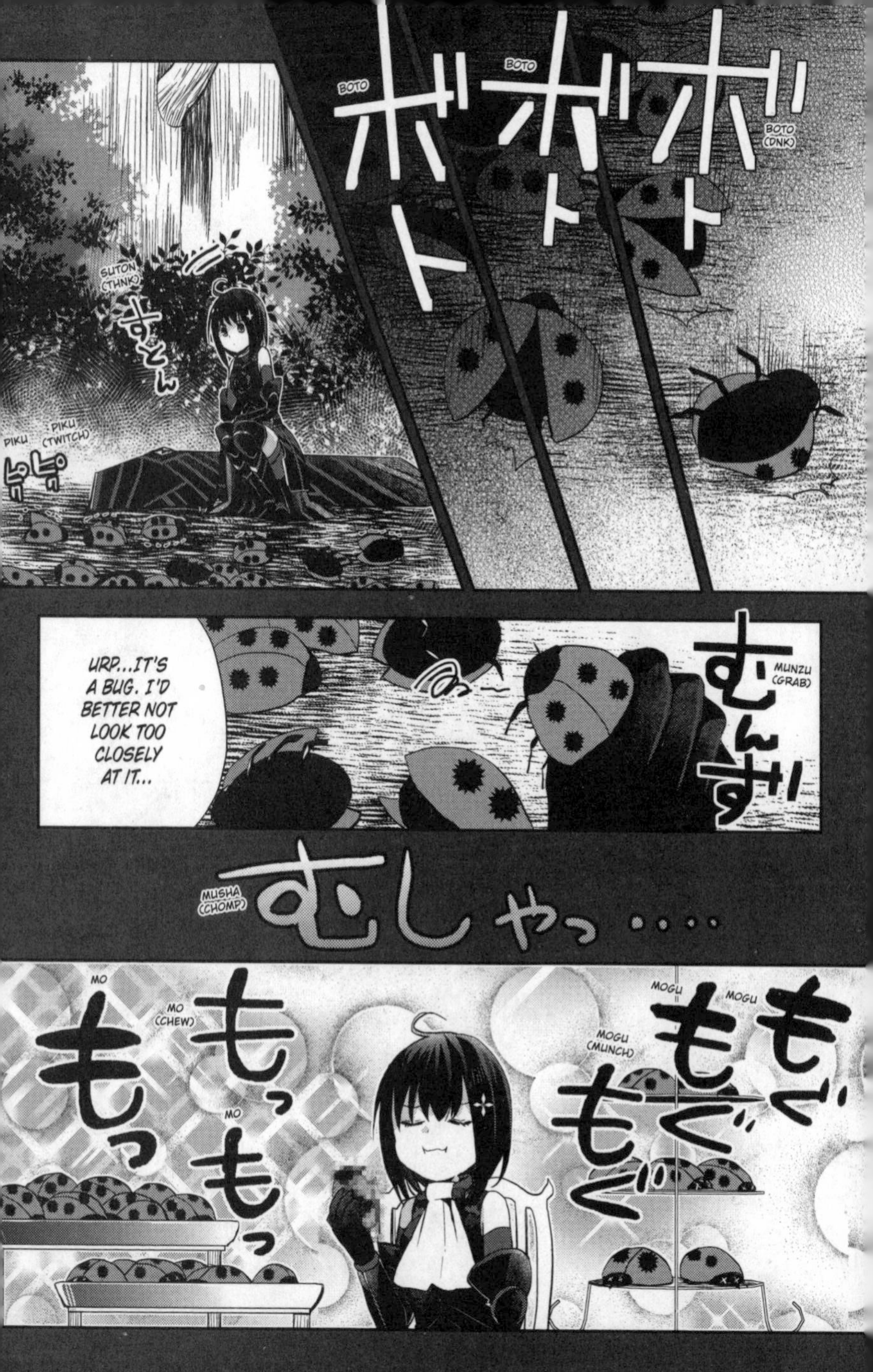
BOTO
BOTO
BOTO (DNK)
SUTON (THNK)
すとん
PIKU
PIKU (TWITCH)
ぴくぴく
MUNZU (GRAB)
むんず
URP...IT'S A BUG. I'D BETTER NOT LOOK TOO CLOSELY AT IT...
MUSHA (CHOMP)
むしゃっ....
MOGU
MOGU
MOGU (MUNCH)
もぐもぐもぐ
MO
MO (CHEW)
MO
もっもっもっ

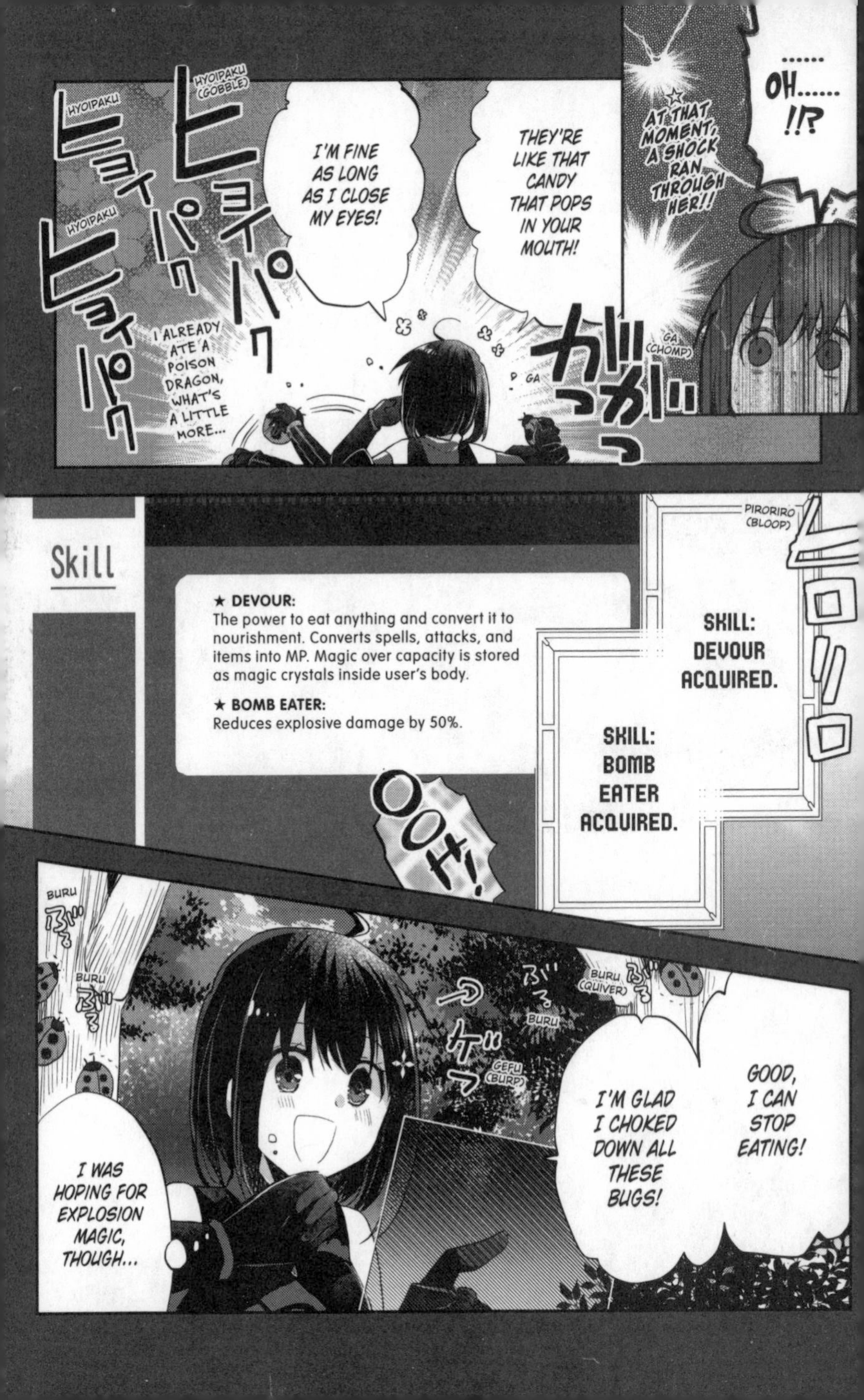

......
OH......!!?
AT THAT MOMENT, A SHOCK RAN THROUGH HER!!
THEY'RE LIKE THAT CANDY THAT POPS IN YOUR MOUTH!
I'M FINE AS LONG AS I CLOSE MY EYES!
HYOIPAKU (GOBBLE)
HYOIPAKU
HYOIPAKU
I ALREADY ATE A POISON DRAGON, WHAT'S A LITTLE MORE...
GA (CHOMP)
GA
PIRORIRO (BLOOP)
SKILL: DEVOUR ACQUIRED.
SKILL: BOMB EATER ACQUIRED.
Skill
★ DEVOUR:
The power to eat anything and convert it to nourishment. Converts spells, attacks, and items into MP. Magic over capacity is stored as magic crystals inside user's body.
★ BOMB EATER:
Reduces explosive damage by 50%.
OOH!
GOOD, I CAN STOP EATING!
I'M GLAD I CHOKED DOWN ALL THESE BUGS!
BURU (QUIVER)
BURU
GEFU (BURP)
BURU
BURU
I WAS HOPING FOR EXPLOSION MAGIC, THOUGH...

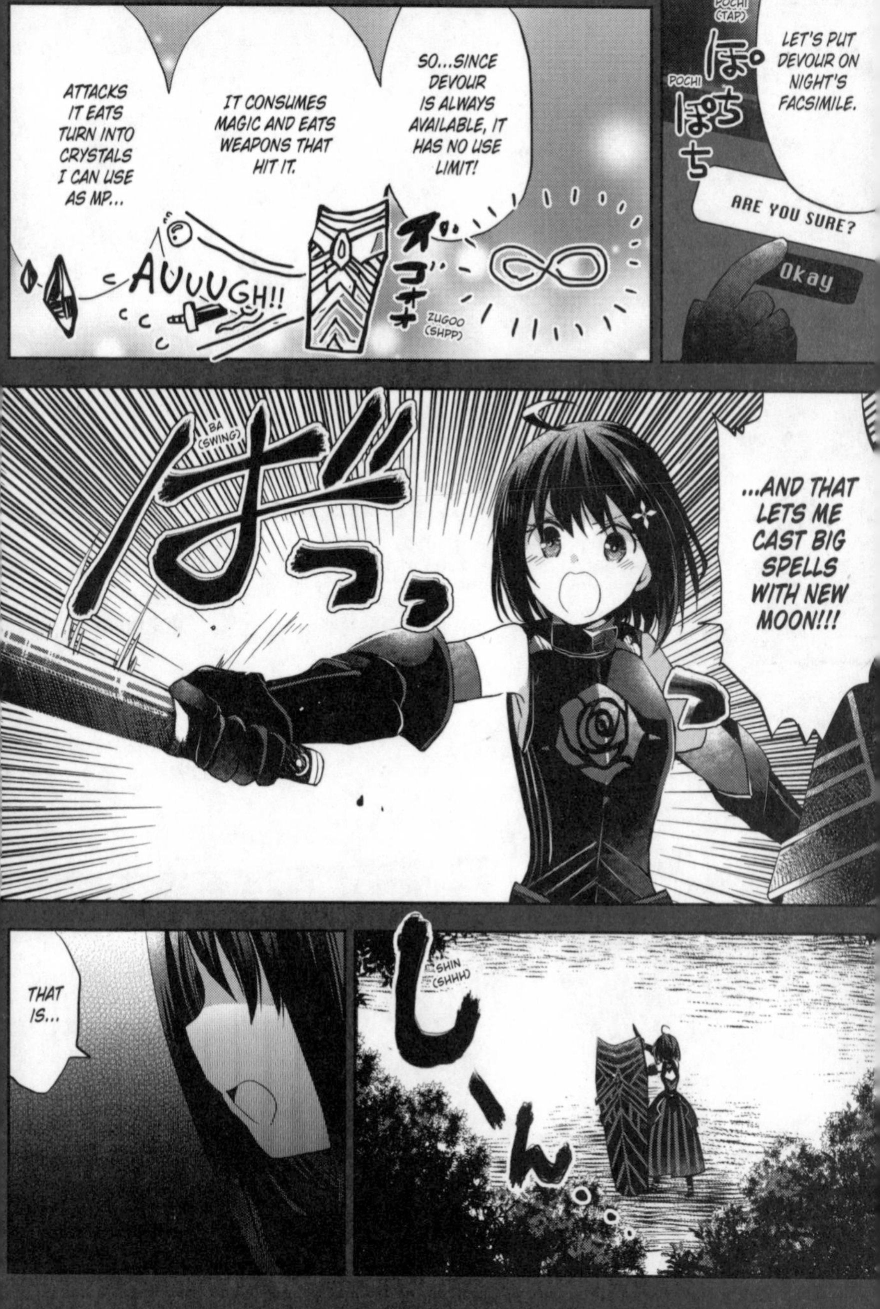
LET'S PUT DEVOUR ON NIGHT'S FACSIMILE.
ぽ。 POCHI (TAP)
ぽち POCHI
ARE YOU SURE?
Okay
SO...SINCE DEVOUR IS ALWAYS AVAILABLE, IT HAS NO USE LIMIT!
IT CONSUMES MAGIC AND EATS WEAPONS THAT HIT IT.
ATTACKS IT EATS TURN INTO CRYSTALS I CAN USE AS MP...
ZUGOO (SHPP)
AUUUGH!!
...AND THAT LETS ME CAST BIG SPELLS WITH NEW MOON!!!
BA (SWING)
SHIN (SHHH)
THAT IS...

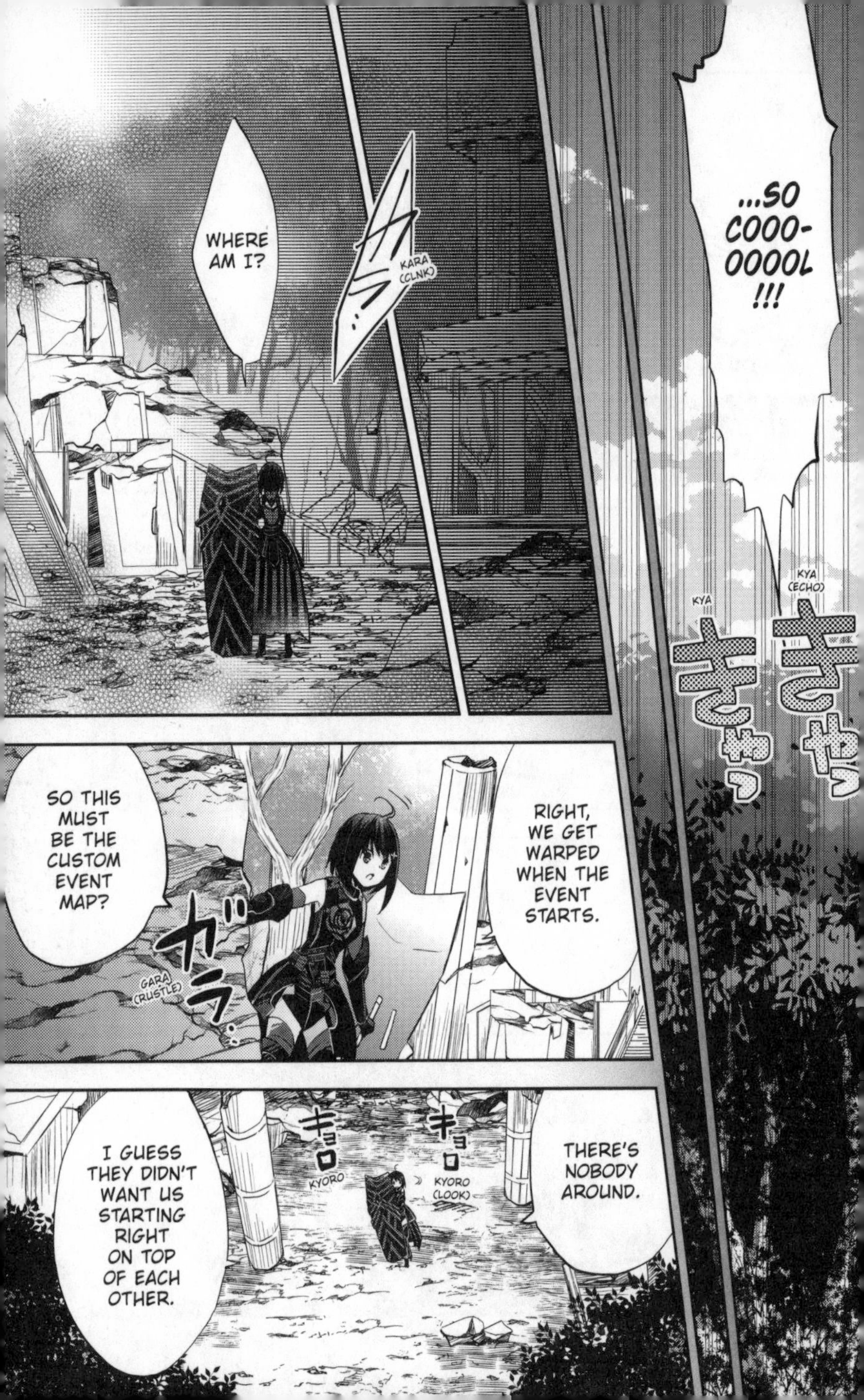
...SO COOO-OOOOL!!!
きゃっ
KYA (ECHO)
きゃっ
KYA
カラ
KARA (CLNK)
WHERE AM I?
RIGHT, WE GET WARPED WHEN THE EVENT STARTS.
SO THIS MUST BE THE CUSTOM EVENT MAP?
ガラ
GARA (RUSTLE)
THERE'S NOBODY AROUND.
キョロ
KYORO (LOOK)
キョロ
KYORO
I GUESS THEY DIDN'T WANT US STARTING RIGHT ON TOP OF EACH OTHER.

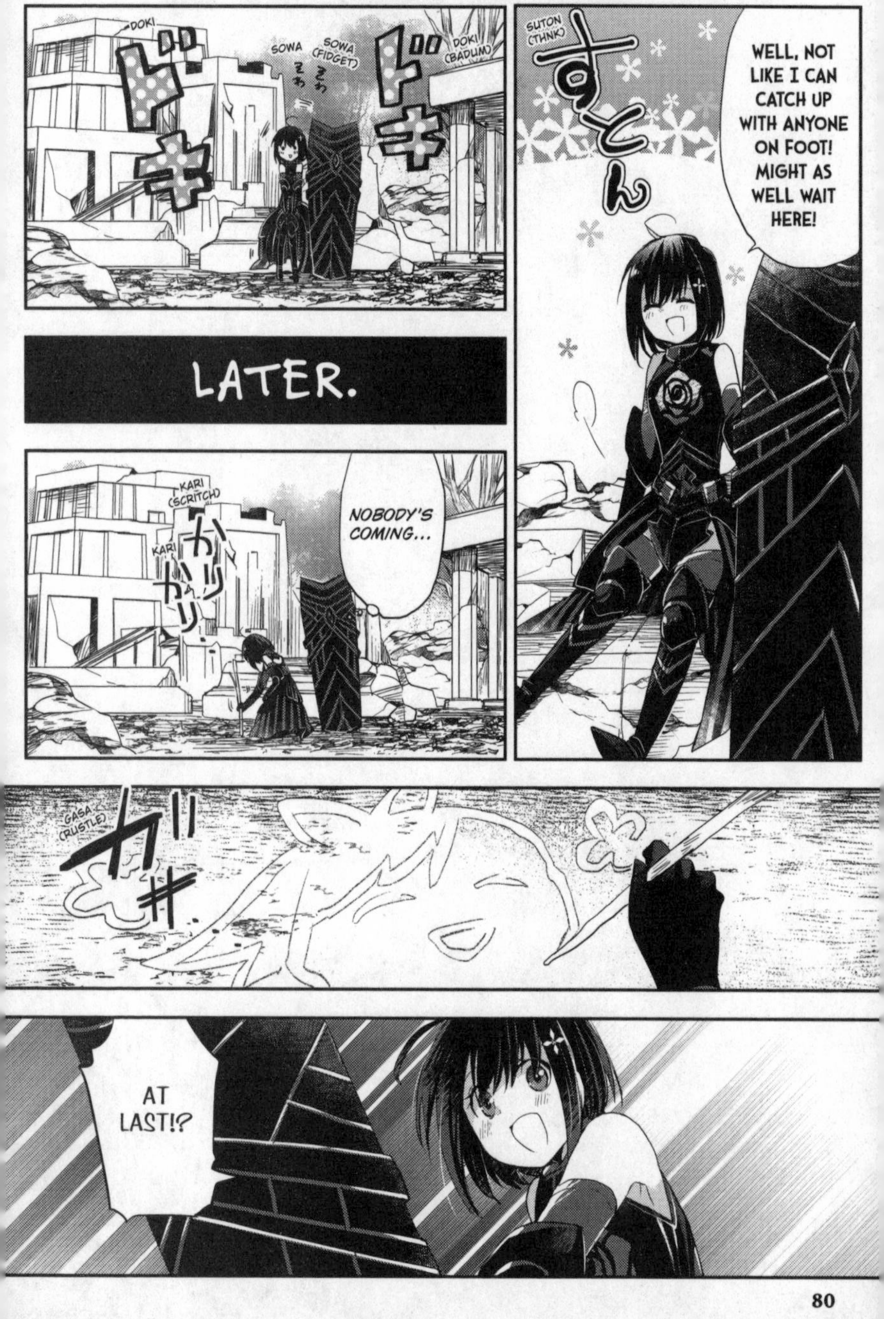
SUTON (THNK)
WELL, NOT LIKE I CAN CATCH UP WITH ANYONE ON FOOT! MIGHT AS WELL WAIT HERE!
DOKI (BADUM)
SOWA (FIDGET)
SOWA
DOKI
LATER.
NOBODY'S COMING...
KARI (SCRITCH)
KARI
GASA (RUSTLE)
AT LAST!?

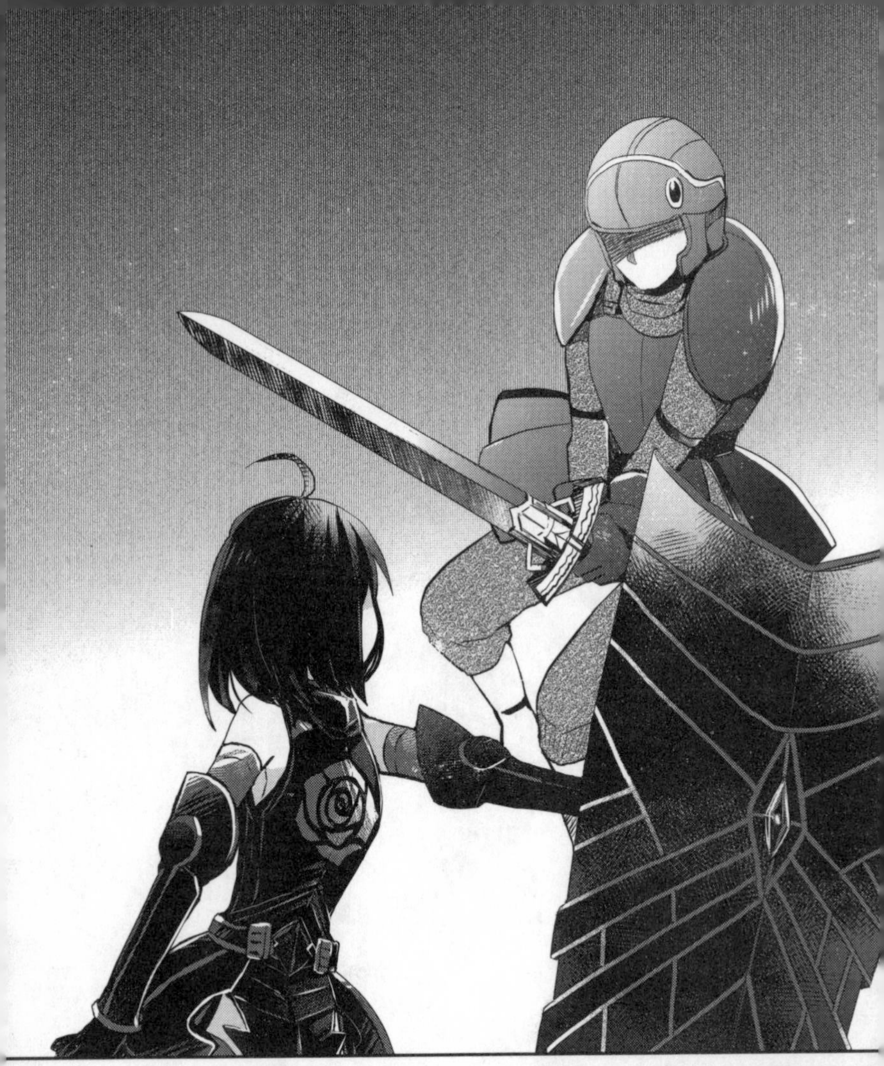

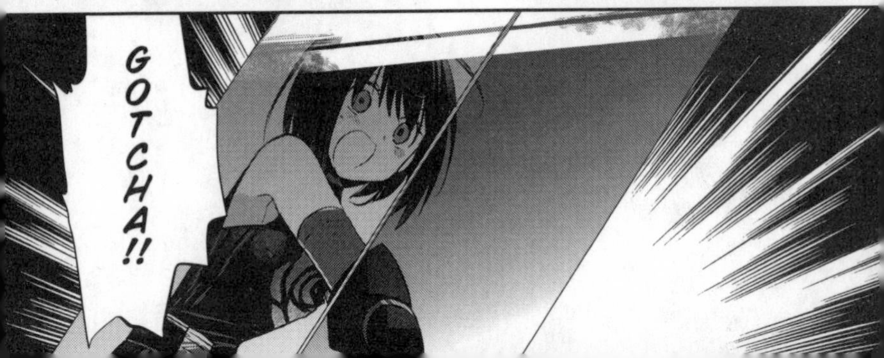
GOTCHA!!

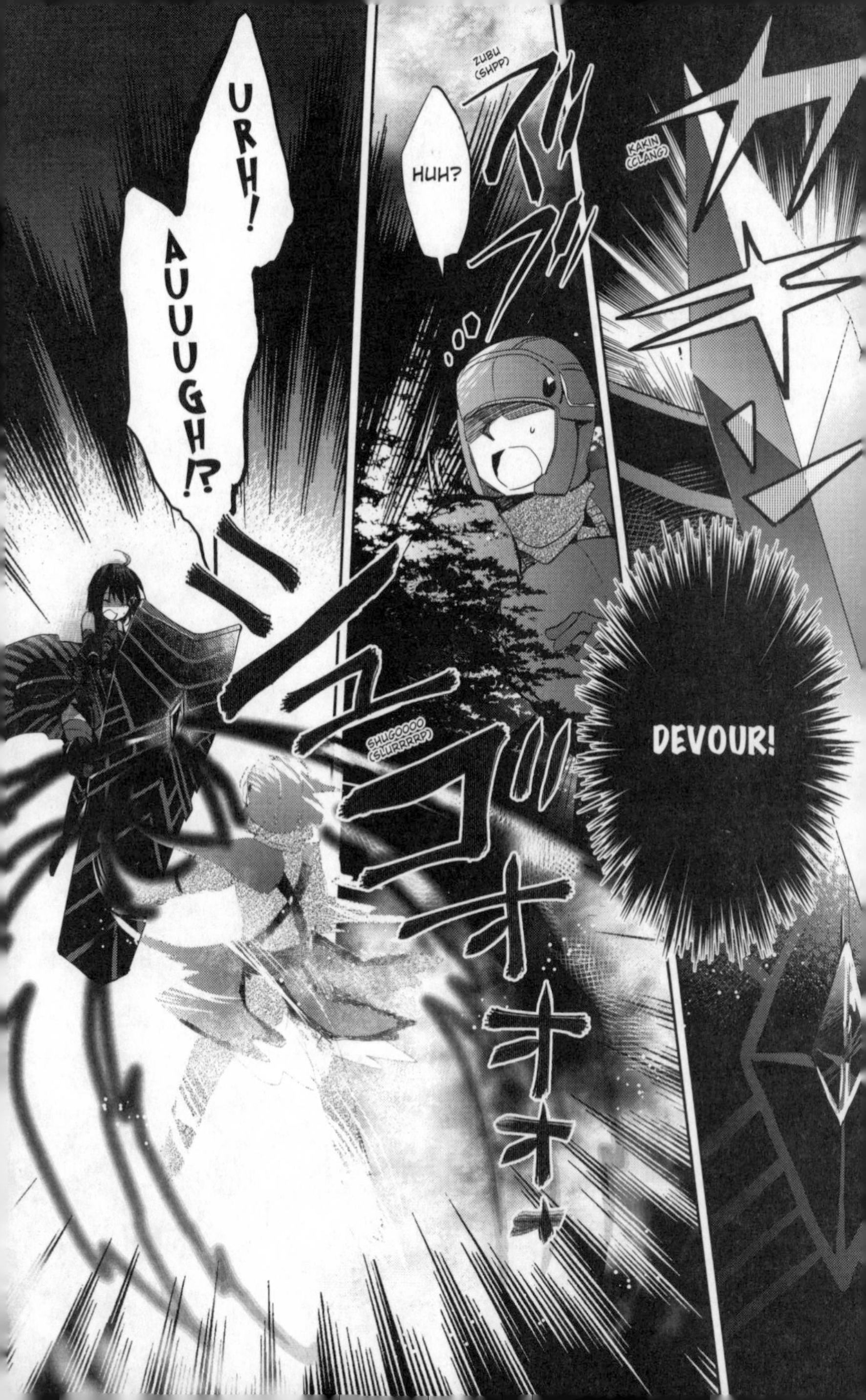
KAKIN (CLANG)
DEVOUR!
ZUBU (SHPP)
HUH?
SHUGOOOO (SLURRRRP)
URH! AUUUGH!?

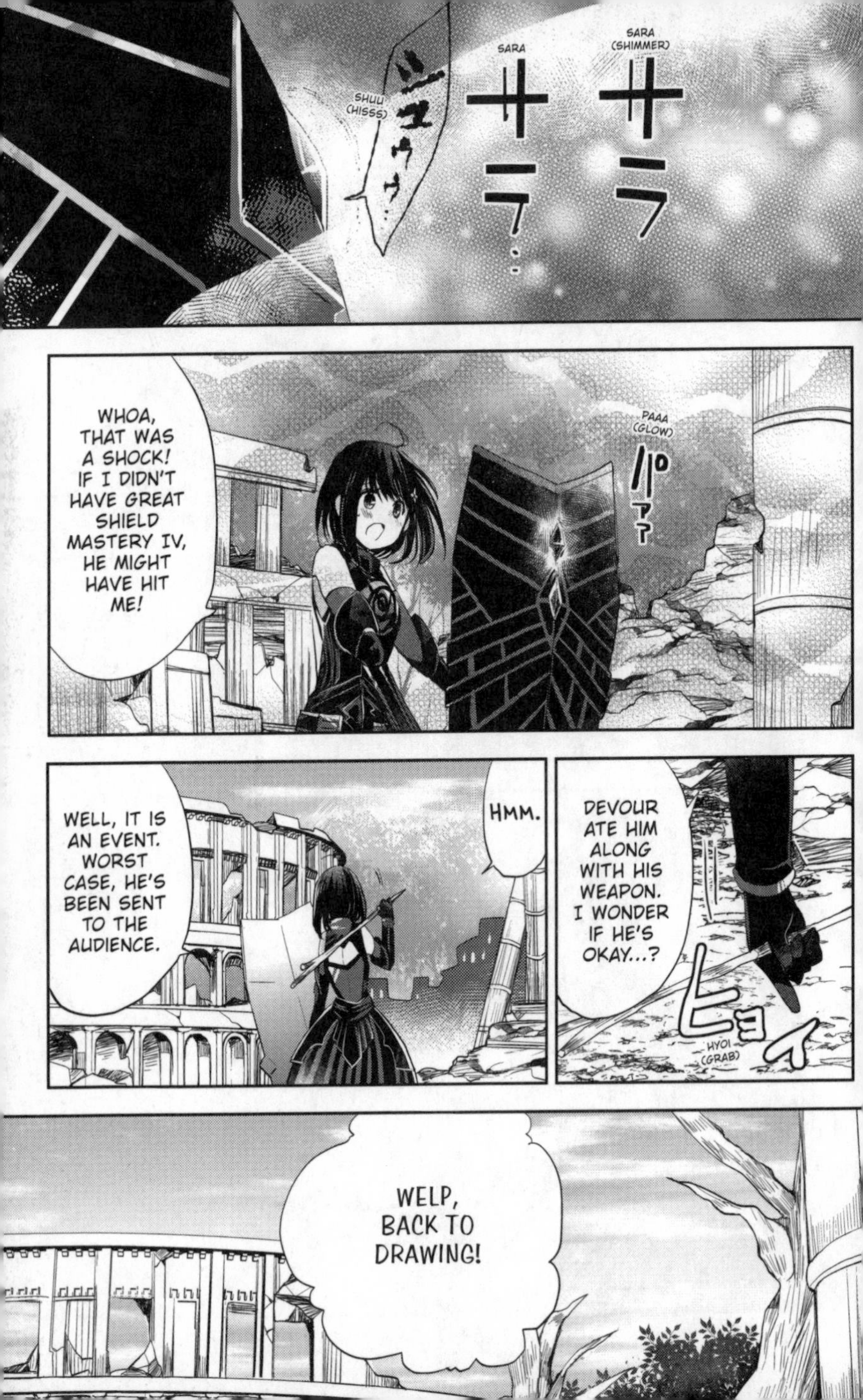
サラ
SARA (SHIMMER)
サラ…
SARA
シュウウ…
SHUU (HISSS)
WHOA, THAT WAS A SHOCK! IF I DIDN'T HAVE GREAT SHIELD MASTERY IV, HE MIGHT HAVE HIT ME!
パァア
PAAA (GLOW)
DEVOUR ATE HIM ALONG WITH HIS WEAPON. I WONDER IF HE'S OKAY...?
ヒョイ
HYOI (GRAB)
HMM.
WELL, IT IS AN EVENT. WORST CASE, HE'S BEEN SENT TO THE AUDIENCE.
WELP, BACK TO DRAWING!

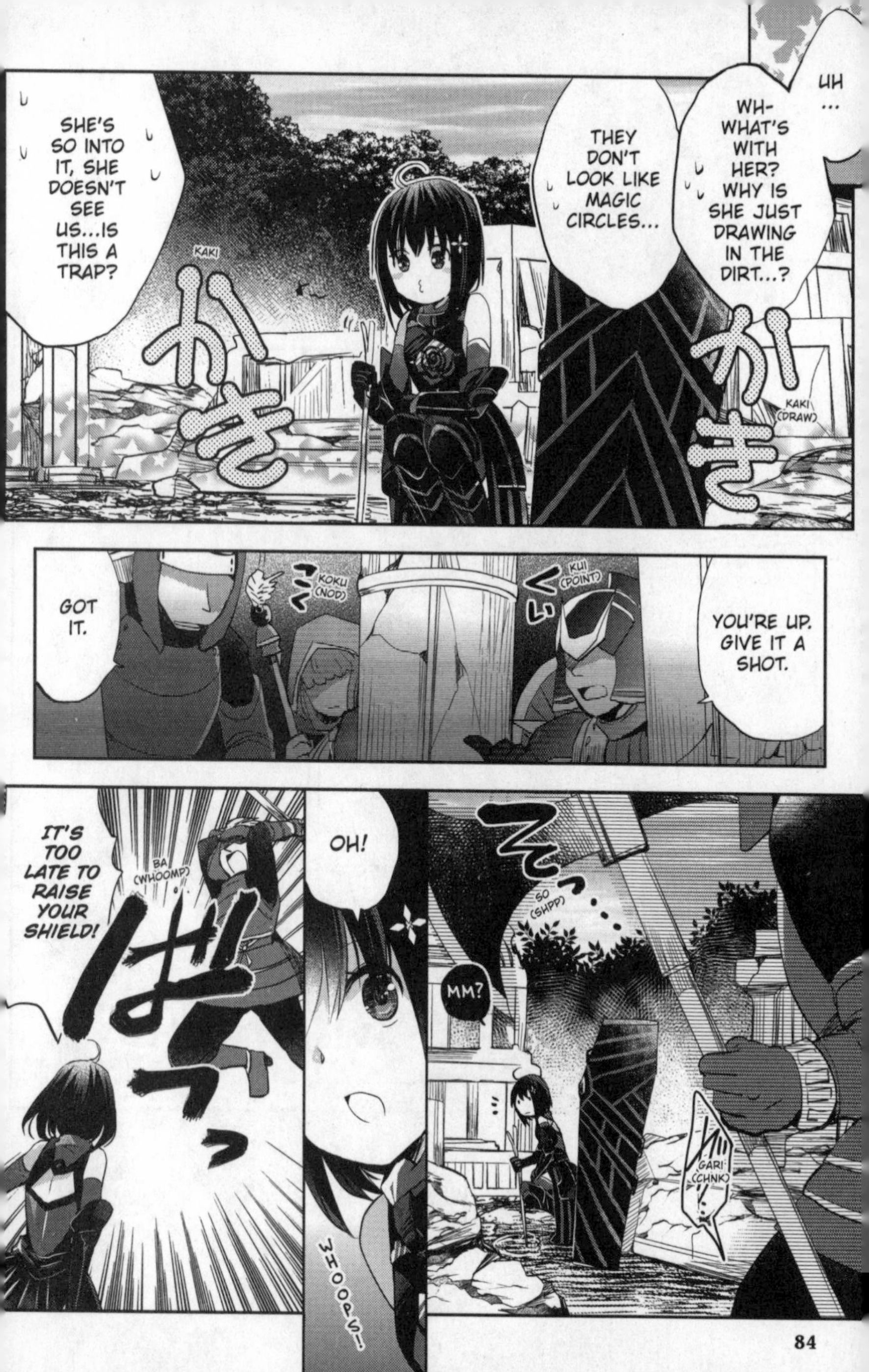
UH...
WH-WHAT'S WITH HER? WHY IS SHE JUST DRAWING IN THE DIRT...?
THEY DON'T LOOK LIKE MAGIC CIRCLES...
かき
KAKI (DRAW)
SHE'S SO INTO IT, SHE DOESN'T SEE US...IS THIS A TRAP?
かき
KAKI
YOU'RE UP. GIVE IT A SHOT.
くい
KUI (POINT)
こく
KOKU (NOD)
GOT IT.
SO (SHPP)
MM?
GARI (CHNK)
OH!
WHOOPS!
BA (WHOOMP)
IT'S TOO LATE TO RAISE YOUR SHIELD!

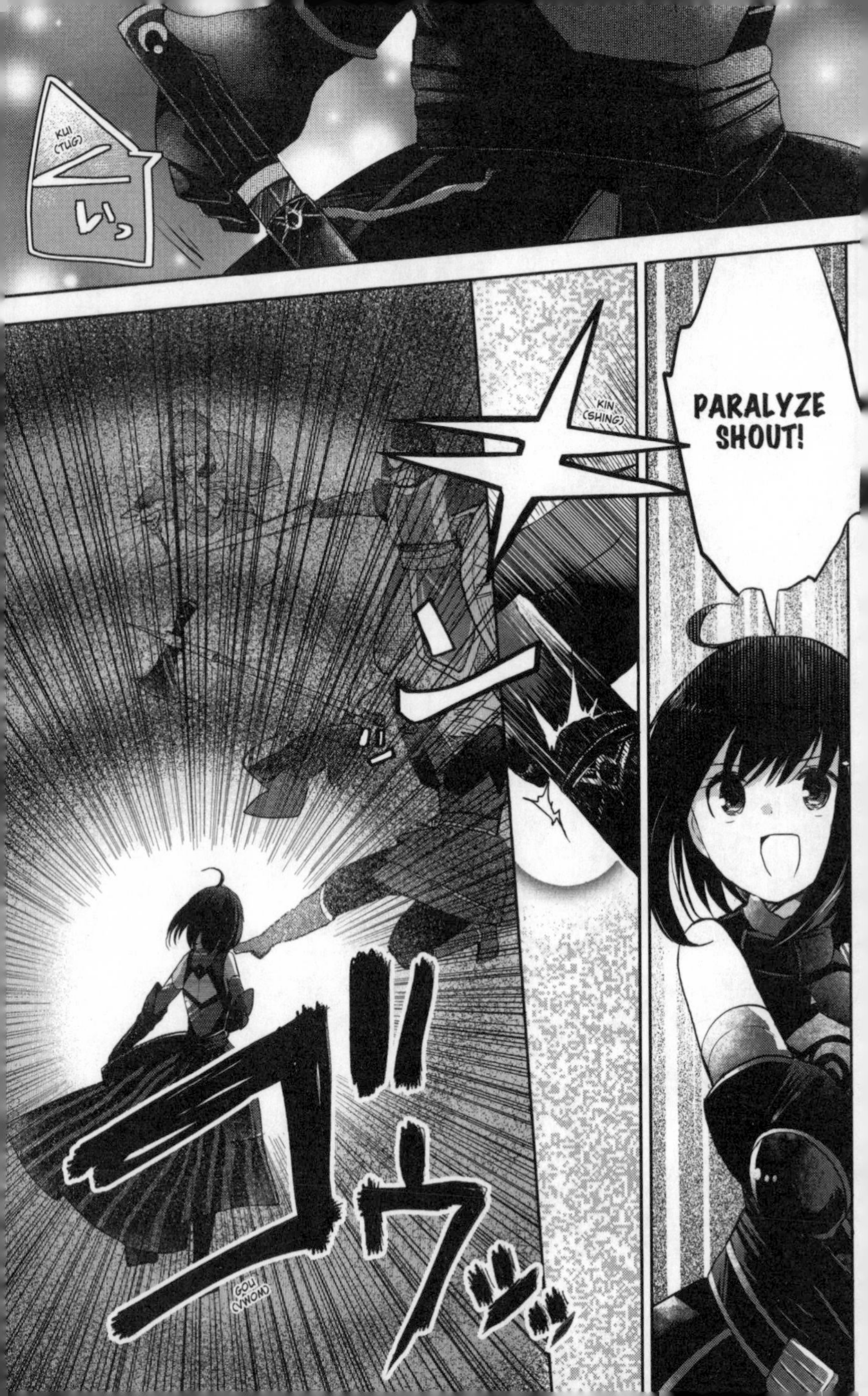
くいっ
KUI (TUG)
PARALYZE SHOUT!
KIN (SHING)
ゴウッ
GOU (VWOM)

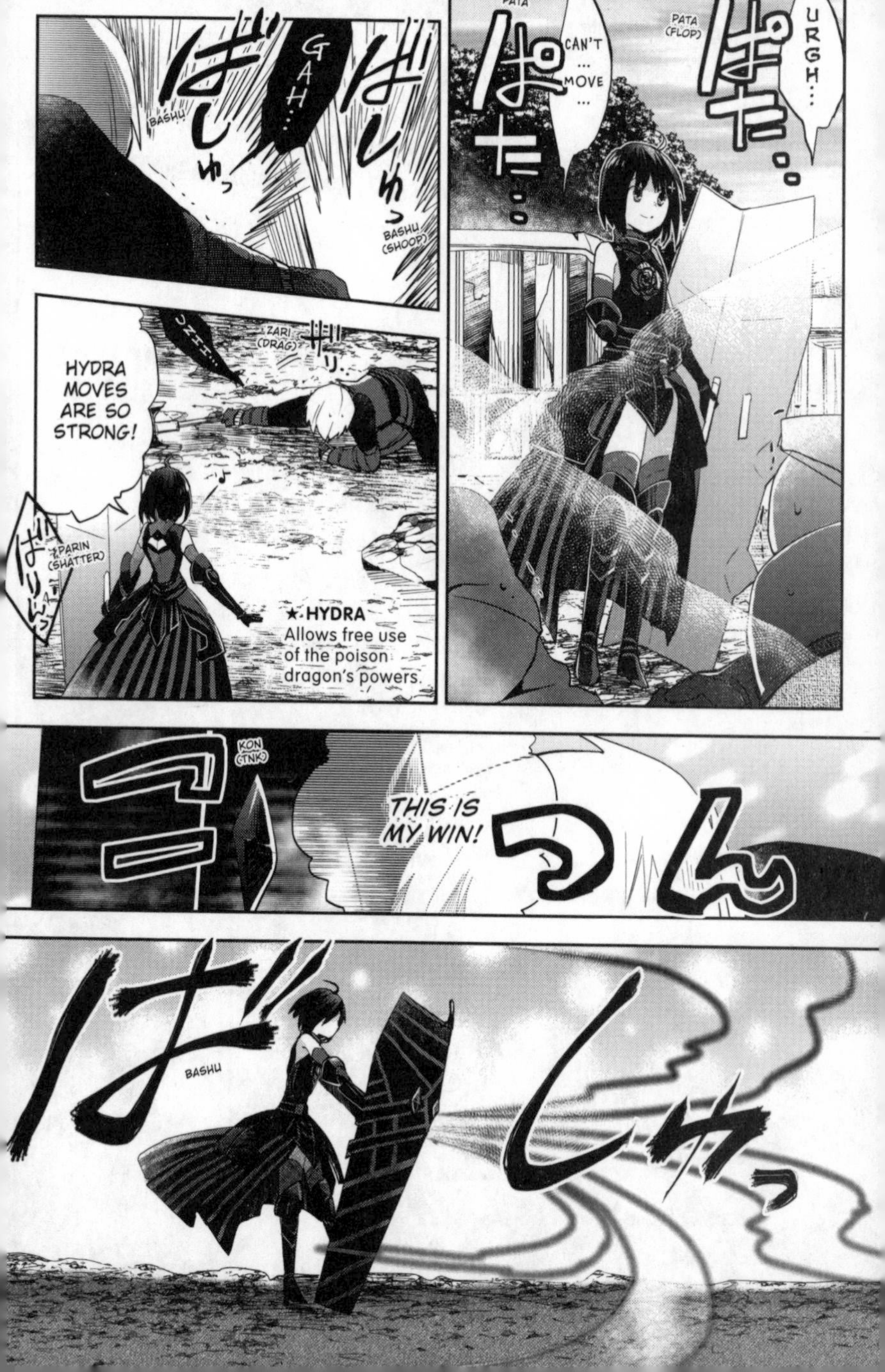
URGH…
PATA (FLOP)
CAN'T … MOVE …
PATA
GAH…
BASHU!
BASHU (SHOOP)
HYDRA MOVES ARE SO STRONG!
ZARI (DRAG)
…ZZIII
PARIN (SHATTER)
★ HYDRA
Allows free use of the poison dragon's powers.
KON (TNK)
THIS IS MY WIN!
BASHU

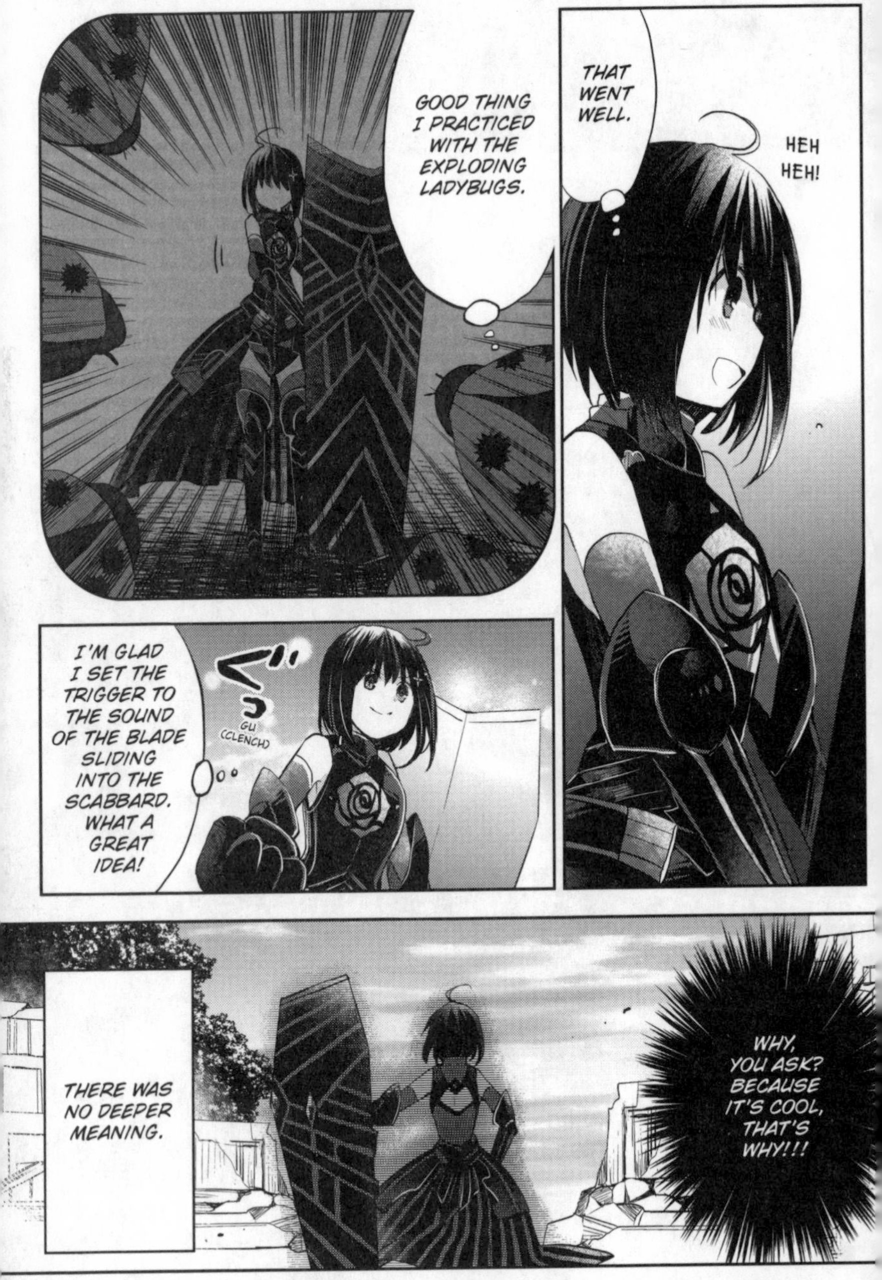
THAT WENT WELL.
HEH HEH!
GOOD THING I PRACTICED WITH THE EXPLODING LADYBUGS.
I'M GLAD I SET THE TRIGGER TO THE SOUND OF THE BLADE SLIDING INTO THE SCABBARD. WHAT A GREAT IDEA!
GU (CLENCH)
WHY, YOU ASK? BECAUSE IT'S COOL, THAT'S WHY!!!
THERE WAS NO DEEPER MEANING.

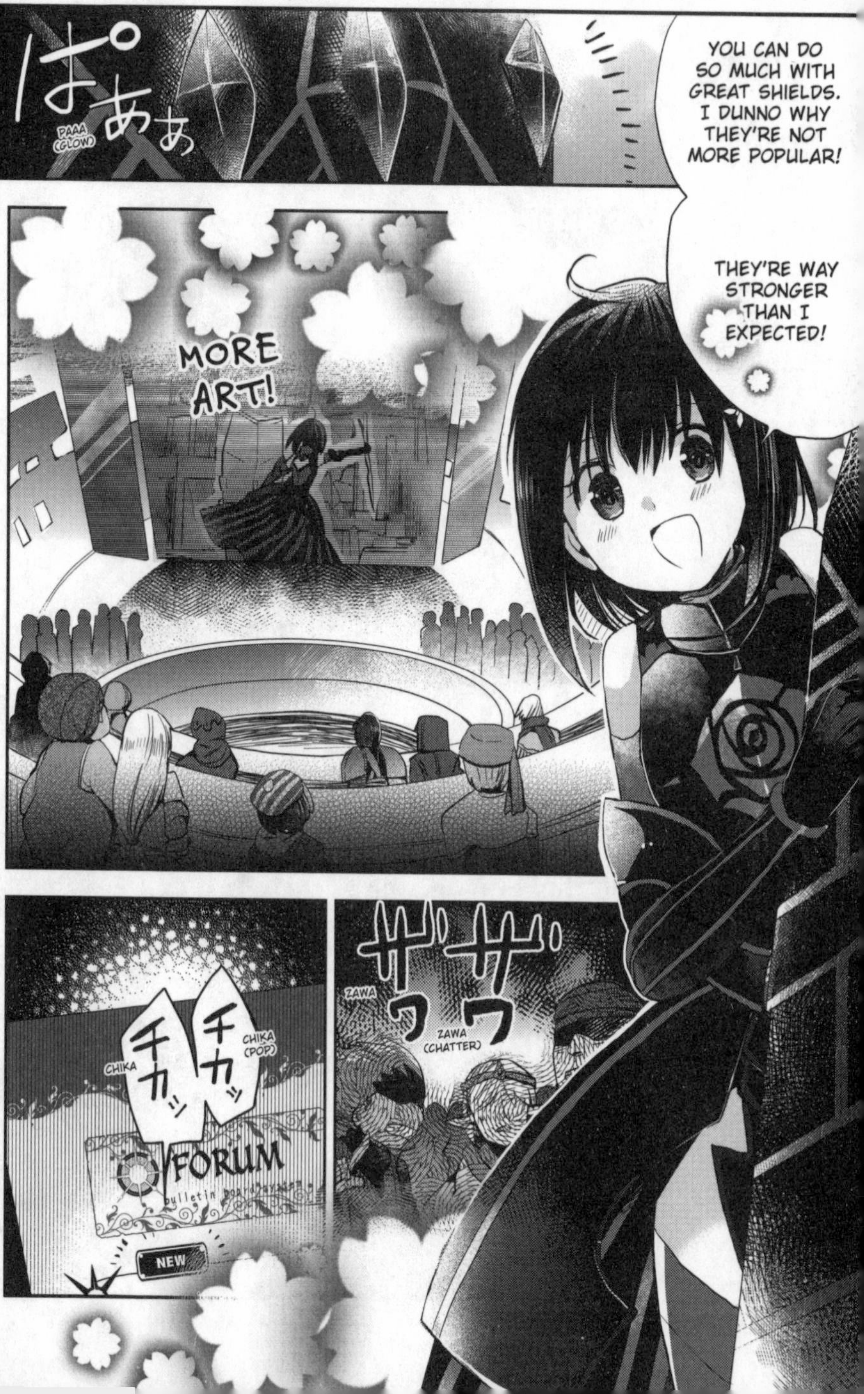
YOU CAN DO SO MUCH WITH GREAT SHIELDS. I DUNNO WHY THEY'RE NOT MORE POPULAR!
ぱあぁ
PAAA (GLOW)
THEY'RE WAY STRONGER THAN I EXPECTED!
MORE ART!
ザワ
ZAWA
ザワ
ZAWA (CHATTER)
チカッ
CHIKA (POP)
チカッ
CHIKA
FORUM
bulletin board
NEW

Bofuri

I Don't Want to Get Hurt, so I'll Max Out My Defense.

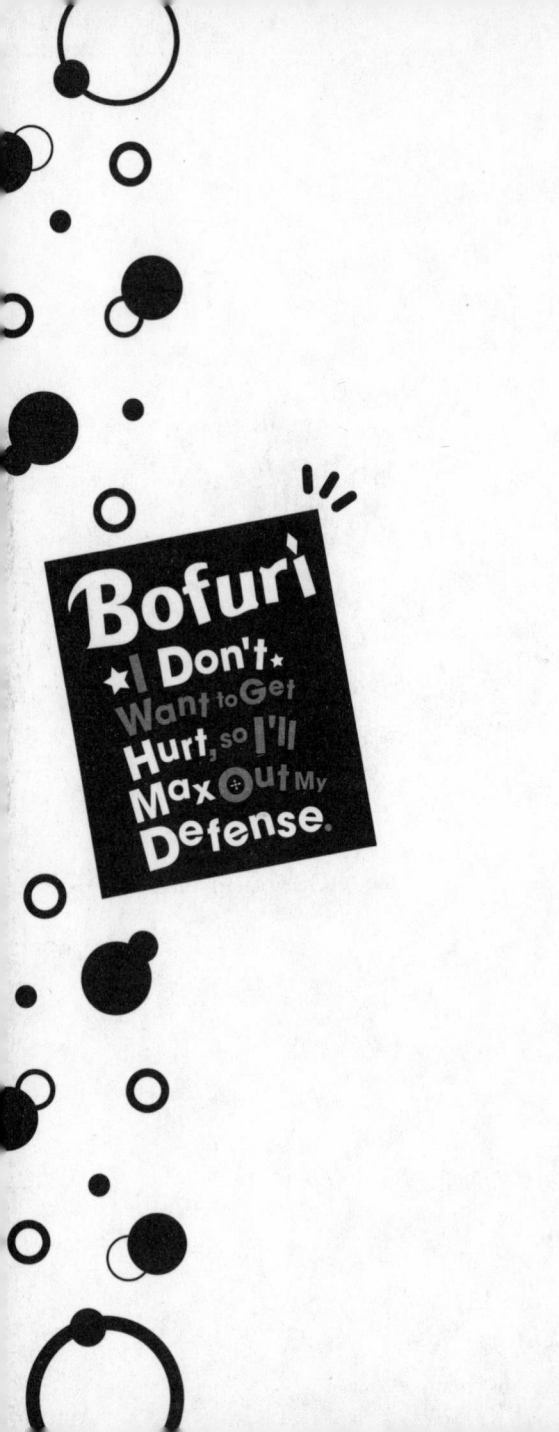

Welcome to NewWorld Online.

I Don't Want to Get Hurt,
so I'll Max Out My Defense.

presented by: JIROU OIMOTO & YUUMIKAN

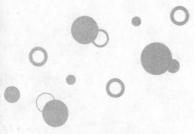

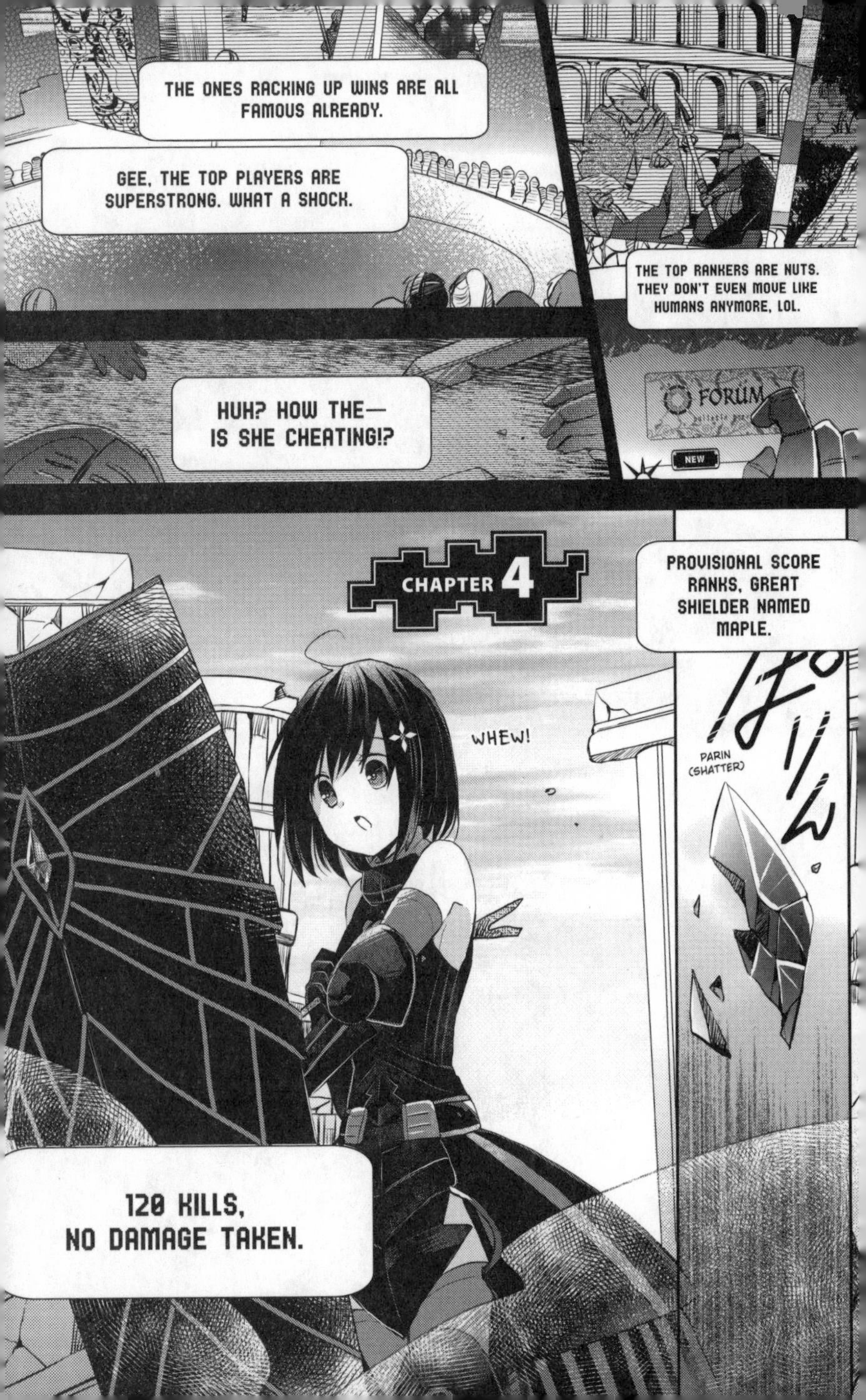
THE TOP RANKERS ARE NUTS. THEY DON'T EVEN MOVE LIKE HUMANS ANYMORE, LOL.
THE ONES RACKING UP WINS ARE ALL FAMOUS ALREADY.
GEE, THE TOP PLAYERS ARE SUPERSTRONG. WHAT A SHOCK.
FORUM
NEW
HUH? HOW THE— IS SHE CHEATING!?
CHAPTER 4
PROVISIONAL SCORE RANKS, GREAT SHIELDER NAMED MAPLE.
ぱりん
PARIN (SHATTER)
WHEW!
120 KILLS, NO DAMAGE TAKEN.

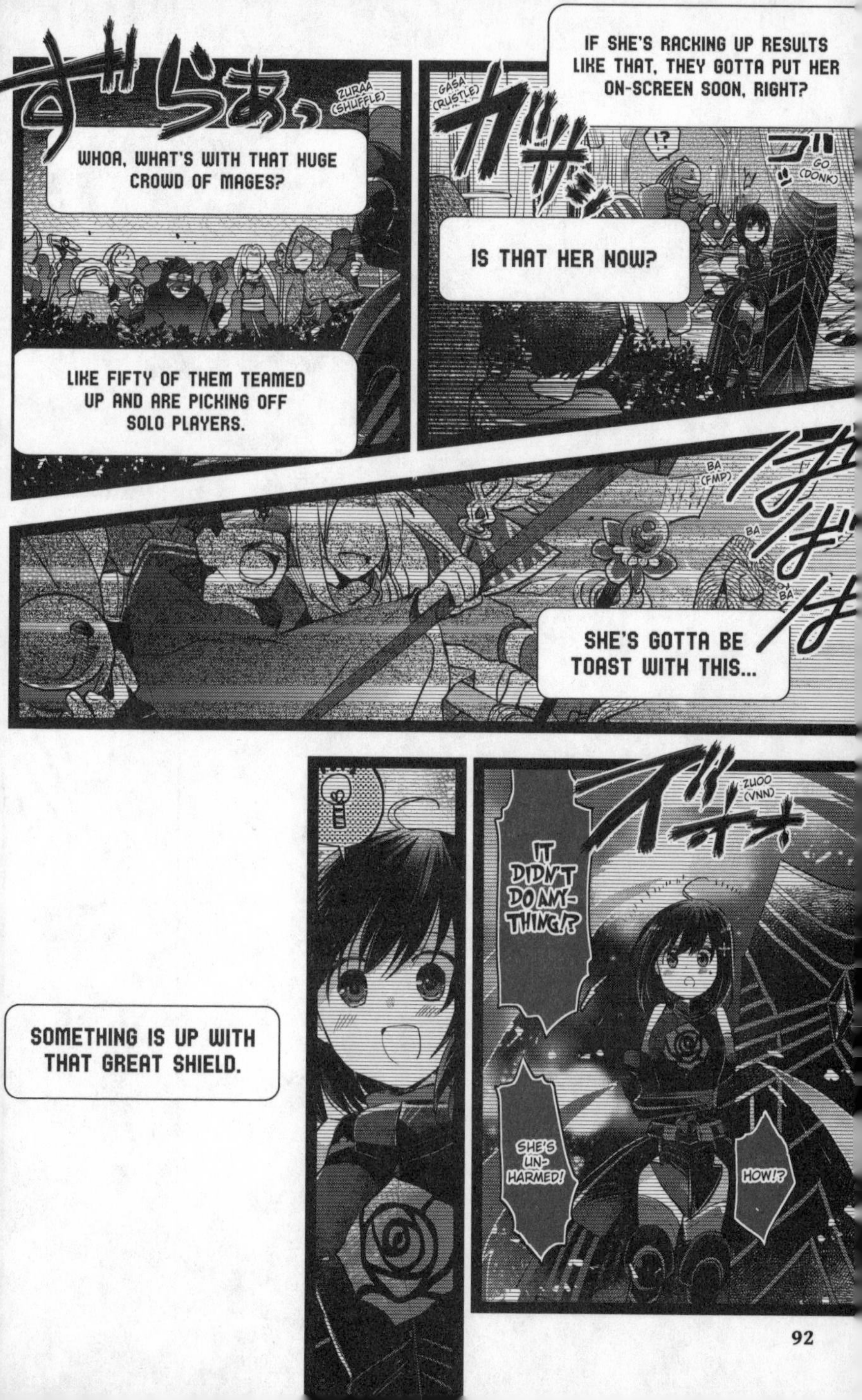
IF SHE'S RACKING UP RESULTS LIKE THAT, THEY GOTTA PUT HER ON-SCREEN SOON, RIGHT?
GASA (RUSTLE)
!?
GO (DONK)
IS THAT HER NOW?
ZURAA (SHUFFLE)
WHOA, WHAT'S WITH THAT HUGE CROWD OF MAGES?
LIKE FIFTY OF THEM TEAMED UP AND ARE PICKING OFF SOLO PLAYERS.
BA (FMP)
BA
BA
SHE'S GOTTA BE TOAST WITH THIS...
ZUOO (VNN)
IT DIDN'T DO ANY-THING!?
SHE'S UN-HARMED!
HOW!?
SOMETHING IS UP WITH THAT GREAT SHIELD.

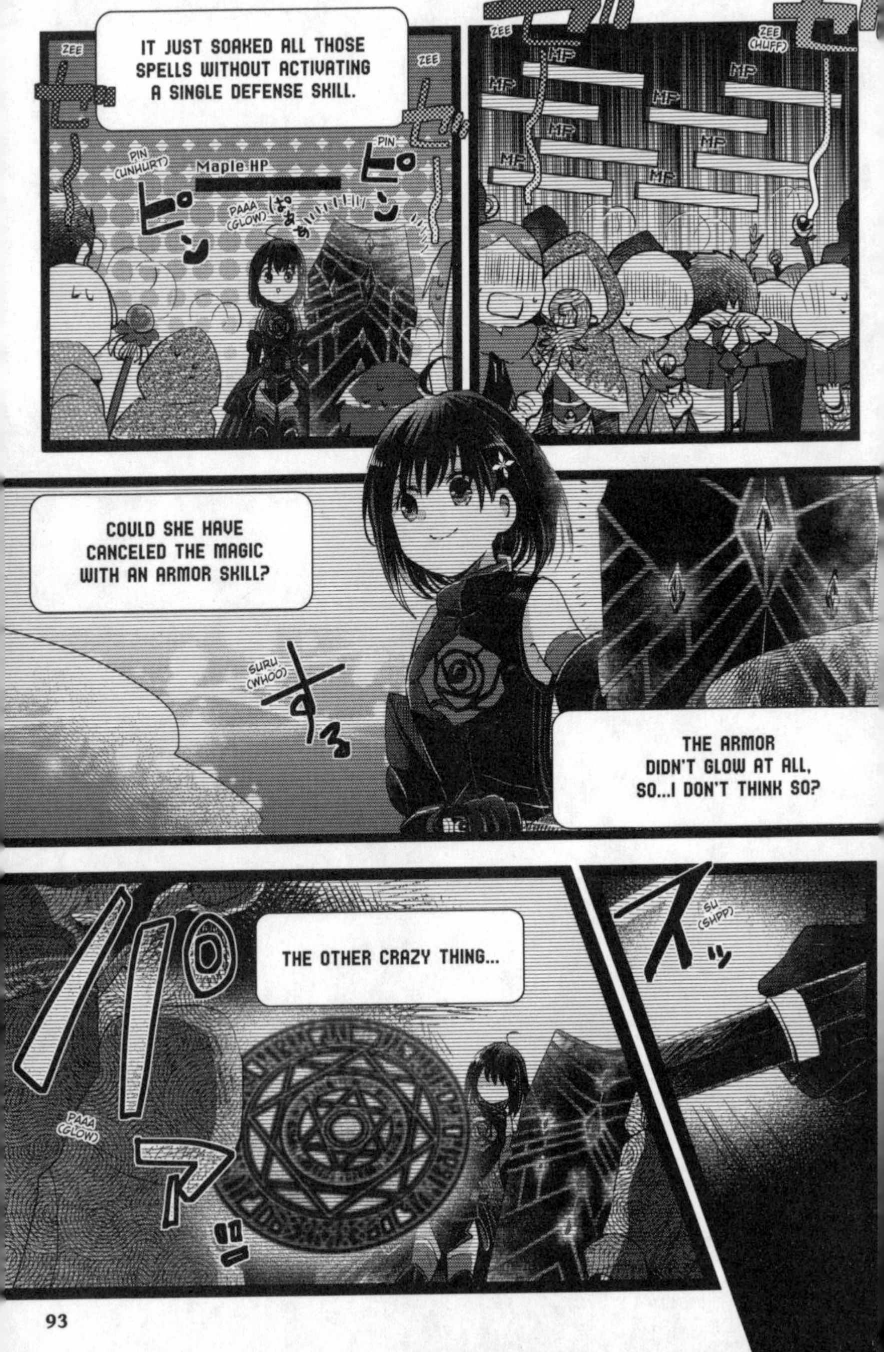
ZEE (HUFF)
ZEE
MP
MP
MP
MP
MP
MP
MP
IT JUST SOAKED ALL THOSE SPELLS WITHOUT ACTIVATING A SINGLE DEFENSE SKILL.
ZEE
ZEE
PIN
PIN (UNHURT)
Maple HP
PAAA (GLOW)
COULD SHE HAVE CANCELED THE MAGIC WITH AN ARMOR SKILL?
SURU (WHOO)
THE ARMOR DIDN'T GLOW AT ALL, SO...I DON'T THINK SO?
SU (SHPP)
THE OTHER CRAZY THING...
PAAA (GLOW)

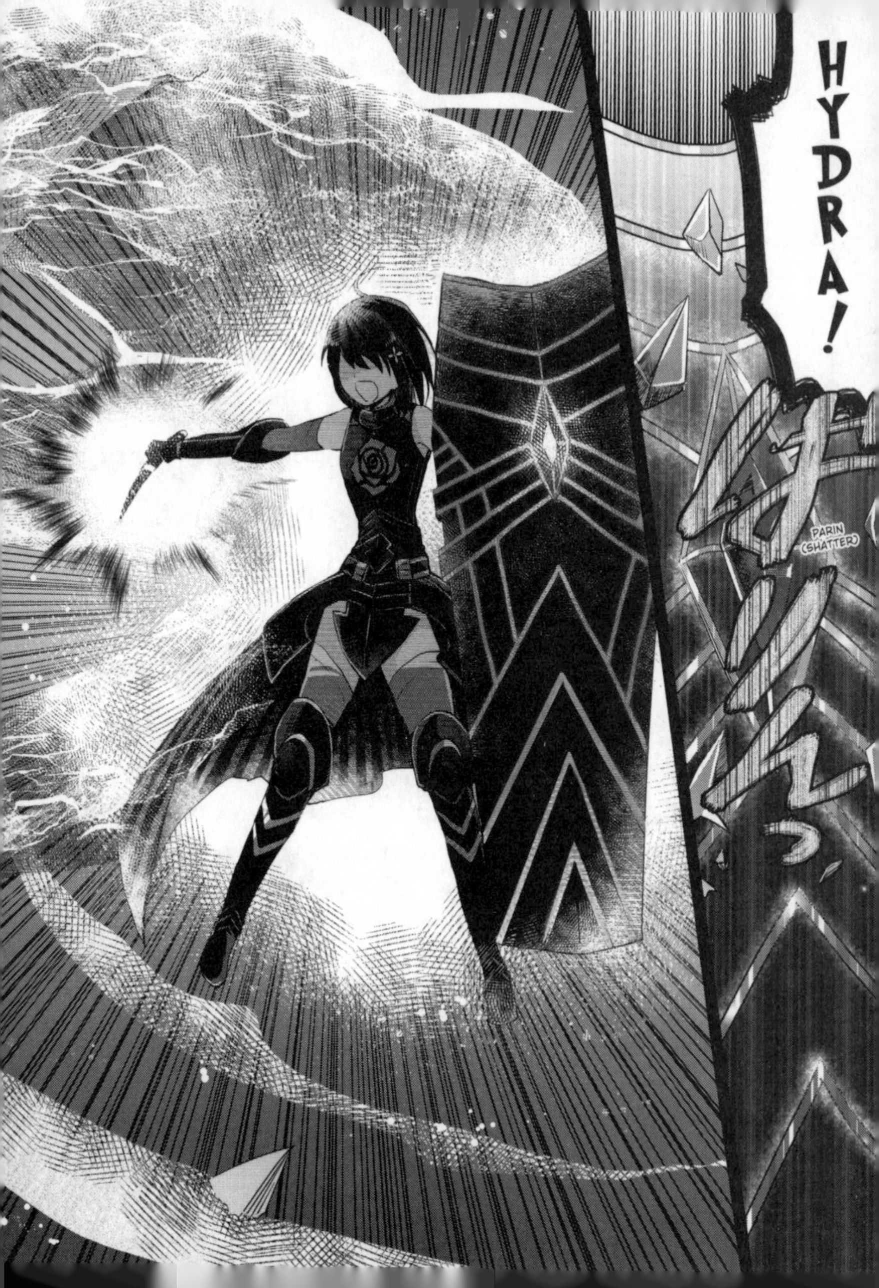
HYDRA!
PARIN (SHATTER)

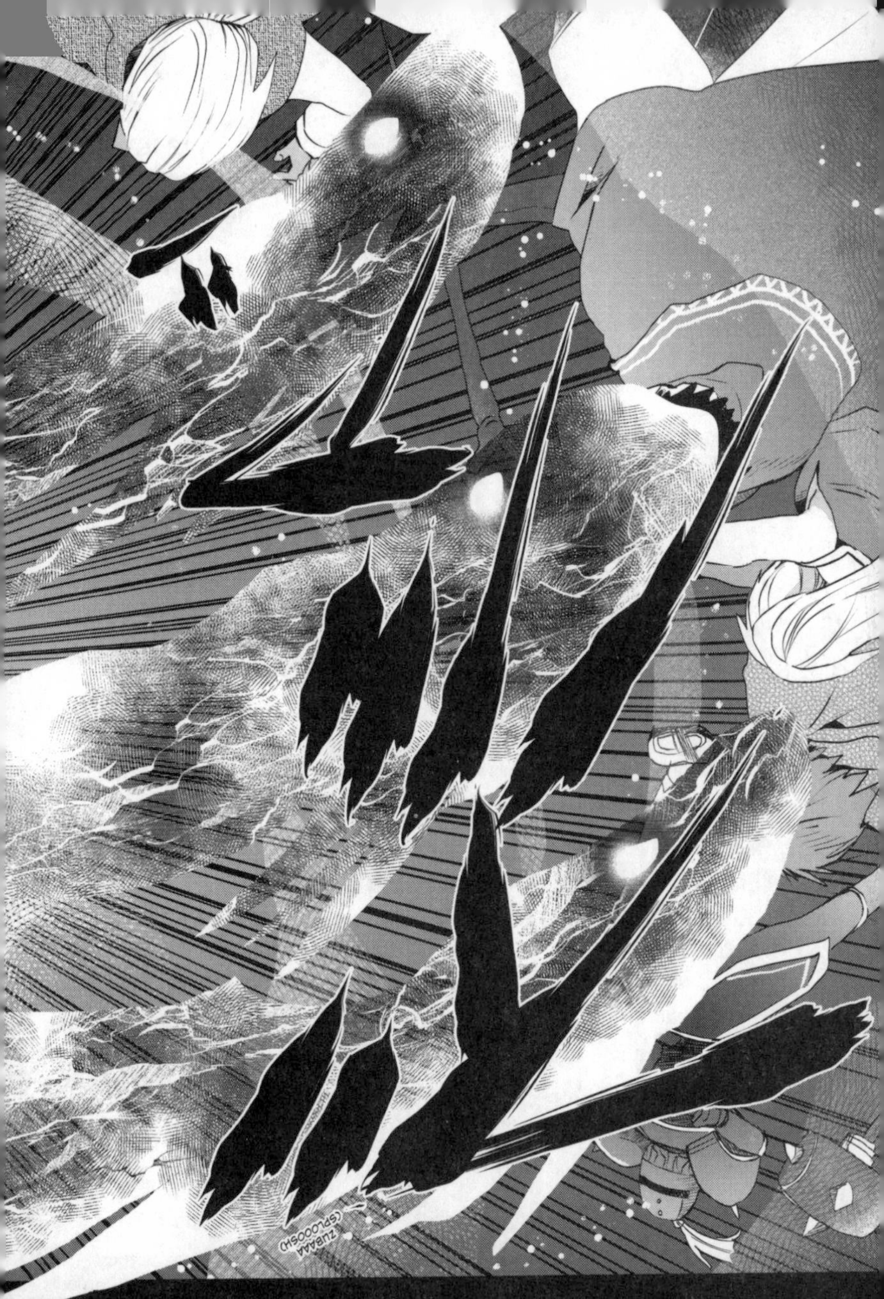
ZUBAAA
(SPLOOOSH)

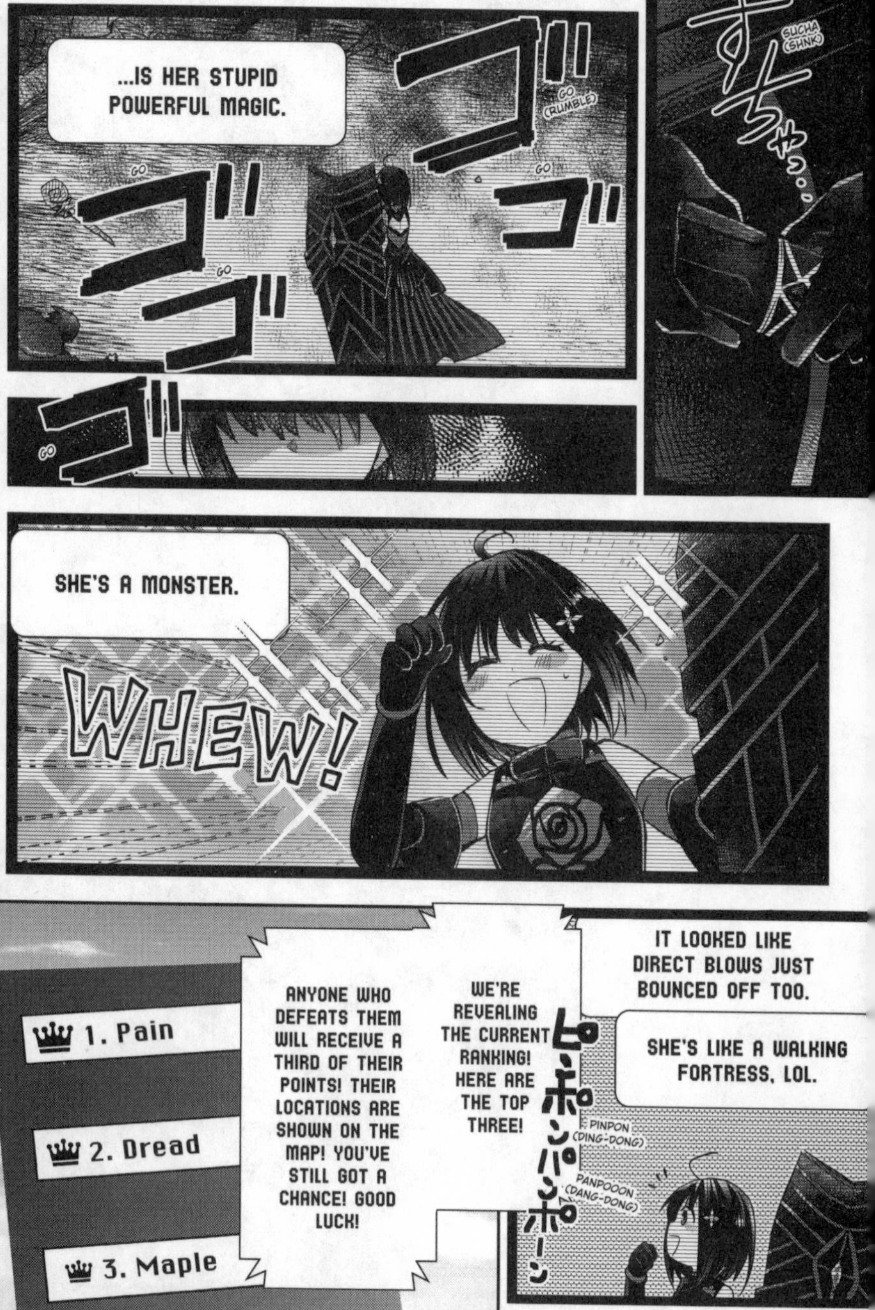
すちゃっ…
SUCHA (SHNK)
…IS HER STUPID POWERFUL MAGIC.
ゴゴゴゴ
GO (RUMBLE)
GO
GO
ゴ
GO
SHE'S A MONSTER.
WHEW!
IT LOOKED LIKE DIRECT BLOWS JUST BOUNCED OFF TOO.
SHE'S LIKE A WALKING FORTRESS, LOL.
ピンポンパンポーン
PINPON (DING-DONG)
PANPOOON (DANG-DONG)
WE'RE REVEALING THE CURRENT RANKING! HERE ARE THE TOP THREE!
ANYONE WHO DEFEATS THEM WILL RECEIVE A THIRD OF THEIR POINTS! THEIR LOCATIONS ARE SHOWN ON THE MAP! YOU'VE STILL GOT A CHANCE! GOOD LUCK!
1. Pain
2. Dread
3. Maple

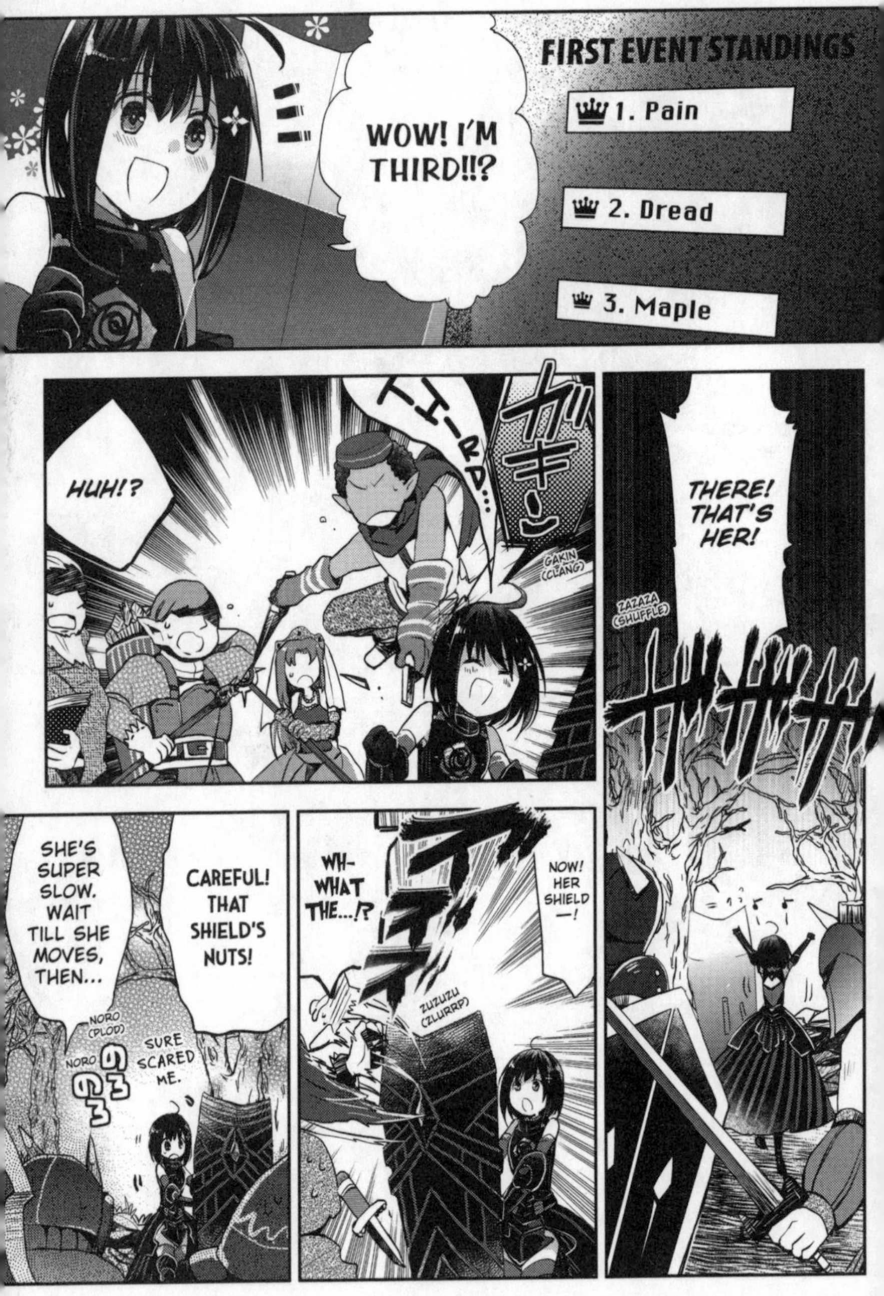
FIRST EVENT STANDINGS
1. Pain
2. Dread
3. Maple
WOW! I'M THIRD!!?
THERE! THAT'S HER!
ZAZAZA (SHUFFLE)
HUH!?
TH-I-RD...
GAKIN (CLANG)
NOW! HER SHIELD—!
WH-WHAT THE...!?
ZUZUZU (ZLURRP)
CAREFUL! THAT SHIELD'S NUTS!
SHE'S SUPER SLOW. WAIT TILL SHE MOVES, THEN...
NORO (PLOD)
NORO
SURE SCARED ME.

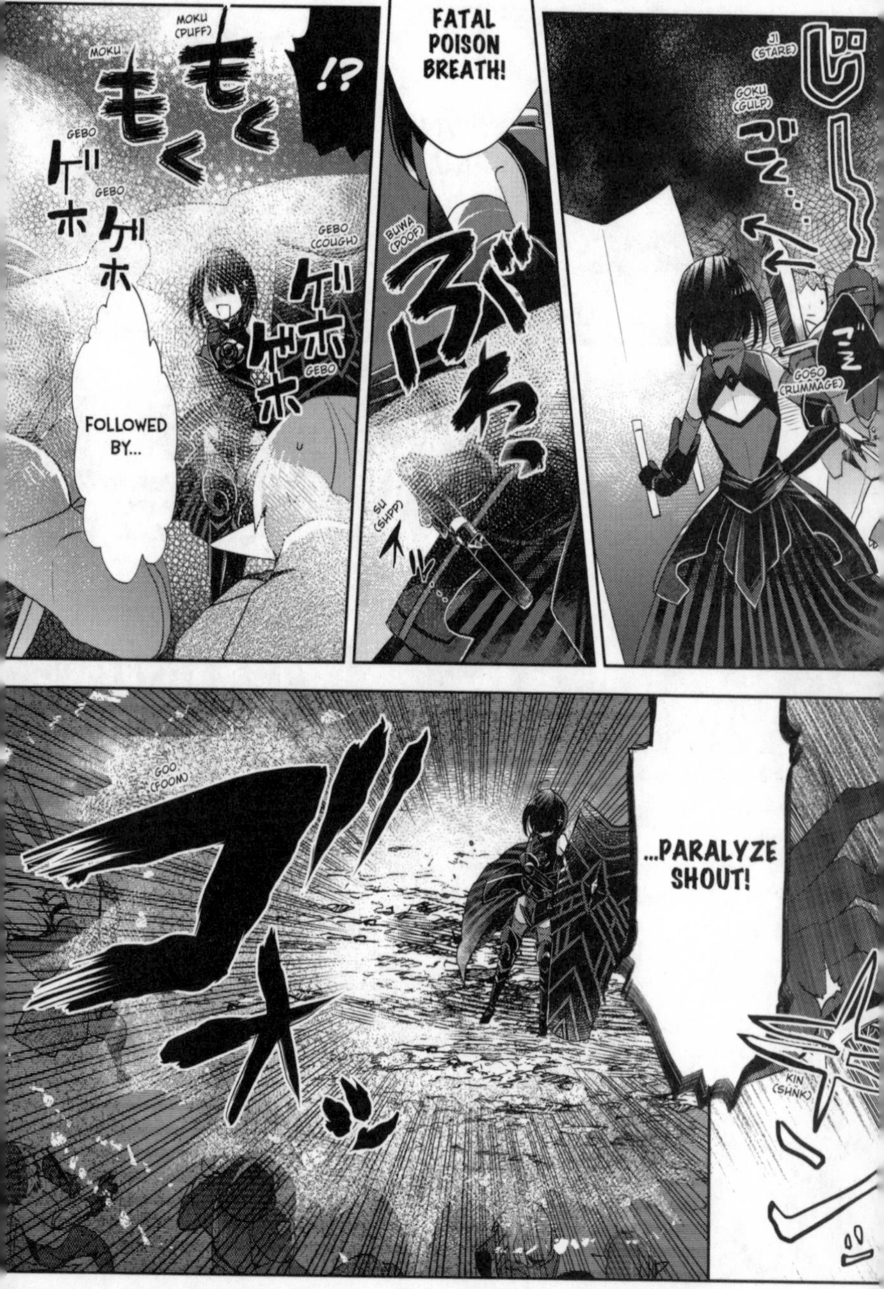
JI (STARE)
GOKU (GULP)
GOSO (RUMMAGE)
FATAL POISON BREATH!
BUWA (POOF)
SU (SHPP)
MOKU (PUFF)
MOKU
!?
GEBO
GEBO
GEBO (COUGH)
GEBO
FOLLOWED BY...
...PARALYZE SHOUT!
KIN (SHNK)
GOO (FOOM)

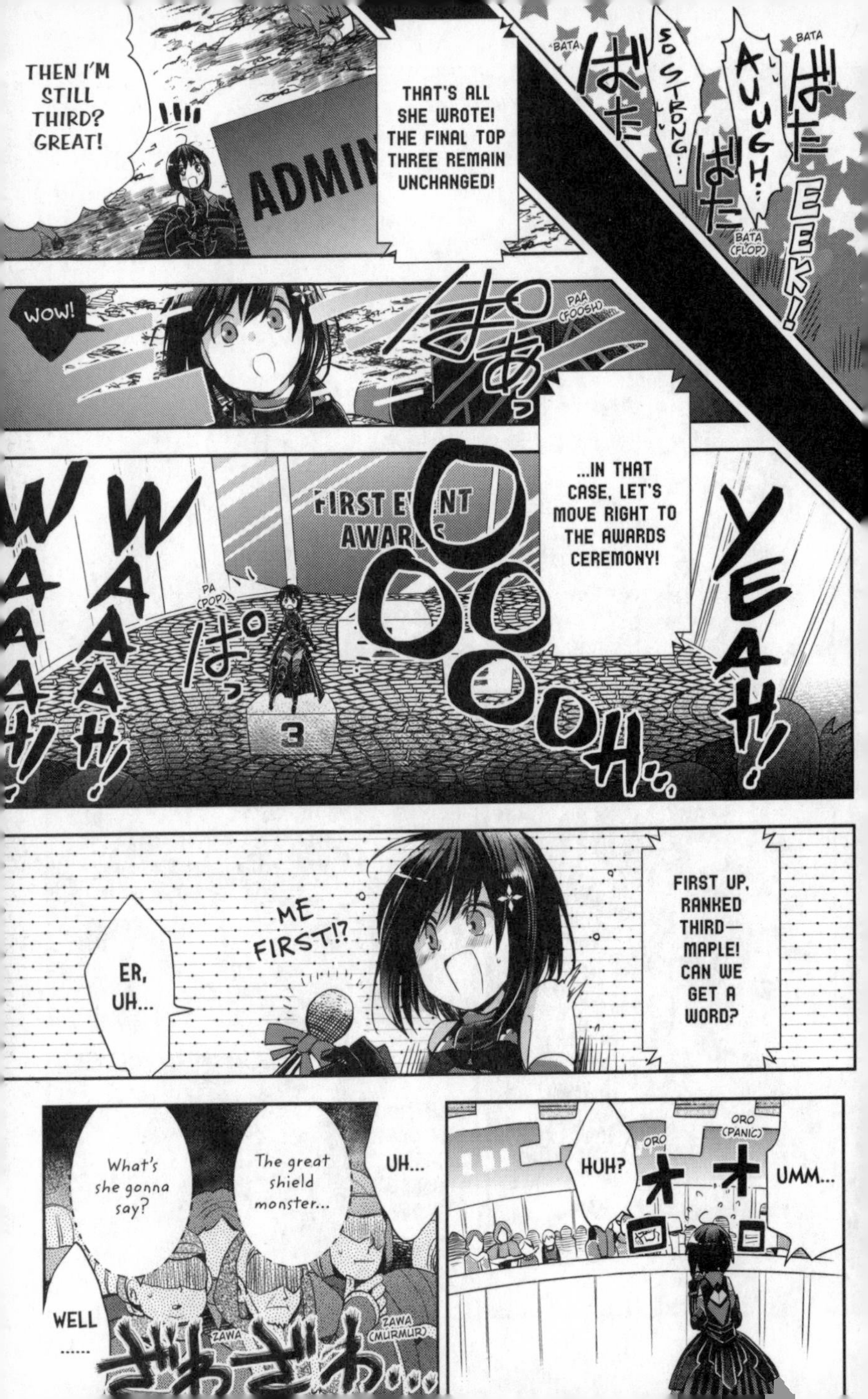
BATA
ばた
EEK!
AUUGH...
SO STRONG...
ばた
BATA (FLOP)
THAT'S ALL SHE WROTE! THE FINAL TOP THREE REMAIN UNCHANGED!
ADMIN
THEN I'M STILL THIRD? GREAT!
PAA (FOOSH)
WOW!
...IN THAT CASE, LET'S MOVE RIGHT TO THE AWARDS CEREMONY!
YEAH!
OOOOOH
FIRST EV NT AWAR
PA (POP)
3
WAAAH!
WAAAAH!
FIRST UP, RANKED THIRD— MAPLE! CAN WE GET A WORD?
ME FIRST!?
ER, UH...
ORO (PANIC)
UMM...
ORO
HUH?
UH...
The great shield monster...
What's she gonna say?
WELL ......
ZAWA (MURMUR)
ZAWA

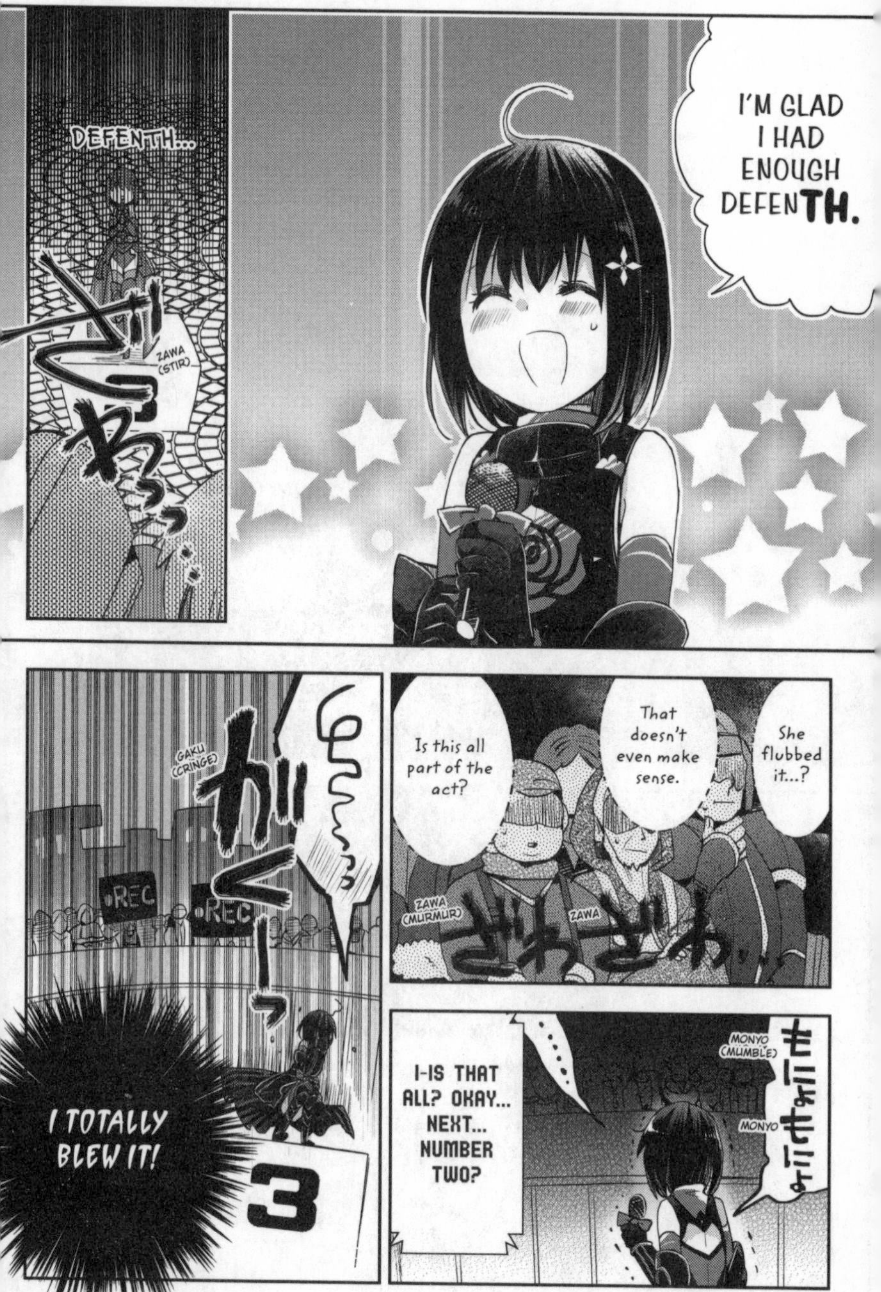
I'M GLAD I HAD ENOUGH DEFENTH.
DEFENTH...
ZAWA (STIR)
She flubbed it...?
That doesn't even make sense.
Is this all part of the act?
ZAWA (MURMUR)
ZAWA
MONYO (MUMBLE)
MONYO
I-IS THAT ALL? OKAY... NEXT... NUMBER TWO?
GAKU (CRINGE)
REC
REC
3
I TOTALLY BLEW IT!

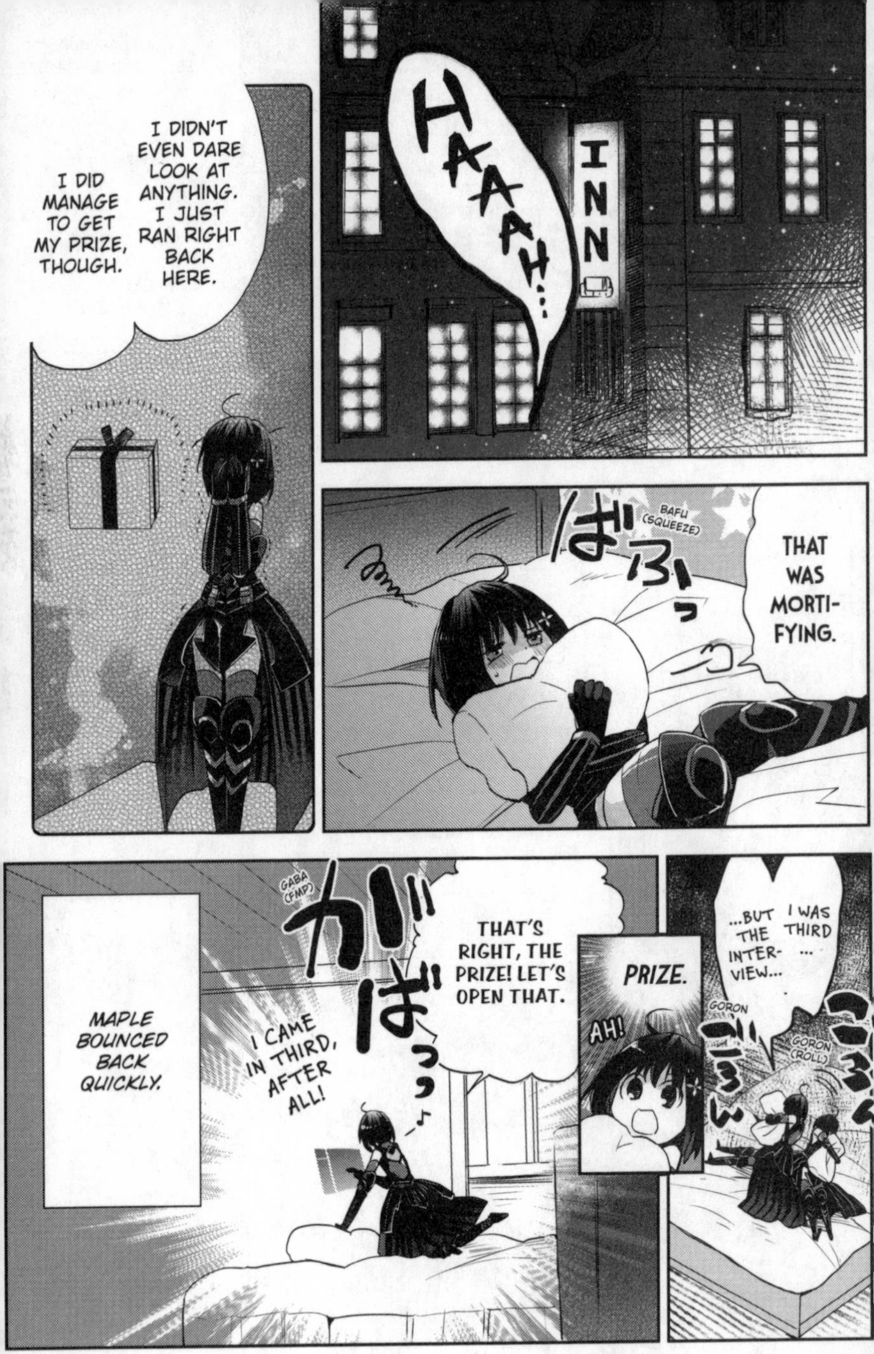
HAAAH...
INN
BAFU (SQUEEZE)
ばふっ
THAT WAS MORTI-FYING.
I DIDN'T EVEN DARE LOOK AT ANYTHING. I JUST RAN RIGHT BACK HERE.
I DID MANAGE TO GET MY PRIZE, THOUGH.
I WAS THIRD ...
...BUT THE INTER-VIEW...
GORON GORON (ROLL)
ごろん ごろん
PRIZE.
AH!
THAT'S RIGHT, THE PRIZE! LET'S OPEN THAT.
GABA (FMP)
がばっ
I CAME IN THIRD, AFTER ALL!
MAPLE BOUNCED BACK QUICKLY.

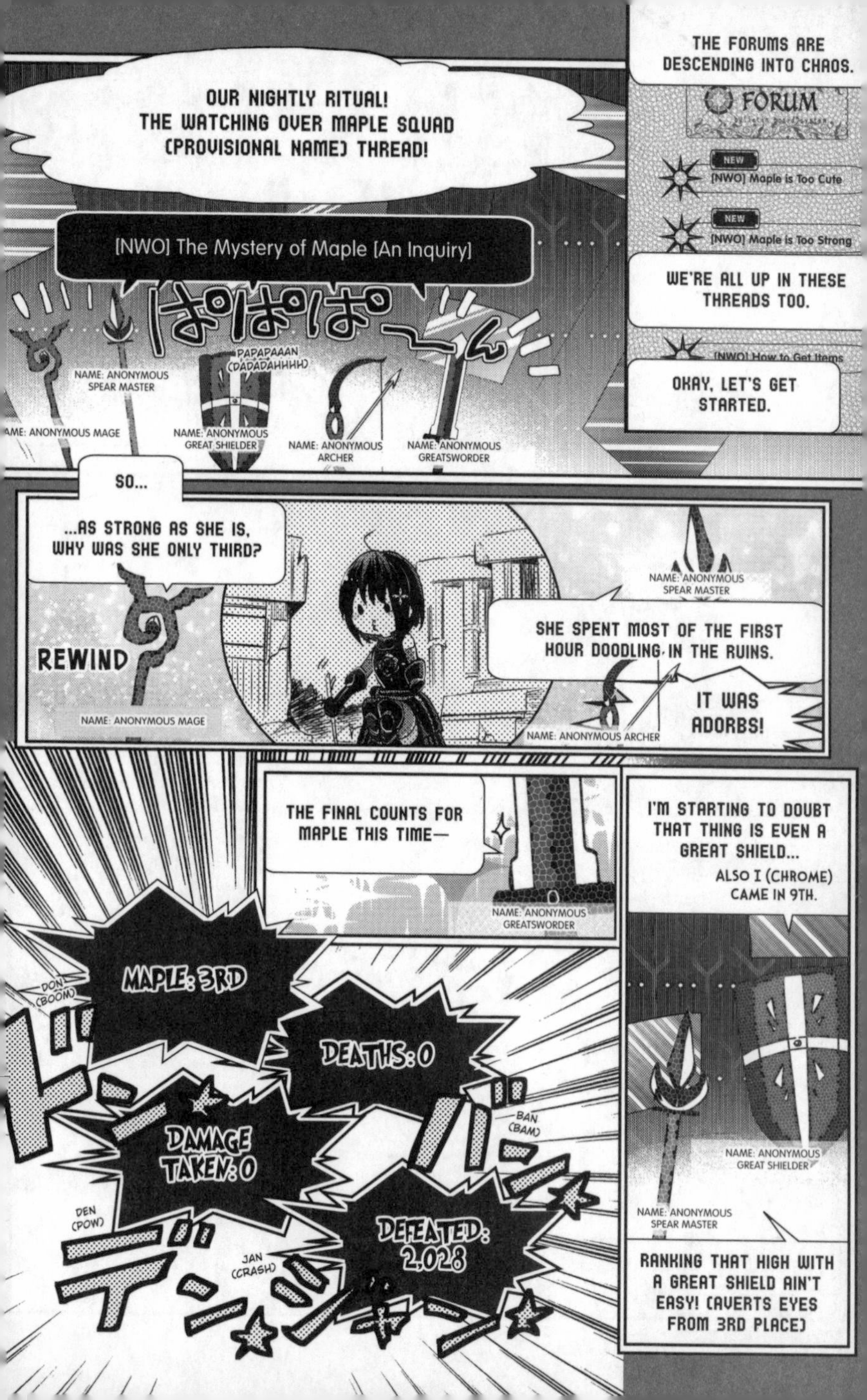
THE FORUMS ARE DESCENDING INTO CHAOS.
FORUM
NEW
[NWO] Maple is Too Cute
NEW
[NWO] Maple is Too Strong
WE'RE ALL UP IN THESE THREADS TOO.
[NWO] How to Get Items
OKAY, LET'S GET STARTED.
OUR NIGHTLY RITUAL! THE WATCHING OVER MAPLE SQUAD (PROVISIONAL NAME) THREAD!
[NWO] The Mystery of Maple [An Inquiry]
PAPAPAAAN (DADADAHHHH)
NAME: ANONYMOUS GREATSWORDER
NAME: ANONYMOUS ARCHER
NAME: ANONYMOUS GREAT SHIELDER
NAME: ANONYMOUS SPEAR MASTER
NAME: ANONYMOUS MAGE
NAME: ANONYMOUS SPEAR MASTER
SHE SPENT MOST OF THE FIRST HOUR DOODLING IN THE RUINS.
IT WAS ADORBS!
NAME: ANONYMOUS ARCHER
SO...
...AS STRONG AS SHE IS, WHY WAS SHE ONLY THIRD?
REWIND
NAME: ANONYMOUS MAGE
I'M STARTING TO DOUBT THAT THING IS EVEN A GREAT SHIELD...
ALSO I (CHROME) CAME IN 9TH.
THE FINAL COUNTS FOR MAPLE THIS TIME—
NAME: ANONYMOUS GREATSWORDER
MAPLE: 3RD
DON (BOOM)
DEATHS: 0
BAN (BAM)
DAMAGE TAKEN: 0
DEN (POW)
DEFEATED: 2,028
JAN (CRASH)
NAME: ANONYMOUS GREAT SHIELDER
NAME: ANONYMOUS SPEAR MASTER
RANKING THAT HIGH WITH A GREAT SHIELD AIN'T EASY! (AVERTS EYES FROM 3RD PLACE)

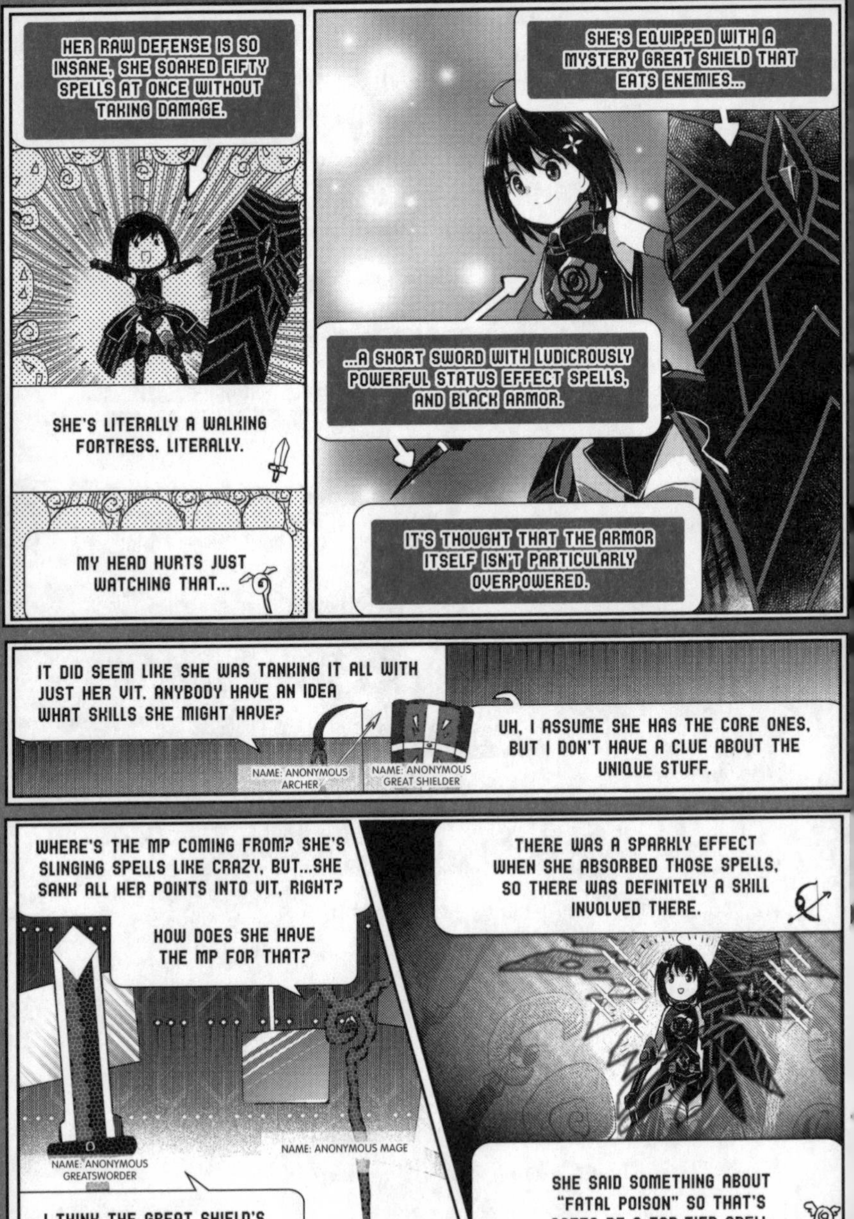
SHE'S EQUIPPED WITH A MYSTERY GREAT SHIELD THAT EATS ENEMIES...
...A SHORT SWORD WITH LUDICROUSLY POWERFUL STATUS EFFECT SPELLS, AND BLACK ARMOR.
IT'S THOUGHT THAT THE ARMOR ITSELF ISN'T PARTICULARLY OVERPOWERED.
HER RAW DEFENSE IS SO INSANE, SHE SOAKED FIFTY SPELLS AT ONCE WITHOUT TAKING DAMAGE.
SHE'S LITERALLY A WALKING FORTRESS. LITERALLY.
MY HEAD HURTS JUST WATCHING THAT...
IT DID SEEM LIKE SHE WAS TANKING IT ALL WITH JUST HER VIT. ANYBODY HAVE AN IDEA WHAT SKILLS SHE MIGHT HAVE?
NAME: ANONYMOUS ARCHER
UH, I ASSUME SHE HAS THE CORE ONES, BUT I DON'T HAVE A CLUE ABOUT THE UNIQUE STUFF.
NAME: ANONYMOUS GREAT SHIELDER
THERE WAS A SPARKLY EFFECT WHEN SHE ABSORBED THOSE SPELLS, SO THERE WAS DEFINITELY A SKILL INVOLVED THERE.
SHE SAID SOMETHING ABOUT "FATAL POISON" SO THAT'S GOTTA BE A TOP-TIER SPELL.
WHERE'S THE MP COMING FROM? SHE'S SLINGING SPELLS LIKE CRAZY, BUT...SHE SANK ALL HER POINTS INTO VIT, RIGHT?
HOW DOES SHE HAVE THE MP FOR THAT?
NAME: ANONYMOUS MAGE
I THINK THE GREAT SHIELD'S A MAGIC RESERVOIR.
NAME: ANONYMOUS GREATSWORDER

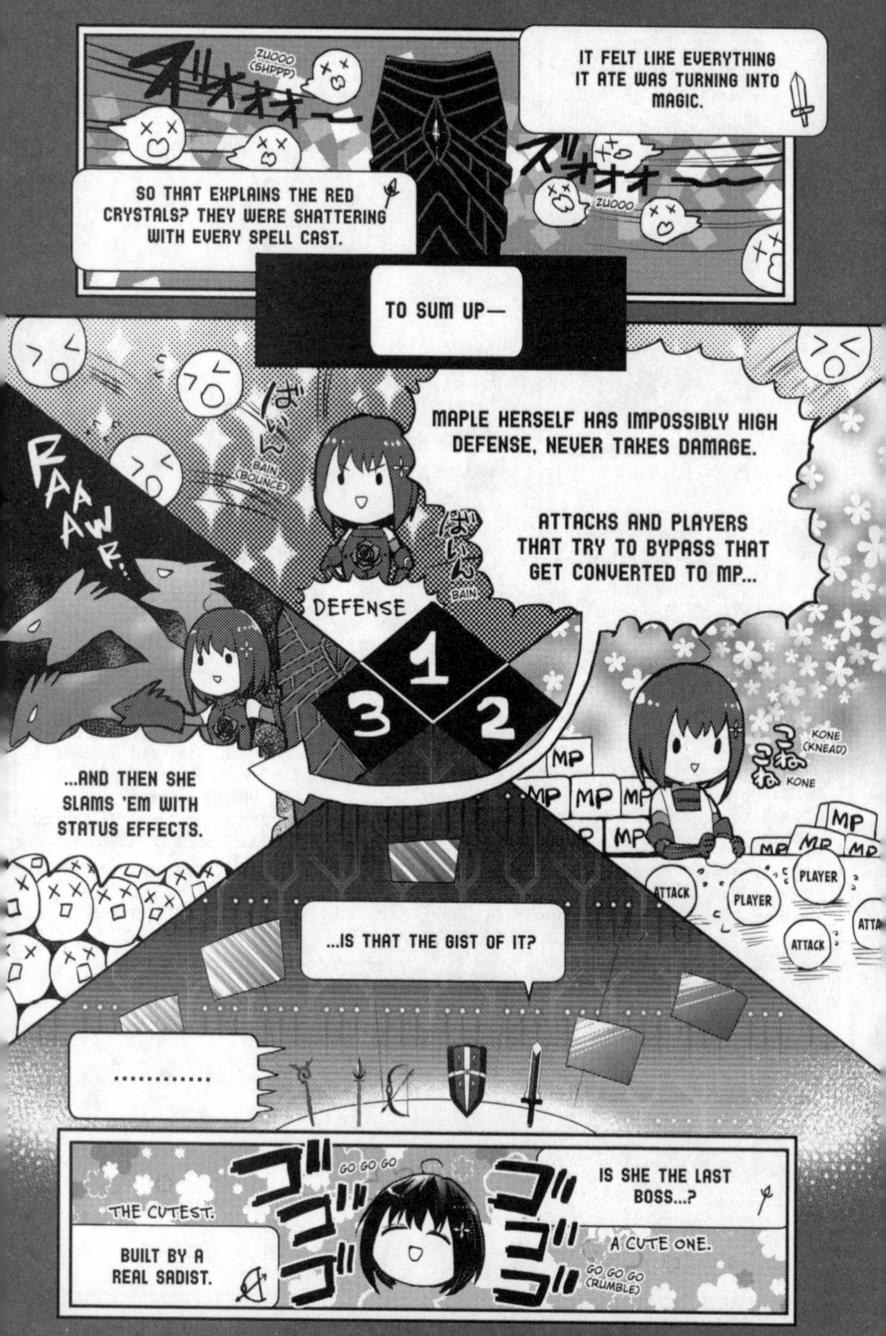
IT FELT LIKE EVERYTHING IT ATE WAS TURNING INTO MAGIC.
ZUOOO (SHPPP)
ZUOOO
SO THAT EXPLAINS THE RED CRYSTALS? THEY WERE SHATTERING WITH EVERY SPELL CAST.
TO SUM UP—
MAPLE HERSELF HAS IMPOSSIBLY HIGH DEFENSE, NEVER TAKES DAMAGE.
BAIN (BOUNCE)
BAIN
ATTACKS AND PLAYERS THAT TRY TO BYPASS THAT GET CONVERTED TO MP...
DEFENSE
1
2
3
KONE (KNEAD)
KONE
MP
PLAYER
ATTACK
RAAAWR...!
...AND THEN SHE SLAMS 'EM WITH STATUS EFFECTS.
...IS THAT THE GIST OF IT?
....
IS SHE THE LAST BOSS...?
A CUTE ONE.
GO GO GO
GO GO GO (RUMBLE)
THE CUTEST.
BUILT BY A REAL SADIST.

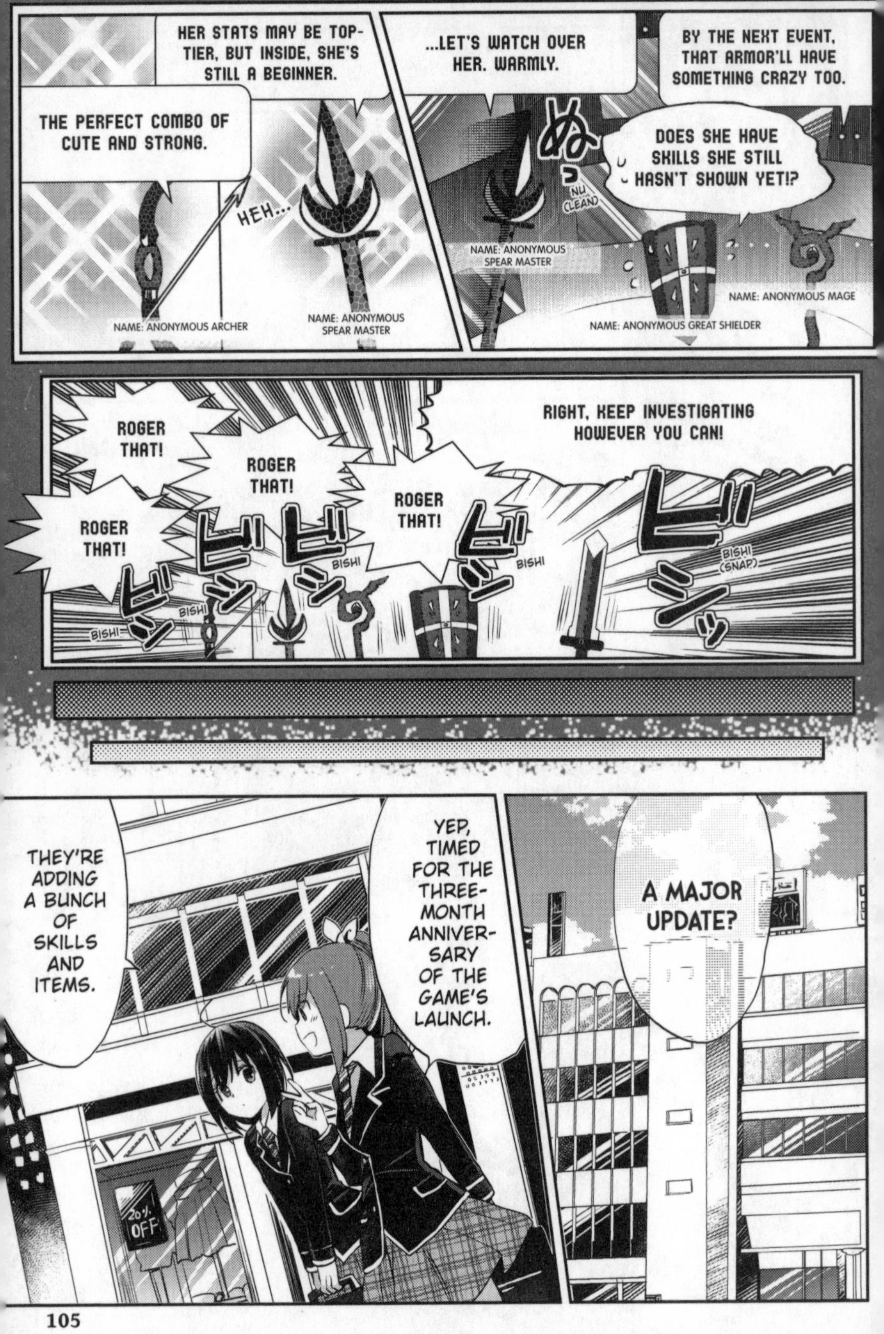
BY THE NEXT EVENT, THAT ARMOR'LL HAVE SOMETHING CRAZY TOO.
DOES SHE HAVE SKILLS SHE STILL HASN'T SHOWN YET!?
NU (CLEAN)
...LET'S WATCH OVER HER. WARMLY.
NAME: ANONYMOUS SPEAR MASTER
NAME: ANONYMOUS MAGE
NAME: ANONYMOUS GREAT SHIELDER
HER STATS MAY BE TOP-TIER, BUT INSIDE, SHE'S STILL A BEGINNER.
THE PERFECT COMBO OF CUTE AND STRONG.
HEH...
NAME: ANONYMOUS SPEAR MASTER
NAME: ANONYMOUS ARCHER
RIGHT, KEEP INVESTIGATING HOWEVER YOU CAN!
BISHI (SNAP)
ROGER THAT!
BISHI
ROGER THAT!
BISHI
ROGER THAT!
BISHI
ROGER THAT!
BISHI
A MAJOR UPDATE?
YEP, TIMED FOR THE THREE-MONTH ANNIVERSARY OF THE GAME'S LAUNCH.
THEY'RE ADDING A BUNCH OF SKILLS AND ITEMS.
20% OFF

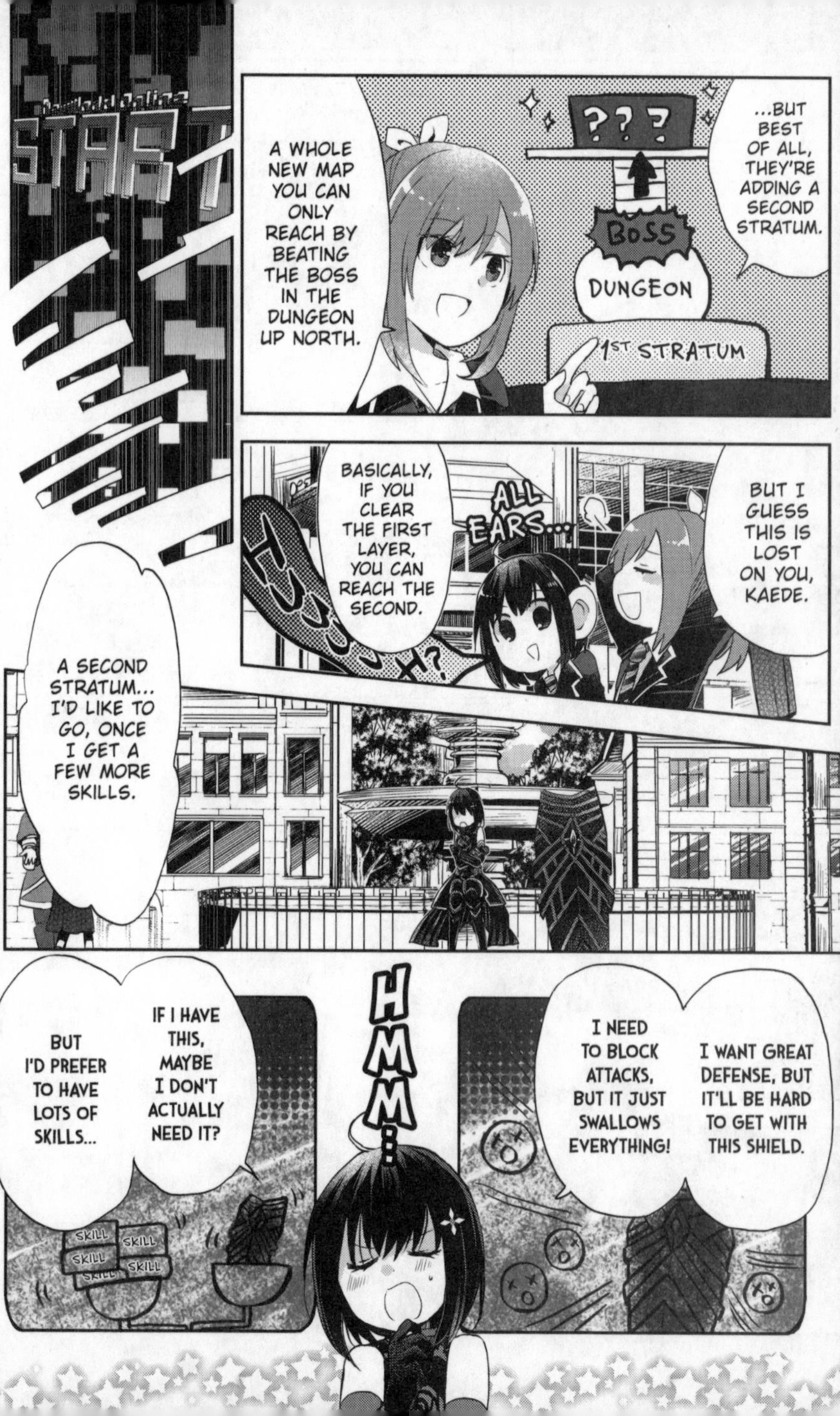
...BUT BEST OF ALL, THEY'RE ADDING A SECOND STRATUM.
???
BOSS
DUNGEON
1ST STRATUM
A WHOLE NEW MAP YOU CAN ONLY REACH BY BEATING THE BOSS IN THE DUNGEON UP NORTH.
START
BUT I GUESS THIS IS LOST ON YOU, KAEDE.
ALL EARS...
BASICALLY, IF YOU CLEAR THE FIRST LAYER, YOU CAN REACH THE SECOND.
HUH?
A SECOND STRATUM... I'D LIKE TO GO, ONCE I GET A FEW MORE SKILLS.
I WANT GREAT DEFENSE, BUT IT'LL BE HARD TO GET WITH THIS SHIELD.
I NEED TO BLOCK ATTACKS, BUT IT JUST SWALLOWS EVERYTHING!
HMM...
IF I HAVE THIS, MAYBE I DON'T ACTUALLY NEED IT?
BUT I'D PREFER TO HAVE LOTS OF SKILLS...
SKILL
SKILL
SKILL
SKILL

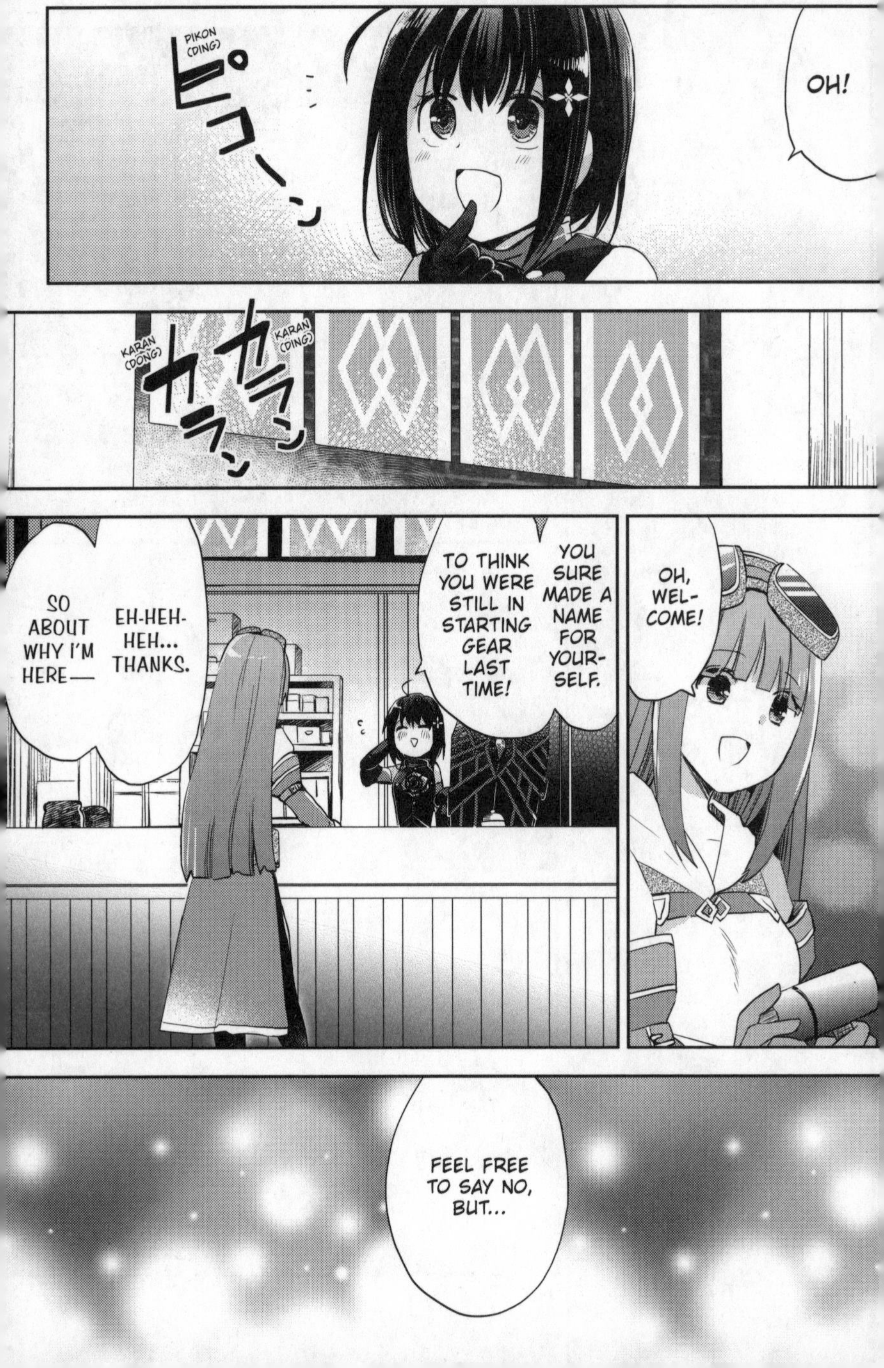
OH!
PIKON (DING)
KARAN (DING)
KARAN (DONG)
OH, WEL-COME!
YOU SURE MADE A NAME FOR YOUR-SELF.
TO THINK YOU WERE STILL IN STARTING GEAR LAST TIME!
EH-HEH-HEH... THANKS.
SO ABOUT WHY I'M HERE—
FEEL FREE TO SAY NO, BUT...

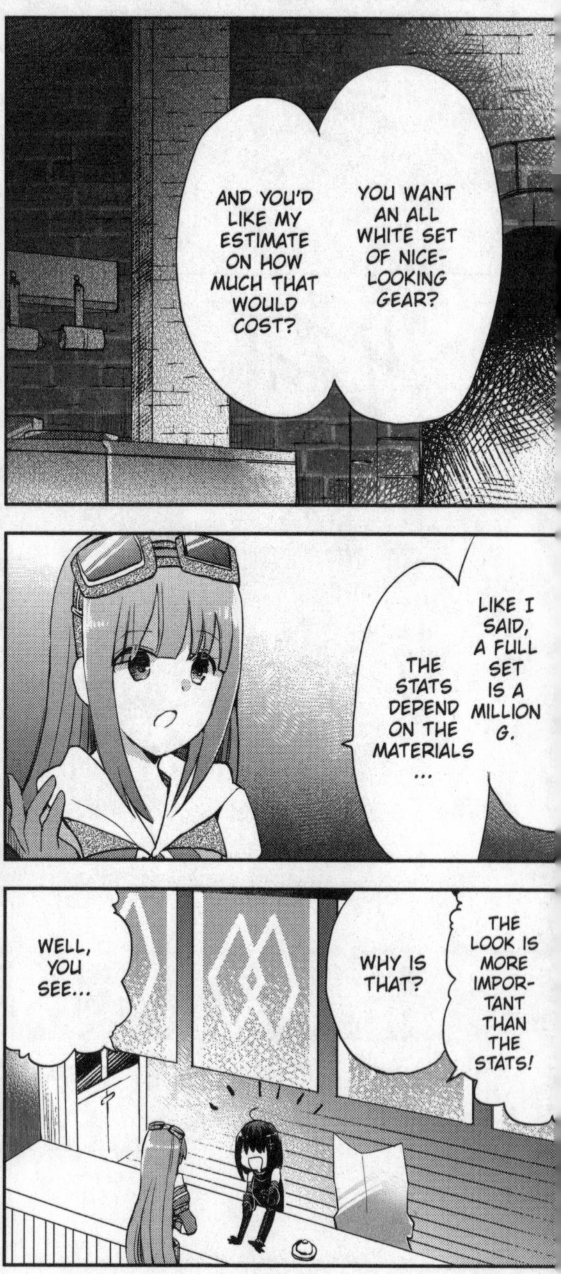
YOU WANT AN ALL WHITE SET OF NICE-LOOKING GEAR?
AND YOU'D LIKE MY ESTIMATE ON HOW MUCH THAT WOULD COST?
LIKE I SAID, A FULL SET IS A MILLION G.
THE STATS DEPEND ON THE MATERIALS ...
THE LOOK IS MORE IMPORTANT THAN THE STATS!
WHY IS THAT?
WELL, YOU SEE...

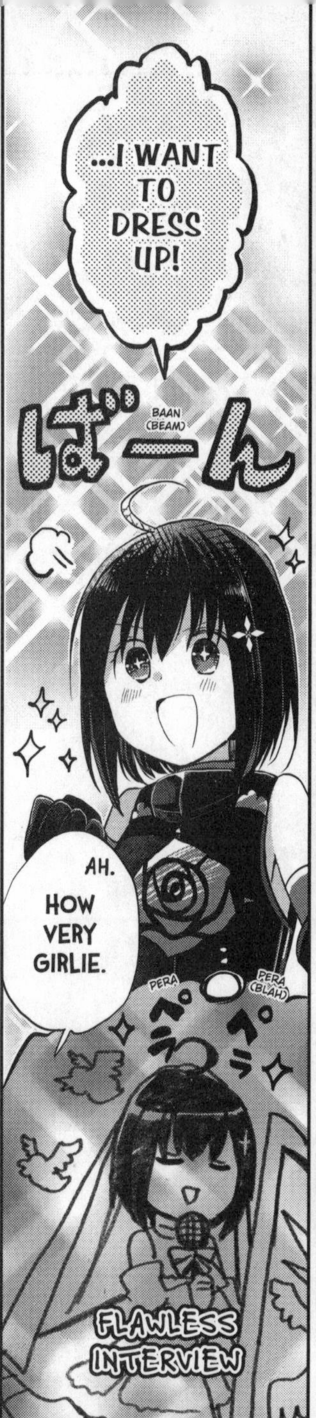
...I WANT TO DRESS UP!
ばーん
BAAN (BEAM)
AH. HOW VERY GIRLIE.
PERA (BLAH)
PERA
ペラペラ
FLAWLESS INTERVIEW

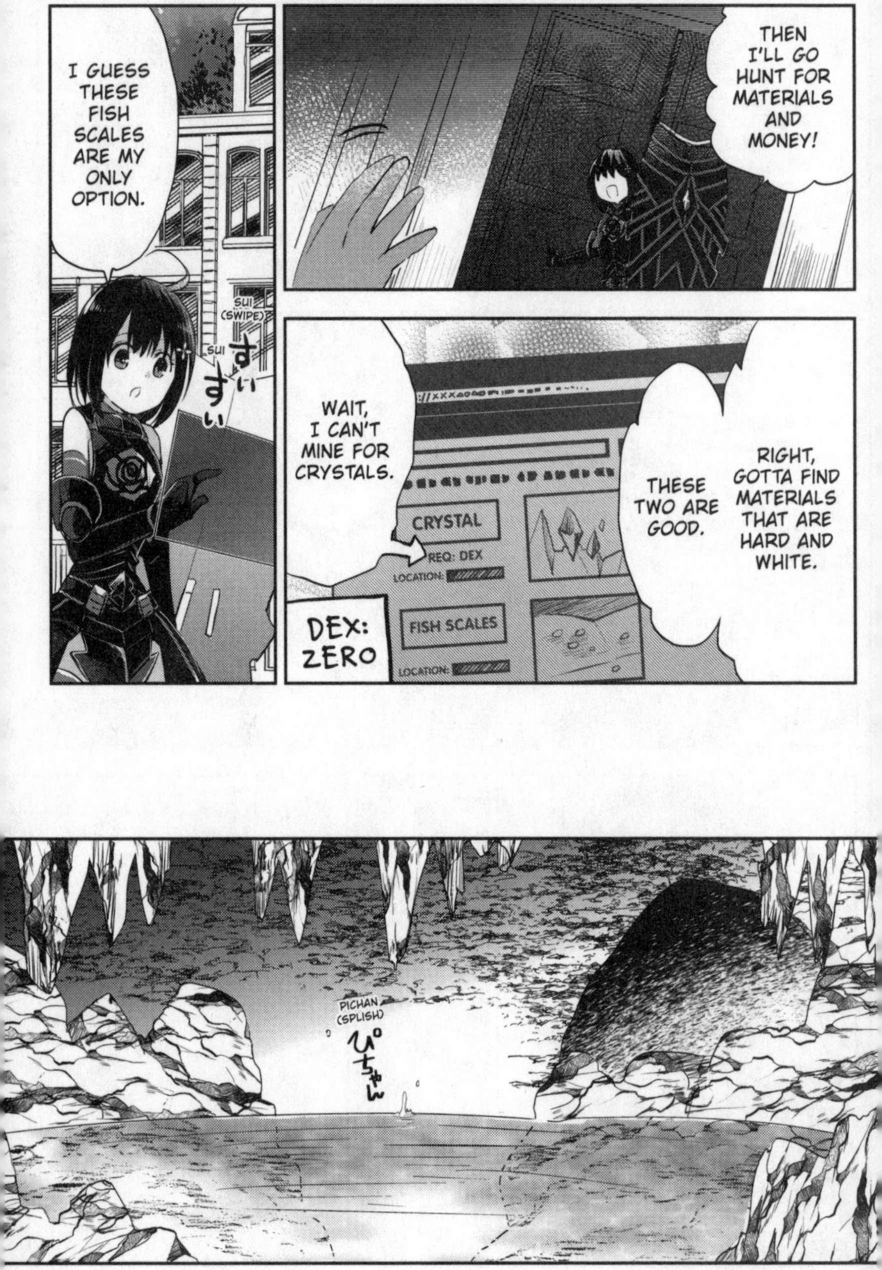
THEN I'LL GO HUNT FOR MATERIALS AND MONEY!
RIGHT, GOTTA FIND MATERIALS THAT ARE HARD AND WHITE.
THESE TWO ARE GOOD.
WAIT, I CAN'T MINE FOR CRYSTALS.
CRYSTAL
REQ: DEX
LOCATION:
FISH SCALES
LOCATION:
DEX: ZERO
I GUESS THESE FISH SCALES ARE MY ONLY OPTION.
SUI (SWIPE)
すい
SUI
すい
PICHAN (SPLISH)
ぴちゃん

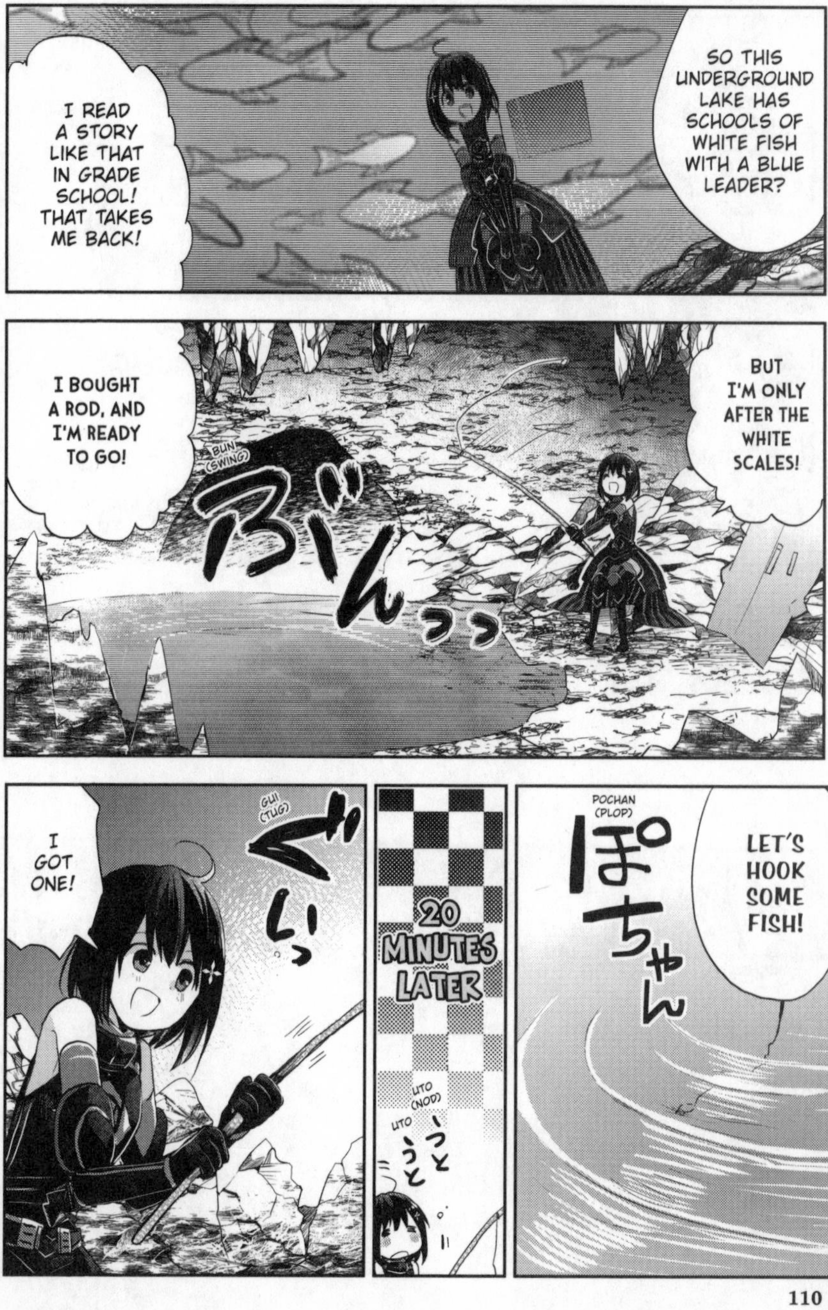
SO THIS UNDERGROUND LAKE HAS SCHOOLS OF WHITE FISH WITH A BLUE LEADER?
I READ A STORY LIKE THAT IN GRADE SCHOOL! THAT TAKES ME BACK!
BUT I'M ONLY AFTER THE WHITE SCALES!
I BOUGHT A ROD, AND I'M READY TO GO!
BUN! (SWING)
ぶんっっっ
LET'S HOOK SOME FISH!
POCHAN (PLOP)
ぽちゃん
20 MINUTES LATER
UTO (NOD)
UTO
うと うと
GUI (TUG)
ぐいっ
I GOT ONE!

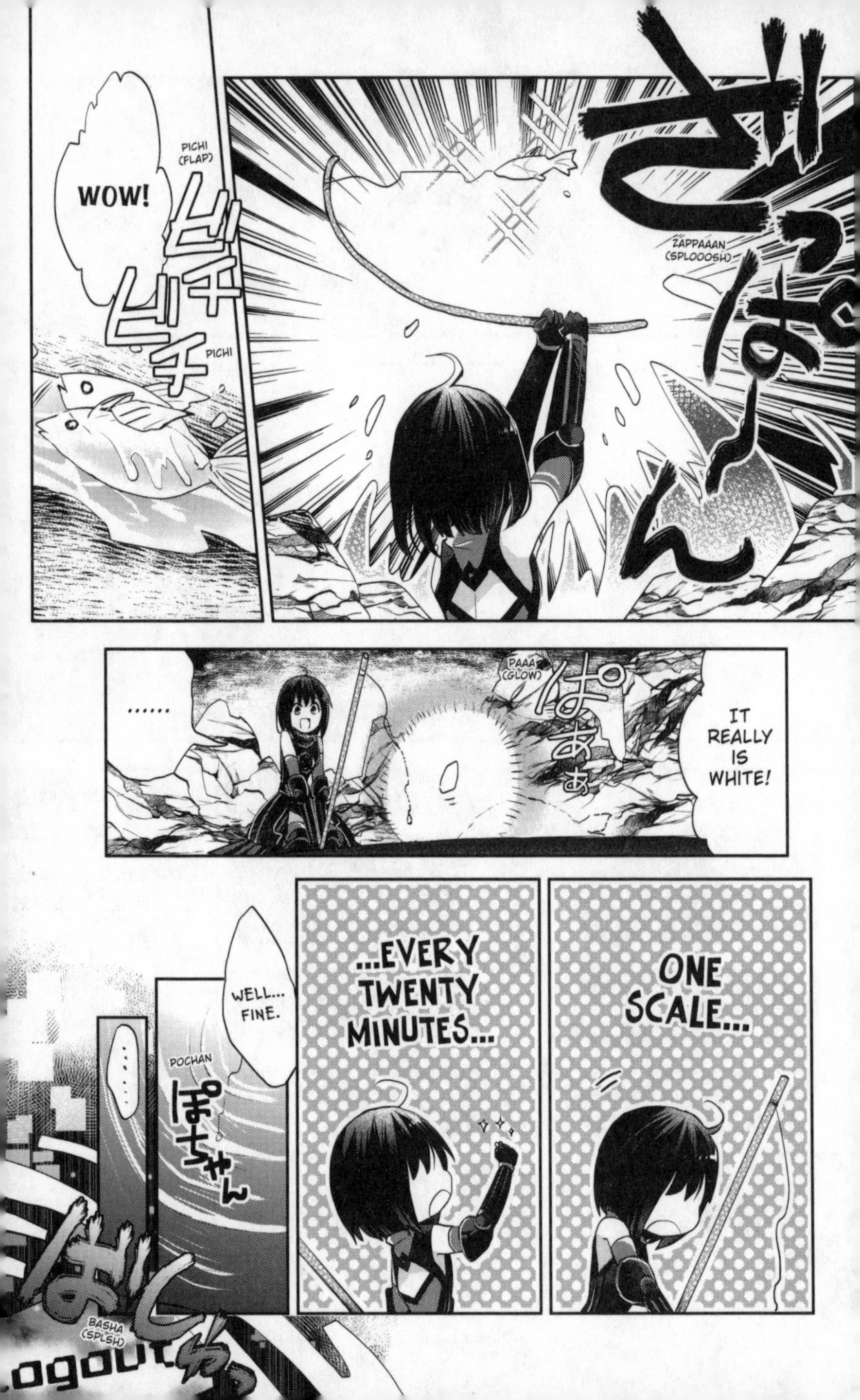
ざっぱ～ん
ZAPPAAAN (SPLOOOSH)
WOW!
ピチピチ
PICHI (FLAP) PICHI
IT REALLY IS WHITE!
ぱぁぁ
PAAA (GLOW)
......
ONE SCALE...
...EVERY TWENTY MINUTES...
WELL... FINE.
ぽちゃん
POCHAN
......
BASHA (SPLSH)

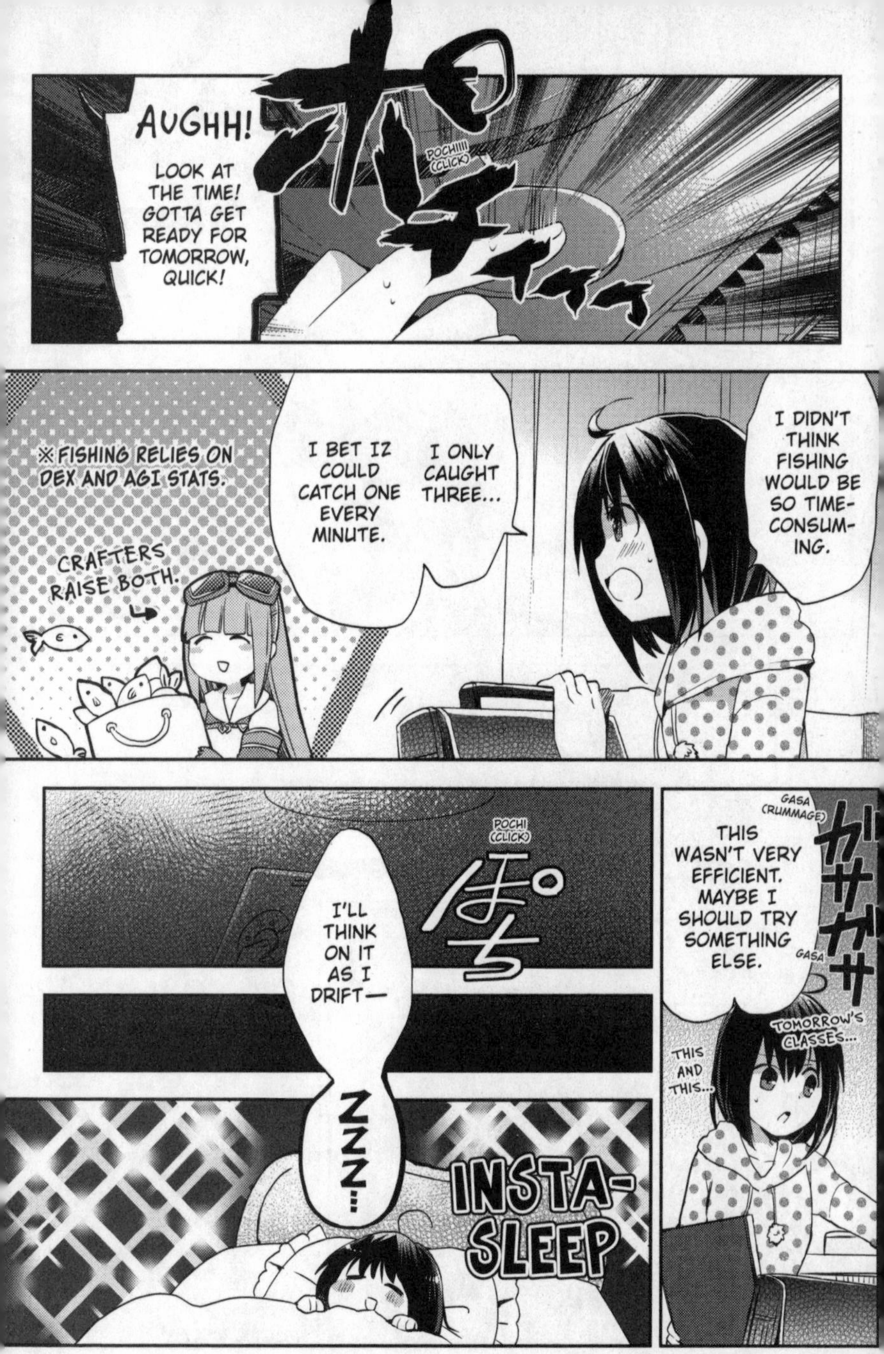
AUGHH!
LOOK AT THE TIME! GOTTA GET READY FOR TOMORROW, QUICK!
POCHIIII (CLICK)
I DIDN'T THINK FISHING WOULD BE SO TIME-CONSUM-ING.
I ONLY CAUGHT THREE...
I BET IZ COULD CATCH ONE EVERY MINUTE.
※FISHING RELIES ON DEX AND AGI STATS.
CRAFTERS RAISE BOTH.
GASA (RUMMAGE)
THIS WASN'T VERY EFFICIENT. MAYBE I SHOULD TRY SOMETHING ELSE.
GASA
TOMORROW'S CLASSES...
THIS AND THIS...
POCHI (CLICK)
I'LL THINK ON IT AS I DRIFT—
ZZZ...
INSTA-SLEEP

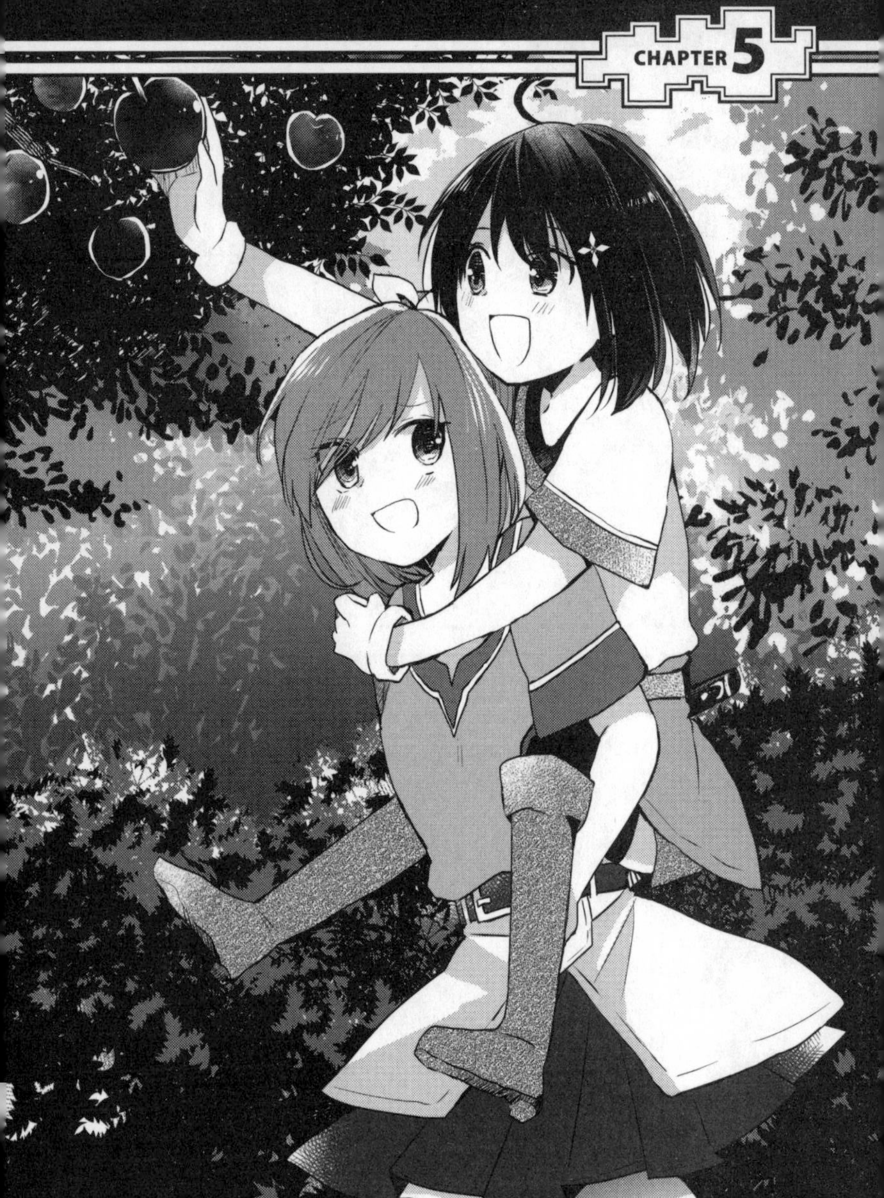
CHAPTER 5

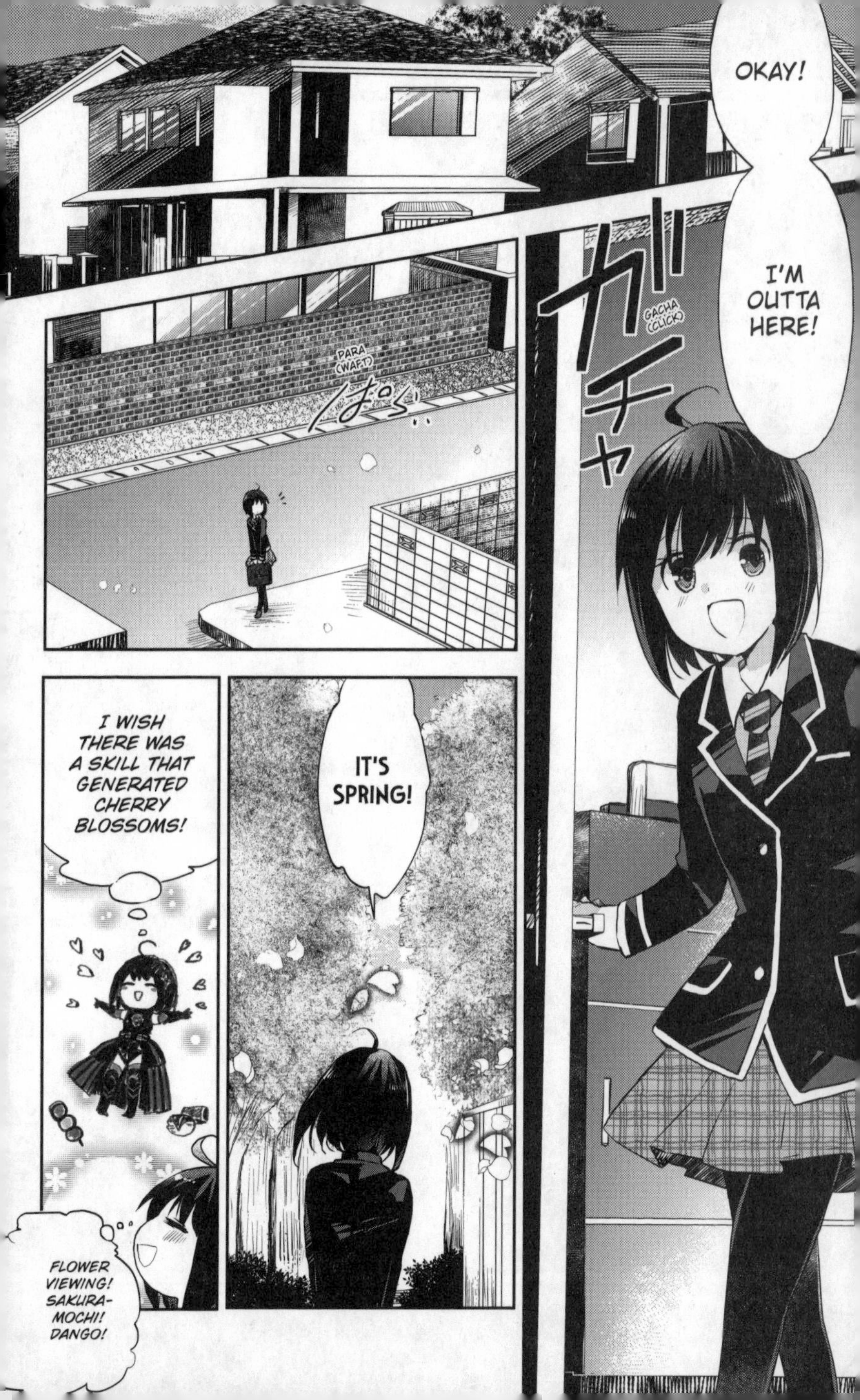
OKAY!
I'M OUTTA HERE!
ガチャ
GACHA (CLICK)
PARA (WAFT)
ぱら
IT'S SPRING!
I WISH THERE WAS A SKILL THAT GENERATED CHERRY BLOSSOMS!
FLOWER VIEWING! SAKURA-MOCHI! DANGO!

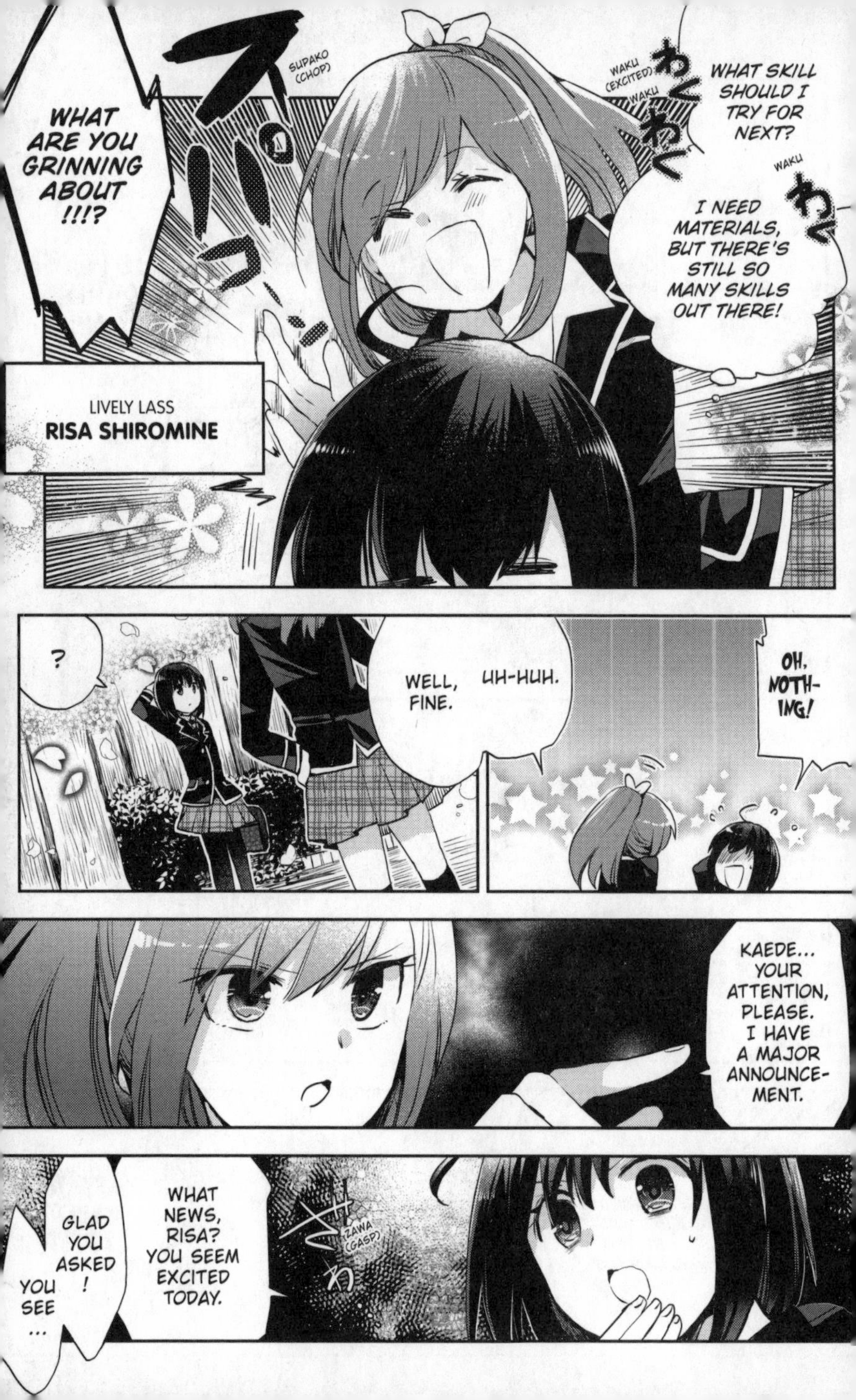
WAKU (EXCITED) WAKU
WHAT SKILL SHOULD I TRY FOR NEXT?
WAKU
I NEED MATERIALS, BUT THERE'S STILL SO MANY SKILLS OUT THERE!
SUPAKO (CHOP)
WHAT ARE YOU GRINNING ABOUT !!!?
LIVELY LASS
RISA SHIROMINE
OH, NOTHING!
UH-HUH.
WELL, FINE.
?
KAEDE... YOUR ATTENTION, PLEASE. I HAVE A MAJOR ANNOUNCEMENT.
ZAWA (GASP)
WHAT NEWS, RISA? YOU SEEM EXCITED TODAY.
GLAD YOU ASKED!
YOU SEE...

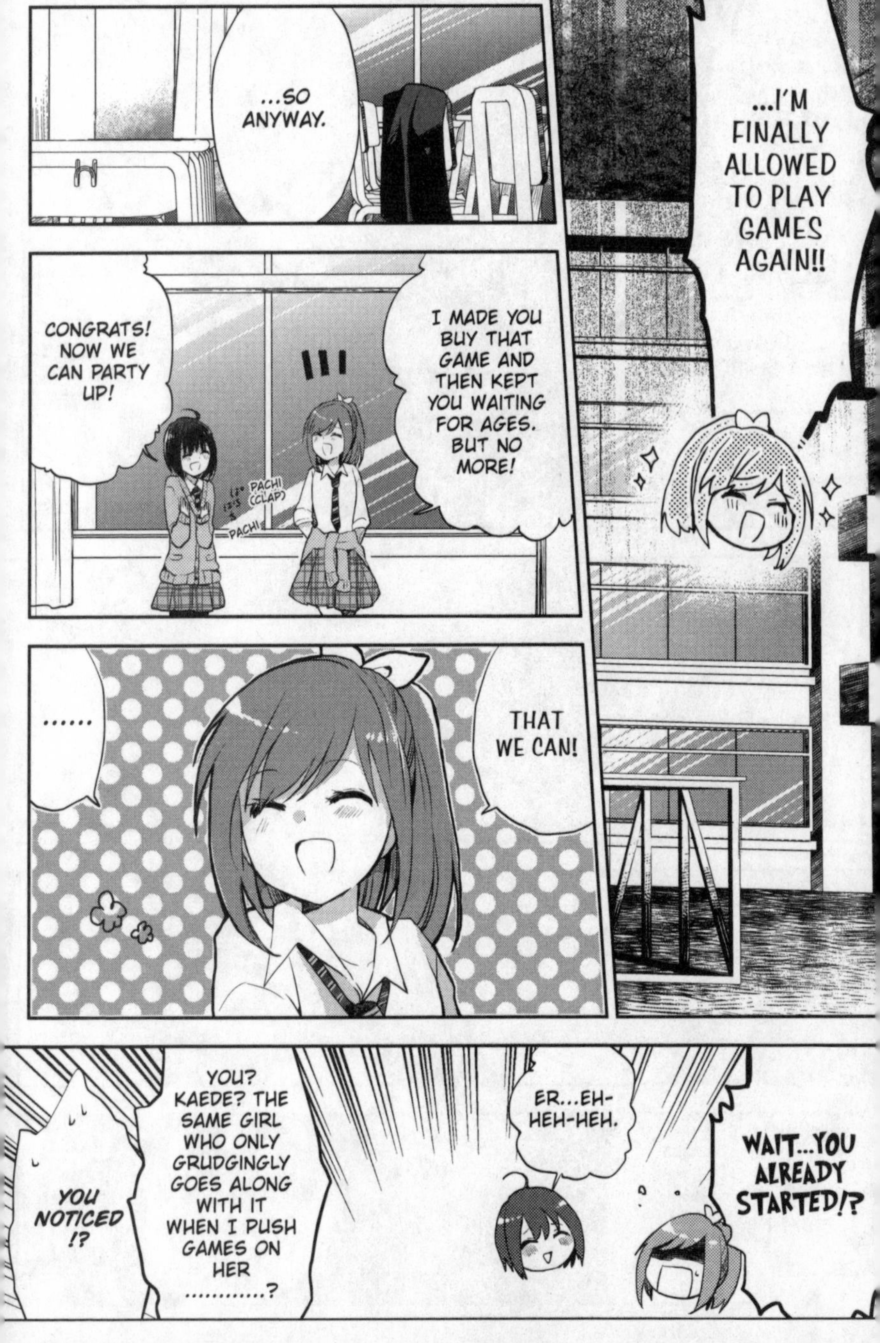
...I'M FINALLY ALLOWED TO PLAY GAMES AGAIN!!
...SO ANYWAY.
I MADE YOU BUY THAT GAME AND THEN KEPT YOU WAITING FOR AGES. BUT NO MORE!
CONGRATS! NOW WE CAN PARTY UP!
PACHI (CLAP) PACHI
THAT WE CAN!
......
WAIT...YOU ALREADY STARTED!?
ER...EH-HEH-HEH.
YOU? KAEDE? THE SAME GIRL WHO ONLY GRUDGINGLY GOES ALONG WITH IT WHEN I PUSH GAMES ON HER ....?
YOU NOTICED !?

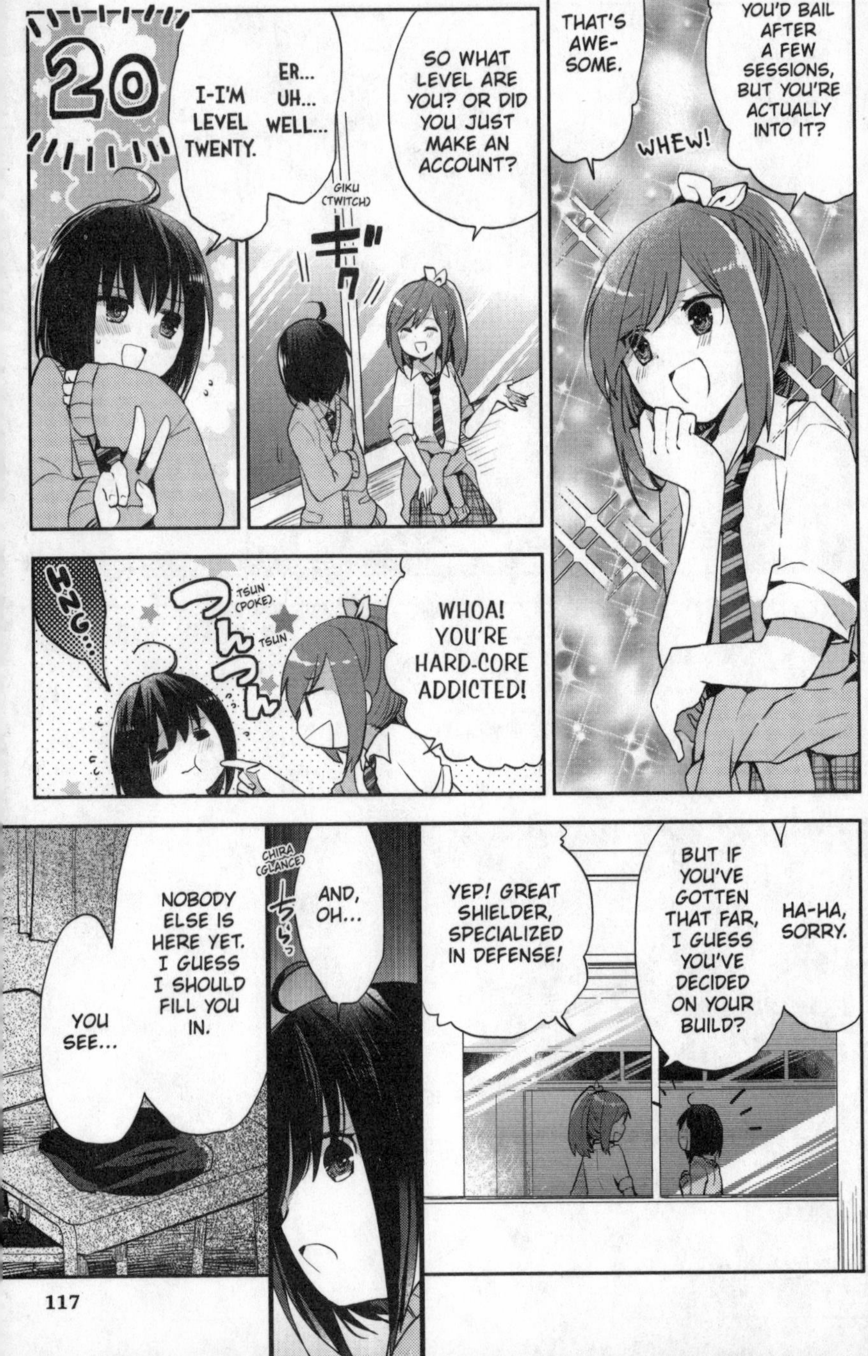
I FIGURED YOU'D BAIL AFTER A FEW SESSIONS, BUT YOU'RE ACTUALLY INTO IT?
WHEW!
THAT'S AWE-SOME.
SO WHAT LEVEL ARE YOU? OR DID YOU JUST MAKE AN ACCOUNT?
GIKU (TWITCH)
ER... UH... WELL...
I-I'M LEVEL TWENTY.
20
WHOA! YOU'RE HARD-CORE ADDICTED!
TSUN
TSUN (POKE)
HNG...
HA-HA, SORRY.
BUT IF YOU'VE GOTTEN THAT FAR, I GUESS YOU'VE DECIDED ON YOUR BUILD?
YEP! GREAT SHIELDER, SPECIALIZED IN DEFENSE!
AND, OH...
CHIRA (GLANCE)
NOBODY ELSE IS HERE YET. I GUESS I SHOULD FILL YOU IN.
YOU SEE...

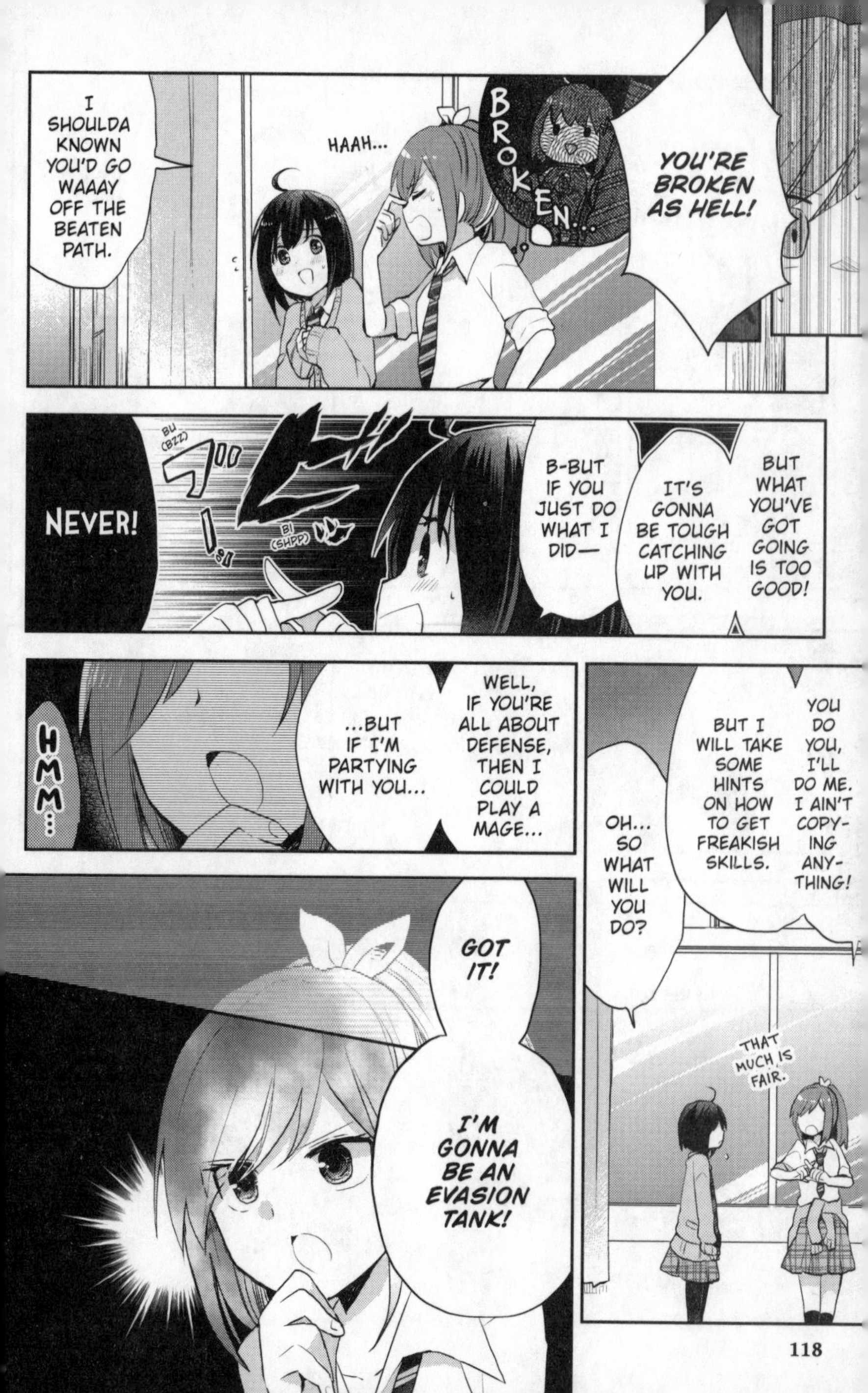
YOU'RE BROKEN AS HELL!
BROKEN...
HAAH...
I SHOULDA KNOWN YOU'D GO WAAAY OFF THE BEATEN PATH.
BUT WHAT YOU'VE GOT GOING IS TOO GOOD!
IT'S GONNA BE TOUGH CATCHING UP WITH YOU.
B-BUT IF YOU JUST DO WHAT I DID—
BI (SHPP)
BU (BZZ)
NEVER!
YOU DO YOU, I'LL DO ME. I AIN'T COPYING ANYTHING!
BUT I WILL TAKE SOME HINTS ON HOW TO GET FREAKISH SKILLS.
OH... SO WHAT WILL YOU DO?
THAT MUCH IS FAIR.
WELL, IF YOU'RE ALL ABOUT DEFENSE, THEN I COULD PLAY A MAGE...
...BUT IF I'M PARTYING WITH YOU...
HMM...
GOT IT!
I'M GONNA BE AN EVASION TANK!

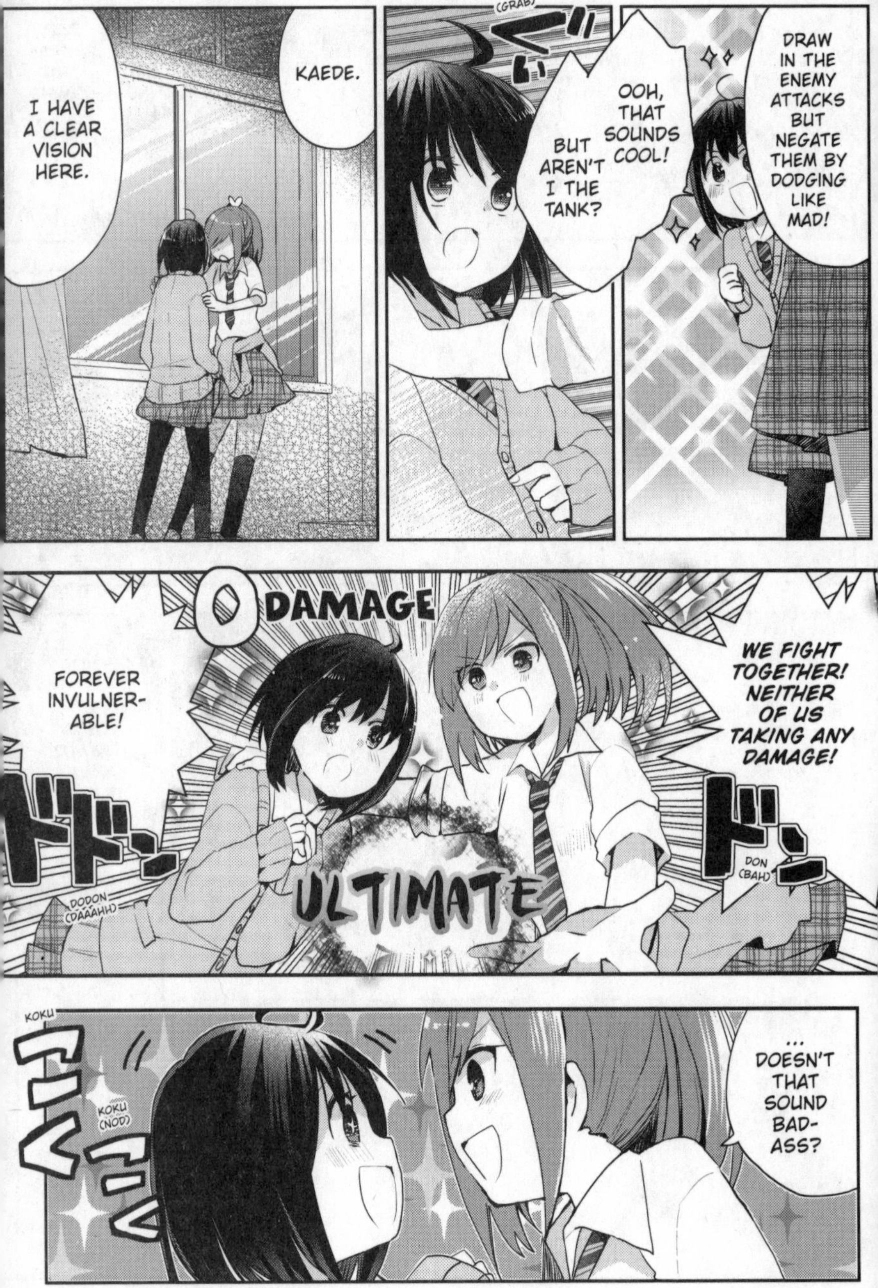
DRAW IN THE ENEMY ATTACKS BUT NEGATE THEM BY DODGING LIKE MAD!
GUI (GRAB)
OOH, THAT SOUNDS COOL!
BUT AREN'T I THE TANK?
KAEDE.
I HAVE A CLEAR VISION HERE.
WE FIGHT TOGETHER! NEITHER OF US TAKING ANY DAMAGE!
DON (BAH)
0 DAMAGE
ULTIMATE
FOREVER INVULNER-ABLE!
DODON (DAAAHH)
... DOESN'T THAT SOUND BAD-ASS?
KOKU
KOKU (NOD)

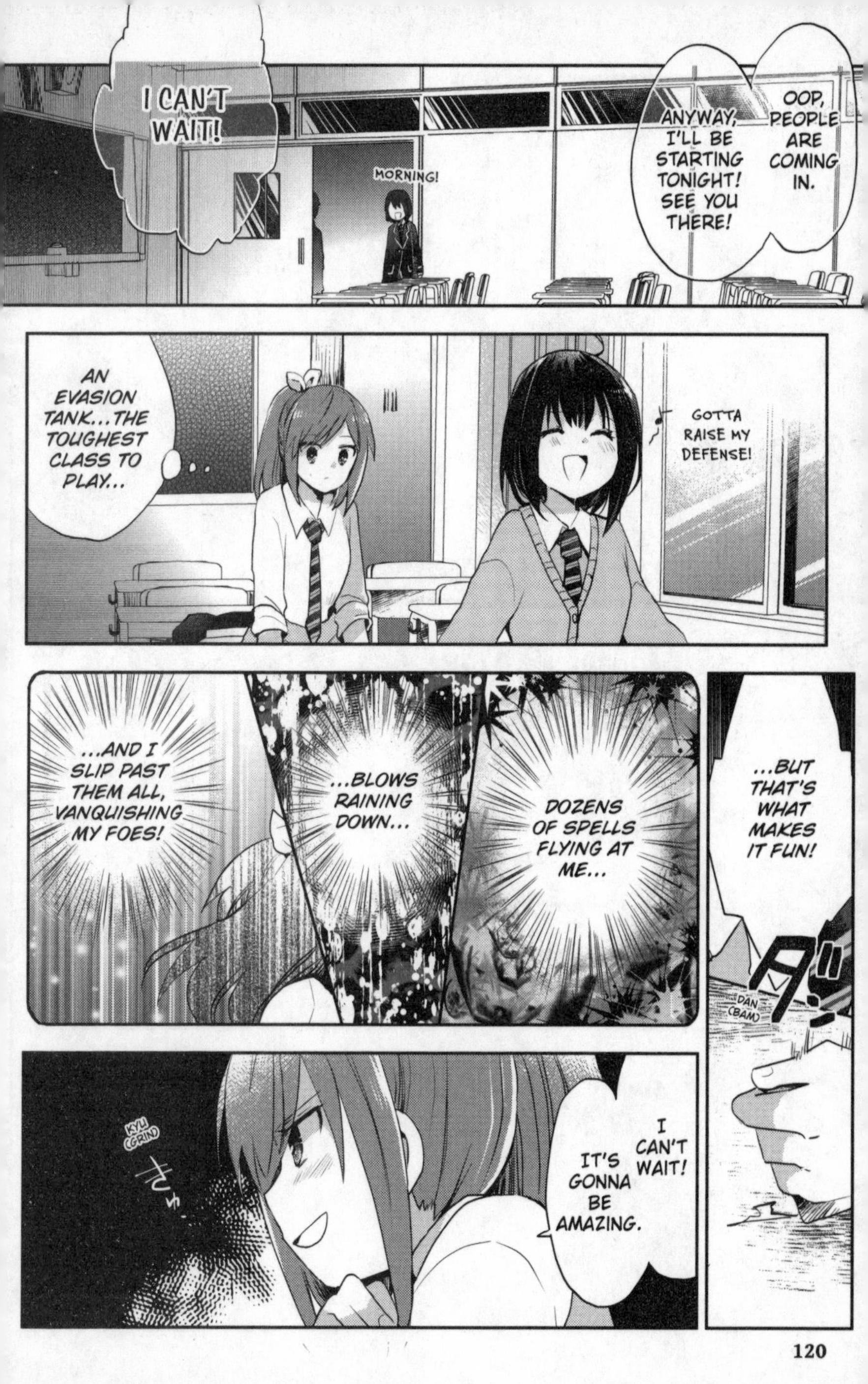
OOP, PEOPLE ARE COMING IN.
ANYWAY, I'LL BE STARTING TONIGHT! SEE YOU THERE!
MORNING!
I CAN'T WAIT!
GOTTA RAISE MY DEFENSE!
AN EVASION TANK...THE TOUGHEST CLASS TO PLAY...
...BUT THAT'S WHAT MAKES IT FUN!
DAN (BAM)
DOZENS OF SPELLS FLYING AT ME...
...BLOWS RAINING DOWN...
...AND I SLIP PAST THEM ALL, VANQUISHING MY FOES!
I CAN'T WAIT!
IT'S GONNA BE AMAZING.
KYU (GRIN)

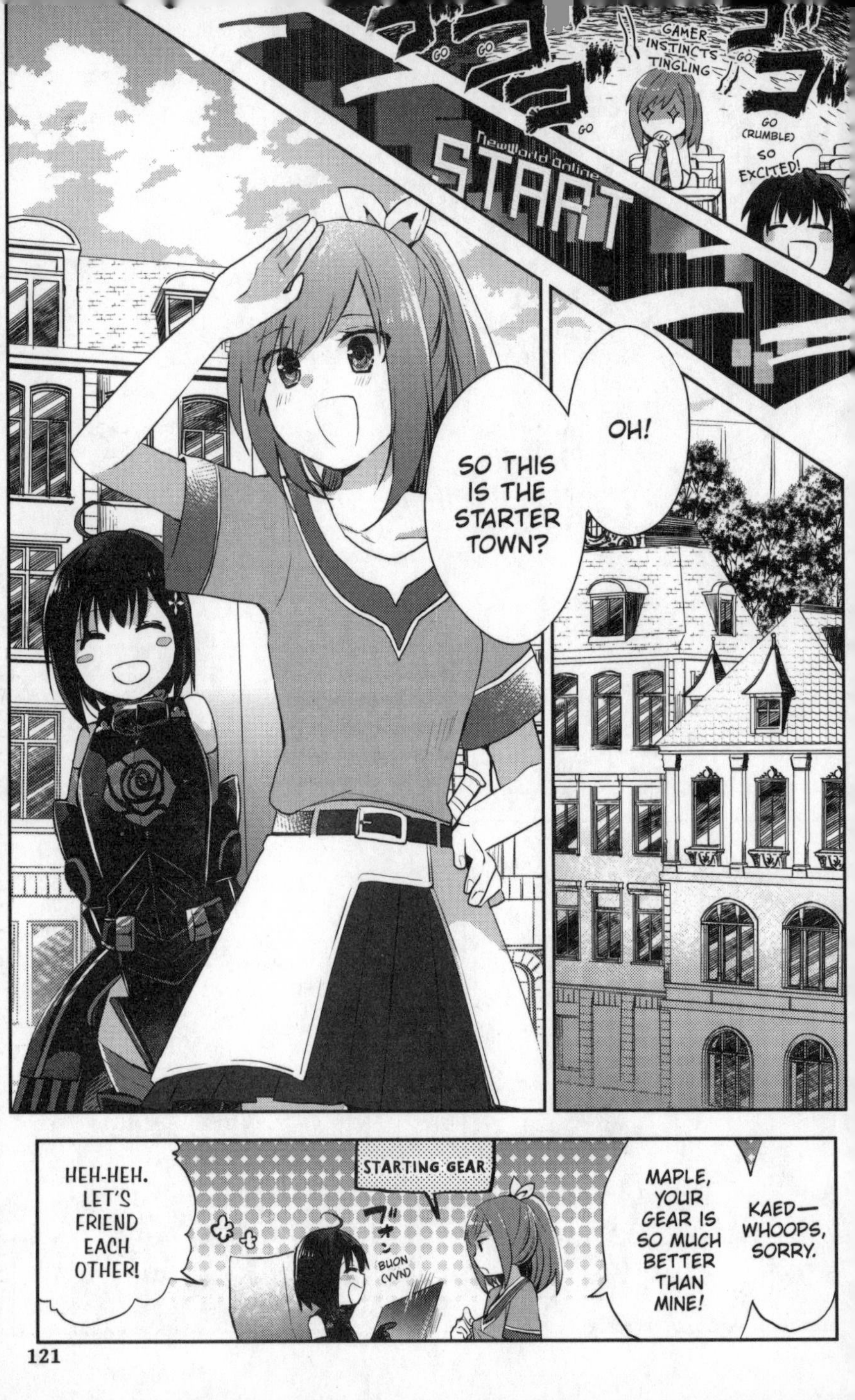
GO GO
GAMER INSTINCTS TINGLING
GO GO
GO (RUMBLE)
SO EXCITED!
NewWorld Online START
OH!
SO THIS IS THE STARTER TOWN?
KAED— WHOOPS, SORRY.
MAPLE, YOUR GEAR IS SO MUCH BETTER THAN MINE!
STARTING GEAR
BUON (VVN)
HEH-HEH. LET'S FRIEND EACH OTHER!

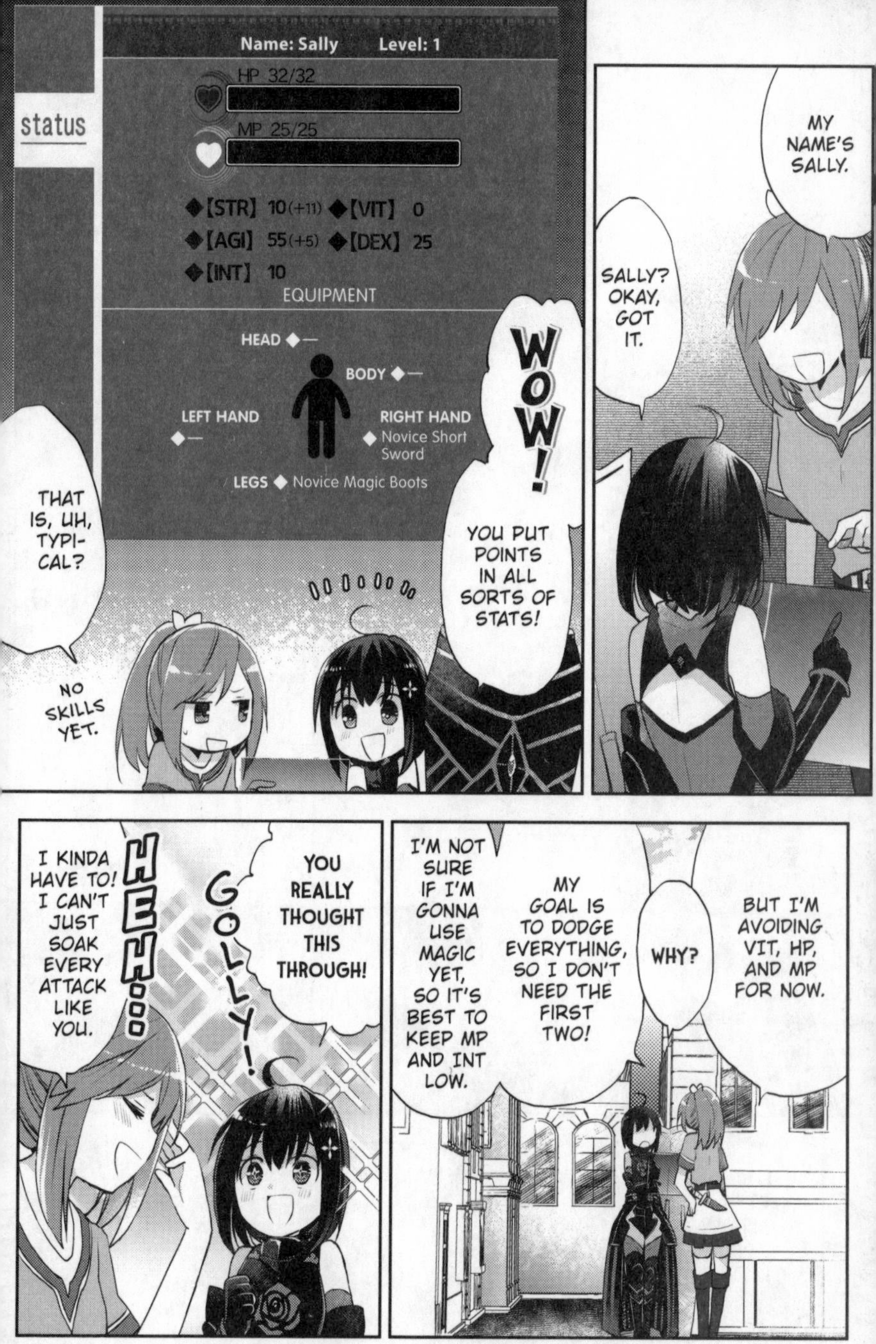
MY NAME'S SALLY.
SALLY? OKAY, GOT IT.
Name: Sally Level: 1
status
HP 32/32
MP 25/25
◆【STR】 10(+11) ◆【VIT】 0
◆【AGI】 55(+5) ◆【DEX】 25
◆【INT】 10
EQUIPMENT
HEAD ◆—
BODY ◆—
LEFT HAND ◆—
RIGHT HAND ◆ Novice Short Sword
LEGS ◆ Novice Magic Boots
WOW!
YOU PUT POINTS IN ALL SORTS OF STATS!
OOOOOOO
THAT IS, UH, TYPI-CAL?
NO SKILLS YET.
BUT I'M AVOIDING VIT, HP, AND MP FOR NOW.
WHY?
MY GOAL IS TO DODGE EVERYTHING, SO I DON'T NEED THE FIRST TWO!
I'M NOT SURE IF I'M GONNA USE MAGIC YET, SO IT'S BEST TO KEEP MP AND INT LOW.
YOU REALLY THOUGHT THIS THROUGH!
GOLLY!
HEHOOO
I KINDA HAVE TO! I CAN'T JUST SOAK EVERY ATTACK LIKE YOU.

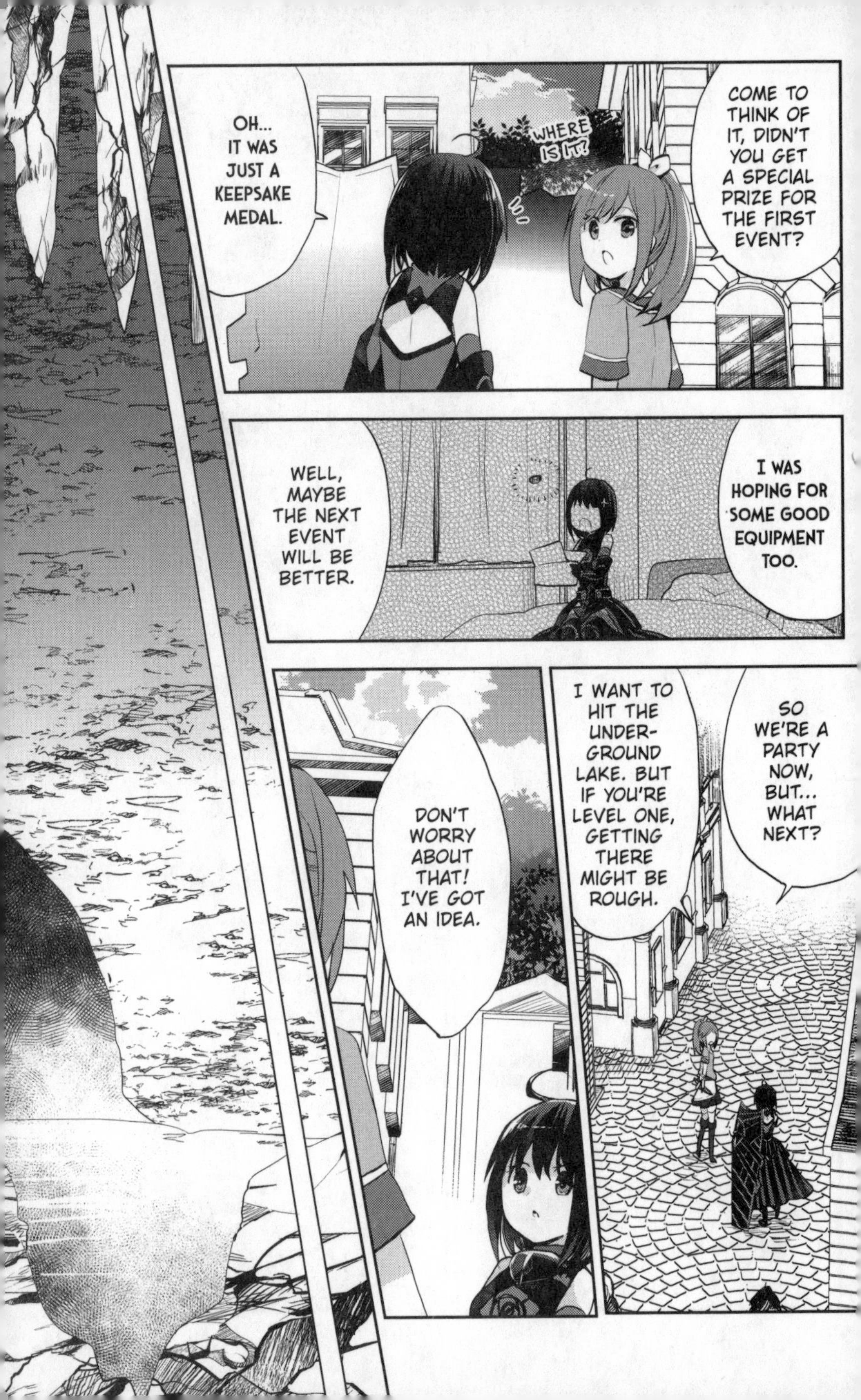
COME TO THINK OF IT, DIDN'T YOU GET A SPECIAL PRIZE FOR THE FIRST EVENT?
WHERE IS IT?
OH... IT WAS JUST A KEEPSAKE MEDAL.
I WAS HOPING FOR SOME GOOD EQUIPMENT TOO.
WELL, MAYBE THE NEXT EVENT WILL BE BETTER.
SO WE'RE A PARTY NOW, BUT... WHAT NEXT?
I WANT TO HIT THE UNDER-GROUND LAKE. BUT IF YOU'RE LEVEL ONE, GETTING THERE MIGHT BE ROUGH.
DON'T WORRY ABOUT THAT! I'VE GOT AN IDEA.

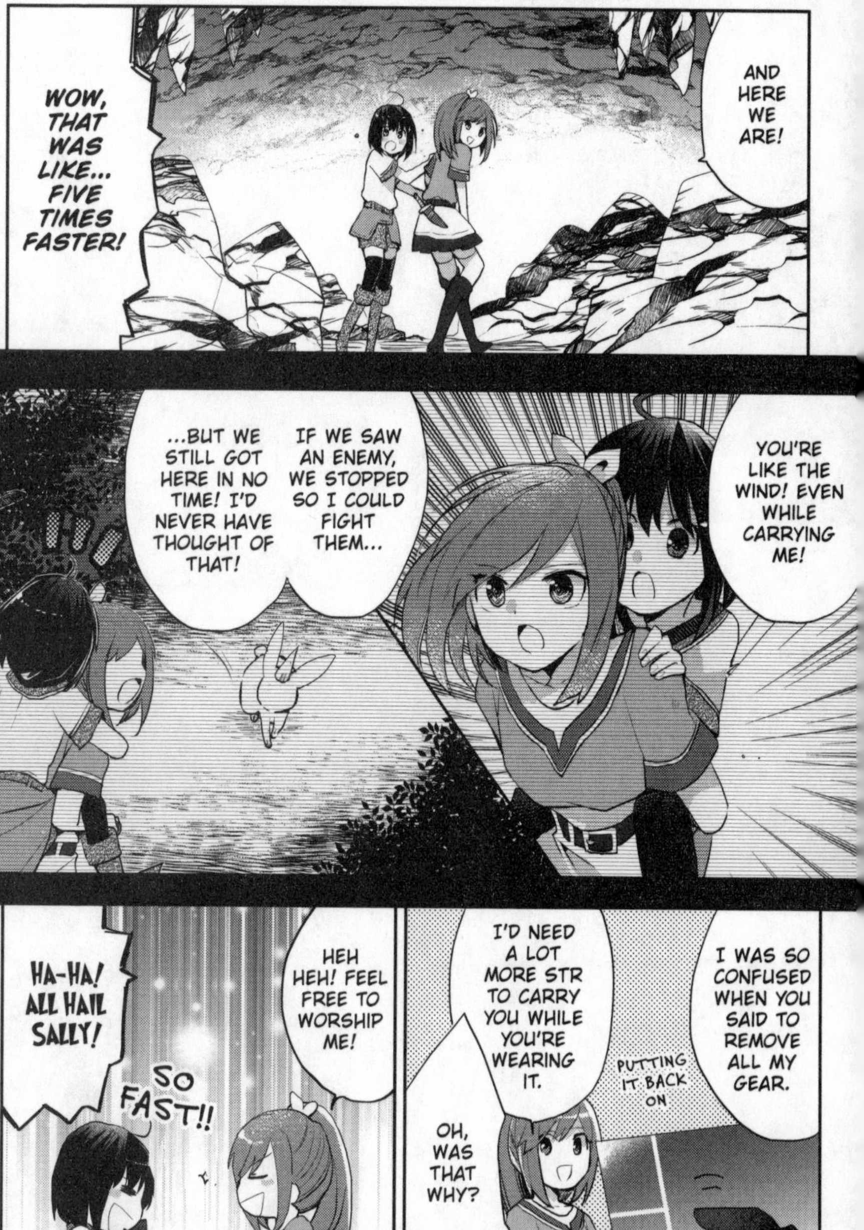
AND HERE WE ARE!
WOW, THAT WAS LIKE... FIVE TIMES FASTER!
YOU'RE LIKE THE WIND! EVEN WHILE CARRYING ME!
IF WE SAW AN ENEMY, WE STOPPED SO I COULD FIGHT THEM...
...BUT WE STILL GOT HERE IN NO TIME! I'D NEVER HAVE THOUGHT OF THAT!
I WAS SO CONFUSED WHEN YOU SAID TO REMOVE ALL MY GEAR.
PUTTING IT BACK ON
I'D NEED A LOT MORE STR TO CARRY YOU WHILE YOU'RE WEARING IT.
OH, WAS THAT WHY?
HEH HEH! FEEL FREE TO WORSHIP ME!
HA-HA! ALL HAIL SALLY!
SO FAST!!

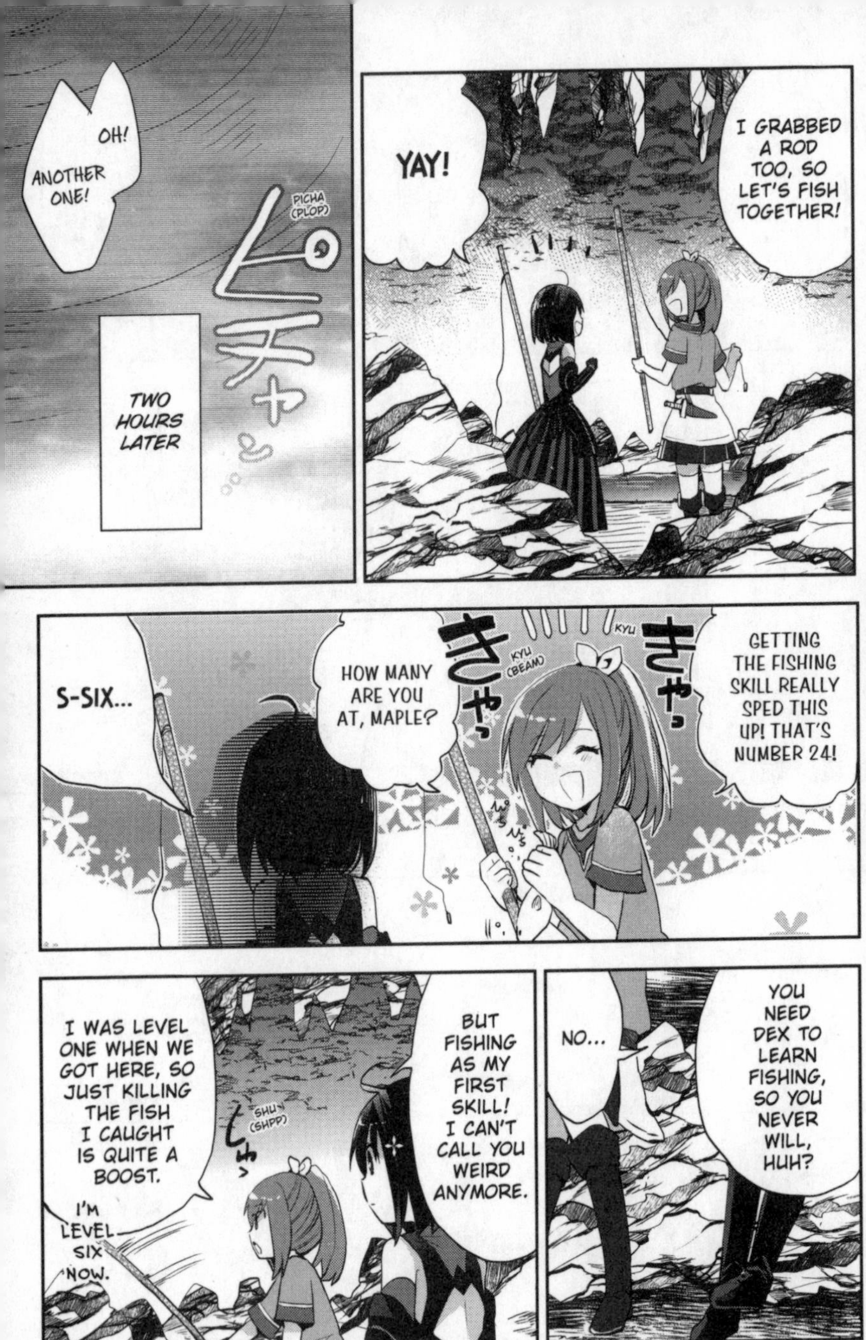
I GRABBED A ROD TOO, SO LET'S FISH TOGETHER!
YAY!
OH! ANOTHER ONE!
PICHA (PLOP)
ピチャ
TWO HOURS LATER
GETTING THE FISHING SKILL REALLY SPED THIS UP! THAT'S NUMBER 24!
KYU
KYU (BEAM)
きゃっきゃっ
HOW MANY ARE YOU AT, MAPLE?
S-SIX...
YOU NEED DEX TO LEARN FISHING, SO YOU NEVER WILL, HUH?
NO...
BUT FISHING AS MY FIRST SKILL! I CAN'T CALL YOU WEIRD ANYMORE.
I WAS LEVEL ONE WHEN WE GOT HERE, SO JUST KILLING THE FISH I CAUGHT IS QUITE A BOOST.
SHU (SHPP)
しゅ
I'M LEVEL SIX NOW.

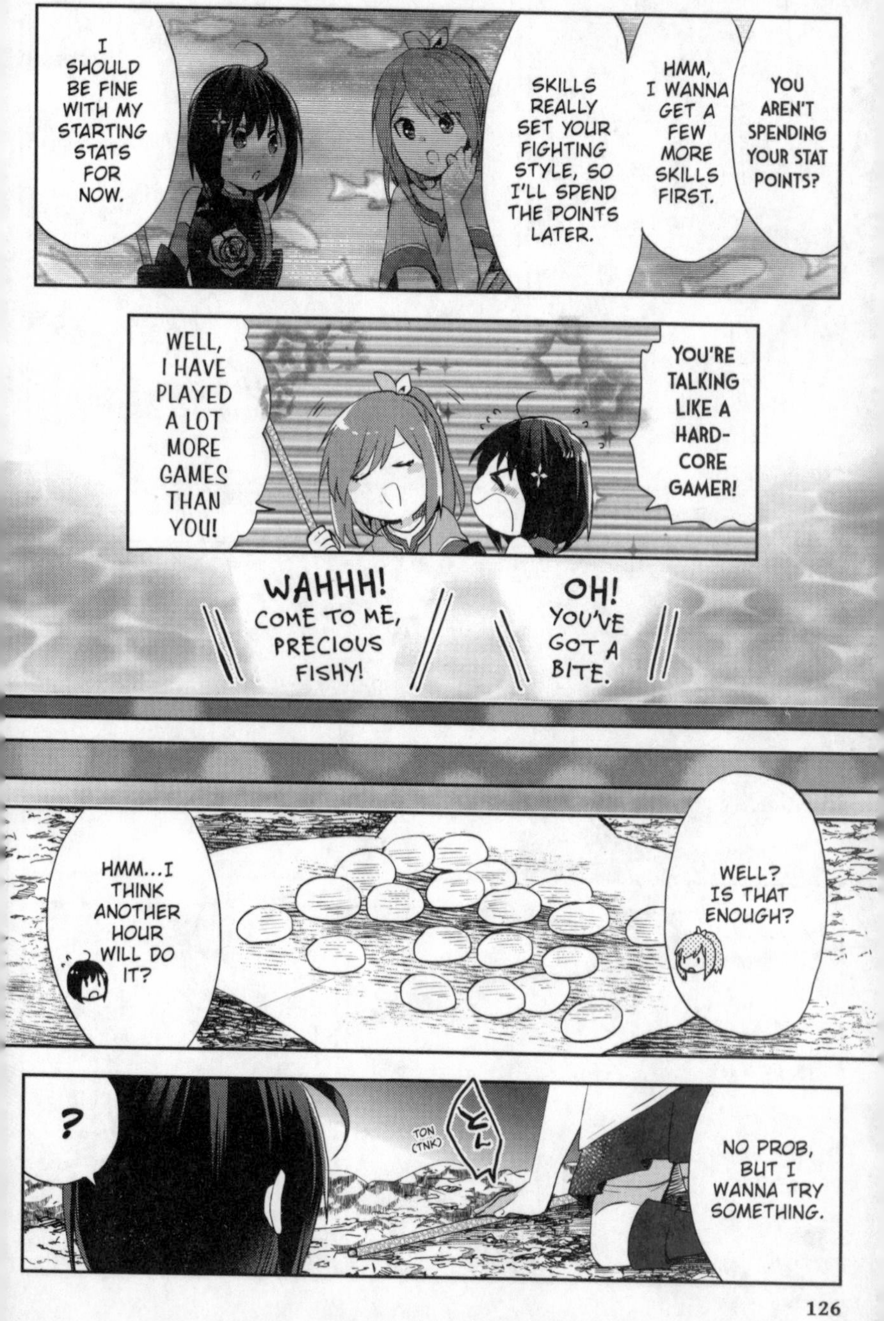
YOU AREN'T SPENDING YOUR STAT POINTS?
HMM, I WANNA GET A FEW MORE SKILLS FIRST.
SKILLS REALLY SET YOUR FIGHTING STYLE, SO I'LL SPEND THE POINTS LATER.
I SHOULD BE FINE WITH MY STARTING STATS FOR NOW.
YOU'RE TALKING LIKE A HARD-CORE GAMER!
WELL, I HAVE PLAYED A LOT MORE GAMES THAN YOU!
OH! YOU'VE GOT A BITE.
WAHHH! COME TO ME, PRECIOUS FISHY!
WELL? IS THAT ENOUGH?
HMM...I THINK ANOTHER HOUR WILL DO IT?
NO PROB, BUT I WANNA TRY SOMETHING.
TON (TNK)
?

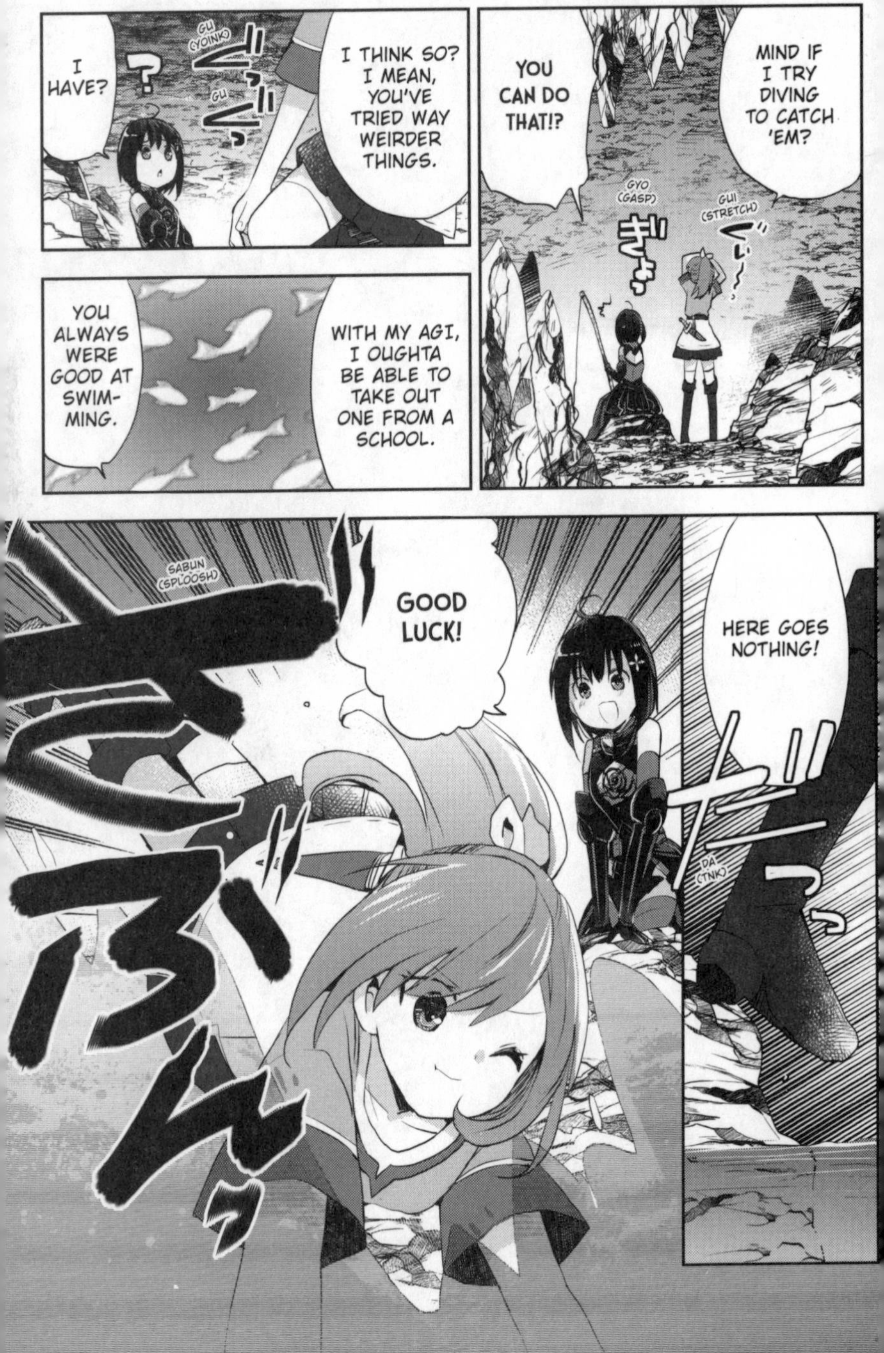
MIND IF I TRY DIVING TO CATCH 'EM?
GUI (STRETCH)
YOU CAN DO THAT!?
GYO (GASP)
I THINK SO? I MEAN, YOU'VE TRIED WAY WEIRDER THINGS.
GU (YOINK)
GU
I HAVE?
WITH MY AGI, I OUGHTA BE ABLE TO TAKE OUT ONE FROM A SCHOOL.
YOU ALWAYS WERE GOOD AT SWIM-MING.
HERE GOES NOTHING!
DA (TNK)
GOOD LUCK!
SABUN (SPLOOSH)

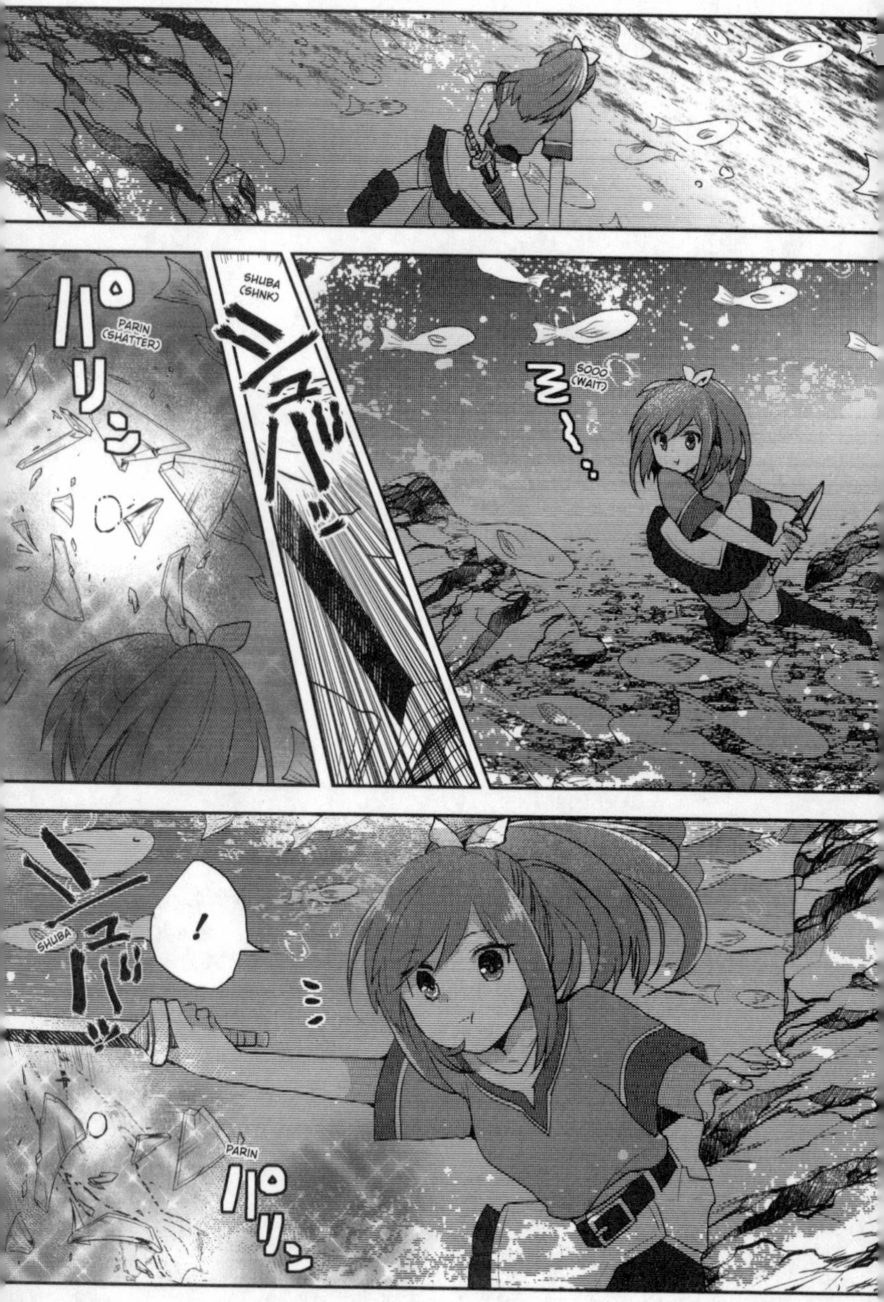
ミ~‥
SOOO (WAIT)
シュバッ
SHUBA (SHNK)
パリン
PARIN (SHATTER)
シュバッ
SHUBA
!
パリン
PARIN

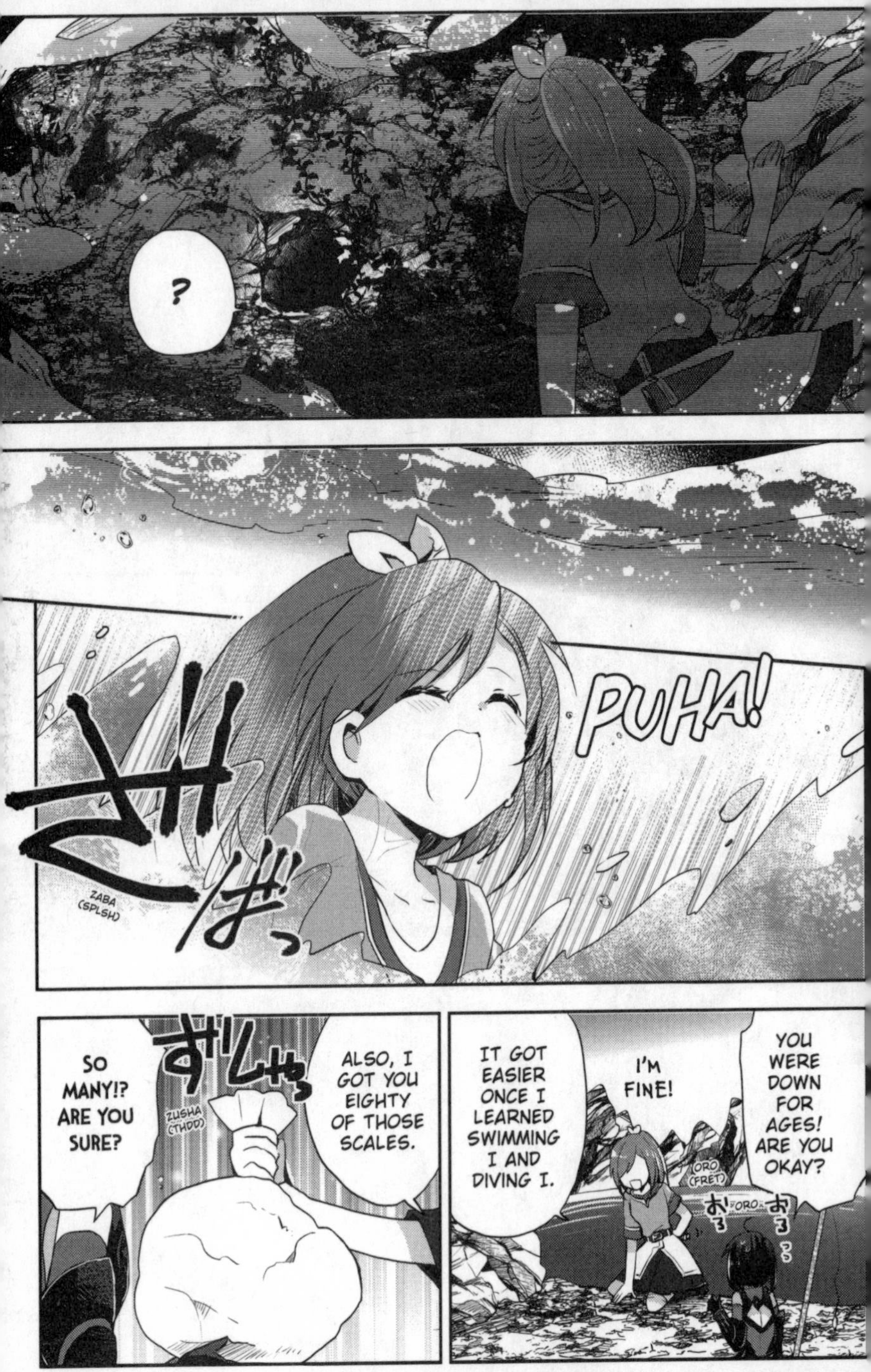
?
PUHA!
ざばっ
ZABA (SPLSH)
YOU WERE DOWN FOR AGES! ARE YOU OKAY?
おろ おろっ
ORO ORO (FRET)
I'M FINE!
IT GOT EASIER ONCE I LEARNED SWIMMING I AND DIVING I.
ALSO, I GOT YOU EIGHTY OF THOSE SCALES.
ずしゃっ
ZUSHA (THDD)
SO MANY!? ARE YOU SURE?

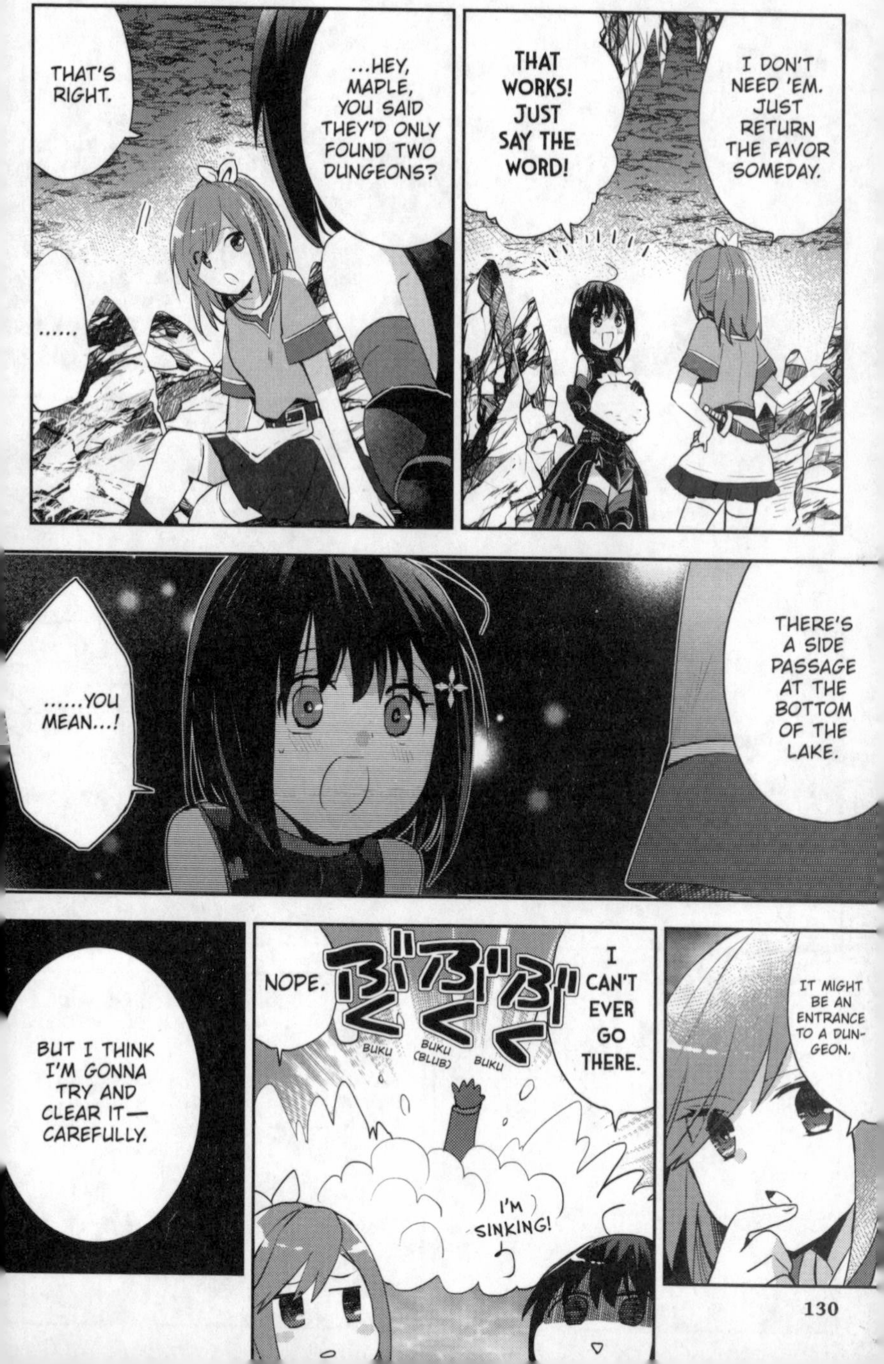
I DON'T NEED 'EM. JUST RETURN THE FAVOR SOMEDAY.
THAT WORKS! JUST SAY THE WORD!
...HEY, MAPLE, YOU SAID THEY'D ONLY FOUND TWO DUNGEONS?
THAT'S RIGHT.
......
THERE'S A SIDE PASSAGE AT THE BOTTOM OF THE LAKE.
......YOU MEAN...!
IT MIGHT BE AN ENTRANCE TO A DUN-GEON.
I CAN'T EVER GO THERE.
BUKU BUKU (BLUB) BUKU
NOPE.
I'M SINKING!
BUT I THINK I'M GONNA TRY AND CLEAR IT—CAREFULLY.

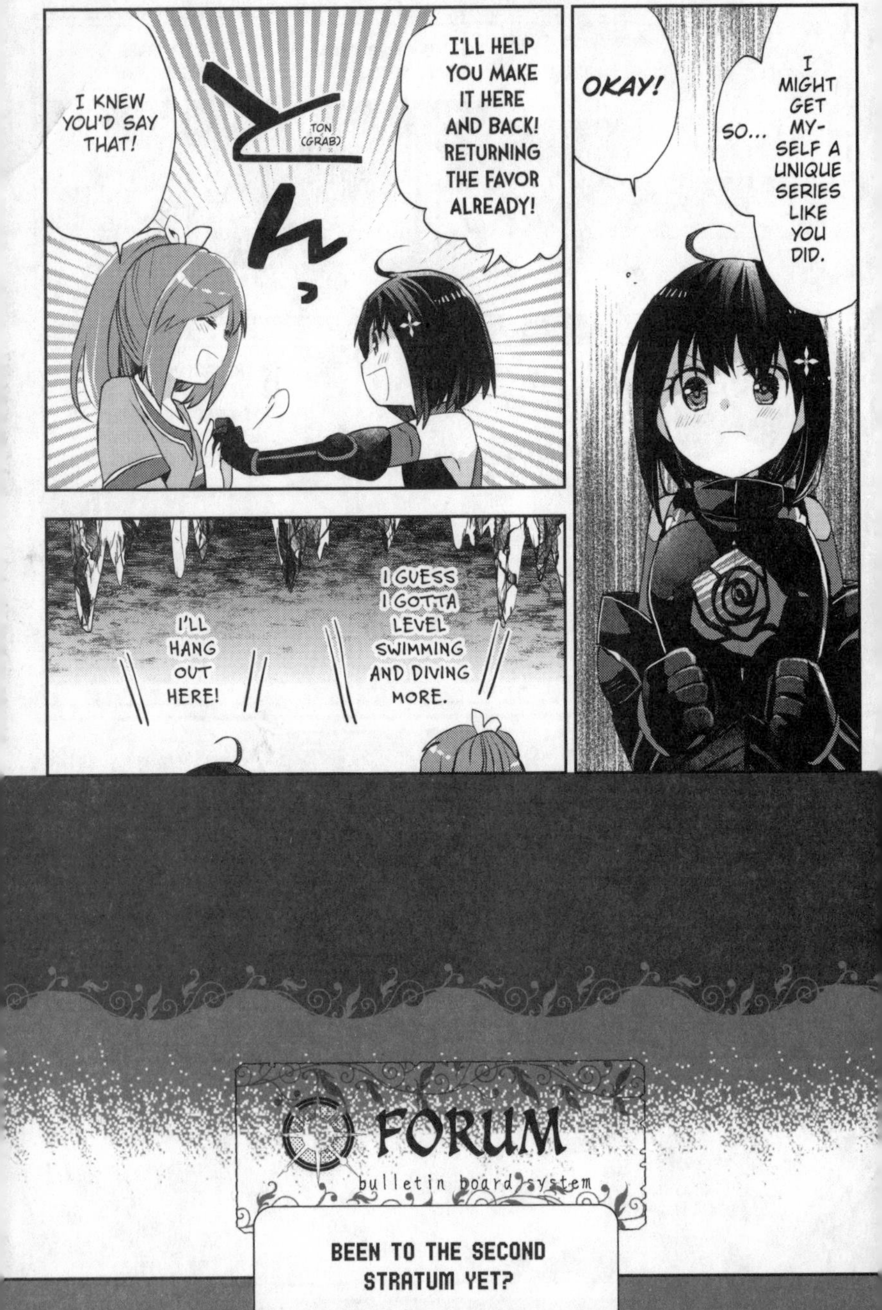
I MIGHT GET MY-SELF A UNIQUE SERIES LIKE YOU DID.
SO...
OKAY!
I'LL HELP YOU MAKE IT HERE AND BACK! RETURNING THE FAVOR ALREADY!
TON (GRAB)
I KNEW YOU'D SAY THAT!
I GUESS I GOTTA LEVEL SWIMMING AND DIVING MORE.
I'LL HANG OUT HERE!
FORUM
bulletin board system
BEEN TO THE SECOND STRATUM YET?

I JUST MADE IT THERE MYSELF.
NAME: ANONYMOUS GREAT SHIELDER
JUST CLEARED THAT BOSS EARLIER.
NAME: ANONYMOUS GREATSWORDER
I MANAGED IT TOO.
NAME: ANONYMOUS SPEAR MASTER
YUP, DOWNED THE THING.
NAME: ANONYMOUS ARCHER
I MADE IT THROUGH SOMEHOW.
NAME: ANONYMOUS MAGE
I THOUGHT MAPLE WOULD HIT IT FIRST THING, SO I'VE BEEN GRINDING LEVELS TO KEEP UP...AND NOW I'M A FRONT-RUNNER.
SAME.
NAME: ANONYMOUS GREATSWORDER
NAME: ANONYMOUS ARCHER
MAPLE HASN'T HIT THE SECOND STRATUM YET, I DON'T THINK.
ACTUALLY, ACCORDING TO MY FRIEND LIST, SHE'S FORMED A PARTY.
DEETS. NOW.
NAME: ANONYMOUS GREAT SHIELDER
NAME: ANONYMOUS MAGE
DUNNO HER NAME, BUT SHE WAS IN STARTING GEAR. LOOKED CLOSE, PROBABLY IRL FRIENDS.
WEAPONS?
DAGGERS.
SURPRISING. I'D HAVE PREDICTED A MAGE OR AN ARCHER.
NAME: ANONYMOUS SPEAR MASTER
NAME: ANONYMOUS MAGE
NAME: ANONYMOUS GREAT SHIELDER
NOT A BAD PLAN FOR A TWO-PERSON PARTY.
BUT...SHE'S MAPLE'S FRIEND, RIGHT?

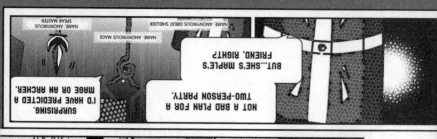

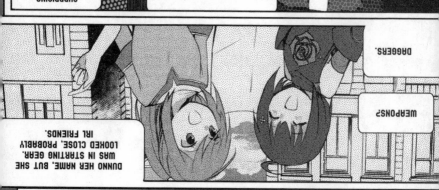

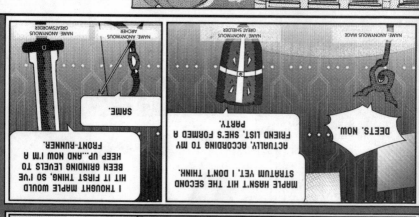

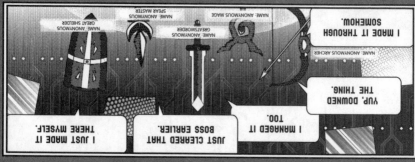

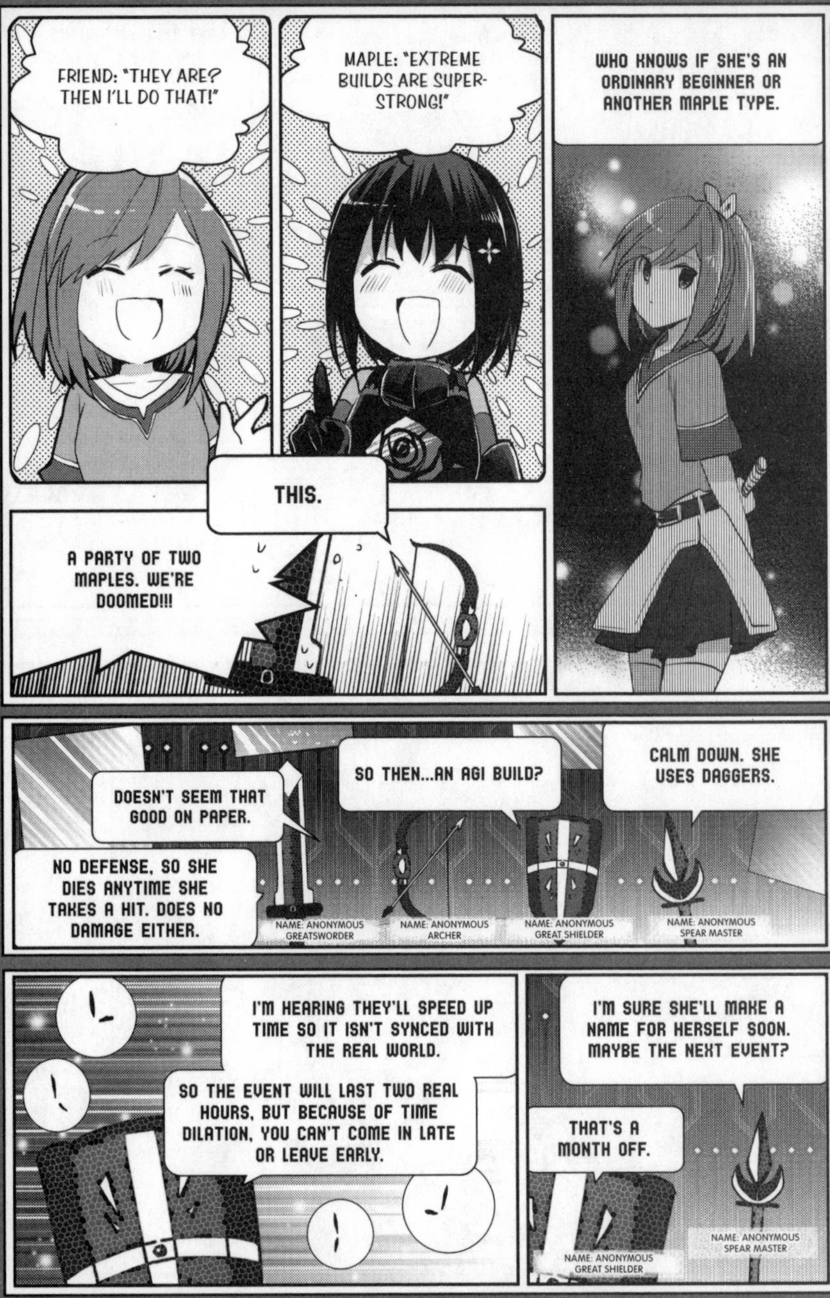
WHO KNOWS IF SHE'S AN ORDINARY BEGINNER OR ANOTHER MAPLE TYPE.
MAPLE: "EXTREME BUILDS ARE SUPER-STRONG!"
FRIEND: "THEY ARE? THEN I'LL DO THAT!"
THIS.
A PARTY OF TWO MAPLES. WE'RE DOOMED!!!
CALM DOWN. SHE USES DAGGERS.
SO THEN...AN AGI BUILD?
DOESN'T SEEM THAT GOOD ON PAPER.
NO DEFENSE, SO SHE DIES ANYTIME SHE TAKES A HIT. DOES NO DAMAGE EITHER.
NAME: ANONYMOUS SPEAR MASTER
NAME: ANONYMOUS GREAT SHIELDER
NAME: ANONYMOUS ARCHER
NAME: ANONYMOUS GREATSWORDER
I'M SURE SHE'LL MAKE A NAME FOR HERSELF SOON. MAYBE THE NEXT EVENT?
THAT'S A MONTH OFF.
NAME: ANONYMOUS SPEAR MASTER
NAME: ANONYMOUS GREAT SHIELDER
I'M HEARING THEY'LL SPEED UP TIME SO IT ISN'T SYNCED WITH THE REAL WORLD.
SO THE EVENT WILL LAST TWO REAL HOURS, BUT BECAUSE OF TIME DILATION, YOU CAN'T COME IN LATE OR LEAVE EARLY.
!
!
!
!

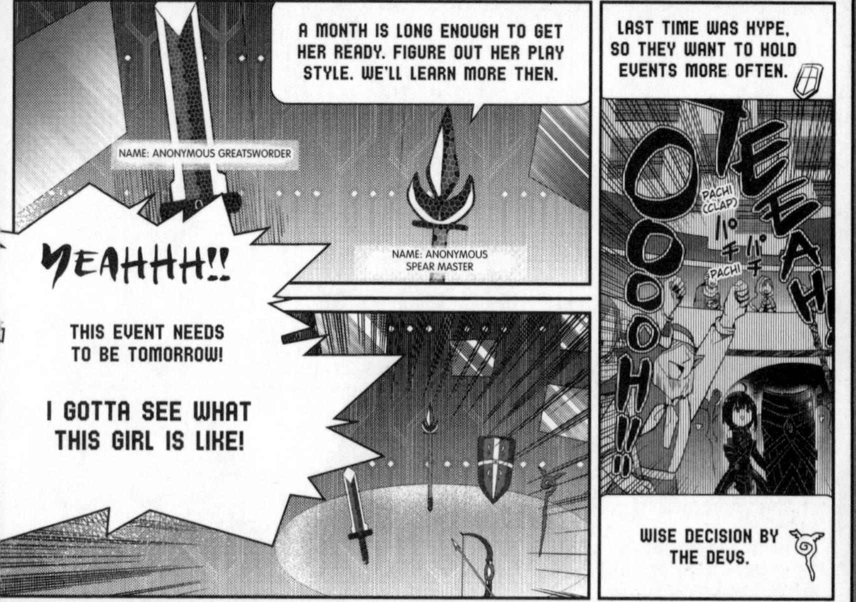
LAST TIME WAS HYPE, SO THEY WANT TO HOLD EVENTS MORE OFTEN.
TEEEAH! OOOOOH!!
PACHI (CLAP)
PACHI
WISE DECISION BY THE DEVS.
A MONTH IS LONG ENOUGH TO GET HER READY. FIGURE OUT HER PLAY STYLE. WE'LL LEARN MORE THEN.
NAME: ANONYMOUS GREATSWORDER
NAME: ANONYMOUS SPEAR MASTER
YEAHHH!!
THIS EVENT NEEDS TO BE TOMORROW!
I GOTTA SEE WHAT THIS GIRL IS LIKE!
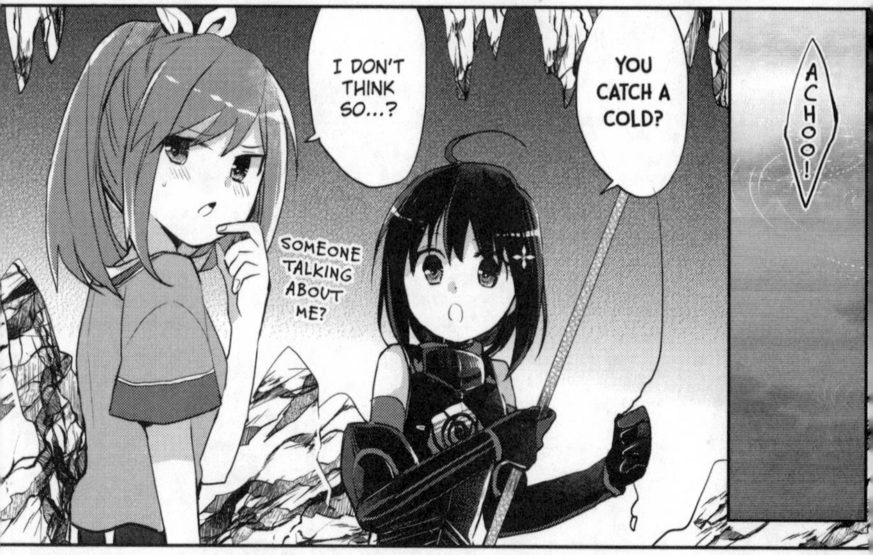
ACHOO!
YOU CATCH A COLD?
I DON'T THINK SO...?
SOMEONE TALKING ABOUT ME?

Bofuri

I Don't Want to Get Hurt, so I'll Max Out My Defense.

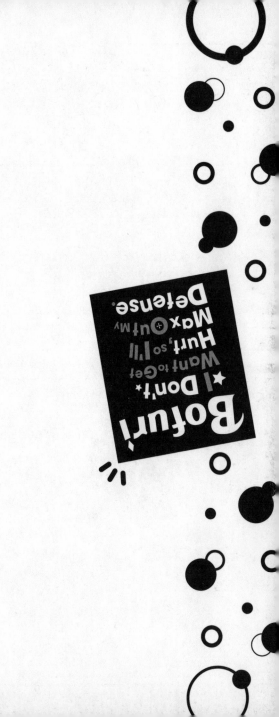

Welcome to *NewWorld Online*.

I Don't Want to Get Hurt,

so I'll Max Out My Defense.

presented by: JIROU OIMOTO & YUUMIKAN

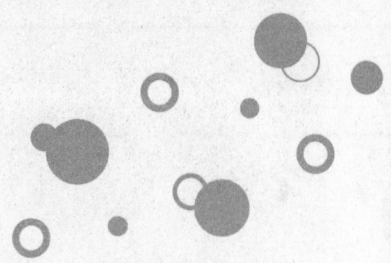

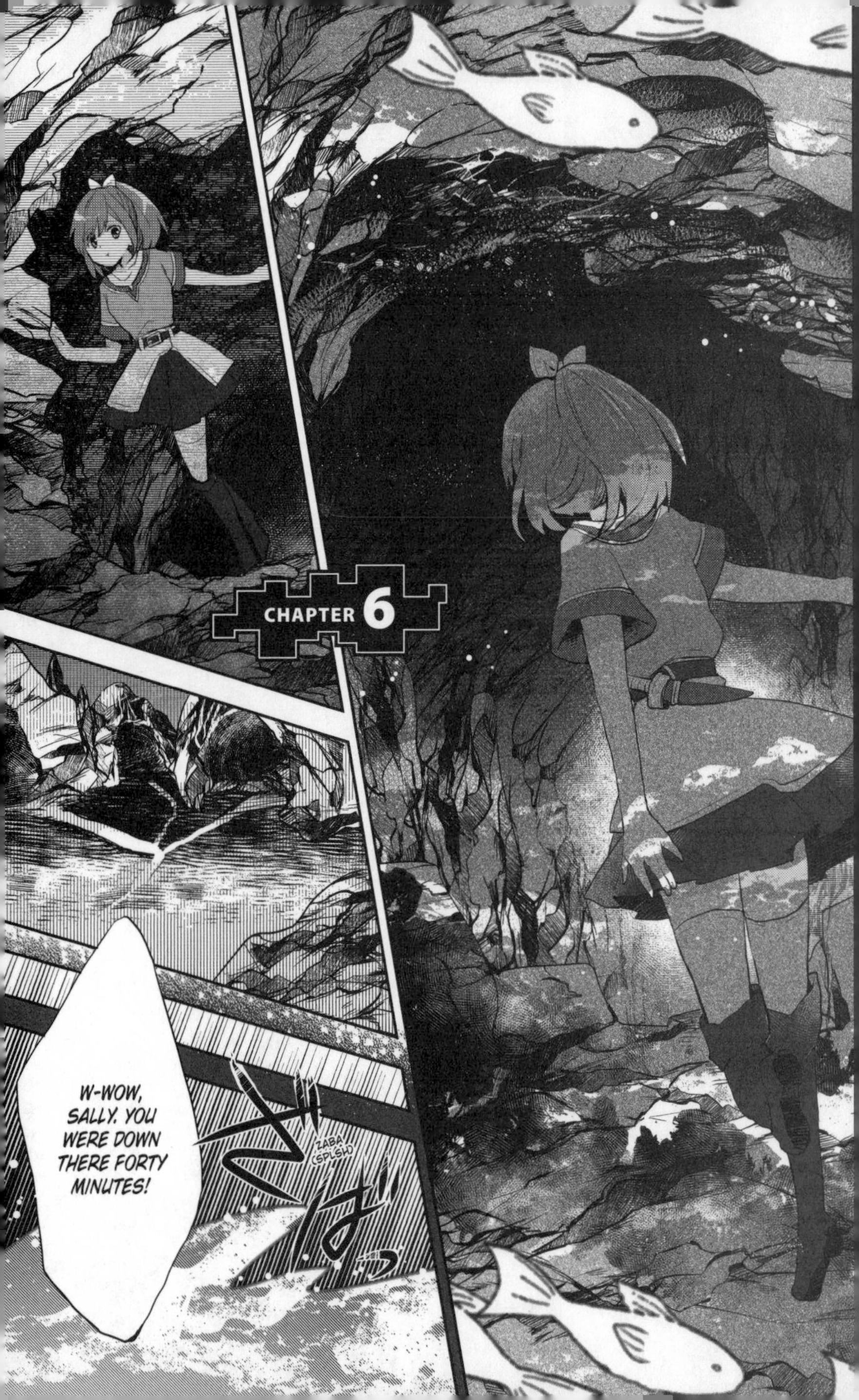
CHAPTER 6
ZABA (SPLSH)
W-WOW, SALLY. YOU WERE DOWN THERE FORTY MINUTES!

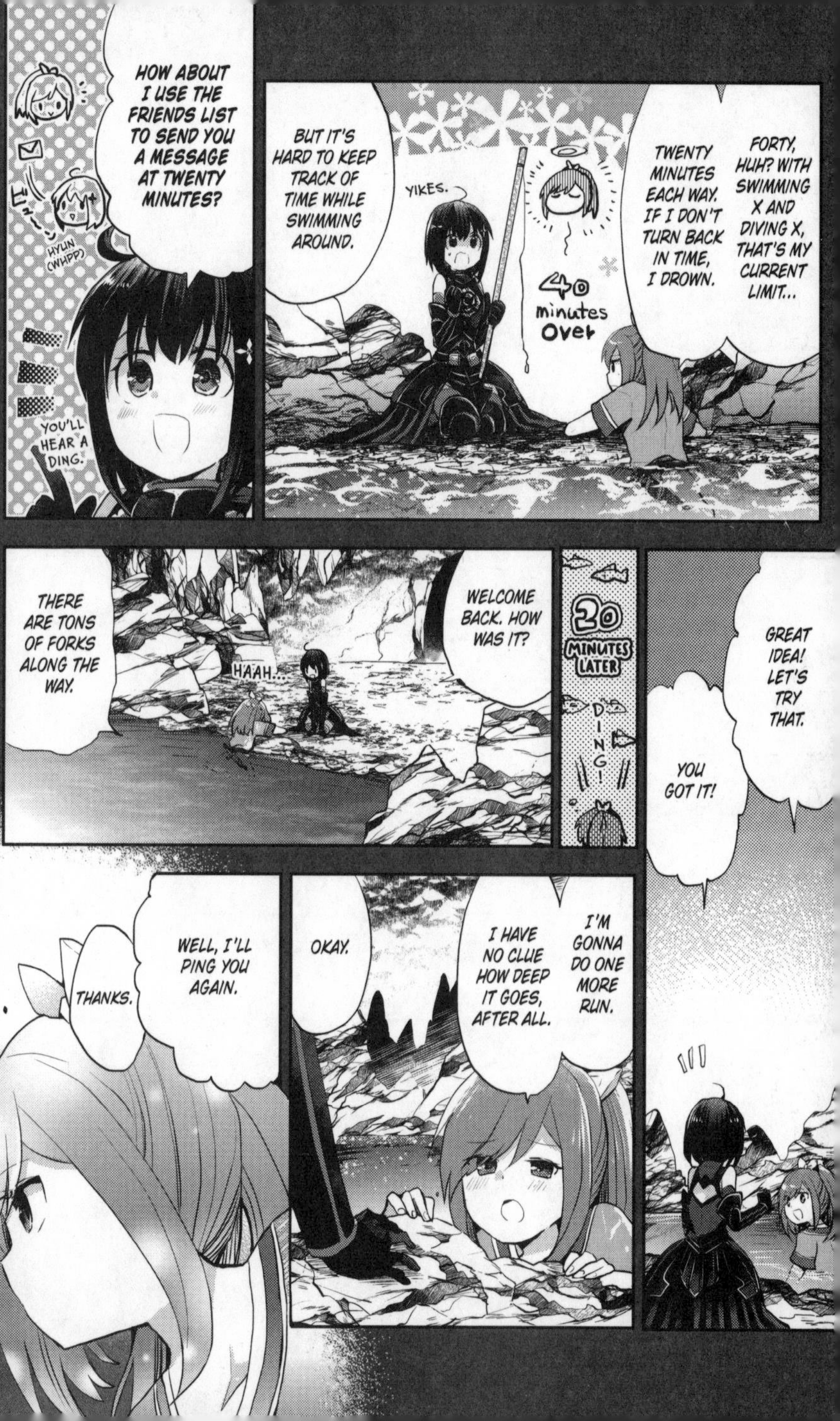
FORTY, HUH? WITH SWIMMING X AND DIVING X, THAT'S MY CURRENT LIMIT...
TWENTY MINUTES EACH WAY. IF I DON'T TURN BACK IN TIME, I DROWN.
40 minutes Over
YIKES.
BUT IT'S HARD TO KEEP TRACK OF TIME WHILE SWIMMING AROUND.
HOW ABOUT I USE THE FRIENDS LIST TO SEND YOU A MESSAGE AT TWENTY MINUTES?
HYUN (WHPP)
YOU'LL HEAR A DING.
GREAT IDEA! LET'S TRY THAT.
YOU GOT IT!
20 MINUTES LATER
DING!
WELCOME BACK. HOW WAS IT?
HAAH...
THERE ARE TONS OF FORKS ALONG THE WAY.
I'M GONNA DO ONE MORE RUN.
I HAVE NO CLUE HOW DEEP IT GOES, AFTER ALL.
OKAY.
WELL, I'LL PING YOU AGAIN.
THANKS.

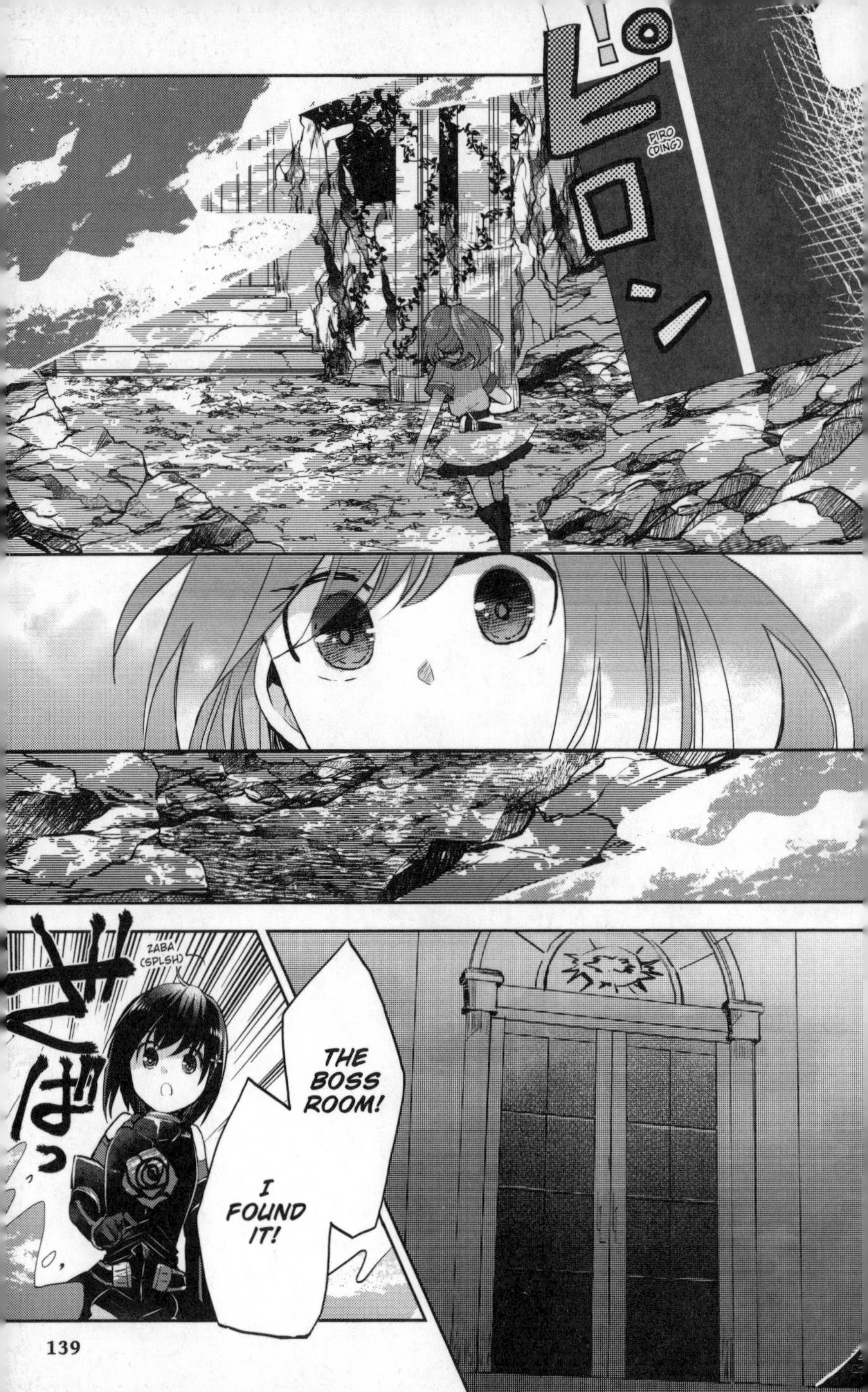
PIRO (DING)
THE BOSS ROOM!
I FOUND IT!
ZABA (SPLSH)

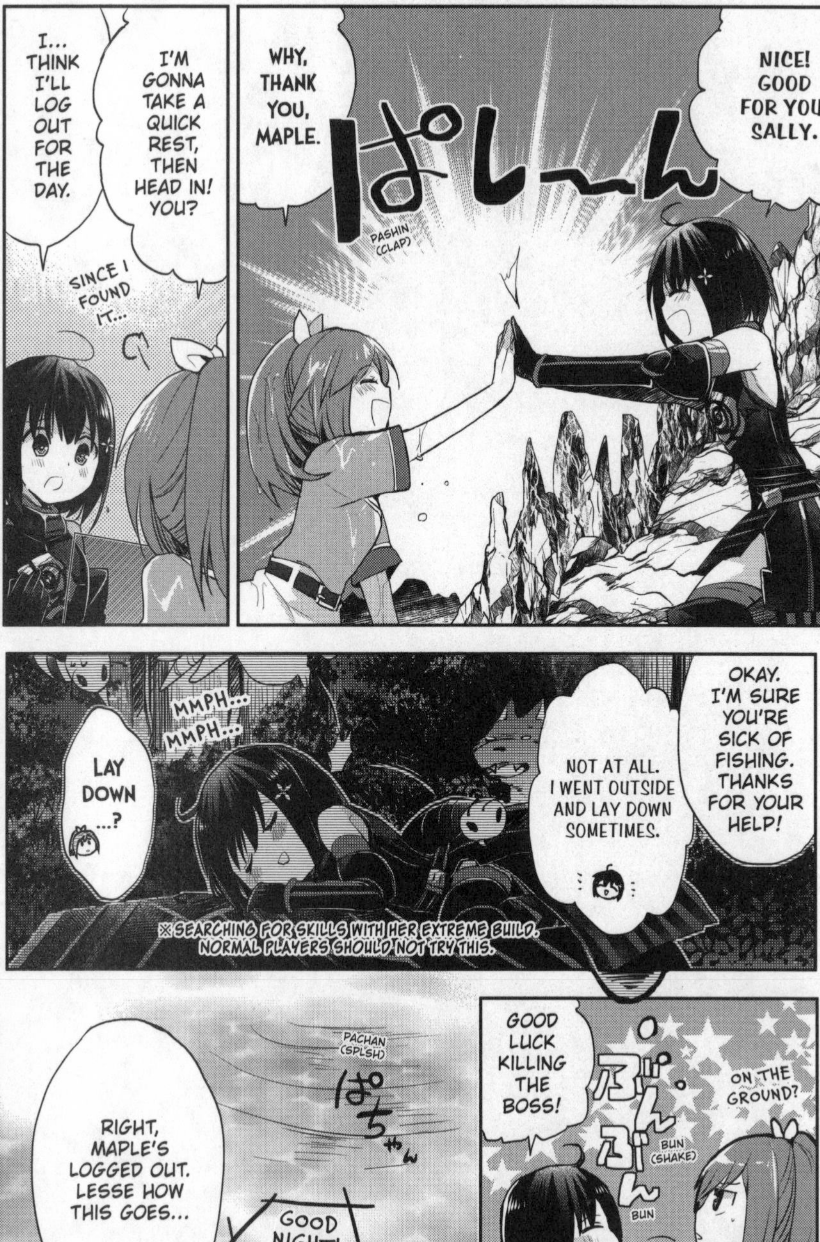
NICE! GOOD FOR YOU, SALLY.
ぱしーん
PASHIN (CLAP)
WHY, THANK YOU, MAPLE.
I'M GONNA TAKE A QUICK REST, THEN HEAD IN! YOU?
I... THINK I'LL LOG OUT FOR THE DAY.
SINCE I FOUND IT...
OKAY. I'M SURE YOU'RE SICK OF FISHING. THANKS FOR YOUR HELP!
NOT AT ALL. I WENT OUTSIDE AND LAY DOWN SOMETIMES.
MMPH... MMPH...
LAY DOWN ...?
※ SEARCHING FOR SKILLS WITH HER EXTREME BUILD. NORMAL PLAYERS SHOULD NOT TRY THIS.
ON THE GROUND?
GOOD LUCK KILLING THE BOSS!
ぶんぶん
BUN (SHAKE)
BUN
GOOD NIGHT!
ぱちゃん
PACHAN (SPLSH)
RIGHT, MAPLE'S LOGGED OUT. LESSE HOW THIS GOES...

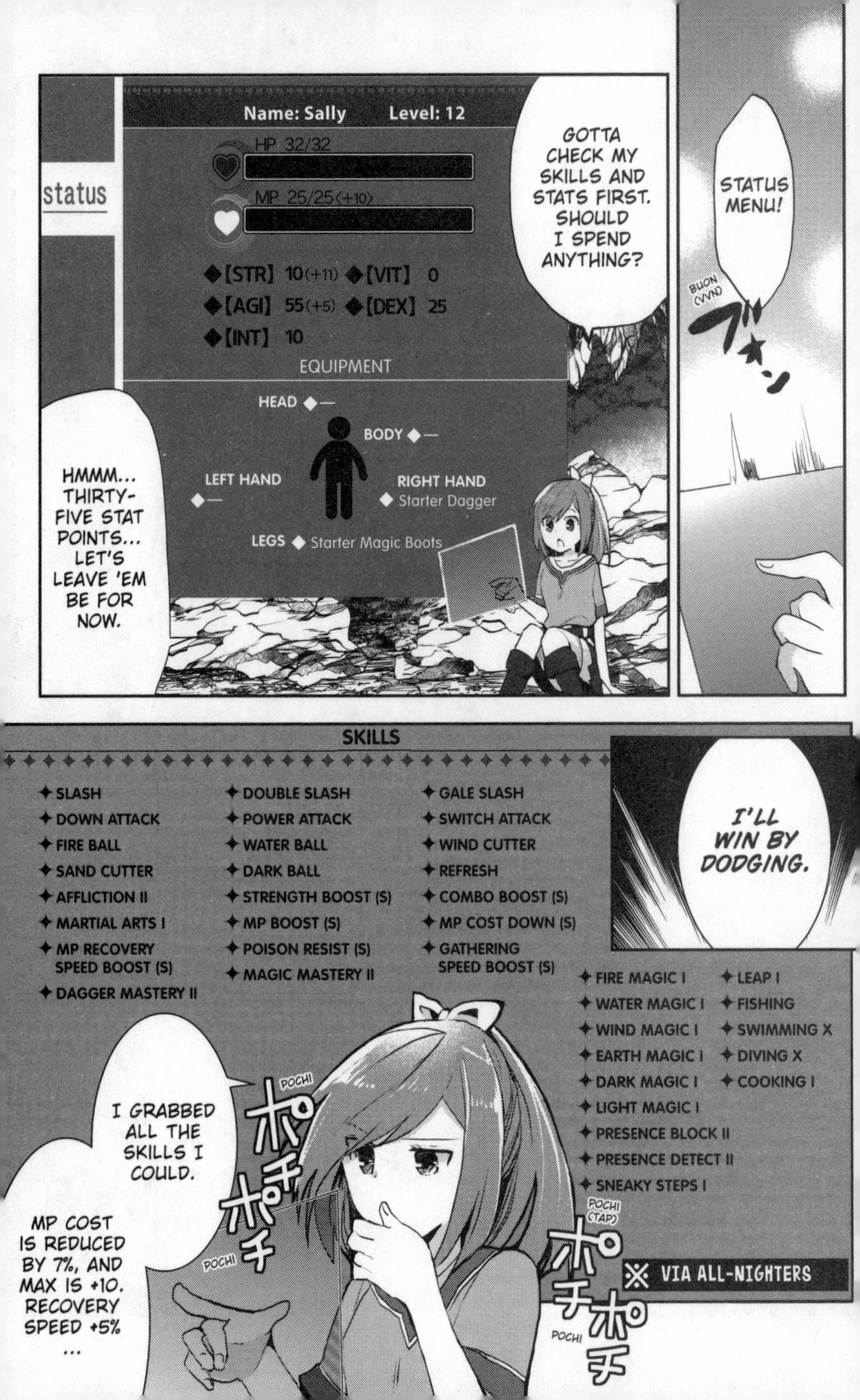
STATUS MENU!
BUON (VVN)
ブォン
GOTTA CHECK MY SKILLS AND STATS FIRST. SHOULD I SPEND ANYTHING?
Name: Sally Level: 12
status
HP 32/32
MP 25/25〈+10〉
◆【STR】 10(+11) ◆【VIT】 0
◆【AGI】 55(+5) ◆【DEX】 25
◆【INT】 10
EQUIPMENT
HEAD ◆—
BODY ◆—
LEFT HAND ◆—
RIGHT HAND ◆ Starter Dagger
LEGS ◆ Starter Magic Boots
HMMM... THIRTY-FIVE STAT POINTS... LET'S LEAVE 'EM BE FOR NOW.
I'LL WIN BY DODGING.
SKILLS
✦SLASH
✦DOWN ATTACK
✦FIRE BALL
✦SAND CUTTER
✦AFFLICTION II
✦MARTIAL ARTS I
✦MP RECOVERY SPEED BOOST (S)
✦DAGGER MASTERY II
✦DOUBLE SLASH
✦POWER ATTACK
✦WATER BALL
✦DARK BALL
✦STRENGTH BOOST (S)
✦MP BOOST (S)
✦POISON RESIST (S)
✦MAGIC MASTERY II
✦GALE SLASH
✦SWITCH ATTACK
✦WIND CUTTER
✦REFRESH
✦COMBO BOOST (S)
✦MP COST DOWN (S)
✦GATHERING SPEED BOOST (S)
✦FIRE MAGIC I
✦WATER MAGIC I
✦WIND MAGIC I
✦EARTH MAGIC I
✦DARK MAGIC I
✦LIGHT MAGIC I
✦PRESENCE BLOCK II
✦PRESENCE DETECT II
✦SNEAKY STEPS I
✦LEAP I
✦FISHING
✦SWIMMING X
✦DIVING X
✦COOKING I
※ VIA ALL-NIGHTERS
POCHI (TAP)
ポチポチ
POCHI
I GRABBED ALL THE SKILLS I COULD.
POCHI
ポチ
POCHI
ポチ
MP COST IS REDUCED BY 7%, AND MAX IS +10. RECOVERY SPEED +5% ...

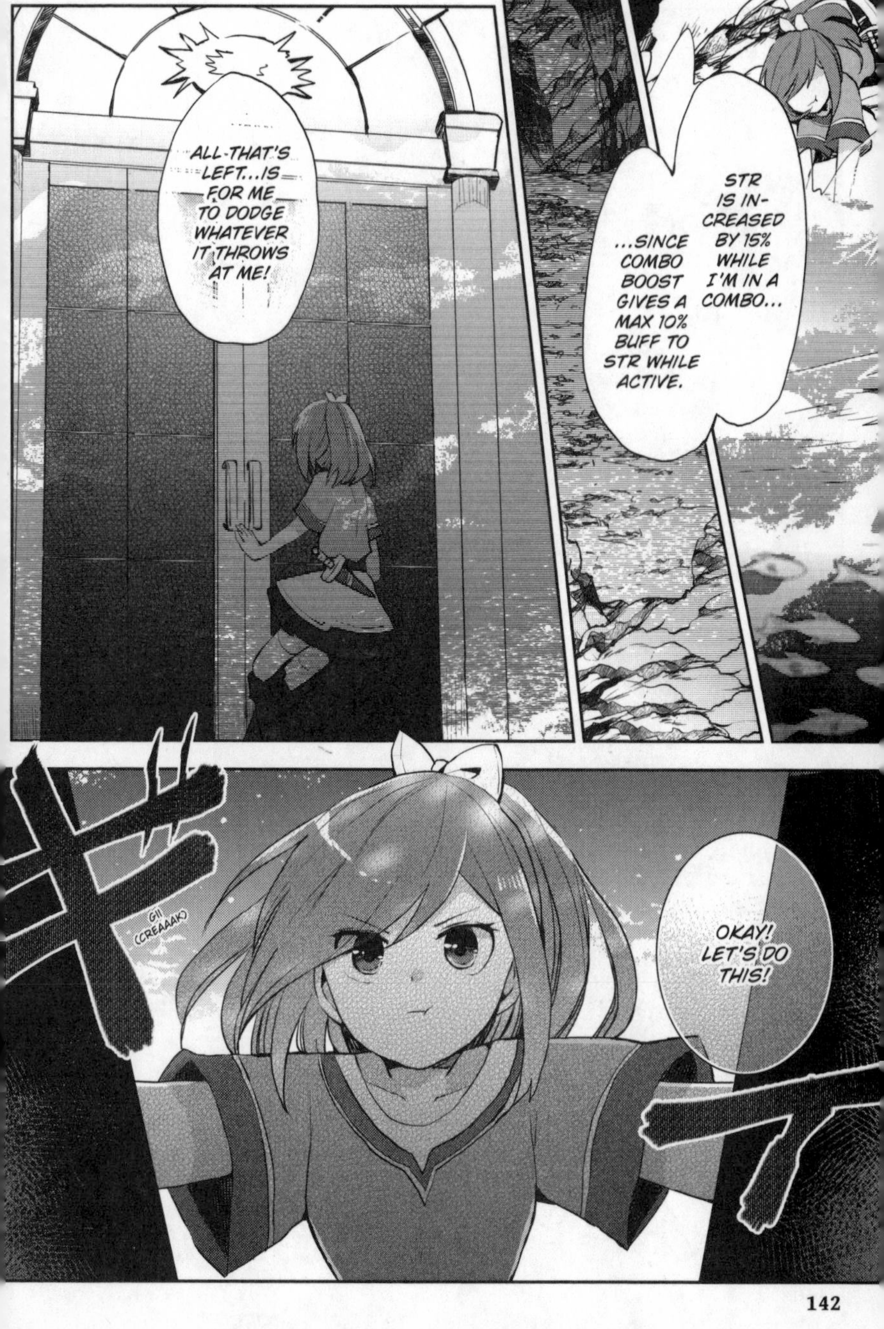
STR IS IN-CREASED BY 15% WHILE I'M IN A COMBO... ...SINCE COMBO BOOST GIVES A MAX 10% BUFF TO STR WHILE ACTIVE.
ALL THAT'S LEFT...IS FOR ME TO DODGE WHATEVER IT THROWS AT ME!
OKAY! LET'S DO THIS!
GII (CREAAAK)

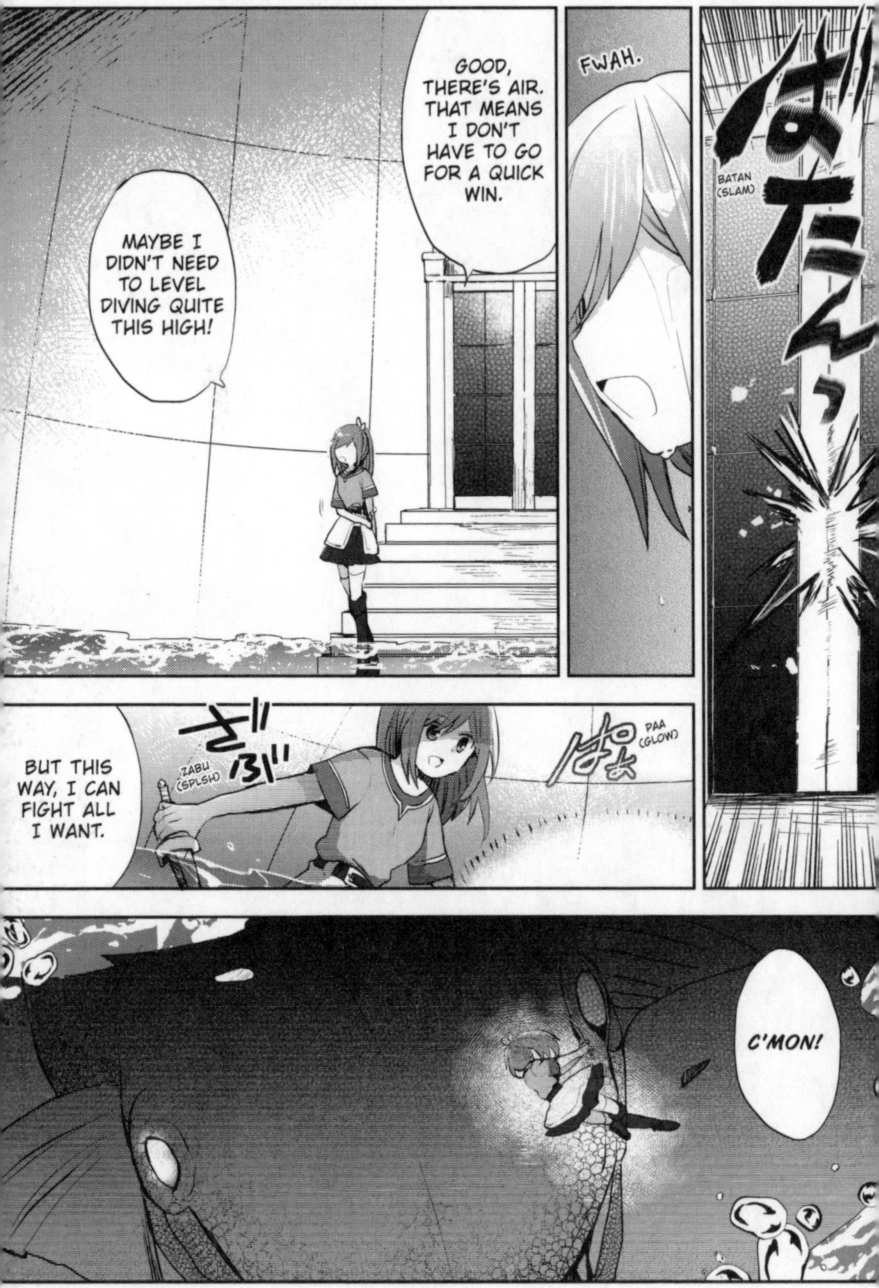
ばたんっ
BATAN (SLAM)
FWAH.
GOOD, THERE'S AIR. THAT MEANS I DON'T HAVE TO GO FOR A QUICK WIN.
MAYBE I DIDN'T NEED TO LEVEL DIVING QUITE THIS HIGH!
ぱぁ
PAA (GLOW)
ざぶ
ZABU (SPLSH)
BUT THIS WAY, I CAN FIGHT ALL I WANT.
C'MON!

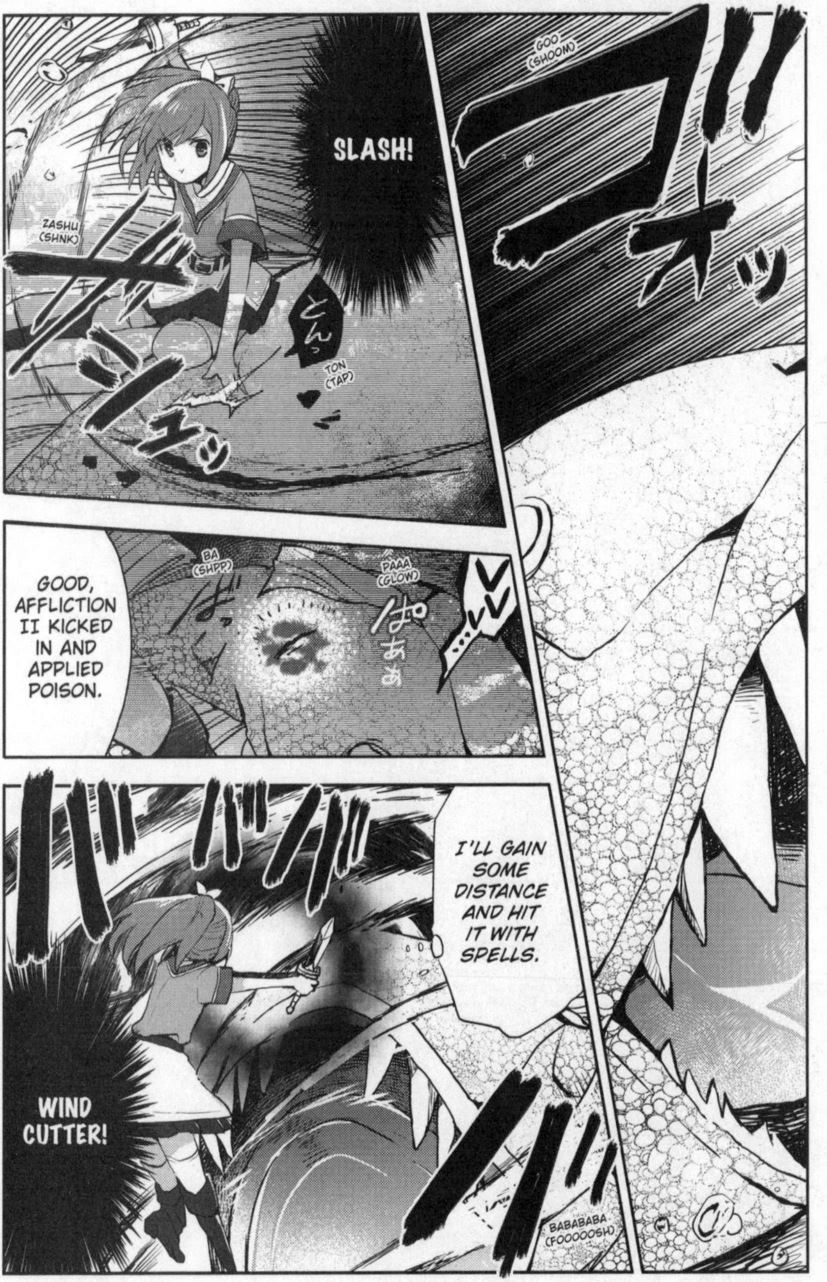
GOO (SHOOM)
SLASH!
ZASHU (SHNK)
TON (TAP)
GOOD, AFFLICTION II KICKED IN AND APPLIED POISON.
BA (SHPP)
PAAA (GLOW)
I'LL GAIN SOME DISTANCE AND HIT IT WITH SPELLS.
BABABABA (FOOOOOSH)
WIND CUTTER!

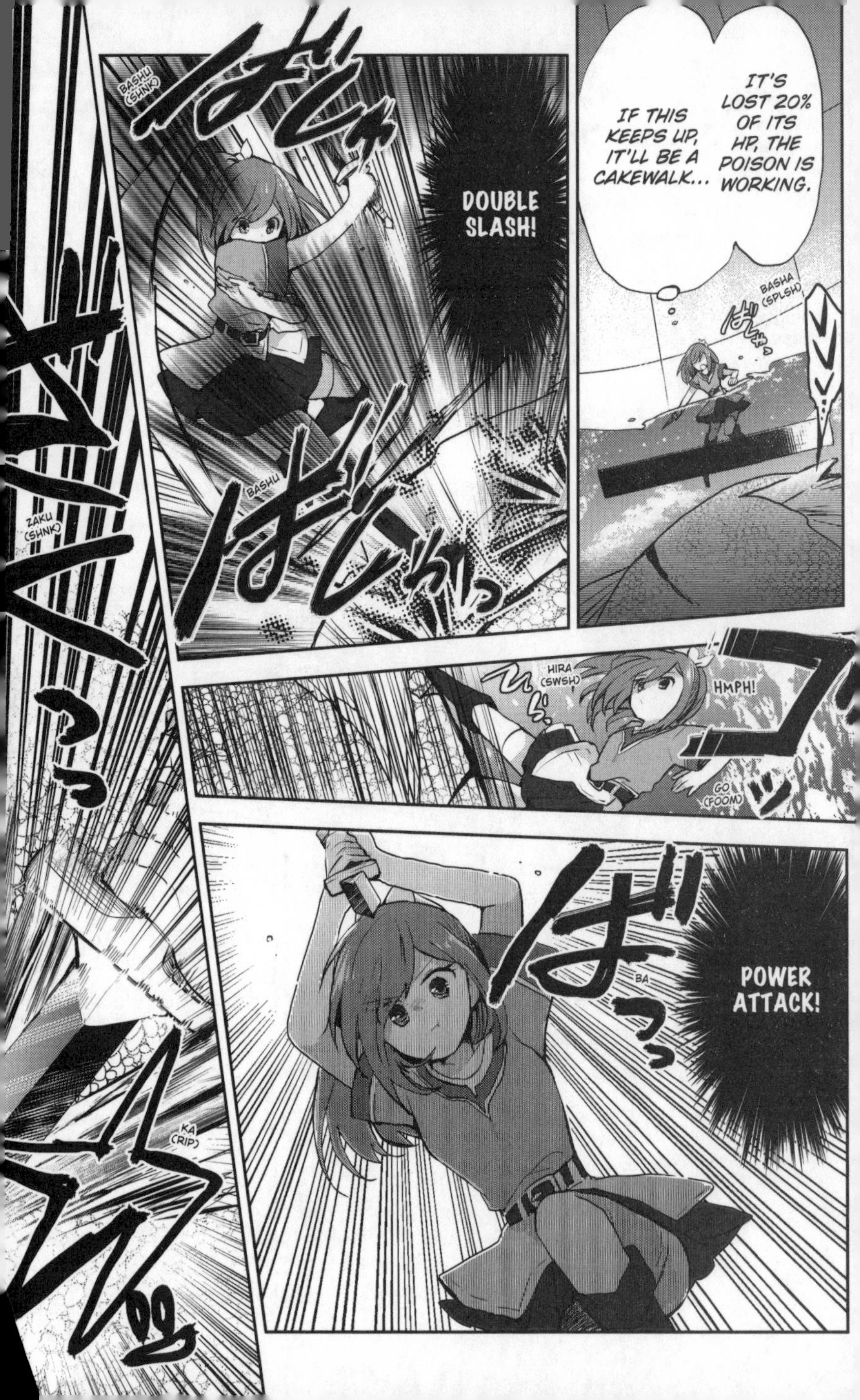
IT'S LOST 20% OF ITS HP, THE POISON IS WORKING.
IF THIS KEEPS UP, IT'LL BE A CAKEWALK...
BASHA (SPLSH)
BASHU (SHNK)
DOUBLE SLASH!
BASHU
HMPH!
HIRA (SWSH)
GO (FOOM)
POWER ATTACK!
BA
ZAKU (SHNK)
KA (RIP)

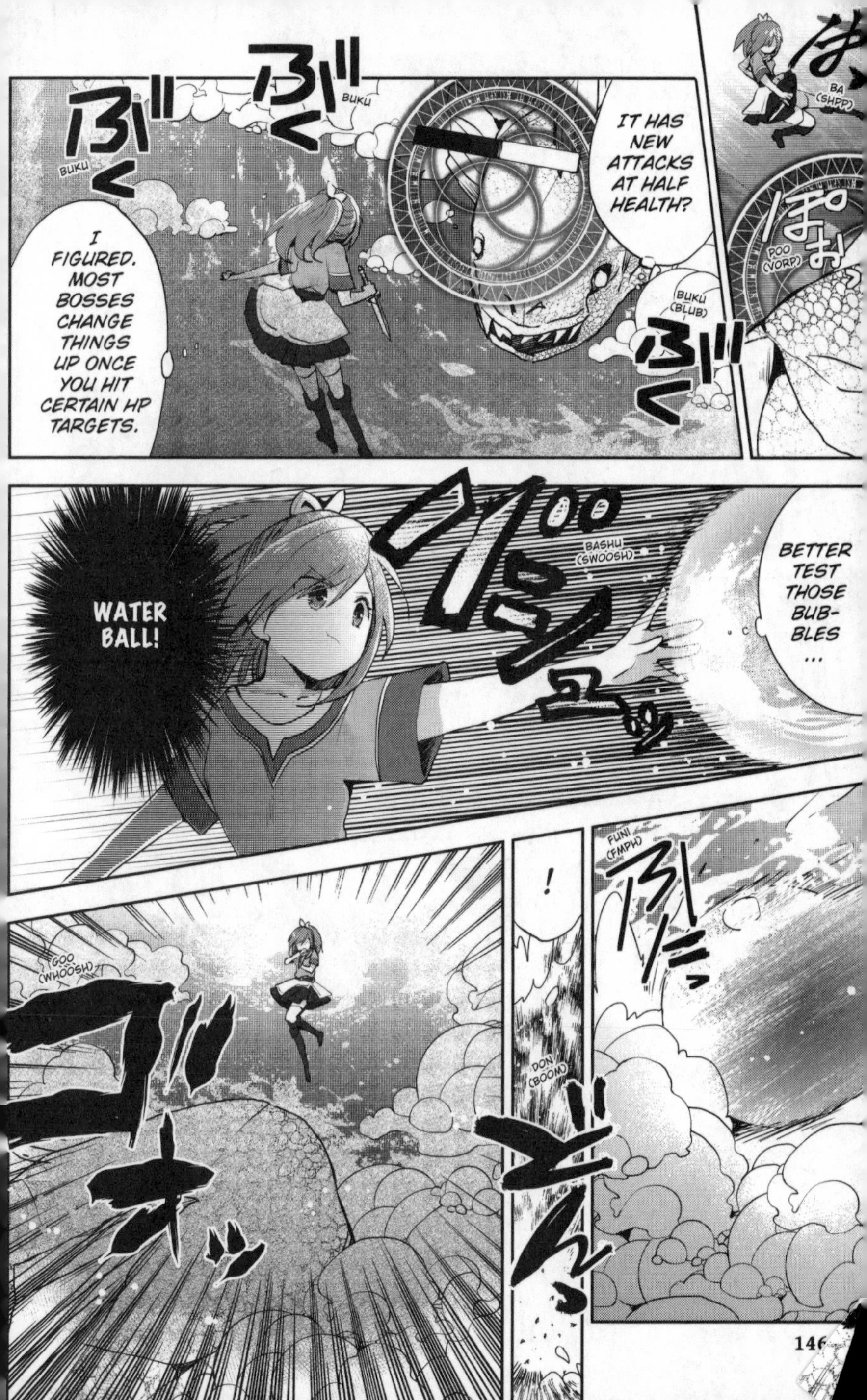
BA (SHPP)
POO (VORP)
BUKU (BLUB)
IT HAS NEW ATTACKS AT HALF HEALTH?
BUKU
BUKU
I FIGURED. MOST BOSSES CHANGE THINGS UP ONCE YOU HIT CERTAIN HP TARGETS.
BETTER TEST THOSE BUB-BLES...
BASHU (SWOOSH)
WATER BALL!
FUNI (FMPH)
!
DON (BOOM)
GOO (WHOOSH)

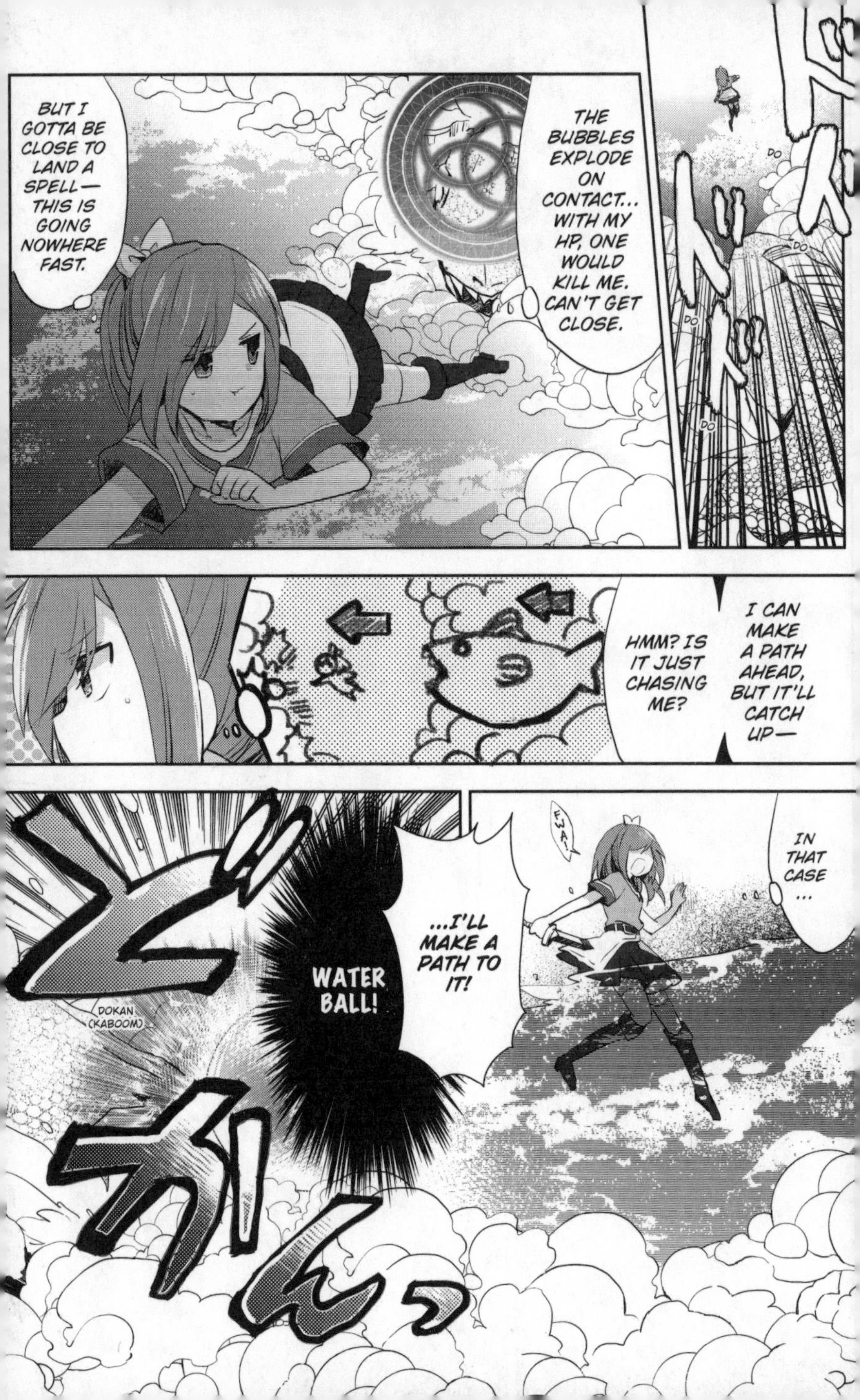
DO
DO
DO
DO
DO
THE BUBBLES EXPLODE ON CONTACT... WITH MY HP, ONE WOULD KILL ME. CAN'T GET CLOSE.
BUT I GOTTA BE CLOSE TO LAND A SPELL—THIS IS GOING NOWHERE FAST.
I CAN MAKE A PATH AHEAD, BUT IT'LL CATCH UP—
HMM? IS IT JUST CHASING ME?
IN THAT CASE...
FWA!
...I'LL MAKE A PATH TO IT!
WATER BALL!
DOKAN (KABOOM)

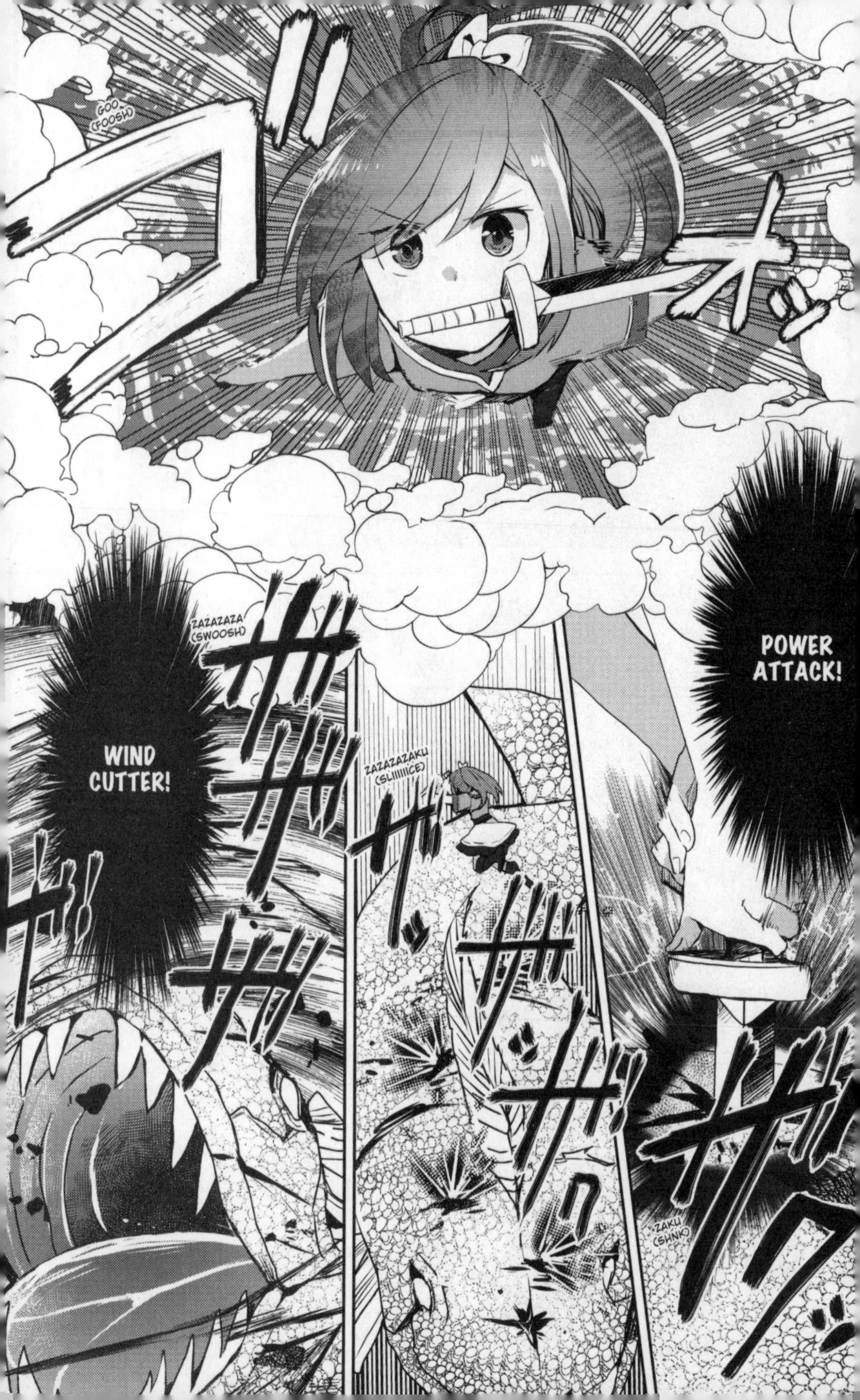
GOO (FOOSH)
POWER ATTACK!
ZAKU (SHNK)
ZAZAZAZAKU (SLIIIIIICE)
WIND CUTTER!
ZAZAZAZA (SWOOSH)

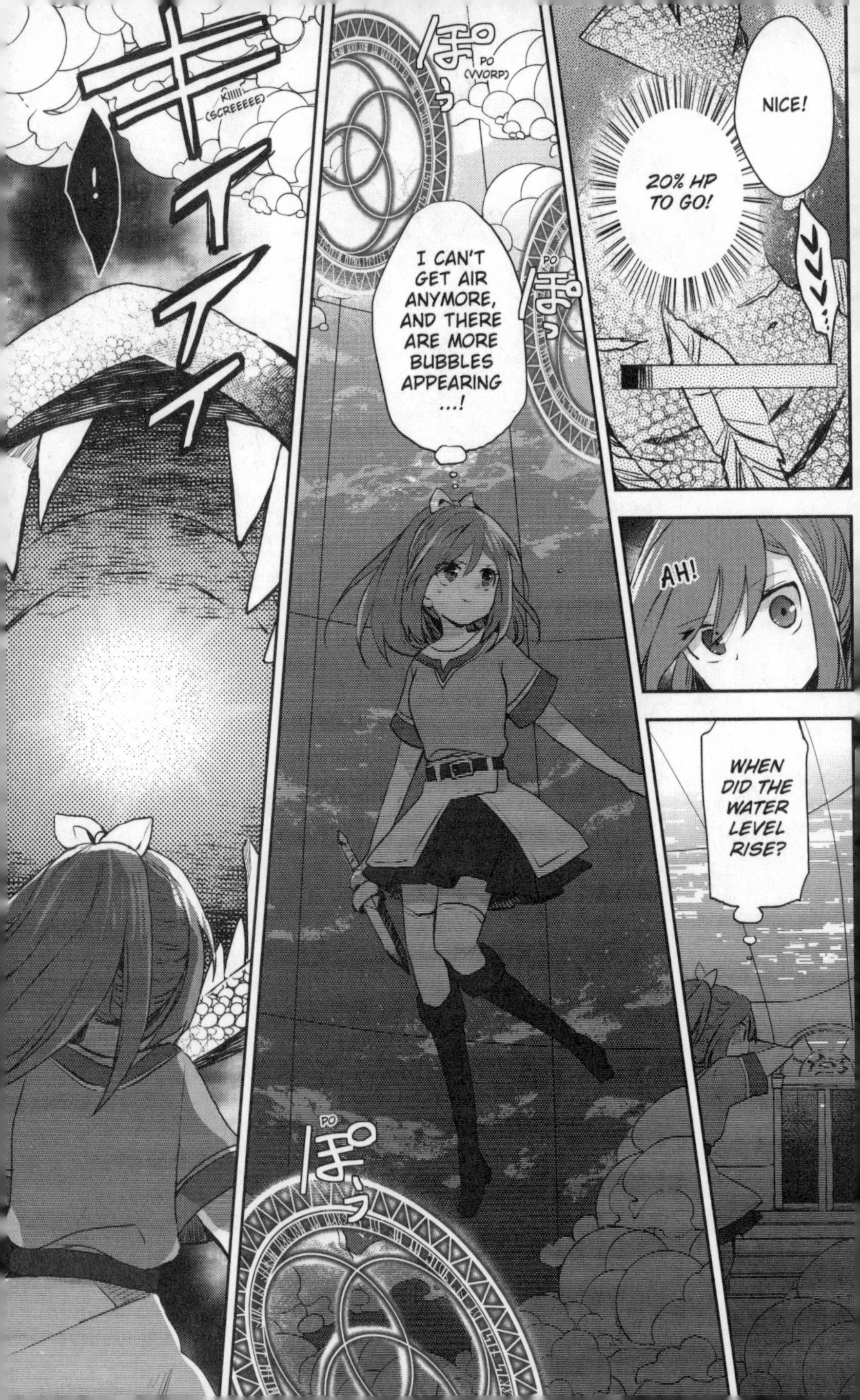
NICE!
20% HP TO GO!
AH!
WHEN DID THE WATER LEVEL RISE?
PO (VVORP)
PO
I CAN'T GET AIR ANYMORE, AND THERE ARE MORE BUBBLES APPEARING ...!
PO
KIIIII (SCREEEEE)

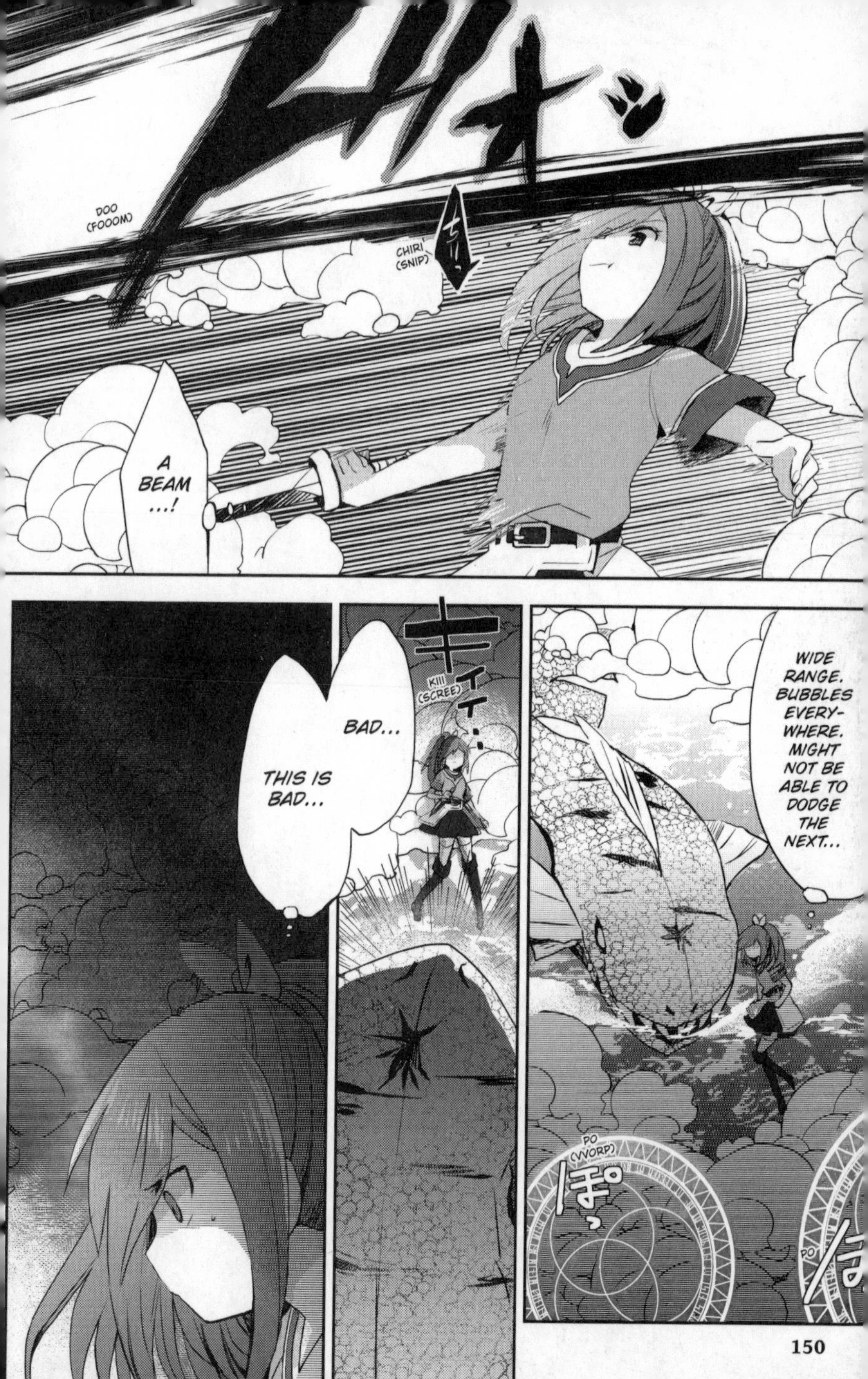
DOO (FOOOM)
CHIRI (SNIP)
A BEAM ...!
WIDE RANGE. BUBBLES EVERY-WHERE. MIGHT NOT BE ABLE TO DODGE THE NEXT...
PO (VVORP)
PO
KIII (SCREE)
BAD...
THIS IS BAD...

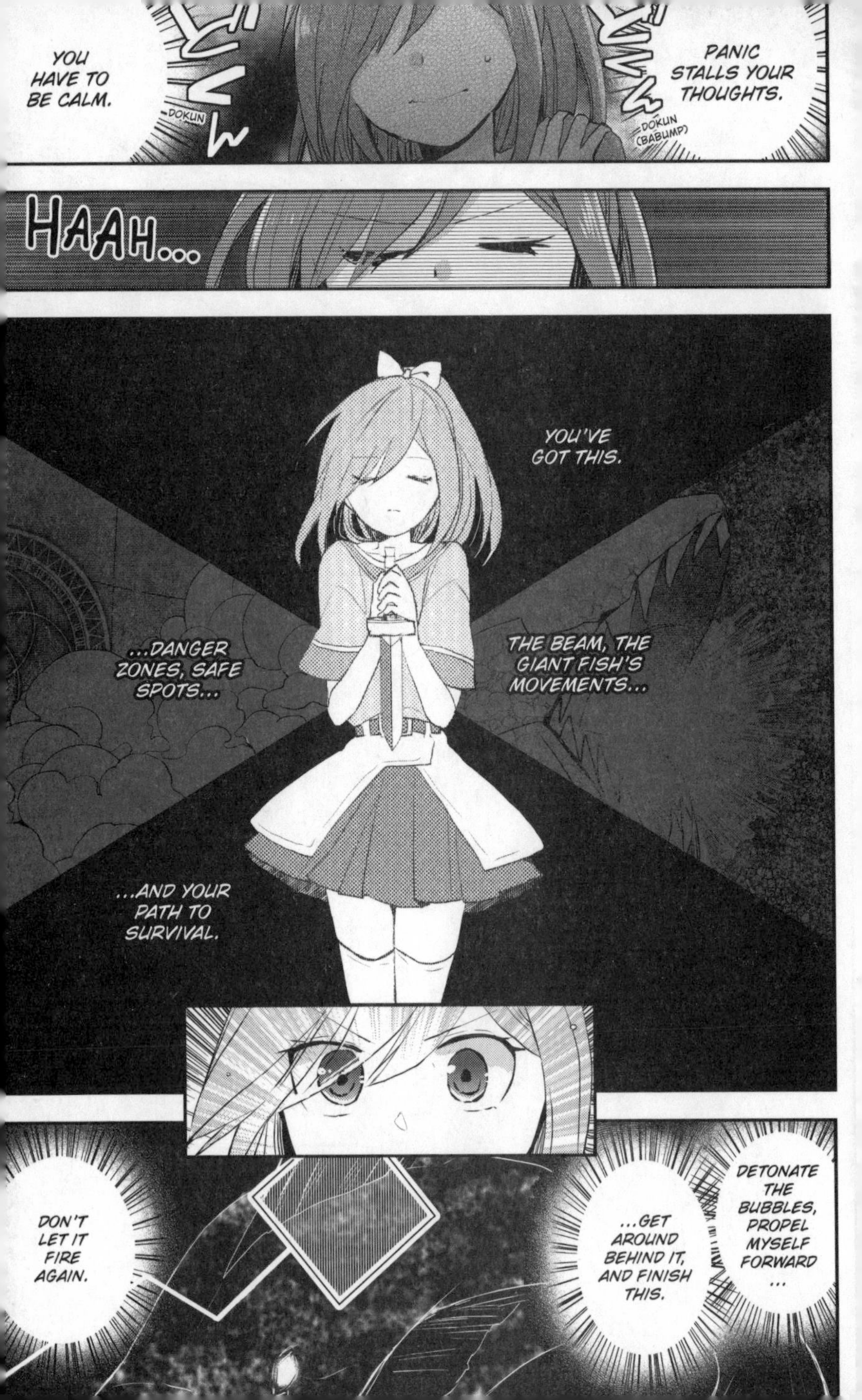
PANIC STALLS YOUR THOUGHTS.
DOKUN (BABUMP)
YOU HAVE TO BE CALM.
DOKUN
HAAH...
YOU'VE GOT THIS.
THE BEAM, THE GIANT FISH'S MOVEMENTS...
...DANGER ZONES, SAFE SPOTS...
...AND YOUR PATH TO SURVIVAL.
DETONATE THE BUBBLES, PROPEL MYSELF FORWARD...
...GET AROUND BEHIND IT, AND FINISH THIS.
DON'T LET IT FIRE AGAIN.

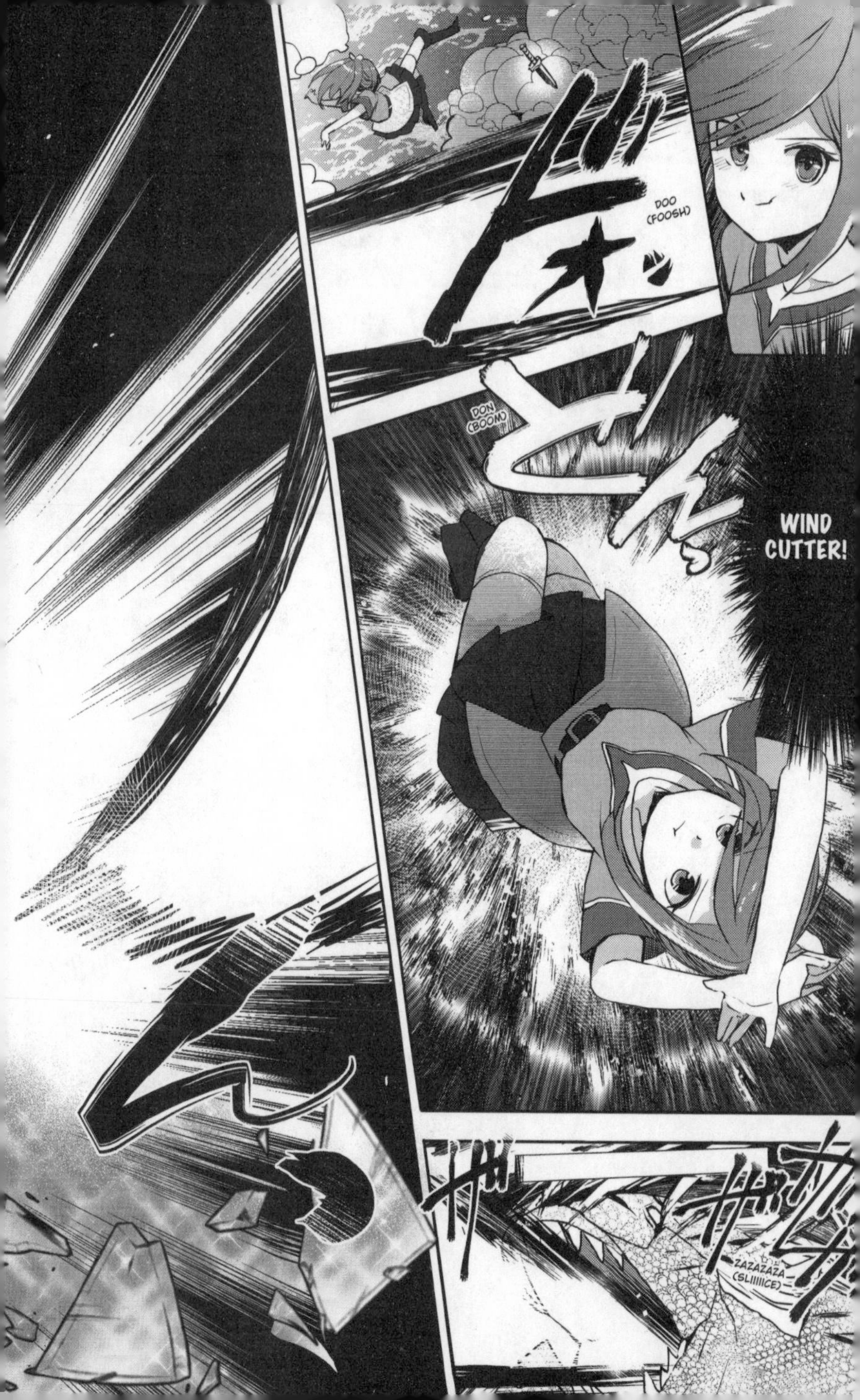
DOO
(FOOSH)
DON
(BOOM)
WIND
CUTTER!
ZAZAZAZA
(SLIIIIICE)

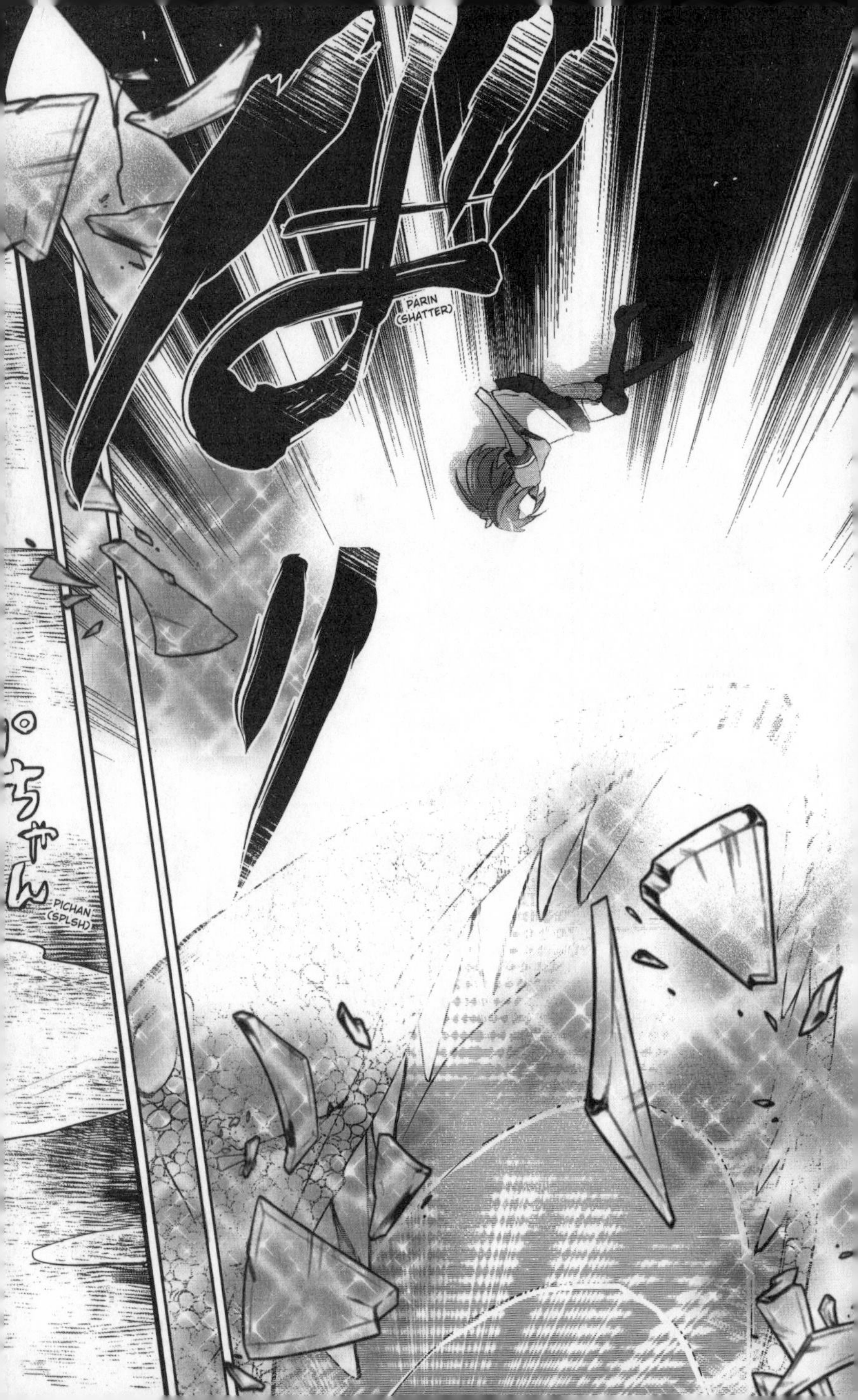
PARIN (SHATTER)
ぴちゃん
PICHAN (SPLSH)

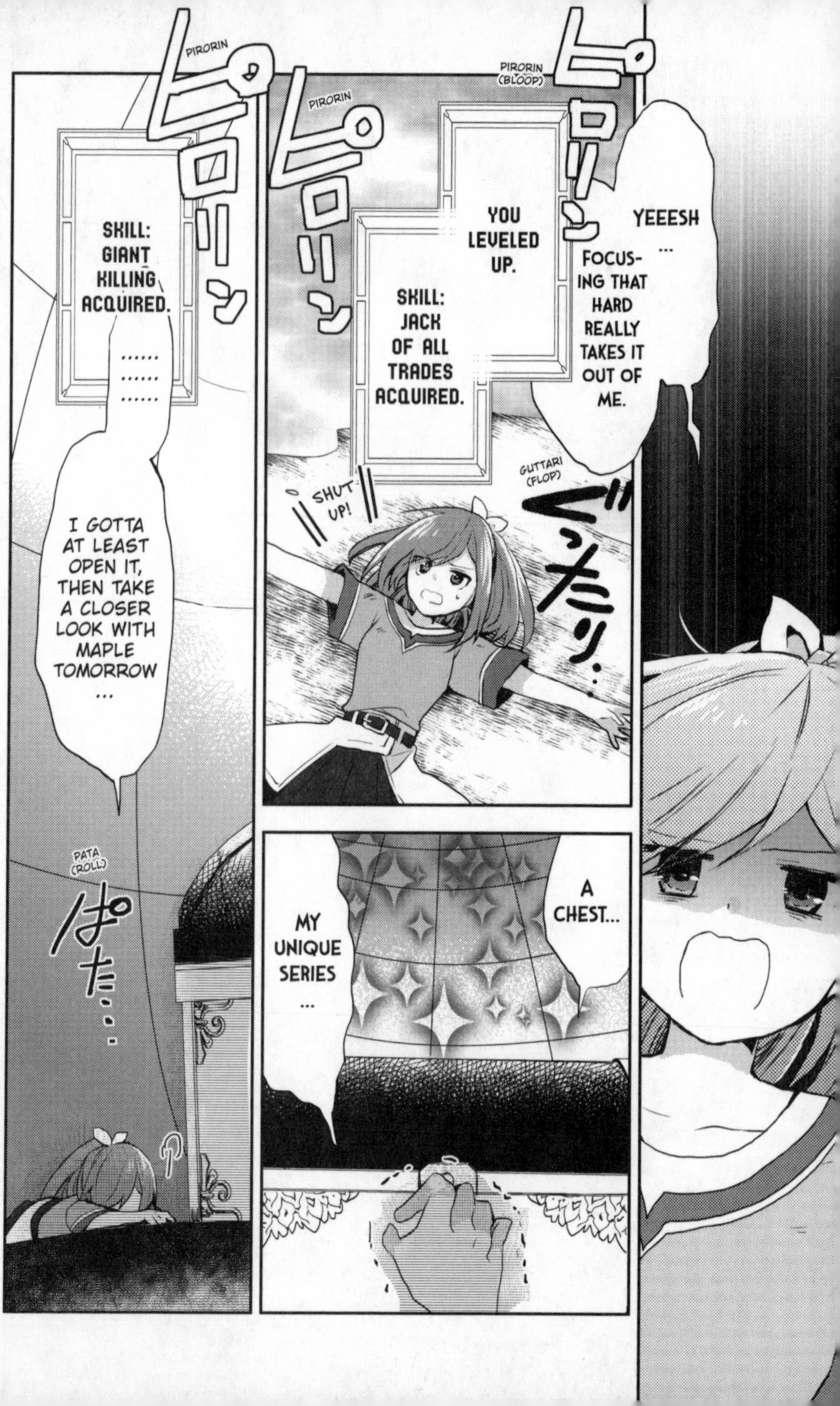
PIRORIN (BLOOP)
YEEESH... FOCUSING THAT HARD REALLY TAKES IT OUT OF ME.
PIRORIN
YOU LEVELED UP.
SKILL: JACK OF ALL TRADES ACQUIRED.
GUTTARI (FLOP)
SHUT UP!
A CHEST...
MY UNIQUE SERIES...
PIRORIN
SKILL: GIANT KILLING ACQUIRED.
....
I GOTTA AT LEAST OPEN IT, THEN TAKE A CLOSER LOOK WITH MAPLE TOMORROW...
PATA (ROLL)

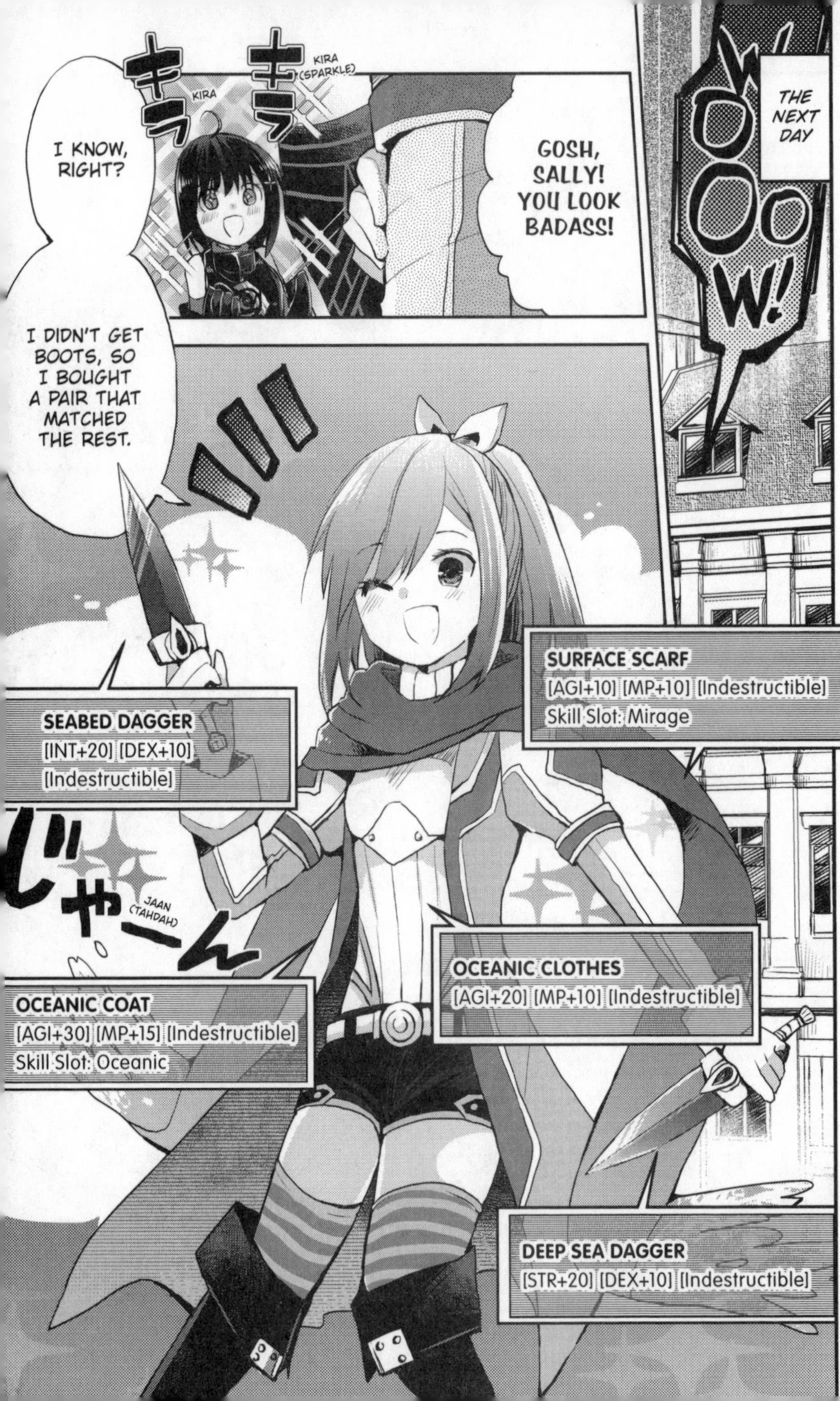
THE NEXT DAY
WOOOOW!
GOSH, SALLY! YOU LOOK BADASS!
キラ KIRA (SPARKLE)
キラ KIRA
I KNOW, RIGHT?
I DIDN'T GET BOOTS, SO I BOUGHT A PAIR THAT MATCHED THE REST.
SURFACE SCARF
[AGI+10] [MP+10] [Indestructible]
Skill Slot: Mirage
SEABED DAGGER
[INT+20] [DEX+10]
[Indestructible]
じゃーん JAAN (TAHDAH)
OCEANIC CLOTHES
[AGI+20] [MP+10] [Indestructible]
OCEANIC COAT
[AGI+30] [MP+15] [Indestructible]
Skill Slot: Oceanic
DEEP SEA DAGGER
[STR+20] [DEX+10] [Indestructible]

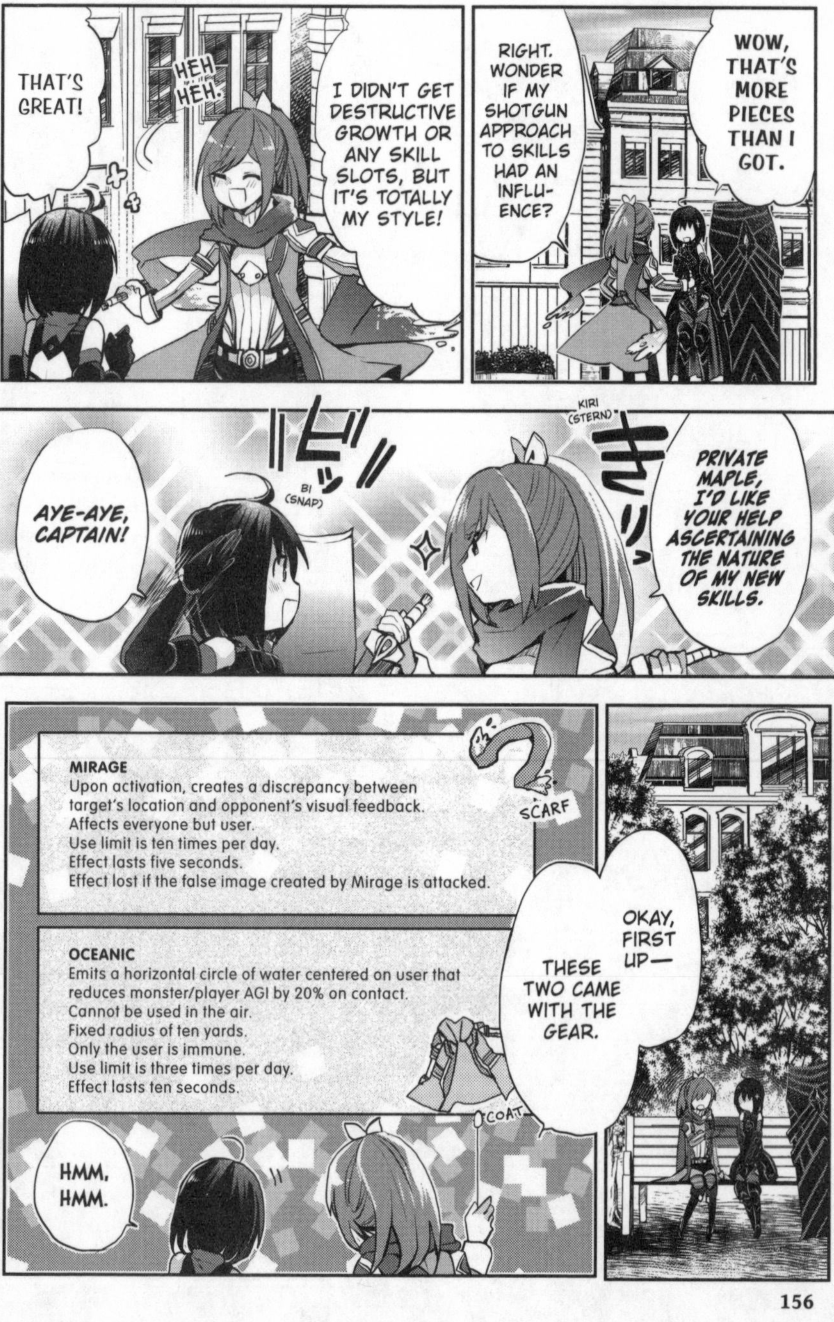
WOW, THAT'S MORE PIECES THAN I GOT.
RIGHT. WONDER IF MY SHOTGUN APPROACH TO SKILLS HAD AN INFLU-ENCE?
I DIDN'T GET DESTRUCTIVE GROWTH OR ANY SKILL SLOTS, BUT IT'S TOTALLY MY STYLE!
HEH HEH.
THAT'S GREAT!
KIRI (STERN)
PRIVATE MAPLE, I'D LIKE YOUR HELP ASCERTAINING THE NATURE OF MY NEW SKILLS.
BI (SNAP)
AYE-AYE, CAPTAIN!
OKAY, FIRST UP—
THESE TWO CAME WITH THE GEAR.
SCARF
MIRAGE
Upon activation, creates a discrepancy between target's location and opponent's visual feedback.
Affects everyone but user.
Use limit is ten times per day.
Effect lasts five seconds.
Effect lost if the false image created by Mirage is attacked.
COAT
OCEANIC
Emits a horizontal circle of water centered on user that reduces monster/player AGI by 20% on contact.
Cannot be used in the air.
Fixed radius of ten yards.
Only the user is immune.
Use limit is three times per day.
Effect lasts ten seconds.
HMM, HMM.

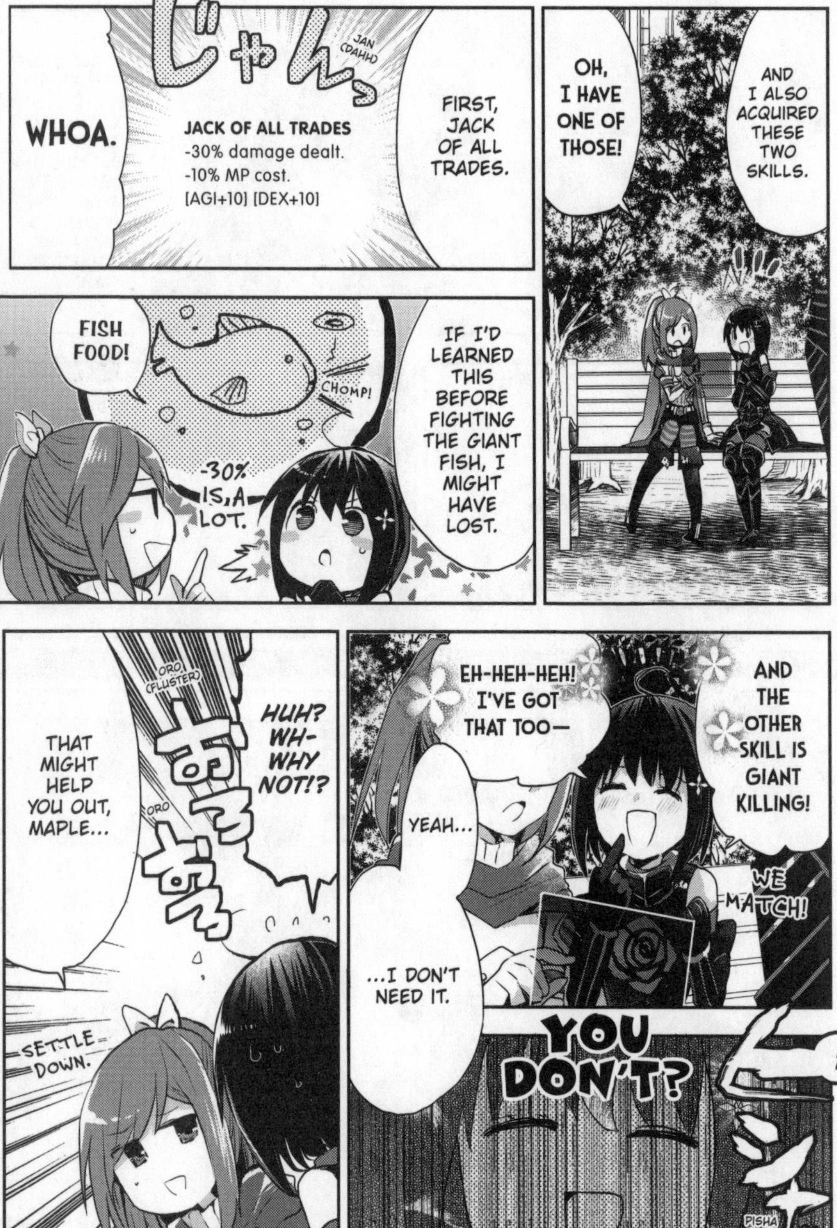
AND I ALSO ACQUIRED THESE TWO SKILLS.
OH, I HAVE ONE OF THOSE!
FIRST, JACK OF ALL TRADES.
じゃん
JAN (DAHH)
WHOA.
JACK OF ALL TRADES
-30% damage dealt.
-10% MP cost.
[AGI+10] [DEX+10]
IF I'D LEARNED THIS BEFORE FIGHTING THE GIANT FISH, I MIGHT HAVE LOST.
CHOMP!
FISH FOOD!
-30% IS A LOT.
AND THE OTHER SKILL IS GIANT KILLING!
EH-HEH-HEH! I'VE GOT THAT TOO—
WE MATCH!
YEAH...
...I DON'T NEED IT.
YOU DON'T?
PISHA (RIP)
HUH? WH-WHY NOT!?
ORO (FLUSTER)
ORO
THAT MIGHT HELP YOU OUT, MAPLE...
SETTLE DOWN.

★ **GIANT KILLING:** If four or more stats (other than HP/MP) are below those of your opponent, double all stats (except HP/MP).

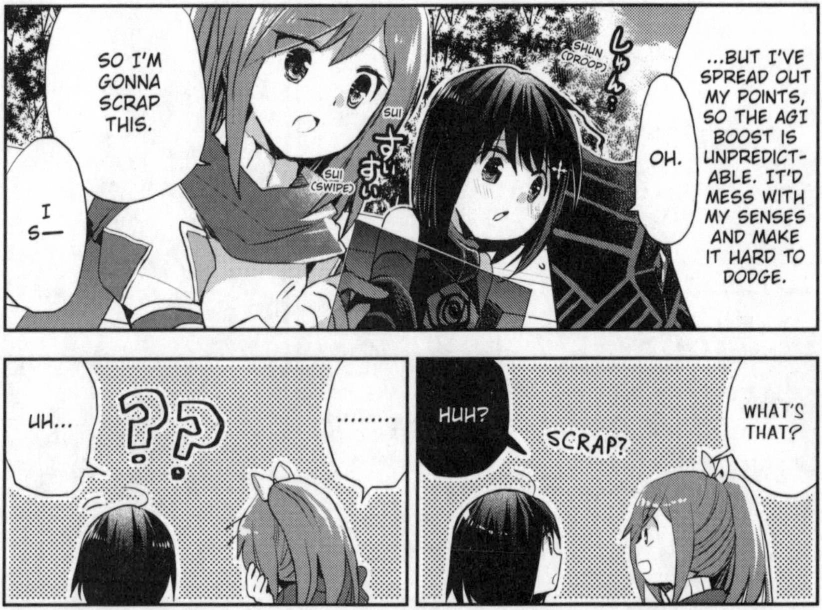
...BUT I'VE SPREAD OUT MY POINTS, SO THE AGI BOOST IS UNPREDICT-ABLE. IT'D MESS WITH MY SENSES AND MAKE IT HARD TO DODGE.
SHUN (DROOP)
OH.
SUI SUI (SWIPE)
SO I'M GONNA SCRAP THIS.
I S—
WHAT'S THAT?
SCRAP?
HUH?
....
??
UH...

EXPLANATION TIME

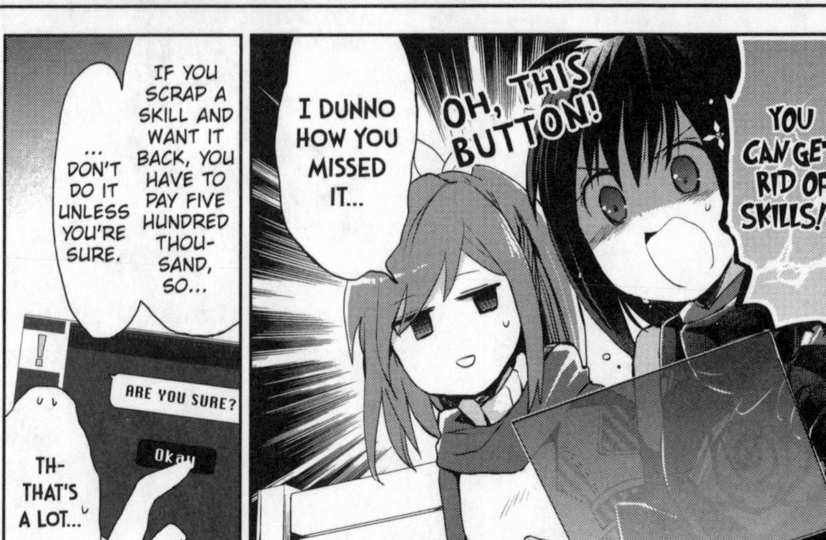
YOU CAN GET RID OF SKILLS!?
OH, THIS BUTTON!
I DUNNO HOW YOU MISSED IT...
IF YOU SCRAP A SKILL AND WANT IT BACK, YOU HAVE TO PAY FIVE HUNDRED THOU-SAND, SO...
...DON'T DO IT UNLESS YOU'RE SURE.
ARE YOU SURE?
Okay
TH-THAT'S A LOT...

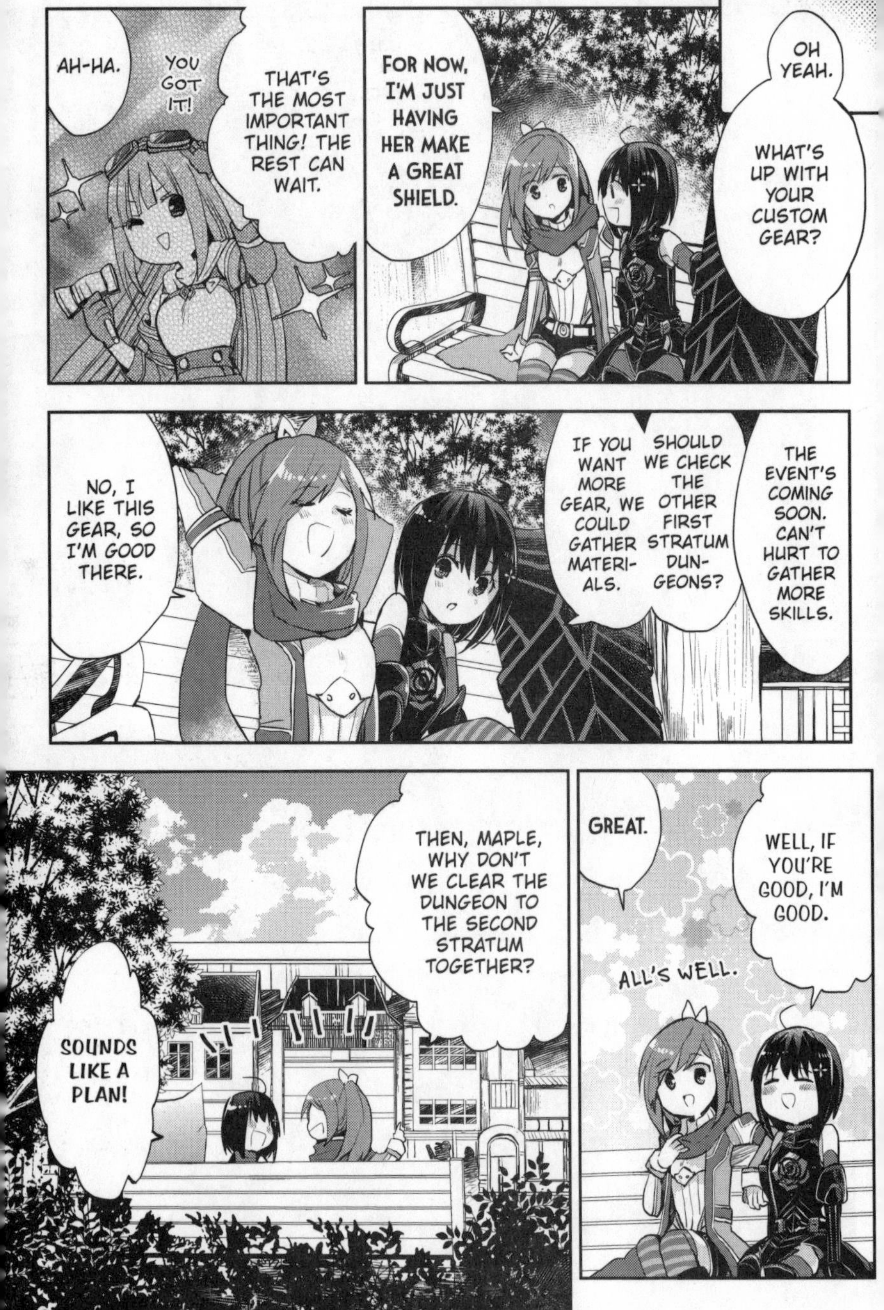
OH YEAH.
WHAT'S UP WITH YOUR CUSTOM GEAR?
FOR NOW, I'M JUST HAVING HER MAKE A GREAT SHIELD.
THAT'S THE MOST IMPORTANT THING! THE REST CAN WAIT.
YOU GOT IT!
AH-HA.
THE EVENT'S COMING SOON. CAN'T HURT TO GATHER MORE SKILLS.
SHOULD WE CHECK THE OTHER FIRST STRATUM DUN-GEONS?
IF YOU WANT MORE GEAR, WE COULD GATHER MATERI-ALS.
NO, I LIKE THIS GEAR, SO I'M GOOD THERE.
WELL, IF YOU'RE GOOD, I'M GOOD.
GREAT.
ALL'S WELL.
THEN, MAPLE, WHY DON'T WE CLEAR THE DUNGEON TO THE SECOND STRATUM TOGETHER?
SOUNDS LIKE A PLAN!

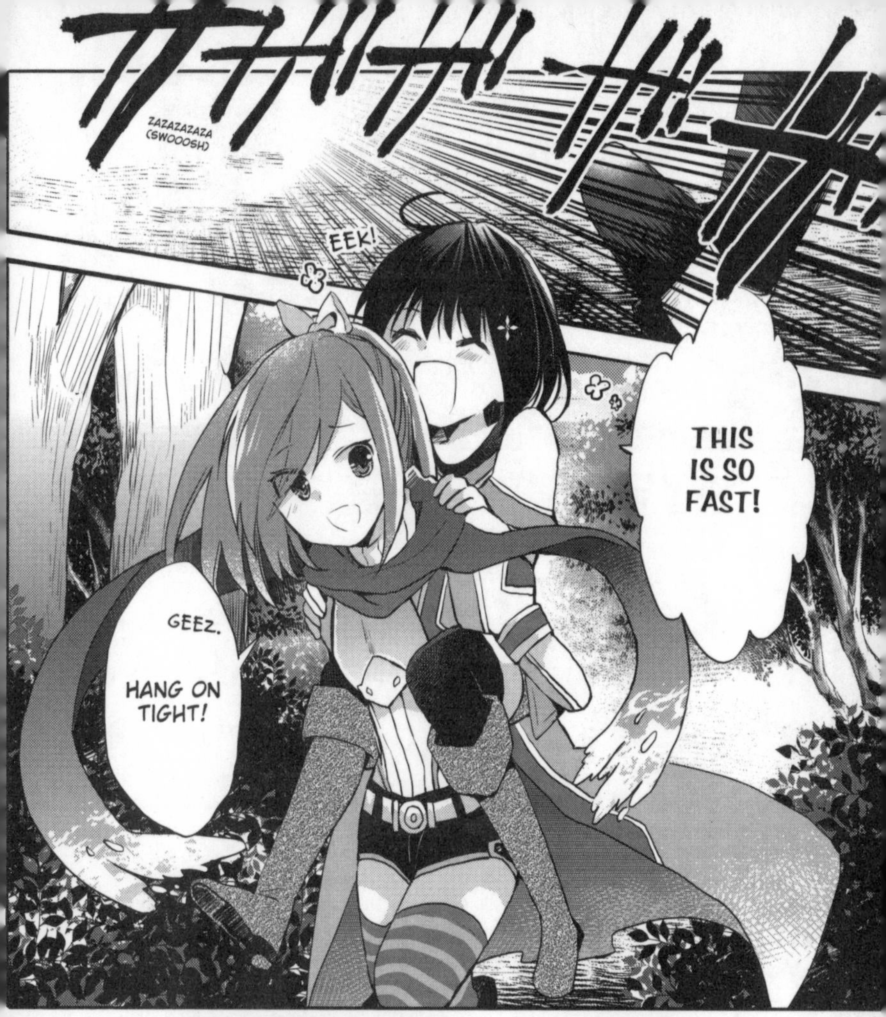
ZAZAZAZAZA (SWOOOSH)
EEK!
THIS IS SO FAST!
GEEZ.
HANG ON TIGHT!

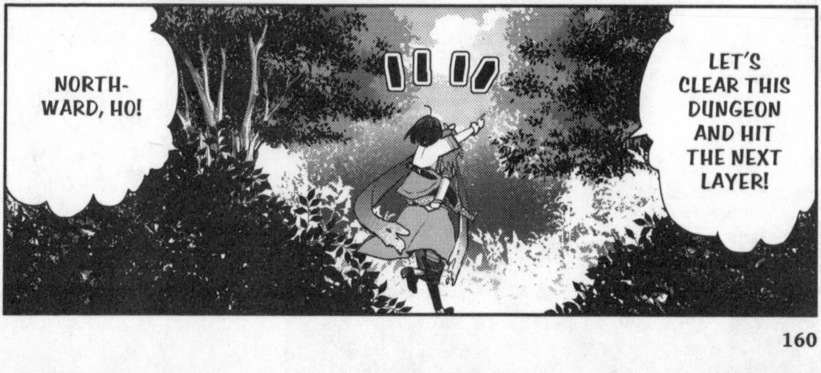
LET'S CLEAR THIS DUNGEON AND HIT THE NEXT LAYER!
NORTH-WARD, HO!

MAPLE: THE HISTORY

HOW'D SHE GET HER SKILLS?

------- ACQUISITION CONDITIONS -------

ABSOLUTE DEFENSE
Be attacked for one hour without taking damage
or doing any damage with spells or weapons.

GIANT KILLING
Solo kill a monster with four or more stats (other than HP/MP)
more than double your own.

MEDITATION
Meditate for three hours while under attack.

TAUNT
Have ten or more monsters' attention on you at once.
Item usage permitted.

MAPLE: THE HISTORY

HOW'D SHE GET HER SKILLS?

ACQUISITION CONDITIONS

SHIELD ATTACK
Finish off fifteen monsters with shield attacks.

HYDRA EATER
Defeat a poison dragon with HP Drain.

HYDRA
Defeat a poison dragon with HP Drain after acquiring Poison Nullification.

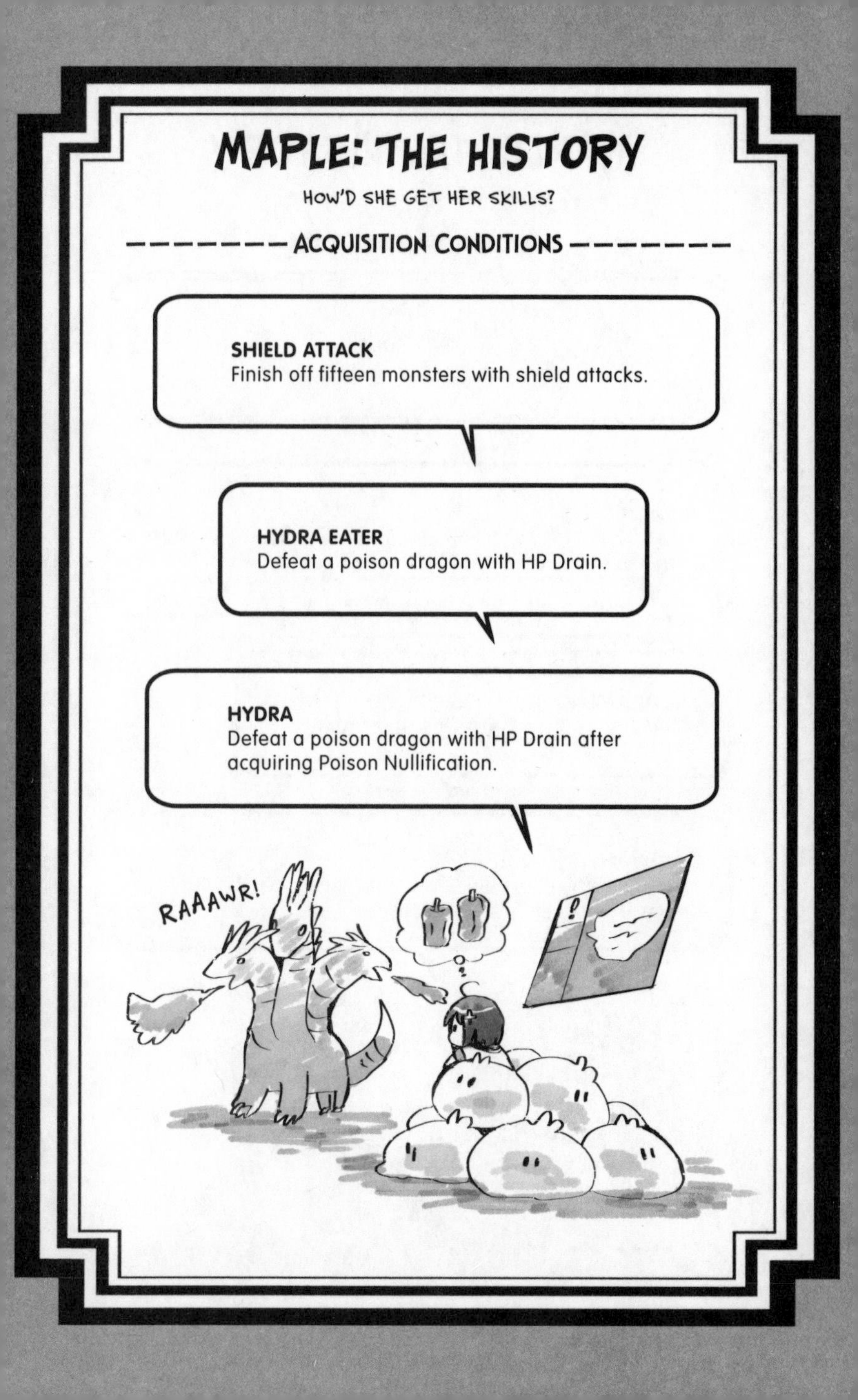
RAAAWR!
!

MAPLE: THE HISTORY

HOW'D SHE GET HER SKILLS?

—————— ACQUISITION CONDITIONS ——————

MORAL TURPITUDE
Exceed a set value for time spent soaking attacks from defeatable foes, while not previously receiving a death penalty.

DEVOUR
Orally ingest a set amount of lethal substances.

BOMB EATER
Defeat Explosing Ladybugs with HP Drain.

BONUS!
(SALLY'S CONDITIONS)

JACK OF ALL TRADES
Ten weapon/attack skills acquired.
Ten magic/MP skills acquired.
Ten other skills acquired.
Ten or more of these skills are at the lowest level.
Defeat a monster with these conditions met.

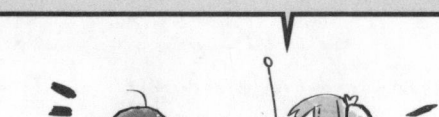

Bofuri ★ I Don't Want to Get Hurt, so ★ I'll Max Out My Defense.

[1]

[Art] **JIROU OIMOTO**
[Original Story] **YUUMIKAN**
[Character Design] **KOIN**

Translation: **Andrew Cunningham** ★ Lettering: **Rochelle Gancio**

This book is a work of fiction. Names, characters, places, and incidents are the product of the author's imagination or are used fictitiously. Any resemblance to actual events, locales, or persons, living or dead, is coincidental.

ITAINO WA IYA NANODE BOGYORYOKU NI KYOKUFURI SHITAITO OMOIMASU Vol. 1
©Jirou Oimoto 2018 ©Yuumikan 2018 ©Koin 2018
First published in Japan in 2018 by KADOKAWA CORPORATION, Tokyo. English translation rights arranged with KADOKAWA CORPORATION, Tokyo through TUTTLE-MORI AGENCY, INC., Tokyo.

English translation © 2021 by Yen Press, LLC

Yen Press
150 West 30th Street, 19th Floor
New York, NY 10001

Visit us!
yenpress.com • facebook.com/yenpress • twitter.com/yenpress
yenpress.tumblr.com • instagram.com/yenpress

First Yen Press Edition: April 2021

Yen Press is an imprint of Yen Press, LLC.
The Yen Press name and logo are trademarks of Yen Press, LLC.

The publisher is not responsible for websites (or their content) that are not owned by the publisher.

Library of Congress Control Number: 2020953028

ISBNs: 978-1-9753-2386-8 (paperback)
978-1-9753-2387-5 (ebook)

10 9 8 7 6 5 4 3 2 1

WOR

Printed in the United States of America